THE Stan Lee UNIVERSE

Danny Fingeroth and Roy Thomas
Editors

Edited by
Danny Fingeroth
&
Roy Thomas

Contributing Editor
Robert Greenberger

Research Consultant
Barry Pearl

Designer
David Greenawalt

Transcriber
Steven Tice

Proofreading by:
Rob Smentek

Publisher
John Morrow

TwoMorrows Publishing
10407 Bedfordtown Drive
Raleigh, North Carolina 27614

www.twomorrows.com

e-mail: twomorrow@aol.com

First Printing, September 2011
Printed in Canada
Softcover ISBN: 978-1-60549-029-8
Hardcover ISBN: 978-1-60549-030-4

Special Thanks to:

Ger Apeldoorn
Mike Bourne
Jerry K. Boyd
Tom Brevoort
Bob Brodsky
Gill Champion
David Bennett Cohen
Neal Conan
Richard Corben
Kevin Dooley
Gary Dunaier
Roger Ebert
Barry Farber
Mike Feder
Eric Fein
Jim Fingeroth
Pat Fingeroth
Jaimee Greenawalt
Scott Hanna
David Kasakove
Michael Kelly
Jackie Knox

Stan Lee
Joan Lee
Joan Cecilia Lee
Nancy Maneely
Country Joe McDonald
Jay Maeder
Russ Maheras
Jeff McLaughlin
Barry Melton
John Morrow
Barry Pearl
Steve Post
John Romita, Jr.
Bob Rozakis
Paul Ryan
Peter Sanderson
Mark Sinnott
Joe Sinnott
Varda Steinhardt
Dann Thomas
Seven Tice
Michael Uslan

Dr. Michael J. Vassallo
Ted White
Will Eisner Studios, Inc.:
Nancy & Carl Gropper
Ken Wong

Staff at the
American Heritage Center at the
University of Wyoming at Laramie:

Susan Gilmore
Mark A. Greene
William Hopkins
Ginny Kilander
Gregory J. Kocken
Shannon Maier
Mark Potter
Keith Reynolds
Sarah Rundall
John R. Waggener
Rick Walters

CONTENTS

About the material that makes up
THE STAN LEE UNIVERSE

Some of this book's contents originally appeared in TwoMorrows' ***Write Now!*** #18 and ***Alter Ego*** #74, as well as various other sources. This material has been redesigned and much of it is accompanied by different illustrations than when it first appeared.

Some material is from **Roy Thomas's** personal archives. Some was created especially for this book.

Approximately **one-third** of the material in the **SLU** was found by **Danny Fingeroth** in June 2010 at the **Stan Lee Collection** (aka "**The Stan Lee Archives**") of the **American Heritage Center** at the University of Wyoming in Laramie, and is material that has rarely, if ever, been seen by the general public. The transcriptions—done especially for this book—of audiotapes of 1960s radio programs featuring Stan with other notable personalities, should be of special interest to fans and scholars alike.

Dedications

To the memory of Blanche S. Fingeroth, who, above and beyond the call of maternal duty, bought comic books for me, per my detailed written instructions, during those sweltering Julys and Augusts.

And to Stan Lee, who wrote and edited the best of those comics, and continues to amaze to this day.

—DF

To Stan—
for being an inspiration and often mentor for the past half century.

—RT

Introduction:
Who is Stan Lee

... and why does he have a Universe when you don't?

by Danny Fingeroth and Roy Thomas, editors

If you're reading this book, odds are you know who Stan Lee is. But the Universe is a strange and mysterious place, and perhaps you *don't* know who Stan Lee is. It's a good bet, though, that, if nothing else, his name is familiar to you, even if you're not sure why.

So if you just have a few seconds, here's the lowdown:

Stan Lee is the co-creator of some of the most significant popular culture characters in existence. Among those are Spider-Man, the X-Men, Iron Man, Thor, and the Incredible Hulk. Beyond that, Stan Lee made sure that the whole world knew about the characters, about the Marvel Comics Group, and about the medium of comic books in general.

To get more specific: Stan was the writer, editor, and art director of Marvel Comics who, with artist-collaborators, conceived those characters and chronicled their earliest adventures in the pages of said comics. He created most of those characters with Jack Kirby, some of them with Steve Ditko, and a bunch of others with artists like Don Heck, John Romita, Sr., Gene Colan, and Bill Everett. Together, they created characters people the world over know and love.

Stan was also the guy who spread the word about Marvel and about comics in general to the world. He spoke at colleges and on radio and TV shows. He was interviewed for countless publications, from the most obscure local pamphlets to internationally known newspapers and websites. For many decades—up to the present, actually—Stan promoted a feeling among his readers that comics were great, Marvel was great, the artists and writers (the "Bullpen") were great, that YOU were great just for reading those comics—and that he, himself, wasn't so bad, either.

And then he went back to his desk and made sure the comics he wrote and edited were so good that they lived up to the publicity he was scoring for them.

In the course of all the above, Stan (a classic "overnight success" who took 20 years of hard work and craft-honing to get there) became arguably the most well known practitioner of comic books in the world. As such, he came into contact with accomplished, famous, and prominent people in media, entertainment, and politics. The kid from DeWitt Clinton High School would hobnob with culture makers and big shots—while never forgetting the folks whose twelve-cent comic book purchases put him on the map.

And then, Stan went on to become a major force in the translation of Marvel's characters into TV and movie and gaming adaptations, and today—after more than 70 years as a professional storyteller—is still the moving force behind a seemingly endless stream of new characters and concepts through his own Pow! Entertainment company, while also serving as Chairman Emeritus of Marvel. Heck, he even has his own star on Hollywood Boulevard now!

The Stan Lee you know may be the guy in the Frank Sinatra hat, perched on a stool on the inside cover of ***Fantasy Masterpieces*** #1—the first time many of us had seen a photo of Stan. Or he may be the guy who came to lecture at your college. He may be the fellow who convinced you that Personna was the razor blade for *you.* He may be familiar as the sage advice-giver in Kevin Smith's ***Mallrats,*** or the gentleman who stops Ben Affleck from stepping into traffic in the ***Daredevil*** movie. He may be the guy overseeing the goings on of ***Who Wants to Be a Superhero?,*** or Craig Ferguson's "nemesis" on ***The Late Show.*** For many more than a few of us, he was the written voice telling us tales of drama, adventure, and romance that fueled our imaginations.

So Stan Lee's universe came to encompass not just the "Marvel Universe," as he dubbed the interrelated

The classic shot of Stan from the inside cover of ***Fantasy Masterpieces*** #1 (February 1966). [©2011 Marvel Characters, Inc.]

world of his characters, but also the wider universe of people whose lives were—and continue to be—somehow affected by Stan the creator, the icon... and "The Man."

This book, then, is a collection of items by, with, and about Stan. They range from reminiscences of working with him from people from the 1940s through today, to transcripts of "lost" radio interviews with him and other key figures in the history of popular culture such as Jack Kirby and Hilde Mosse (more on her later)—to a letter he wrote in praise of a helpful flight attendant! Some of the items herein appeared a few years back in the Stan 85th birthday tribute issues of TwoMorrows' ***Write Now!*** and ***Alter Ego,*** but that material has been combined with lots of other amazing stuff—more than 50% of the book—some never before seen, or not seen for decades. Together, it makes for an incredible compendium of writings and visuals about the phenomenon that is Stan Lee. Some of the highlights of this book are the rare gems found in Stan's archives housed at the University of Wyoming. (Why there? Because Jack Benny's archives are there, and Stan figured, "Good enough for Jack Benny? Good enough for me!" As for why Benny's archives are there... your guess is as good as ours!) Archives highlights include the transcript of a 1968 ***Barry Farber Show*** of Stan debating anti-comics psychiatrist Frederic Wertham's research partner, Dr. Hilde Mosse, which is worth the price of admission all by itself. It's from a radio program that was aired once and never heard since. Then there's Stan's script from the screenplay he wrote for Alain Resnais; Woodstock rockers Country Joe and the Fish's recollections of their visit with Stan at the Bullpen; script, pencil art, and personal notes from Lee and Kirby's 1978 ***Silver Surfer*** graphic novel; and so much more.

Dean Martin once famously said of his ratpack cohort, regarding his effect on the world's popular culture, "It's Sinatra's world. We just live in it." That may or may not be true. But one thing's for sure:

It's Stan Lee's universe. We just *dream* in it.

Danny Fingeroth

DANNY **and** Roy

Roy Thomas

May, 2011

Photo: Peter Nelson.

Danny Fingeroth *was a longtime editor and writer at Marvel Comics, where he was Group Editor of the Spider-Man line, and where he worked with Stan on a variety of projects, including* **Amazing Spider-Man Annual** *#18, which featured the wedding of J. Jonah Jameson,* **Amazing Spider-Man** *#s 363 (the 30th anniversary issue), and the milestone issue #400. After he left Marvel for Byron Preiss Multimedia, Danny worked with Stan on the comics version of the* **Stan Lee's Riftworld** *book series. Over the past decade, Stan has generously given Danny his time for various interviews and has been gracious enough to write introductions to several of Danny's books, including* **Superman on the Couch, Disguised as Clark Kent,** *and* **The Best of Write Now,** *the latter culled from the magazine that Danny produced for TwoMorrows and which Stan was interviewed for several times. While Danny has worked with many talented creators over his career, the times he's worked with Stan are the unquestioned highlights. Danny has spoken about comics and superheroes at Columbia University, the Smithsonian Institution, and The Metropolitan Museum of Art. These days, Danny is Sr. V.P. of Education at New York's Museum of Comic and Cartoon Art (MoCCA), where he also teaches comics writing, trying to pass on the elements of the art and craft that Stan so remarkably advanced.*

Photo: Alan Waite

Roy Thomas *became perhaps Stan Lee's first real "protégé" in mid-1965, when he was hired by Stan (15 minutes after they met) to be a staff writer, a position which quickly evolved into that of editorial assistant. For years he stood at Stan Lee's left hand several mornings a week, getting an impromptu lesson in writing and editing comics as Stan explicated the script and art pages that he (Stan) had written the day before—or applied an editorial pencil to work Roy or others had written—or expounded the strong points (or decried the weak ones) of artwork turned in by artists from Jack Kirby to the veriest beginner. Over time and under Stan's tutelage, Roy became one of Marvel's foremost writers, inheriting directly from him the scripting of such titles as* **Amazing Spider-Man, The X-Men, The Avengers, Daredevil,** *and others. From 1972 to 1974, after Stan was promoted to publisher, Roy served as Marvel's editor-in-chief. In 1978, he wrote a number of scripts for Stan for DePatie-Freleng's* **Fantastic Four** *animated TV series. Even after Roy left Marvel in 1980, the two remained on friendly terms, and in the past decade or so he has interviewed Stan for TwoMorrows magazines such as* **Comic Book Artist** *and his own* **Alter Ego.** *Since 2000 Roy has worked with Stan on the daily-and-Sunday* **Spider-Man** *newspaper comic strip, and considers his association with Stan Lee the highlight of his more than 45 years in the comics field.*

Cub Scouts' Strip Rates Eagle Award

Interview with Stan Lee and Joe Maneely

From *Editor & Publisher* magazine, December, 1957 via *The Menomonee Falls Gazette*, 1972

Joe Maneely at work. [Photo courtesy of Nancy Maneely.]

__Joe Maneely__ was a remarkably gifted and fast artist who was Stan's "go-to" guy in the 1950s for everything from crazy humor to deadly serious adventure stories. In addition, Joe and Stan were close friends. Tragically, Maneely died in a 1958 commuter-train accident. One of the big "What Ifs" if comics history is "What if Joe Maneely had lived to help create the Marvel Universe of the 1960s?"

The article reprinted here, "Cub Scouts Strip Rates Eagle Award," first appeared in **Editor & Publisher** *magazine in December, 1957, but the version seen is adapted from a reprint of it that appeared in the* **Menomonee Falls Gazette** *in 1972. It's a profile of Stan and Joe that spotlights their syndicated strip* **Mrs. Lyons' Cubs**, *that was distributed by the Chicago Sun-Times Syndicate. (And "Eagle Award" here refers to the Cub Scouts honor, not the British comics fan award.)*

Stan Lee and Joe Maneely as drawn by Joe to promote ***Mrs. Lyons' Cubs***. [©2011 the copyright holders]

The conversation piece mostly concerned everything but their work. The protagonists spoke of alley cats, books that could be written on photography, children, Irish coffee, newspapers, interviewing the interviewer.

It was difficult pinning these two witty fellows down. They laughed hard in their excitement, and words rippled like water in a fast-moving brook.

They are young. This is the moment, the opportunity. You do it now or else. You understood how Stan Lee, writer, and Joe Maneely, artist, felt.

Out of the confusion of the spirited chitchat came these facts, finally: On Feb. 10 the Chicago Sun-Times Syndicate will release their daily and Sunday humor strip, ***Mrs. Lyons' Cubs,*** timed to coincide with Boy Scout Week.

"Let me tell you about our purpose," Stan, 35, said. "It's to furnish a vehicle for the countless humorous situations which occur to Cub Scouts and those associated with them, as well as those situations which occur to all youngsters in the age group of 8-10, and the effect on those who have contact with these youngsters."

He said there is no more closely-knit family than the family in which there are Cubs.

Stan is tall, Madison-Avenue-ish in appearance, with a smile that reaches across the room. He smiled: "It's a source of very great satisfaction to me to know that our strip has been approved by the chief Scout executive, Dr. Arthur A. Schuck."

He said he has spent months studying Cub Scout manuals and various scouting publications, and talking with scout leaders, den mothers, Cubs themselves.

"But," he explained, "there will be nothing pedantic about the strip—nothing dry, nothing self-laudatory. For I deeply believe that the best way to reach the vastest audience is through the medium of humor. We hope 'Mrs. Lyons' Cubs' will be humor with a heart, with warmth and feeling."

"I suppose we shouldn't admit this," Joe said, "but this is

A *Mrs. Lyons' Cubs* daily strip, written by Stan, drawn by Joe. [©2011 the copyright holders]

Here's a gag cartoon Joe did in 1958, commenting on his creative partner's editing and coloring styles.

5/2/58 "Stan Lee coloring" gag cartoon by Joe Maneely, Stan Lee Collection, box #31, folder #2, American Heritage Center, University of Wyoming.

not our first attempt. Stan and I have worked out other strip ideas that didn't get anywhere."

"Yeah," Stan agreed. "I remember one especially, that we thought was pretty good, but we never got it out of the shop. I pasted it up in my daughter's room and forgot about It."

The art is good enough to win scoutdom's highest award, and a daily gag will go like this:

Mother at dinner with two Cubs: "How's the onion soup, boys?" "Fine, but it's turtle soup!" one of them answers. "No, it's onion soup," mother insists. "Don't Cubs always have to tell the truth?" the boy asks. "Yes," mother says, "but—" "Well, when you were in the kitchen," the Cub grins, "I let my turtle take a swim in it!"

Joe, 32, modestly played down his talent. "All I hope," he said, "is that every reader will see a little bit of his own family in ***Mrs. Lyons' Cubs*** and will, chuckle at the type of situations he himself has gotten into.

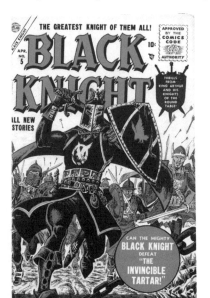

When he wasn't drawing cute cub scouts, Joe Maneely could draw sensational action-adventure, such as this cover to 1956's ***Black Knight*** #5 (April 1956). [© 2011 Marvel Characters, Inc.]

"We have a wonderful foundation on which to build a strip with true humor based upon the real-life experiences of real kids—a strip that will reflect the wonder and warmth of the Cubs themselves."

The boys are newcomers to syndication, but they certainly have been around. Stan, editorial and art director of a New York publishing company, has authored more than 1,000 comic magazines, written and produced specialized magazines for the government and industry and put in time as a freelance writer, publicist, and promotion writer. During the war he wrote training films and film strips.

Married to a former British actress and model, Stan and family live on Long Island. As he says, they have one daughter, two German shepherds, two French poodles and "one utterly disinterested alley cat."

Joe is the quieter of the two partners. He wears glasses, a serious look and a few hairs. He is a product of both the ***Philadelphia Bulletin*** and the ***Philadelphia Daily News*** art departments and now freelances out of New Shrewsbury, N. J., where he, his wife and three daughters live.

Stan Lee Meets [Castle of] Frankenstein

An early Marvel Age interview with Stan, conducted by Ted White

This interview first appeared in 1965's ***Castle of Frankenstein*** #12. Note how it was so early in the Marvel Age that the cover bills it as an "Interview with Marvel Comics." [Castle of Frankenstein and non-Marvel characters ©2011 the copyright holders. Spider-Man ©2011 Marvel Characters, Inc.]

"A Conversation with the Man behind Marvel Comics: Stan Lee," as this piece was called when it first appeared, was one of the earliest Stan interviews of substance ever done. This is only to be expected, since the 1965 interviewer was Ted White, a sophisticated science-fiction and comics fan. Ted's early-1950s one-shot fanzine **The Facts behind Superman** *was, as Bill Schelly writes in his 1997 book* **The Golden Age of Comic Fandom**, *"one of the earliest known attempts to write an authoritative in-depth article about a comic book superhero." In 1960 he wrote the second installment of [the fanzine]* **Xero's** *innovative "All in Color... for a Dime" series—and in the mid-1960s and after, he was becoming a published science-fiction author (***Phoenix Prime**, *et al.) and would soon be the editor of the sf magazine* **Amazing**.

Here's what Ted said about the interview in 2007, with several decades' perspective:

"I have very few memories of the actual interview... but looking back on it, and rereading it, I think it went well and opens a window into Stan before he was the darling of the college lecture circuit and a media celebrity in his own right."

—DF & RT

[A version of this interview appeared in **Alter Ego** *#74.]*

Interviewer Ted White circa 1966, acting as auctioneer at an early comics convention. This photo originally appeared in Larry Ivie's magazine ***Monsters and Heroes***, and later in ***Alter Ego*** #58. [©2011 the respective copyright holders.]

TED WHITE: *You've been with Marvel since what...1944?*
STAN LEE: I'm pretty rotten at dates. But it's been about 25 years, 27 years ... something like that. *[*NOTE: *Actually, as is now well known, Stan came to work for Timely Comics in 1941. –DF & RT.]*

TW: *But the new look in Marvel occurred relatively recently. To what do you attribute this?*
LEE: Well, I guess it started with the first issue of ***Fantastic Four*** about five years ago. They were our first real offbeat superheroes. They sort of started the trend.

TW: *What led you to do those? Up until then there had been no superheroes for about five or six years in this company.*
LEE: Before I answer... would anybody like a sourball?

TW: *Thanks... .*
LEE: What color? I seem to have red, yellow, orange... couple of greens.

TW: *I feel very strange conducting an interview with a sourball in my mouth.*
LEE: Well, I guess we were looking for something to hook some new readers. Also, I think boredom had a little to do with it. We had been turning out books for about 20 years. Same old type all the time... so I figured, let's try something a little more offbeat. Let's try to... I think the big policy was to avoid the clichés. For example, in the ***Fantastic Four***, the first cliché was: all superheroes wore costumes [so we didn't use them]. We soon learned that was a mistake because, much as the readers like offbeat things, there are certain basics that we must have, and apparently superhero fans do demand costumes, as we learned in the subsequent mail.

TW: *They've been after you to change costumes around ever since.*

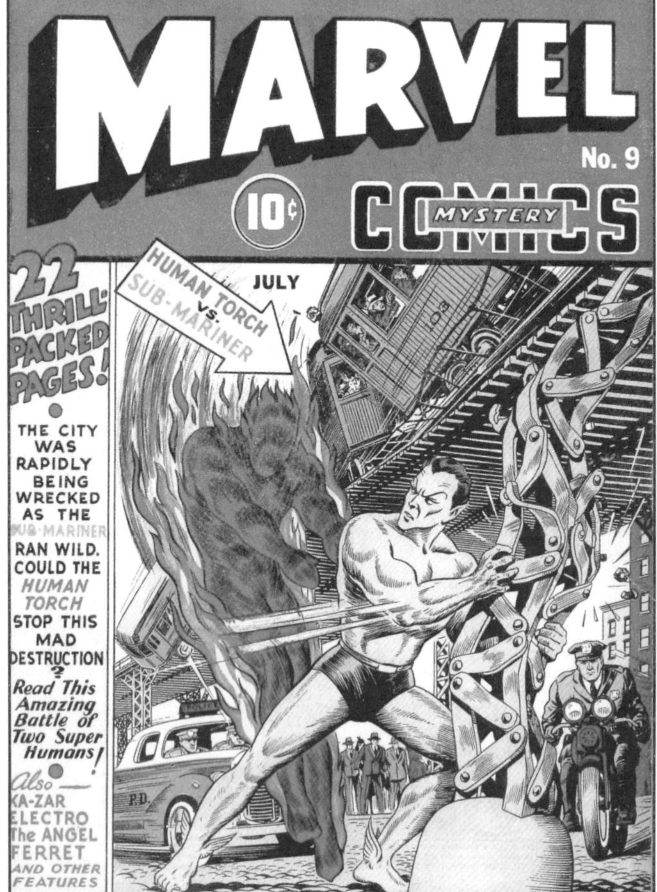

Sub-Mariner, who Stan here refers to as "sort of a hero-villain," battling the original Human Torch in the July 1940 ***Marvel Mystery Comics*** #9. Pencils by Sub-Mariner creator Bill Everett, inks by Alex Schomburg. [©2011 Marvel Characters, Inc.]

LEE: Yes. In fact, they... costumes were nothing that I ever worried much about, but I see that the rabid fans are tremendously interested in the attire of their superheroes. The other cliché that we... I think we were probably the first outfit to break... was the cliché of all the superheroes being goody-goody and friendly with each other. If they're members of a team, they're all nice and polite, and... . We had our Fantastic Four argue amongst themselves. They didn't always get along well and so forth. And this seems to have caught on very well.

TW: *Actually, doesn't this go back to company policy back in the days in the '40s, when The Sub-Mariner and The Human Torch were fighting with each other?*
LEE: Well, the only thing is... then, The Sub-Mariner wasn't that much of a good guy. It was sort of his personality that he would not get along well. They were natural enemies. Fire and water.

TW: *Well, this was pretty unusual. I guess we can say that, in the comics, Marvel pioneered the whole idea of the anti-hero... the superhero who isn't really a hero.*
LEE: Yes, I think you could say that, because I think certainly Sub-Mariner is the first one that I... that I can remember. Bill Everett did the first "Sub-Mariner"... he was sort of a hero-villain. He was really more hero than villain... but he wasn't 100% hero in the sense that the heroes are today.

TW: *The readers would see things from his point of view, of course. Now you've got a full-fledged line, and you're doing very little besides the superheroes. Of course, you have branched out a good bit. You've got* **Sgt. Fury**, *which is about 50% superhero and about 50% non-superhero, depending upon whether you read his adventures in World War II or his adventures today. And the newest thing you're doing is the TV series. Can you tell us a little about that? How much work do the animators do on the original art?*
LEE: Well, quite a bit. They use the actual story and art from the magazines. Basically, it's using our still figures, our still pictures, our panels, and then animating the panels.

TW: *They go back to your original black-&-whites?*
LEE: Yes. [*phone buzzer interrupts*] Excuse me. Yeah?... Why, sure... Just one little interruption. Would you mind opening the door? I think it locks automatically, and Sol Brodsky is coming in. Thanks, yeah. He'll be in in a minute. [*BUZZ*] Whoops! [*into phone*] Yeah? I'll give Sol something, something to look at. [*Production manager Sol Brodsky enters stage left and confers with Stan over a comics page*]
SOL BRODSKY: Stan, he's supposed to be catching him here on the rebound?
LEE: Or reaching for him.
BRODSKY: Reaching for him...
LEE: He doesn't have to be actually catching him...
BRODSKY: Now he's flying by this way... and the hand like this looks as if he's throwing.
LEE: I thought the hand could just be like that, as if it's going to...
BRODSKY: Like this...
LEE: Sure. just reaching. Any way that will make sense... see ... 'cause here he grabbed him. Instead of it being this way, we'll turn it that way... and now he's reaching to grab him, see?
BRODSKY: Yeah... we just drew it wrong.
LEE: Right. I just want to give you something. I understand Steranko is here. I'll probably be another 20 minutes... so possibly he might want to look this over and then I'll talk to him. [*Brodsky exits*]

TW: *We're curious to know the exact procedure you follow when you brainstorm a story, especially one that will continue over several issues.*
LEE: Well, what we usually do is, with most of the artists, get a rough plot... I mean as much as I can write in longhand on the side of one sheet of paper... who the villain will be, what the problem will be, and so forth. Then I call the artist—whoever's going to draw the strip... I read to him what I've written down, these few notes... and we discuss it. By the time we're through talking for about 20 minutes, we usually have some plot going. And we talk it out. Lately, I've had

Stan's 1960s right hand man, Sol Brodsky, portrayed on the cover of the January 1985 ***Marvel Age*** #22, published shortly after Brodsky's 1984 death. By that time, the talented artist had become a VP of Marvel. Art by John Romita, Sr. [©2011 Marvel Characters, Inc.]

By ***Thor*** #153 (June 1968), Stan had for a while been calling himself and Jack Kirby by their Stan-given nicknames, "the Man" and "The King." Also by this point, he had stopped designating which of them did what tasks, simply saying the story was "by" the two of them. Inks by Vince Colletta.

Roy Thomas come in, and he sits and makes notes while we discuss it. Then he types them up, which gives us a written synopsis. Originally—I have a little tape recorder—I had tried taping it, but I found that nobody on the staff has time to listen to the tape again later... so it's just too much of a waste. But this way he makes notes, types it quickly, I get a carbon, the artist gets a carbon... so we don't have to worry that we'll forget what we've said. Then the artist goes home... or wherever he goes... and he draws the thing out, brings it back, and I put the copy in after he's drawn the story based on the plot I've given him. Now, this varies with the different artists. Some artists, of course, need a more detailed plot than others. Some artists, such as Jack Kirby, need no plot at all. I mean, I'll just say to Jack, "Let's let the next villain be Dr. Doom"... or I may not even say that. He may tell *me*. And then he goes home and does it. He's so good at plots, I'm sure he's a thousand times better than I. He just about makes up the plots for these stories. All I do is a little editing... I may tell him that he's gone too far in one direction or another. Of course, occasionally I'll give him a plot, but we're practically both the writers on the things.

TW: *He actually did do a script while you were away on vacation.*
LEE: Yes. We had both plotted that out before I left, but he put the copy in on that one. I did a little editing later, but it was his story. Jack is just fantastic. We're lucky. Most of our men are good story men. In fact, they have to be. A fellow who's a good artist, but isn't good at telling a story in this form... in continuity form... can't really work for us. Unless we get somebody to do the layouts for him and he just follows the layouts. We've done that in the past.

TW: *That's what it means when you have a little note saying "Layouts by Kirby, art by So-and-So"... ?*
LEE: Yes. Now, that isn't always because the artist can't do layouts. There are many extenuating circumstances. For example, an artist who hasn't done a certain strip may have to do it because suddenly the other artist who is going to do it is ill or something. He isn't familiar with the story line, and I don't have time to explain it. Now Jack has been in on most of these things with me. I can call Jack down. I can say, "Jack, make it a 12-page story, and, roughly, this is the plot." Jack can go home, and the next day he has the whole thing broken down. He gives it to the artist, and the artist just has to worry about drawing his work on the breakdowns. It's a lot easier than me spending a whole day discussing the philosophy of the strip with a new artist. Also, there are some fellows who are starting a new strip, who are a little unfamiliar. They'd rather have Jack break it down for them once or twice until they get the feeling of it.

TW: *Of course, Jack has a very good sense of action.*
LEE: The greatest...

TW: *And his perspective... things seem to be coming out at you on the page. It seems to me that his layouts are a lot more dynamic... less static than a lot of the other artists who are working on their own.*
LEE: Well, we refer to Jack—it started as a gag, calling him Jack "King" Kirby, but actually I mean it. I think that this guy is absolutely... in this particular field, he's the master.

TW: *Of course, he's been working with Marvel on and off practically since Marvel started. He did the original* **Captain America**, *of course but he was doing work back before* **Captain America**, *back before he had his long collaboration with Joe Simon.*
LEE: I don't know anything about that because I wasn't here at the time... and I think he had been with another company before Marvel.

TW: *He did* **Blue Bolt**.
LEE: Yeah... I think that was for Fox. They're now out of business. But Jack...

TW: *No, actually that was for Curtis.*
LEE: That who it was?

TW: *They had a different name for the company.*
LEE: Might have been...

TW: *...because* **The Saturday Evening Post** *didn't have anything to do with comic books.*
LEE: Yeah, I seem to remember now. You're right. But Jack... I'm probably Jack's biggest fan. And, of course, we have many other

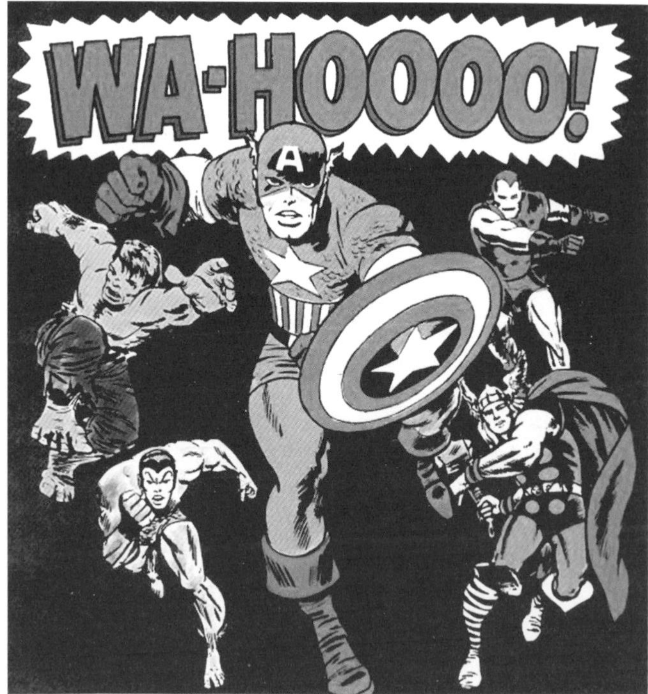

WA-HOOOO!
"MARVEL SUPER-HEROES"
are coming your way on TV!
THE GREATEST ARRAY OF COMIC BOOK
SUPER STARS EVER TO BLAST THEIR WAY
INTO MILLIONS OF TELEVISION HOMES!

Cover to the booklet produced to market the 1966 ***Marvel Super-Heroes*** cartoon to TV stations around the U.S. [©2011 Marvel Characters, Inc.]

talented men—[*phone buzzes*] I think the staff we have now is really pretty terrific. Excuse me. 'Lo? Er ... listen, ask him if it's urgent. If it isn't, I'll get back to him in about a half hour... I'm in that conference now. Okay? Thanks.

TW: *Getting back to the TV shows, you're using your own original script from the books?*
LEE: Actually, they have to be changed to some degree because some of them aren't complete in themselves. And the animation studio has to change the ending or... it has to seem as if it's a complete episode.

TW: *How closely do you oversee this?*
LEE: Pretty closely. In fact, I have some storyboards here. They give them to me in this form, you see, and I take them home with me and check them.

TW: *Those are Photostats of the original panels? Is that it? Then, of course, they're going to work with those from the point of view of the animation.*
LEE: Yes. So I... I'm actually, I guess you might say, the story editor on the TV series.

TW: *How closely do you feel that their animation has followed the style of the original artist, bearing in mind that so much of an artist's style is in his handling of thickness of line and...*
LEE: Oh, very closely. They shoot the actual picture, and all that they animate is opening the mouths and shutting and opening the eyes and moving the arms and legs... but it's the basic drawing that we've got there. I don't see how anything could be more faithful to the original artwork. Now, naturally, they had to make some little changes... but I've had experience with other people who've taken properties. They usually don't even bother with the people whose property they've taken. They just go out on their own. This particular outfit, Grantray-Lawrence, they've been an absolute joy to work with. They check with us on everything, and they're tremendously anxious to keep to the spirit of our own strips and stories. I couldn't be more satisfied with what they've been doing. They're trying their best to keep it in the style, for better or for worse—the style that we have in our books.

TW: *Did you ever see* **Jonny Quest**?
LEE: Yes.

TW: *What did you think of that? Would you prefer to see that type of animation?*
LEE: That type of animation didn't bother me. I think it has a certain charm. In many ways I think I prefer that to full animation which can ruin a human-type character. It's so hard to animate a human being. Technically, I think this is a very interesting... The way they're doing our show technically. I'm delighted with that. I wouldn't have been happy if it were animated like, you know, like ***Mickey Mouse***... just regular animation.

TW: *Do you feel that the form of animation they're using is, in another sense, somehow related to the mass audience concept of camp which has had something to do with Marvel's success with adults?*
LEE: I hadn't thought of it that way, but now that you mention it, it very well could be.

TW: *How do you feel about the way in which the Marvel audience breaks down into age groups? Have you made any effort to find out just what percentage is what age group?*
LEE: No. I can just guess by the mail we receive, and the people I meet and so forth. I couldn't give you a figure, but I would say we have a tremendous amount of young adults reading our books. Now whether this is 50% of our readership or 10% or so, I don't know. But, as far as the mail is concerned, it's about 50% of our mail... college students, soldiers...

TW: *You've gotten a lot of attention on college campuses... I know a lot of the college magazines have devoted space to the Marvel characters.*
LEE: And it seems to be growing all the time...

TW: *It's nice to see the Marvel shows taking away the lead* **Batman** *had two years ago..*
LEE: That television show is so much the style of our comic magazines that, if we did our comic magazines live, we would almost look as if we were imitating ***Batman***.

TW: *Except that you do not present your characters in the light in which ABC presents* **Batman**. *It's almost as if the producer is asking the audience to join him in sneering at the hero.*
LEE: I agree 100%. You get the feeling that they're ridiculing or

laughing at their own characters. I would love for some of our characters to be done with the kind of budget that ***Batman*** has. But I have no idea whether that's in the works or not.

TW: *It would be wonderful to see* **Fantastic Four** *done that way. Can you think of the special effects of the Human Torch?*
LEE: Yeah. Or I would settle for any of them. For something even simpler... like ***Spider-Man***. I can see ***Spider-Man*** making a magnificent show.

TW: *Have you had any nibbles from the movie studios for full-length movies?*
LEE: No, not that I know of. Again, I don't know. The front office may have had some... It's nothing that I really discuss with them until the thing is definite. But I haven't been told of any. I wouldn't be surprised, though.

TW: *Has there been any conflict between your title* **The Avengers** *and the ABC-TV [live-action] show?*
LEE: No. Apparently it didn't mean anything to anybody.

TW: *You were there first in this country.*
LEE: Yeah.

Marvel's success led to other companies popping up and trying to imitate what they saw as the Marvel style. Here's the Wally Wood cover to one of the more successful—and interesting—of those companies, Tower Comics' ***Thunder Agents*** #5 (June 1966). [©2011 the copyright holders.]

TW: *What is your feeling about the way in which the Marvel Group has grown in terms of circulation? You see any leveling off? Is it still growing?*
LEE: It's just incredible. We just seem to be growing at the same steady rate year after year.

TW: *Does it put more pressure on you? Does it take pressures off you?*
LEE: Well, the only thing that puts more pressure on us is if we physically produce more titles, and we're not. We're sort of limited to the titles we have now. If our sales increase, the only pressure is one of jubilation. About five years ago, I guess we were selling about 13 million. Now we're selling about 45 million a year... and this has been a steady rise over the past five years... and there seems to be no end in sight, I'm happy to say. I think we're only limited by how many we can physically print and how many we can physically distribute. I think we can really sell many more if we can print them and distribute them.

TW: *Well, you're getting more competition all the time, of course. New companies keep coming into the superhero field. There are the Tower people... and Harvey Comics... Those are the most flagrant imitators. How do you feel in general about the imitators?*
LEE: I wish they would peddle their papers elsewhere. The flattery kick—we've gotten over that years ago. We realize that we are rather popular now. We appreciate it. But the thing that bothers me... corny as it may sound... we really are trying to make comics as good as comics can be made. We're trying to elevate the medium. We're trying to make them as respectable as possible. Our goal is that someday an intelligent adult would not be embarrassed to walk down the street with a comic magazine. I don't know whether we can ever bring this off, but it's something to shoot for. At any rate, we try to do this. Now when other companies come out... and they try to make their books seem like our books, as if they're all in the same class, the same milieu... and yet the quality is inferior, the art is inferior, the writing is inferior, the plotting is inferior, I feel this does nothing but hurt us. The adults who don't read comics, but whose youngsters try to convince them that comics are really pretty good... you know, who may read ours and like them, say "Why don't you read one? They're really good." And the people who are uninitiated but who have heard about comics and might want to pick one up and see what all the talk is about are very apt to mistakenly pick up one of these imitations, look at them, and say, "Aw, I knew it. That fellow who told me comics are good is really an idiot. They're as bad as they ever were." In this way I think we can be hurt by imitators.

TW: *The imitators make themselves look so much like your line that many readers may think they've gotten hold of a Marvel Comic.*
LEE: Exactly. Now, silly as this may sound, or hard to believe as it may sound, I wish our imitators did better books. If they put out books of comparable quality to ours... . Now, I don't like this to sound as if I'm an egomaniac, but I think you see what I mean. If I felt myself that the art and stories were as good as our books, I would be happier, because I would feel that we're all elevating the field... and we're all going to benefit by it.

TW: *It would put more pressure on you to get even better...*

EVEN AT THE HEIGHT OF THEIR ACCURSED POWER, THEY WERE BARELY A MATCH FOR ME!
BUT NOW... HAVING RENDERED THEM HELPLESS VIA MY HYPNO-PERSUADER, THE GAME IS FINALLY ENDED... THE VICTORY FINALLY MINE!
EVEN THOUGH THE HYPNOTIC EFFECT SHALL SOON WEAR OFF... BY THEN IT WILL BE TOO LATE!
BY THEN... THEY'LL BE AT THE MERCY OF MY INVINCIBLE, OMNIPURPOSE ROBOTS!
BUT, EVEN THE PLAN OF DR. DOOM HAS NOT BEEN TOTALLY FLAWLESS...!
5

In this interview, Stan says that, "Some artists, such as Jack Kirby, need no plot at all... I'll just say to Jack, 'Let the next villain be Dr. Doom'... and then he goes home and does it." Here, a Kirby-Joe Sinnott full-page splash of the not-so-good Doctor (did he ever get his degree, anyway?) from ***Fantastic Four*** #86 (May 1969). The words, of course, are by Stan. [© 2011 Marvel Characters, Inc.]

LEE: Right. But, as it is, at this particular moment, I still think that we are doing the only somewhat significant work in this field. There's the occasional exception.

TW: *You're up against something which is a periodic phenomenon in the comic book industry. Back in the early '50s, the EC group set really high standards. I don't think you've beat them on art yet. When* **Mad** *came out, and it was a sleeper, someone realized, "My God! That thing is selling!" Suddenly, the stands were covered with* **Mad** *imitations. Whenever someone notices that someone is doing something original that is making money, they'll all jump on the bandwagon. But for some reason none of them bother doing anything which has the quality of the original. It would seem that if someone wants to capture the Marvel audience... or enlarge upon it in any way... they should be less concerned with the superficialities... such as having "chatty" covers. That's a gimmick they've taken from you, and now you've dropped it. They never attempt the quality of writing you're doing. And you've kept changing your approach, evolving your characters. In* **Thor**, *for instance, you've gotten into some great mythological conflicts... and away from the nonsense with alter egos, the doctor turning into Thor, and...*

LEE: We've gotten many letters from readers who say, "Heyl We haven't seen Dr. Blake in a while!" So we're trying to see how we can get back to that a little bit. Although I will admit I myself would like to just keep him Thor and keep the stories as they're going. It makes it easier and more palatable to me.

TW: *Originally* **Thor** *[i.e.,* **Journey into Mystery***] was a very schizophrenic thing. You had the "Thor" feature at the front, essentially a standard superhero with his civilian identity and his civilian lovelife problems, and in the back you had your "Tales of Asgard," which was pretty much pure myth reinterpreted in comic form. Now, although you are dealing less with myth in its original sense, you are including all the mythic figures... you've gotten into Grecian mythology... Pluto and the Underworld. That's marvelous stuff; that's sense-of-wonder stuff.*

LEE: Oh, you're quite right. Quite right. In fact, we don't really have any set plan for anything... so you'll always find changes in our books. One day I'll wake up in the morning... or Jack will... or any of our artists... or Roy Thomas... or anybody... and say, "Hey! Why don't we do thus and such?" We're very lucky that there is nobody clamping down on us and saying, "You have to stay within these prescribed channels." To me, any new idea is worth exploring. Even a bad new idea is better than a good formulized rut you might be in. So I like to change things. As far as the ***FF*** goes, they are getting a little bit science-fictiony. I would like to give them a different feeling than, let's say, ***Spider-Man***, which isn't science-fictiony. I'm very hard-pressed to find out how to make ***Spider-Man*** very different from ***Daredevil***. I, sooner or later, will find a way. I would like all of our books to be different from each other... to have their own individual style. It's difficult... because we still don't have enough artists. Consequently, I have to alternate. One fellow may draw "Hulk" this month... he may have to draw ***Daredevil*** next month... and so forth. We still don't have one artist for one feature except in the case of ***Thor*** and ***Spider-Man*** and a few others.

TW: *Why is this?*

LEE: We just don't have enough men. So if one man is ill... or if one man breaks an arm... or anything... somebody else has to do his strip. Then somebody else's strip is now late. Somebody else has to do this. We're continually running into crises of that sort.

TW: *Is there any way out?*

LEE: Just getting more artists. We're looking all the time. But this is what we're up against. The reason I mention this about the art is that it's one of the reasons that it's a little difficult also to stay with a definite theory for each book. As you change artists, you change your approach, you see. But sooner or later things will level off. Maybe they never will, because we're always in a state of flux. But it keeps it exciting.

TW: *Well, our time is up.*

LEE: I'm awfully sorry. Nobody enjoys this sort of thing more than I do. I wish we had another ten hours to go through it.

A Fantastic First

The Creation of the Fantastic Four – and Beyond

by Roy Thomas

[This article originally appeared in somewhat different form in **Alter Ego** v2, #2.]

One late-1960s day in New York, Stan Lee asked me to step into his office. As his associate editor and left-hand man, I figured the summons probably meant one of three things:

1.) A new comics title had been added to the Marvel schedule (and was doubtless already two weeks late).

2.) It was time to play "musical chairs" again, moving "Artist A" to a new feature (with "Artist B" taking over "A's" current strip, and so on down the line assignment-wise, until a harmonious equilibrium was again achieved—for the moment).

3.) The cover price of comics was going up again (it had already risen since 1961 from 10¢ to 12¢ to 15¢, at the very least; where would it all *end?*).

This time, however, Stan simply had something he wanted to show me: his two-page synopsis for the first half of ***Fantastic Four*** #1!

Jack Kirby's cover to ***Fantastic Four*** #1 has become one of the most famous since the first issue of ***Action Comics***. The inker's identity is uncertain after all these years, although historians have narrowed it down to most likely being George Klein.

He had stumbled onto it the previous day at home, not having realized till then that it still existed. (I'd asked him about such hoary artifacts once or twice, but Stan didn't think he had saved anything. Why should he have? Who could possibly *care?*)

As photocopiers were not then the omnipresent office furniture they've since become—and our Photostat machine was way too precious to waste on non-essentials—it didn't occur to me to try to make a copy of the synopsis. The more fool, me.

But I did read it through, before giving it back and returning to whatever I'd been doing. And I never forgot certain salient details...

Actually, this wasn't the first early-'60s synopsis of Stan's I'd seen (see latter part of article). And when I'd gone to work for him in July 1965, I'd learned that he was increasingly dispensing with written synopses, with Marvel artists often working merely from brief conversations, in person or over the phone.

Still, I knew that in my hands was an important document in comics history. For this was the synopsis for the very first issue of the flagship title of what had later become Marvel Comics.

This was the one that had started it all!

CUT TO: 1998.

Let it be said at this point that I was always reluctant to accost Stan in Los Angeles, where we were both living at the time. Though my erstwhile mentor and I have generally had a good relationship, whether or not I was working for Marvel at the time, I didn't want to impose on him. But I did, anyway.

Biting the proverbial bullet, I dropped him a note asking if by any chance he still had that *F.F.* #1 plot he'd shown me three decades ago, because I'd like to print it in *Alter Ego.* To my amazement, a few nights later I received the following breezy fax:

Hi, Roy!

I found the FF #1 synopsis!

Will mail it off to you on Monday. (It's not clear enough to fax)

Sorry to say I have no other synopses on file. Never thought to save any. To this day, I'll never know what made me save the FF #1 synopsis. I certainly never thought anyone would care about it later on.

In fact, I'm not even sure I did save it. I think someone else might have saved it and given it to me at some much later date. Jack? Martin Goodman? Sol Brodsky? Who knows?

At any rate, it'll soon be winging its way into your eager clutches --that is, if "clutches" can truly be a noun. Well, villains since time immemorial have said "I've got you in my clutches!" (But I still think it's a verb and, anyway, who ever said that villains were good at grammar?)

This is enough nuttiness for one fax-- to be continued in the masterful missive you'll receive next week.

Excelsior!

Two days later, I received a photocopy of the synopsis. It might be a bit hard to read in places, Stan explained, because "It was written on an old Remington which apparently had a lousy ribbon."

The synopsis is printed here. (A retyped version appeared without fanfare in the 30th-anniversary ***F.F.*** #358, Nov. 1991, even duplicating typos such as "synopses" for "synopsis"; but, to the best of our knowledge, this is the first time *the actual document,* including traces of the original words under the crossed-out ones and a few handwritten numbers by Stan, has ever seen print.)

A few easily-guessed letters at the extreme right of both pages were lost at some stage in photocopying; back in 1961 Stan clearly didn't believe in wasting paper by leaving much of a margin on either side. And a few other letters (on the *right,* strangely) were obliterated when perforations were made so the copies—or the original?—could be put in a binder.

So get out your magnifying glasses and/or do a bit of squinting, True Believers (and scoffers, as well)... .

SYNOPSES: THE FANTASTIC FOUR JULY '61 SCHEDULE (#1)

STORY #1. INTRODUCTION. "MEET THE FANTASTIC FOUR"

This story is told in 2 chapters. Chapter one is 6 pages long. Chapter 2 is 5 pages.

There are four main characters: 1) REED RICHARDS. (Mr. Fantastic) He is young, handsome scientist. Leader of the four. Invents a space ship to go to Mars. Hopes to be first man to reach Mars.
2) SUSAN STORM. (Invisible Girl) She is Reed's girl friend. She's an actress. Beautiful, glamorous.
3) BEN GRIMM. (The Thing) Ben is very husky, brutish guy. He's a pilot. He falls for Susan also.
4) JOHNNY STORM. (Human Torch) He is Susan's kid brother. A teen-ager. 17 years old. High school star athlete.

Story might open up with a meeting of Fantastic Four. As meeting starts, caption tells reader that we will go back a few weeks to see how it all began....

Reed Richards tells Susan and her brother Johnny that his space ship is finally completed. He hopes to be first man to Mars. But he needs a pilot. They hire Ben Grimm. Ben is huge, surly unpleasant guy who doesn't want any part of project until he sees Susan. He falls for Susan, and she manages to coax him into piloting ship. Ben is crackerjack pilot, ex-war hero, best pilot available.

As the four are about to begin flight, they are warned against it by authorities. Told that no one yet knows what effect cosmic rays will have on human bodies so far out in space. But they decide to go anyway. They fear that if they don't go, Reds may beat us to it.

(NOTE: At the rate the Communists are progressing in space, maybe we better make this a flight to the STARS, instead of just to Mars, because by the time this mag goes on sale, the Russians may have already MADE a flight to Mars!)

So, without clearance from the authorities, in the dead of night, they take off for the nearest star— very dramatically.

In space, on the way to the stars, POOOF! They are bombarded by cosmic rays which penetrate the ship and which affect all four of the occupants. They can't continue the trip— have to turn back— are lucky to land alive. But they are all different now— they sense it— although they don't yet quite know HOW they've changed.

Suddenly, they can't see Susan! But they know she's there! They can HEAR her. They realize she has become invisible. She can not become visible again. Later, she will buy a mask with a face like the one she had and she will have to wear that mask ~~always~~ in order to be seen. Her clothes of course can be seen, so it is only her flesh that is invisible. When she takes her clothes off, she's completely invisible. (I hope this won't seem to sexy in art work. Better talk to me about it, ~~[illegible]~~ Jack— maybe we'll change this gimmick somewhat).

As for Johnny, Susan's brother, whenever he gets excited, he bursts into flame. Becomes a Human Torch, and can fly, as his body gets lighter than air. BUT doesn't last for more than 5 minutes. At end of five minutes, his flame goes out and he becomes normal again, until he gets excited again. But can't flame on for at least 5 minutes after he's gotten back to normal. Comics Association told me he may never burn anyone with flame, he may only burn ropes, doors, etc.—never people. And, he cannot toss fireballs as the old Human Torch could. His biggest asset is that he can fly.

more—

YOU'RE
=GASP=
FADING AWAY!!
OH, NO!! NO!!
IT'S IMPOSSIBLE!

Susan Storm becomes invisible for the first time. Note the difference between how this is handled in the plot and in the eventual comic. ***FF*** #1 pencils are of course by Kirby, but, as with the cover, the inker's identity is a mystery. [©2011 Marvel Characters, Inc.]

They think Reed Richards, the pilot, is unaffected by cosmic rays, as he seems normal--
UNTIL he tries to reach for something. Then they realize his arm has STRETCHED toward the
thing he reached for. After awhile they realize Reed's body has become like RUBBER. He
can get skinny, elongated, anything that you can do with rubber. He can squeeze thru key-
holes, etc. Of course, the more stretched-out he gets, the weaker he gets-- but the point
remains that he can twist and stretch his body into almost any shape. (He can even alter
the appearance of his face to make himself look like someone else) BUT it is quite pain-
ful to do all this, so he can only maintain the strange shapes for a very short period of
time until the pain gets to be unbearable.

Finally, Ben Grimm steps out of the shadows. They all gasp-- his body has changed in the
most grotesque way of all. He's sort of shapeless-- he's become a THING. And, he's grown
more fantastically powerful than any other living thing. He is stronger than an elephant.
BUT, he is so heavy that he moves very slowly-- he's very ponderous, and these slow, ponderous movements should make him look very dramatic. He cannot alter his appearance as the
others can, so he must wear a coat with turned-up collar, sunglasses, slouch hat, and glove
when he goes out in public. But when he takes 'em off, he is a THING!

So much for who they are and how they got that way. Now, here's a gimmick I think we might
play up to advantage: Let's make The Thing the heavy- in other words, he's not really a
good guy. He's part of the ~~xxxxx~~ Fantastic Four because they all got that way together and
they decide to remain a team, and also because he has a crush on Susan-- but actually, he
is jealous of Mr. Fantastic and dislikes Human Torch because Torch always sides with
Fantastic. ~~xx~~ Let's treat him so that reader is always afraid he will sabotage the
Fantastic Four's efforts at whatever they are doing-- he isn't interested in helping mankind the way the other three are-- he is more interested in winning Susan away from ~~Mxx~~
Mr. Fantastic. (We might indicate that he feels he may return to his normal self at any
time, because none of them know how long their strange powers will last- or whether o
the effect of the cosmic rays will one day wear off them).

Anyway, the four of them decide to form a ~~xxxx~~ unit-- they think it is ~~xxx~~ an act of Fate
which made them as they are and they think they owe it to fate to use their powers to
help mankind. So they adopt their new names: HUMAN TORCH, MR. FANTASTIC, INVISIBLE GIRL,
and THE THING, and vow to spend their lives fighting all sorts of evil menaces which the
normal forces of the world cannot cope with. And, to keep it all from getting too goody-
goody, there is always friction between Mr. Fantastic and The Thing, with Human Torch
siding with Mr. F. Also, the other three are always afraid of The Thing getting out of
their control some day and harming mankind with his amazing strength. Occasionally also,
you might have the Thing wanting to do something for personal profit- and the other 3 try
to stop him. In other words, the Thing doesn't have the ethics that the other three have,
and consequently he will probably be the most interesting one to the reader, because he'll
always be unpredictable.

So much for the introduction--- the preceding should have covered exactly 11 pages,
consisting of 2 chapters. (Chapter one: 6 pages. Chapter 2: 5 pages)

The next two chapters, in which the Fantastic Four undertakes their first case, will ~~also~~
be ~~two~~ 3 chapters for a ~~xxxxx~~ total of ~~10~~ 13 pages-- ~~5 pages to each chapter~~ (3,5,5.)

Ben Grimm's first feat of superhuman strength as the Thing. [©2011 Marvel Characters, Inc.]

And there you have it—less important than the Magna Carta, no doubt, but certainly way more significant than most other comics-related items which have seen the light of day since 1961—or before, for that matter.

In answer to my earlier query, Stan sent a few comments along with the synopsis:

"Incidentally, I didn't discuss it with Jack first. I wrote it first, after telling Jack it was for him because I knew he was the best guy to draw it.

"P.S.: As you are probably aware, the biggest change that was made after the synopsis was written, was—

"I decided to make the Thing more sympathetic than originally intended. After seeing the way Jack drew him, I felt it was too obvious for such an ugly, monstrous-looking guy to act in a typically monstrous, menacing way.

"Jack totally agreed, and the Thing ended up adding more comedy than menace to the strip. (He'd prove to be menacing only to the bad guys—not to our heroes.)

"There! Now scholars of the future and academicians everywhere can relax and breathe easier. The truth is out. The cause of literature hath been well served.

"Only the Pulitzer is wanting!

"(Just to prove corniness doesn't fadeth with the years!)"

Of course, the change in the Thing from threatening to sympathetic wasn't quite total, since Ben Grimm was considered a menace by his compeers for the first few issues, though more because of his unpredictability than because he was evil. Nor was that the only change that occurred between the synopsis and the printed ***Fantastic Four*** #1.

Thus, girding my loins in the interests of the goddess Historia, I faxed Stan a few additional questions, inviting him to respond only if he wished to and had time. The next day, he graciously phoned me from Hollywood in between meetings and quickly went over my queries point by point:

1.) Since the 11 pages allotted for the first part had become 13—with the flashback-origin squeezed into a mere five—I'd asked if Jack had added the action-packed 8-page intro on his own; it shows Reed summoning his three comrades with a signal in the sky, to which they respond in ways that reveal their powers to the reader. Stan said that might have been Jack's idea, or his own later suggestion; he didn't remember, after so many years, though he tended toward giving Jack the credit.

2.) Reed is described as "young," but in the finished comic he sports white hair on his temples. Stan said he'd liked that look on a then-current comic strip hero—"maybe Steve Canyon." (But Milt Caniff's USAF stalwart had all-blond locks, so most likely it was Kerry Drake, Rex Morgan, Judge Parker, or some lesser light of the funny papers.)

3.) Surprisingly, Susan Storm was originally intended to be a beautiful, glamorous "actress." Stan suspects that, since the page-count given to the actual origin had been more than cut in half, and nothing in Jack's pencils overtly indicated an acting career, he probably dropped that notion when writing the dialogue. (Jack's artwork would have supported scripting Sue as either actress or simply "the girl-friend.")

4.) The twin concepts of Ben Grimm as just a pilot Reed hired for a single mission, and of Ben's being smitten with Sue, were both likewise dropped—again perhaps because of the truncation of the origin. Any such information could have been imparted only via dialogue, and would have slowed the story as penciled.

5.) Re the idea of Sue remaining permanently invisible and having to wear a humanoid face-mask to been seen—well, Stan's note at the end of that paragraph indicates he was already re-thinking that bit; he asked Jack to talk with him about it, because "maybe we'll change this gimmick somewhat." Since the writer/editor and artist probably discussed this point before Jack started drawing, any number of other changes—including the notion of starting with a multi-page action sequence—may have been suggested then, as well, by either man. In any event, Sue gained control of her invisibility almost at once.

6.) One of the most intriguing things about the synopsis is that, near the end of the paragraph re Sue's invisibility, Stan addresses the artist—and a word is crossed out before the typed "Jack." The final letter of the marked-out five-letter word seems to be a "y" or "g"—while the second-from-last letter has a vertical "mast" at left, like a "b." Did Stan type "Kirby" for some reason, then cross it out and substitute the more usual "Jack"—or is it maybe, just maybe, possible that Stan originally had a different artist in mind? Stan says it's highly unlikely he ever considered anyone but Jack to draw ***F.F.*** #1—but I'd give a whole run of "Heroes Reborn" to be able to see that crossed-out word!

7.) Clearly, Stan had intended the powers of both Johnny and Reed to be far more limited; in Reed's case, the synopsis indicates that stretching caused him considerable pain. Stan recalls that, when Jack's pencils came in, there was strain but not pain in Reed's face, so he downplayed that notion. (Also, Reed's shape-changing and chameleon powers became considerably more restricted than the synopsis indicates. But then, I recall Stan telling me in '65 that he always felt Reed's power was potentially too humorous and never wanted him to become another Plastic Man.)

Almost as famous as the cover to ***Fantastic Four*** #1 is its splash page. Fortunately for readers, Reed's prayer went unanswered. [©2011 Marvel Characters, Inc.]

8.) One argument often used to "prove" that Jack Kirby created the Fantastic Four pretty much on his own is that the concept of four people going up in a vehicle which crashes back to earth (though without their gaining super-powers), after which they dedicate themselves to serving mankind, had been the basis of DC's "Challengers of the Unknown" origin in ***Showcase*** #5, 1956—an origin story penciled by Jack.

Stan, whom I never knew during the 1960s to pay much attention to what the competition was doing, said he can't recall ever seeing that story, though he couldn't swear he didn't; he laughed self-deprecatingly, saying he'd thought the story he gave Jack was new and wildly original: "Shows what *I* know!"

And indeed, the origin in ***F.F.*** #1 is more different from that in ***Showcase*** #5 than the brief description above indicates, since in 1956 the future Challengers were merely flying through a storm in an airplane which crashed, while in 1961 Reed and Co. went up in a spaceship that was downed by cosmic rays.

Besides, Dave Wood, not Jack, is usually credited with writing the Challengers' origin, though Kirby and even Joe Simon may have been involved. DC editors didn't generally bring non-writing artists into plot conferences in the 1950s. However, if anyone has any hard evidence on this matter, I most definitely want to see it! In any event, Stan repeated once again that he's always considered Jack very much a "collaborator" on ***F.F.*** #1, not just the artist.

Though I didn't query Stan about it, another intriguing item in the synopsis is the switching of destinations in mid-stream!

When Stan started typing, he intended Reed's ship to be bound for Mars. Then suddenly he interrupted the synopsis to muse over whether the Russians might have already reached Mars by the time ***F.F.*** #1 would hit the newsstands (only a few months later!), and the destination became "the stars" instead. This in a day eight years before a landing on the moon!

Here we see, as elsewhere in the synopsis, a creative mind at work in the long-ago days of typewriters instead of word processors. Nowadays, Stan would have simply pressed a "delete" key, and any superceded thoughts would've been forever lost before he sent the synopsis to Jack!

Another fascinating bit of information gleaned from the synopsis is that Stan had obviously checked certain aspects of the story in advance with the Comics Code Authority.

This was probably because Martin Goodman's comics company (which wouldn't call itself "Marvel" till ***F.F.*** #14, cover-dated May 1963) was getting back into the superhero game after six years—for the first time since the cancellation of the revived *Sub-Mariner* mag in '55—and Stan didn't want any problems with regard to the Human Torch!

At the bottom of the first page, Stan says the "Comics Association told me he may never burn anyone with flame, he may only burn ropes, doors, etc.—never people. And, he cannot toss fireballs as the old Human Torch could. His biggest asset is that he can fly."

Yet, by ***F.F.*** #9, Johnny suddenly tossed a "fireball" (actually called that in dialogue!) to fuse the ground ahead into a roadway for his sports car; the Code seemed not to notice, or at least to care—and the "no fireballs" rule became a dead letter.

One other question I couldn't resist asking Stan on the phone:

One of the great early-60s mysteries is the identity of the inker(s) of ***F.F.*** #1-4, before Joe Sinnott and Dick Ayers arrived on the scene with #5-6. Writer Mark Evanier has theorized that #1-2 may have been inked by the talented George Klein, in 1961 mostly a DC inker who would go to work for Marvel late in the decade, not long before his untimely death.

Stan doubted Klein was the inker, but couldn't rule it out. He said he'd "always" assumed Ayers had inked those issues (as had many of us for years), but evidently he was wrong.

I asked if the inker might possibly have been Sol Brodsky, who had become Marvel's full-time production manager by 1965 (see Sol's inking of John Buscema's cover for ***Sub-Mariner*** #1 in 1968).

Stan replied, "Listen, you could tell me anybody, and I wouldn't have the slightest idea."

Case not yet closed... though I kinda hope Mark's right.

As I said earlier, the synopsis for #1 wasn't the first ***F.F.*** plot I'd seen.

Over Thanksgiving weekend in 1963, while the nation mourned the assassination of President John F. Kennedy the week before, I took a train from St. Louis to Detroit to spend a subdued holiday with Jerry Bails, college-prof founder of ***Alter Ego.***

There, he showed me an item Stan Lee had recently sent him: the "script" for ***Fantastic Four*** #8. "Knowing" that comic book artists always worked from a script as detailed as a Hollywood screenplay, I was surprised to see that what Jerry had received was merely a plot, its first page covering the initial 13 pages of the comic, and that it was clearly meant as a blueprint from which the artist would break down the tale into pictures.

> SYNOPSIS for FANTASTIC FOUR #8 "Prisoners of Puppet Master!"
>
> (5 pages): Thing enters headquarters. Mr. F working on something in lab which he doesn't want Thing to see-- tells Torch to keep Thing out. Torch tosses up wall of flame between them. Thing gets angry-- feels they are keeping secrets from him. Says he's thru-- storms out. I.G. runs after him-- to cool him off. Becomes invisible so as not to attract attention to herself in her uniform-- people stare at invisible gal talking to Thing. They suddenly see a guy about to jump off a bridge. I.G. shoots flare over guy's head. Mr. F sees it-- tries to reach out of window to grab guy-- too far to reach-- Torch flies toward guy and saves him. Guy is in a daze-- doesn't know why he did it-- is a congressman. Across town the villain has observed what happened through binoculars--angry-- FF frustrated him. He has a small model of bridge and a small model of congressman on table-- he made congressman walk off bridge by manipulating the small puppet of him. Now Puppet Master will make puppets of FF and destroy them! He has blind daughter-- pretty. (He plans to demonstrate his powers to the world, and then sell his services to nation which is the highest bidder.)
>
> (5 pages): Puppet Master figures easiest thing to do is let FF destroy themselves-- he makes only one puppet-- the Thing. He will let the Thing who is strongest destroy the others. He moves puppet to a model of his own apartment so that Thing will come to him. In street, Thing suddenly gets in to a daze, and heads for Puppet Master's apt., followed by I.G. Thing, under PM's spell, reveals I.G.'s presence, some interesting scenes showing how PM tries to capture her, and he finally succeeds, helped by blind daughter who can sense things unseen. PM commands Thing to return and slay Mr. F and Torch-- he also tells his daughter to go WITH Thing, dressed in I.G.'s costume, to throw them off-guard. Then, PM makes puppet of warden of state prison-- gonna get him to realize all the hundreds of dangerous prisoners, to prove his power. IG strains to escape bonds and stop him.
>
> (3 pages): Thing enters FF headquarters with Blind gal. Starts to fight Mr. F-- knocks out Torch before Torch can burst into flame. Mr. F runs into lab-- Thing follows-- gets exposed to artificial rays-- becomes human-- but only for as long as he is under rays-- Mr. F tells him the rays are what he was working on earlier-- to make Thing human-- but didn't want Thing to know until they were perfected-- because didn't want Thing to be disappointed. Not perfected yet-- still has to find a way to make results more lasting. Blind gal can't understand-- tells Thing she thinks he is handsome-- his voice-- his character-- etc.-- while in human form the Puppet Master's spell is broken-- he is now ashamed of himself. Mr. F realizes blind gal is not I.G.-- wonders where I.G. is-- we switch to Puppet Master-- he has opened prison gates (thru control of warden) and now is making a doll to finish off I.G.

Page 5 of ***Fantastic Four*** #8. From plot to printed comic, both Lee and Kirby made changes from what was described in the original plot synopsis. Inks by Dick Ayers. [©2011 Marvel Characters, Inc.]

"Marvel artists work from this?" I asked. Jerry said apparently so; Stan added dialogue and captions later. I shook my head; it seemed to me like a helluva way to run a railroad. (Yeah, as it turned out—a *good* one!) Evidently Stan Lee trusted artists like Kirby, Ditko, *et al.*, to both pace out and flesh out the story.

Truth to tell, neither Jerry nor I can recall whether he ever possessed the entire synopsis, or merely the first of two pages—because, in an early comics "apa" ("amateur press association," a breed of low-circulation fanzine 'way too esoteric to explain here), he retyped and printed only page one. Jerry feels that, if he'd had the whole synopsis, he would probably have printed both pages.

Check out the synopsis on the previous page(retyped for clarity) for Pages 1-13 of ***Fantastic Four*** #8, as seen in ***Kappa-Alpha*** #2, Nov. 1964.

And there the page ends.

So much like the synopsis I would later see years later for ***F.F.*** #1—and yet so much unlike, at the same time! For, on that single sheet, Stan Lee had laid out more than half the story for Jack Kirby in 3- to 5-page segments, something he hadn't done for #1.

The whole basic storyline for those 13 pages was there; and while there was ample room for the artist to embellish the story while breaking it down into pictures, the synopsis was quite detailed in its compact way, even though the "blind gal" is not yet named Alicia (let alone Alicia Masters).

Take the rescue of the suicidal man controlled by a villain soon identified as the Puppet Master: When Sue ("I.G.") runs out of FF-HQ after the Thing, Stan specifies not only that she becomes invisible but that people stare at the Thing talking to apparently nobody. The synopsis indicates that Reed tries to stretch to save the man when he jumps off a bridge, but it's too far to reach, so the Torch has to grab him. All this was faithfully rendered in the artwork.

Still, Jack added his own pacing and a couple of important details. He introduces the Puppet Master before the Torch saves the man, rather than after, so we can see how the villain controls his victim, by pushing a tiny image of him off a model bridge. And—a nice visual touch!—Jack has the Puppet Master burn his fingers on the miniature figure when the Torch catches the man. (Dramatic license, really, since Johnny hadn't burned the victim, so there was no logical reason for the PM's pinkies to get burned!)

Instead of the victim being a "congressman," in the published comic he becomes (in the Puppet Master's phrase) "a nameless nobody." Did Jack indicate this demotion in the border notes which he (and other artists) generally wrote to guide the scripter? Or did Stan decide, when writing dialogue, that he wasn't drawn to look like a congressman, nor was such political status in any way germane to the story?

If photostats of Jack's original pencils still exist, they would answer that question; but either way, this shows Stan and Jack working together as a well-oiled machine at the time of ***F.F.*** #8.

Stan wasn't simply giving his best artist a storyline and expecting him to draw it without adding or subtracting (or thinking), nor at that stage was he asking Jack to do much more than tell the synopsized story in exciting pictures.

Jack, for his part, wasn't just mindlessly illustrating another man's plot; neither was he making up major portions of the story as he went along. That would come later, as Marvel expanded and Stan (like Reed Richards) stretched himself thinner and thinner—with or without accompanying pain.

F.F. #8 was Stan Lee's story at the outset, but Jack Kirby was a trusted and talented collaborator in every way. By the end, it had become not Stan's story, not Jack's story, but *their* story.

As I said, Stan and Jack's method of working together was already changing by the time I came to work at Marvel in mid-'65, and it continued to evolve until Jack abruptly left for DC in 1970.

However, these two synopses provide a tantalizing window on the first year and a half of what became the Marvel Comics Group—and on the Lee/Kirby team that changed comics forever.

Gold and Silver Memories

Comics royalty talk about working with Stan

by Danny Fingeroth

Transcribed by Steven Tice, except the Dick Ayers interview, which was transcribed by Danny Fingeroth

Hundreds, maybe thousands, of writers and artists made their way through the halls of Timely/Atlas/Marvel since Stan Lee started working there in 1941. I spoke with some of these talented super-seniors and asked them, not simply their memories of Stan, but as much detail as they could remember about what the actual working process of making comics with him was like.

Because most of the recollections in this section are 40 to 70 years in the past, they may contradict each other or even generally accepted history. One thing is certain: the deep positive feelings these folks have for Stan and his work.

[This article originally appeared in **Write Now!** *#18.]*

—DF

John Romita, Sr.

John Romita, Sr. *was Marvel's art director and Stan's longtime creative collaborator, not just on* **Spider-Man** *and* **Fantastic Four,** *but on countless covers and special projects, and of course the* **Spider-Man** *newspaper strip, which they started together in 1977. John has been interviewed at length many times about his special relationship with Lee. John e-mailed me about how Stan influenced him creatively.*

—DF

"I never had full confidence in my pencil pages. When deadlines forced me to send out the work, I had doubts whether it was sound, clear storytelling. When the lettered pages came in, I was invariably amazed at how well planned and clever my story looked.

"Stan Lee challenged me to do a story so bad that he couldn't make look good. He also went way out of his way to avoid using any 'clever' lines [I'd put] in the margins I'd be proud of. My ego took a jolt, but those stories, you may recall, were dynamite."

And, in ***The Comics Journal*** #252, John had this to say about what he learned from Stan:

"Stan's approach was basically this: Think silent movies. In other words, all your characters have to act overtly and very clearly. You don't do anything mildly. You don't have somebody with his arm bent, pointing a finger. You have him thrust his arm out in space. The Jack Kirby way. Every sinew of a body is involved even if you're saying, 'Go down the street two blocks and make a right on the next corner'...

"Some of it was Jack Kirby's natural approach. Some of it was Stan Lee's acting school, the way he used to act out the plots... He used to jump up on the couch, he used to jump up on the desk, he would run around the office, he would strangle himself, he would use voices."

John Romita, Sr.'s cover to ***Daredevil*** #16 (May, 1966). This issue was where John first drew Spider-Man. [©2011 Marvel Characters, Inc.]

Larry Lieber

***Larry Lieber** is Stan's younger brother. He's a skilled writer, artist, and editor in his own right. Larry produced countless Western, war, and monster stories (the latter often drawn by Jack Kirby) before becoming one of the first writers other than Stan to toil in the Marvel Universe. His* **Thor** *stories—for which he coined the term "Uru hammer"—are fondly remembered in the thunder god's canon. Larry also had a long run as writer and penciler on* **The Rawhide Kid.** *Today, Larry pencils—as he has for over 20 years—the* **Spider-Man** *newspaper strip, which is still written by frère Stan. I spoke via phone to Larry on January 28 and 29, 2008. (On a personal note, Larry was my first boss at Marvel, and I couldn't have had a better mentor to introduce me to the comics business.)*

—DF

***DANNY FINGEROTH:** When you would write for Stan, Larry, the credits would say, "plot by Stan Lee, script by Larry Lieber, pencils by whoever." Take me through how that worked.*
LARRY LIEBER: Stan would give me a plot, usually typed. Just a paragraph or so. "Thor does this and that," and then he'd say, "Now, go home and write me a script." When I started writing for him in 1958, I hadn't written before, and I didn't just sit down at the typewriter. I used to take a pad, and sit up at the park at Tudor City, where I lived at that time. I wanted to be an artist, so I thought like an artist. I would break the story down into thumbnail sketches, panel by panel by panel, six panels, usually, on a page, and I'd write what was in there. You know, "He does this, he does that, he does this." And then I would write in the captions and the dialogue, and then later type it up.

Stan liked the civilian names that I made up, when I was writing all those ***Journey into Mystery*** stories for Jack Kirby. So for the superheroes he also left their civilian names up to me. So I created the name "Don Blake." I created "Tony Stark." I created the Uru hammer. Everybody must know that story by now. *[For details see Larry's interview in Roy Thomas' TwoMorrows-published* **Alter Ego** *v2, #2.]* I also created Ant-Man's name, Henry Pym.

***DF:** So when the credits say that a story was plotted by Stan, and scripted by you, it was never a matter of Stan talking it out with, say, Kirby, and then you getting the pencils and putting the dialogue in?*
LL: Oh, no, no, no. It was always a *full script* done by me. I never worked in what later became known as "the Marvel style."

***DF:** You know, I would have guessed that, because your stories are paced differently than Stan's stuff from that period.*
LL: When I started, I said, "Stan, I'm not a writer." He said, "Oh, you can write. I read your letters from the Air Force. I'll

Splash page to the Thor origin story from ***Journey Into Mystery*** #83, plotted by Stan, scripted by Larry. Art by Jack Kirby and Joe Sinnott. [©2011 Marvel Characters, Inc.]

teach you to write comics." And he *did* teach me. I don't think he had to do that much by the time I did ***Thor*** or any of the other superheroes. But when I was starting off, I started with, what is it, "Grog the Creature" *[laughter]*, you know, those monster things that Jack drew so well.

***DF:** Were those inspired by monster movies or TV shows of the time?*
LL: I would imagine they probably were. Stan would give me something like that, and I would write. And that's when he taught me, things like "use the positive instead of the negative." For instance, if somebody was running away, and I'd write, "The monster was coming and the guy ran away," Stan would say, "No, no. Not 'ran away.' He *'fled.'*" He would always do that and get the *positive,* by which I mean, instead of a character saying what he *won't* do, he says what he *will* do.

And I remember Stan saying to me, when I was starting to write, that I was using too many words. He'd say, "This is a comic book. There's not enough room, enough space." So I learned. And then Stan would go over my script, and he'd say, "Look, you could have said it *this* way, or you could have said it *that* way, or you could have said it *that* way." And everything he said was much better than what I wrote. He could give me four or five ways of saying something, because he did it so easily, and he did it so much better than I was doing it in his choice of words. And in those days he didn't write in the style that he used later on, with the humor in it. It was just straight writing. He said to me, "I don't care what style you use, I don't care how you do it, but there are certain basics in writing." And so I worked, I worked, and I learned a lot from him, as far as the comics went.

My real compliment came years later when I was writing the ***Hulk*** newspaper strip. I was penciling it and Stan was writing it, but at a certain point, he said, "Look, you can write it as well as draw it." I always enjoyed writing *and* drawing more than just drawing, because I felt it was all mine, I could coordinate it. I really enjoyed doing that with the ***Hulk,*** and I put myself into it. So one day, Stan read it, and he said, "I think the ***Hulk*** is very good. Alas, I think it's even more dramatic than my ***Spider-Man*** strip."

Gene Colan

[©2011 Gene Colan.]

Gene Colan *may be best known for his dynamic work on* **Daredevil, Iron Man, Dracula** *and* **Howard the Duck** *in the 1960s and '70s, but he began his artistic career working for Stan Lee and Timely Comics in the '40s. Most of Gene's Iron Man output was recently released in two* **Iron Man Omnibus** *books, and he won an Eisner award (together with writer Ed Brubaker) for Best Single Issue for drawing the lead feature in 2009's* **Captain America** *#601. Sadly, he passed away on June 23, 2011.*

—DF

DANNY FINGEROTH: *When did you first meet Stan and work with him, Gene?*
GENE COLAN: Around 1946 or '47.

DF: *You started out as a Bullpen artist, hired to work on staff, right? Instead of a page rate, you were working for a weekly salary?*
GC: I was on salary, right. All the guys in the Bullpen were. Syd Shores was there, and Vince Alascia, who inked all his stuff. Syd was kind of the overseer. If anyone had any problems, you'd go to Syd and he'd help you get through it.

DF: *Who were the scripts written by then?*
GC: By Stan, as well as by other people.

DF: *When you'd get a script then, it was a standard full script?*
GC: Full script, and no more than maybe six pages. Some war material, and then crime stories; I had a lot of crime stories. Other people inked me, but after a while, I got permission from Stan to ink some of my own pencils.

DF: *Did you have much interaction with Stan while you were working there?*
GC: Not a heck of a lot. Every now and then I would speak with him for one thing or another, or he'd call me in and correct something that I was doing. Stan was a very jolly guy, always like a kid. And if he wanted to express himself fully, he would actually stand on his desk and get into a pose so that we had an idea of what he was looking for.

The very first time I ever met him, even then he had on his head a beanie cap with a propeller on the top, and the window was open. That thing would just spin around. I couldn't believe it. *[laughs]* I always got along well with him.

I started to freelance around 1950. I did ***Hopalong Cassidy*** for DC Comics. I had wanted to get into DC from the very start. To me, and I was very young, I thought they were the best

From ***Daredevil Annual*** #1 (1967): a page from Stan and Gene's tongue-in-cheek version of one of their plot conferences. (Note: Stan no longer smokes—and neither should you!) Inks by John Tartaglione.
[©2011 Marvel Characters, Inc.]

outfit around then, because ***Superman*** came out of that company, and many other good comic books. So I figured, well, that's the MGM of comic books. But I couldn't get work from them. So I enrolled at the Art Students League in Manhattan, on the GI Bill. I spent a few years there, and then I decided, the heck with DC. I found Stan's place, Timely Comics. It was like a revolving door. You could go in and out of the company.

DF: *I know at a certain point, after the Marvel heroes had hit, Stan started doing what was called "Marvel style," where you would work from a brief spoken or written plot, and you came back as "Adam Austin." How did you like working in that new style?*
GC: Stan had taken on a huge writing load because the company had, a few years earlier, been having financial problems, and he decided to write most of his scripts. But he didn't have time to sit down and type out a full-blown script, so he would dictate it to me over the telephone, and I would record it with a tape recorder or a wire recorder. I think I had a wire recorder.

Gene's first ***Daredevil*** cover was to #21 (October 1966), although he had started penciling the title the issue before. Inks are by Frank Giacoia. [©2011 Marvel Characters, Inc.]

He would say to me, "Well, it's roughly like this..." It's amazing he had that kind of faith in me at that time. And he'd continue something like, "A couple of guys break into a bank and they steal some money." And then there was an "in between" of the plot—the middle. And then there's an *ending* to the plot. So it was broken down in three parts, the beginning, the middle, and the end.

DF: *And he would give you the details of the beginning, the middle, and the end?*
GC: No details. "And then there's a couple of bad guys here and there." So he left the characterization up to me. Once in a while he might describe a character, but mostly he gave me my heading. I could do whatever I wanted, so long as I kept within the margins he described in our conference.

DF: *So, say if a romance subplot was developing, how would the two of you keep track of what was going on and where it was at? Or was it mostly up to you?*
GC: It was mostly up to me, I believe, and when a story was finished, I would just drive into the city and deliver it to him.

DF: But he would tell you who the villain was, he would tell you what the main action scene was?
GC: Yes. I wouldn't suggest any storylines at all.

DF: *I think when he worked with Kirby, Ditko, guys like that, they would.*
GC: Oh, yeah, he was very close with Jack Kirby, and then the two of them would hash things out.

DF: *That's interesting, because I always had the impression that he worked similarly with all you guys, but apparently it sounds like it was different with some people than with others. You did a lot of innovative things with panel and page layout. Did Stan encourage that?*
GC: Well, he didn't like zigzag panels or the crazy things that I would put on the page to excite the reader, because it was hard to follow. Everything goes from left to right, and when you have to start figuring out where the fourth panel is, if there are three panels on the top, or two panels on the top, and all of a sudden the panels turn into triangles, sometimes circles. I mean, I had them all over the place. You almost had to number the panels in order for the reader to know what came next.

DF: *Did he make you redraw that kind of stuff?*
GC: No. He asked me to "please cool it. Be a little more traditional." And I did for a short while, but I just gravitated back to it. To this day I'm still doing it.

DF: *But you two seemed to have a good rapport, creatively.*
GC: Oh, yes. I mean, Stan was wonderful to work with. He did a lot of kidding around. As I say, he's young today, just like he was then. He acts just like he always did. He's pretty amazing. Very funny. He always reminded me of Jack Lemmon.

DF: *I could see that.*
GC: I remember he had a problem with that ***Captain America*** story we did where I was inspired by the classic chase scene in the movie ***Bullitt.*** Captain America was either trying to catch up with someone, or getting away from someone. And I think it was the Red Skull. Instead of just taking a few panels and showing the car chase, I took about five, six pages to do it, and Stan flipped out over it. "Not good." He said, "Look, you could have done that in one panel. Why did you take up so much room? Did you forget that you had a plot?"

DF: *But he didn't make you redraw it. He went with it.*
GC: He went with it. It's been my experience, Stan may not have always liked what I did, but he wouldn't scrap the page. He had a deadline. He would just keep the art the way it was, but, of course, I would be jammed up for space at the end of the story because of all the space that I contributed toward the chase scene. I found out I damn near couldn't find room to finish the story!

DF: *Any concluding thoughts about Stan?*
GC: Yeah. He was a gem. I can tell you that. He's one of the nicest people I've ever known in the business. He was not a complainer, and he wouldn't put you down. Other editors I could not say that about.

Jim Mooney

After briefly working for the famed Eisner/Iger Studios, ***Jim Mooney*** *found steady work at Timely Comics and he maintained a working relationship with Timely and Stan Lee that remained intact well into the 1990s. Jim is fondly recalled for his* **Supergirl,** *and his work on* **Spider-Man** *is thought of by many as some of his best. I spoke to Jim via phone in late January 2008. Regrettably, he passed away on March 30th of the same year at age 89.*

—DF

DANNY FINGEROTH: *What was the first work you did with Stan, Jim? Did he write that?*
JIM MOONEY: Yes, it was a character called "E. Claude Pennygrabber." With most of Stan's early stuff, he'd give you an outline of it, and you'd sort of go from there. Like, he'd say, "Page one, let's have him do this, page two, have him do that, and so on, and then we'll climax with this pratfall or something."

DF: *And he would give that to you verbally, or in writing?*
JM: Usually verbally, because I was taking notes, and then, of course, I'd break it down, and then he'd later on put the balloons in.

DF: *So it sounds like in the early '40s he was working in what was later called "Marvel style."*
JM: He was. I think that was the beginning of his modus operandi, the way he worked.

DF: *How many years did you work for Stan in the '40s and '50s, approximately?*
JM: About three or four years, something like that. And then I went to DC.

DF: *And then you must have come back to Marvel in the early or mid-1960s?*
JM: Yeah. At that time I was having a few problems with an editor at DC, and I mentioned to Stan that I really wasn't too happy. He said, "Well, great. Maybe this could be a good time to come on with us again." So I got on the ***Spider-Man*** stuff.

DF: *Now, how did that work?*
JM: I mostly did finishes. I penciled some of them, too.

DF: *John Romita would break down the stories into layouts...*
JM: Sometimes it was tight penciling, sometimes it was loose penciling, sometimes it was just breakdowns.

DF: *Did you ever sit in on any of those famous plot conferences?*
JM: Occasionally. See, John Romita worked in the office, so when I'd come in, sometimes I'd get together with John and Stan. And Stan was always a gas. He'd be jumping on the table and climbing over chairs. *[laughter]* He went through all these histrionics of the way Spider-Man should be doing something.

DF: *What do you think made the Marvel characters different and so popular? Any thoughts on what Stan changed, or what he did differently, and how that happened?*
JM: I think it was just generally Stan's personality. I mean, you stop and think of all the stuff he developed. I mean, all of that was his, and it was his way of doing it.

DF: *You were friendly with Stan outside the office, weren't you?*
JM: Stan used to come up to my place in Woodstock when I lived there, and we were very, very close in those early days. Stan and I, from the very beginning, always got along well. I never had any disputes or harsh words or anything like that. I'd say it was a very, very friendly relationship.

DF: *I just want to thank you—from the time I was a kid, I loved your work, Jim, and then as your editor, and when you drew a story I wrote, too, it was a lot of fun and an honor working with you. And thank you so much for your time today.*
JM: I enjoyed it. You take care now.

The splash page to ***Amazing Spider-Man*** #69 (February 1969), which Jim pencilled and inked from layouts (credited as "storyboards") by John Romita. [© 2011 Marvel Characters, Inc.]

Joe Sinnott

***Joe Sinnott** honed his artistic craft at school in New York, leading him to a career in comics, first as Tom Gill's assistant. Then, in the 1950s, he drew for numerous publishers, including Westerns for Stan Lee. As the superheroes began filling the pages, Stan used Joe first as a penciler on Thor in **Journey into Mystery**, and then switched him to embellisher, his lush lines bringing fresh life to Jack Kirby's **Fantastic Four**. He has since inked every penciler Marvel has used. Currently, Joe is the inker on the Sunday **Spider-Man** strip. I spoke with him via phone on February 6, 2008.*

—DF

***DANNY FINGEROTH:** Joe, you've said [in **Alter Ego** v2, #26] that you'd go in to see Stan in the 1950s, and he would give you a script off the top of a pile of scripts.*
JOE SINNOTT: That's how it used to be, yeah. I'd go down every Friday. I've been with Stan longer than anybody—since 1950.

***DF:** And was there the name of a writer on those scripts?*
JS: Sometimes. Sometimes there were people like Hank Chapman and Ed Jurist. And, of course, Stan wrote a lot of them himself.

***DF:** And was he editing everything at that point?*
JS: Yes, he was the only one—the only editor there.

***DF:** Did he have assistants who worked on stuff?*
JS: There was a guy named Bob Brown. He was a penciler and inker, but he also worked on staff there. I'd go down there, there'd be a little anteroom, and there'd be guys sitting there waiting to see Stan. I can remember Bob Powell and Gene Colan. Gene and I started at roughly the same time. It seemed like Bob would come and say, "All right, Joe, Stan'll see you now." And we'd go in one at a time, bring our finished pages in.

***DF:** Gene must have gone freelance by then.*
JS: I think so. I know John Buscema was on staff there for a while. And they didn't have a big Bullpen, as I remember. Stan had a little drawing table in his office, and if there was something to be done, like a correction, I would do it at that desk.

***DF:** What percentage of those scripts did Stan write?*
JS: Guessing, I would say probably half. In fact, it seemed like you never went into his office where he wasn't sitting there typing on his yellow legal pad.

***DF:** Why did he type on yellow legal paper?*
JS: I don't know. Maybe it was just an idiosyncrasy of his.

***DF:** And would he make a carbon that he'd keep or something?*
JS: No. No.

***DF:** He gave you the only copy of the script? [laughs]*
JS: That's it.

Stan and Joe at the 1995 San Diego Comic-Con. The inscription says: "Joe—You're a really great penciller—a really great inker—but best of all—a really great guy! Excelsior! Your pal, Stan, '95." Photo courtesy of Mark and Joe Sinnott.

***DF:** You've said that you would go in to get the scripts from Stan, you would spend ten or fifteen minutes in his office. Obviously, it was more than him just giving you a script. What would you talk about, typically?*
JS: We'd talk about everything once we were together. Not work, of course. Stan was fun to be with. He really was, y'know? What I remember about working with him, mostly, was his sense of humor. It always came through, it seemed.

When I did ***Fantastic Four*** #5, Stan called me up and said, "Joe, whatever you do, don't leave us." *[laughs]* Once I got started doing ***Thor*** on a regular basis, he would call me. It really wasn't a business call. It was more of a, "How you doin', Joe? We like the work you're doing, and keep it up—and don't go over to DC." *[laughter]* And later on, when I came on ***FF*** permanently, with #44, Stan said to me, "Joe, we like what you're doing with Jack. Whatever you feel like doing, you do."

***DF:** Did Stan ever ask for changes to your art?*

HAIL TO THE CHIEF...STAN THAT IS!
BY: JOLTIN' JOE SINNOTT
EXCELSIOR!

Joe's imagining of Stan among the presidents on Mt. Rushmore, done for ***The Comics Buyer's Guide*** for Stan's 75th birthday in 1997. Courtesy of Mark and Joe Sinnott. [© 2011 Joe Sinnott.]

JS: The only time I ever worked with Stan, all 58 years, that he ever complained of something, was when I was doing a story called "Arrowhead." Arrowhead was an American Indian character. There had been a movie with Burt Lancaster called ***Arrowhead,*** and he was a renegade Indian, just like in the book.

Stan didn't write the script, and the splash said, "Show Arrowhead, a nice, heroic picture of Arrowhead, and around him show a montage of what happens at an Indian camp, the squaws running up a rug, the kids playing ball, and a hunter coming in with a deer on his shoulder," and so on. But as soon as Stan saw the art, he said, "Joe, the splash has no guts. Don't worry about what the script says. Whatever you feel is exciting, you do. Just show me a picture of Arrowhead, running right at the reader with a tomahawk. That'll make you want to turn the page to see what he's going to do with that tomahawk."

That was the only thing I ever had to change for Stan in all the years I've been working with him.

DF: When you penciled in the '60s, you penciled mostly Thor stories, as I recall. So when you'd get a **Thor** *script, say, it wasn't a plot, it was a full script? And those would be by Larry, or Robert Burns, who was Robert Bernstein.*
JS: Right. They were full scripts. I never worked "Marvel style."

DF: Any closing thoughts about Stan, Joe?
JS: Stan, to me at least, was very compassionate. I had some problems during my career, some real bad problems, and Stan couldn't have been any nicer. To me, he was always very generous. And, you know, Stan's a big name, everybody knows him all across the country. But it never affected him. He's completely down to earth.

DF: Joe, this has been a pleasure. Thank you so much.
JS: We could talk all day, Danny.

Mike Esposito

***Mike Esposito** was a penciler and inker who worked for a variety of publishers before teaming with penciler Ross Andru. Together their work, first at DC Comics on books such as* **The Metal Men,** *and later Marvel, and later at Marvel on* **Spider-Man,** *made them among the most distinctive teams in the business. Mike and Ross were also sometime-publishers. Under his own name or as Mickey Demeo, Mike was a prolific inker for Marvel Comics through the 1990s. I spoke with Mike via phone on February 21, 2008. Sad to say, he passed away on October 24, 2010.*

—DF

***DANNY FINGEROTH:** When did you start working with Stan, Mike?*
MIKE ESPOSITO: I started as a penciler for Stan in 1949. I penciled a lot of Westerns. I think I did one of those "Kid" things, maybe ***Rawhide Kid.*** As soon as I went in and I showed him my samples, he said, "Oh, you're a genius as a penciler. Eighty-five dollars a week, one page a day, and I'll put you on Westerns and some crime stuff."

DF: So you were on staff there, or you were freelancing?
ME: I was on staff.

DF: People have said Stan used to have a stack of scripts in his office in the '50s... ?
ME: Oh, yeah. I'd walk in and he'd take one and say, "Hey, do this."

DF: Were you ever in any of those famous story conferences where he'd jump up on a desk and everything like that?
ME: Oh, yes! In fact, it was with me alone one day. I was doing a crime story, and I didn't know how to pencil and exaggerate. And Stan said to me—I think Sol Brodsky was standing around, and Sol was laughing—and Stan gets up on the desk, and he says, "When you've got a gangster, he's got to have big, knotted hands, and a big, wide neck, like a thug." I didn't understand all that. He made sure that the artist understood how to exaggerate.

DF: And he would literally stand on the desk and do that kind of thing?
ME: He was on the desk that particular day, and he was ranting and screaming. And he was very dramatic. He could act anything. He was a good actor. He had a wild imagination, and he was clever. He and Bob Kanigher were similar in that respect. Bob had a brilliant, fast imagination, like Stan, off the top of his head. Stan really was a good, good guy with workers. He never made you feel that you weren't wanted. Ross and I were called up to work for Stan when things were slow, around 1957, when they nearly shut the place. He said, "I'm trying to make a comeback." He gave us some science fiction. He liked it so much he gave us a lot of stuff after that. He made us a team again. We were broken up for a while because work was scarce.

Ross Andru and Mike Esposito worked together for decades as a dynamic creative team, and were also best friends. Here's the splash to ***Amazing Spider-Man*** #153 (February 1976), penciled by Ross and inked by Mike. The script is by Len Wein. [© 2011 Marvel Characters, Inc.]

DF: Any closing observations about Stan, Mike?
ME: One thing about Stan. He was very, very complimentary. He always made you feel better than you were. He never put you on the carpet to tell you that you were bad, did lousy work. Always, "Boy, that's good." Even if it wasn't. So you felt pretty good.

DF: Thanks so much, Mike.
ME: Okay, pal.

Al Jaffee

Since 1955, **Mad Magazine** *and* ***Al Jaffee*** *have been synonymous. He's the man who invented, and continues to this day, the classic (and paper-saving)* ***Mad Fold-In*** *feature. But prior to* **Mad,** *Al began working in comics for Stan Lee at Timely and then Atlas Comics, mostly doing funny animal series. His work has earned him the National Cartoonists Society Advertising and Illustration Award for 1973, Special Features Award for 1971 and 1975, and Humor Comic Book Award for 1979. In 2008, Al won the NCS's Reuben Award for Outstanding Cartoonist of the Year. His biography,* ***Al Jaffee's Mad Life,*** *written by Mary-Lou Weisman, with 75 new illustrations by Al, was published in 2010 by HarperCollins. I spoke with Al via phone on January 28, 2008.*

—DF

DANNY FINGEROTH: *You worked for Stan in the early 1940s, Al?*
AL JAFFEE: I came into the comic business in 1940, prior to World War II, as far as America was concerned, and the United States still lived under terrible discrimination rules against Jews. Of course, against black people it was ten times worse. But my friends and I who were artists, we sat around trying to figure out if we could get into an advertising agency, and the discussion would be something like, "Forget about it, forget about it, you can't go to Benton and Bowles, they'll never hire a Jew." That kind of thing. Then, suddenly, this miracle happened: the comic book business, which was in large part developed by Jewish people, opened up to us. And that's how and why, I think, most of the people like Kirby and Eisner, we all got into it.

Anyway, I was on staff at Timely after I got out of the Army for about four years, from, say, 1946 to '50, when they were in the Empire State Building. I became an associate editor. I took care of all the teenage and animal humor features. About thirty titles. And they were 64 pages then.

DF: *And did you have assistants of your own?*
AJ: I had an assistant, Leon Lazarus. Leon was terrific. He had a very good eye. He was a writer, so he would read the scripts that came in and he would evaluate them for me, and if he said it was really lousy, I wouldn't even bother reading it. But, if he said it was good, then I got it.

DF: *And so did you work there before the war at all?*
AJ: Yes. Before the war, I was completely freelance. I worked at home. How I got to know Stan is that I had been doing a small feature for Will Eisner, and I think there came a point when Eisner either didn't see any reason to carry my feature, or they were retrenching, or something, and Eisner had to let me go. But he sent me over to a friend of his, Ed Cronin, who was handling Quality Comics' stuff, and I did some work for him. But then, through an inker named Chad Grothkopf, I ended up meeting Stan.

I took my portfolio over to Stan Lee, and Stan threw a script at me. I was there at the right place, at the right time, because Stan had just taken over from Simon and Kirby. He was maybe 17, 18, and I was19. Stan grabbed a script and threw it at me and said, "If you can do this, you'll do it regularly." It was a feature called "Squat Car Squad." So I did it, brought it in to Stan, and he says, "Okay, from now on, you do it. And *write* it, also." So I wrote it and brought in the first script, and he said, "Fine. Keep on writing it, and just go ahead and do the script and art, and bring it in finished." He didn't even edit it.

DF: *How do you explain him trusting you like that after so short a time?*
AJ: I had a feeling that we were hitting it off on some level. I can't honestly tell you what it is. You know, it happens from time to time. I don't think my portfolio was anything to rave about. But even while I was doing "Squat Car Squad," when Stan felt that that was running its course, he said, "Create a new feature." So I created "Ziggy Pig and Silly Seal." Actually, I created Silly Seal, and, after a while, Stan said to me, "Why don't we give Silly a partner, and how about a pig called Ziggy?" I said, "Great." And we put the two together, and he gave me a free hand writing those things.

DF: *So were there long meetings where you would discuss stories?*
AJ: No, we never discussed stories. There really isn't a hell of a lot to discuss when you're doing ***Ziggy Pig and Silly Seal.*** Strangely, in most of my stories with those characters, they were fighting the war. Silly Seal was building submarines out of ice cubes. I mean, really weird, but in those days, without television, visual material of any kind was very popular. And, during the war, other people were doing tons of ***Ziggy Pig and Silly Seal,*** and it was going to the military bases.

DF: *When you came in and Stan threw you that script, did you chat for a while to get to know each other?*
AJ: Stan was very friendly with me, and we did chat a little bit. But you have to remember, here's a guy who's 17, 18 years old, who has taken over not only this huge number of animal features, but he was carrying all the

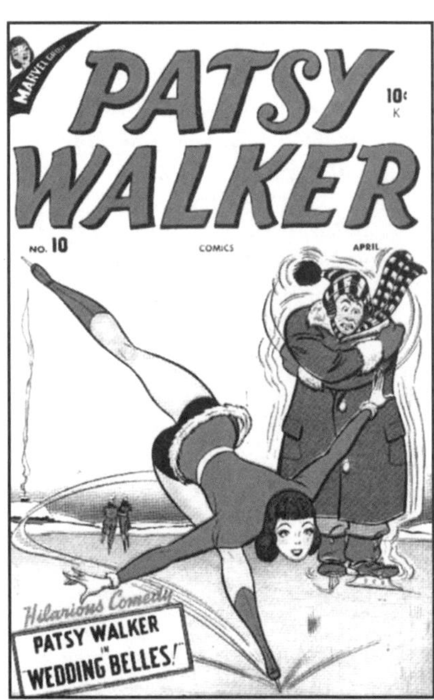

Patsy Walker #10 (April 1947) cover by Al. [© 2011 Marvel Characters, Inc.]

Captain America and ***Human Torch*** and all the rest of that superhero stuff. He was rattling off cover ideas...

DF: *Now, that's what I want to talk to you a little bit about, because you talk, in your 2004* **Alter Ego** *interview, about how the one thing you* did *confer with him about was covers...*
AJ: Oh, yeah. We would have a meeting when the printing schedule would dictate that a whole bunch of new comics were going to come out. I would go in to Stan and I would say, "Well, we need about 20 covers. For ***Patsy Walker,*** and ***Jeannie,*** and ***Frankie***" and so on. So many titles. And Stan was amazing. He would rattle off cover ideas. He just had a great feel for the medium.

DF: *Was it sort of understood that the covers were his domain?*
AJ: Oh, yes. It was his domain.

DF: *Who did the actual cover sketches?*
AJ: The artists who did the series. Say, if Chris Rule was doing ***Patsy Walker*** at the time, he would do the ***Patsy Walker*** cover.

DF: *So you weren't sitting there with him, sketching out each cover as he dictated?*
AJ: No. I was writing down what the ideas were. Stan was very creative, and he was quick-thinking. He didn't really sit and agonize over things.

DF: *Well, he must have been supervising something like 80 or 100 titles a month.*
AJ: And he was on top of everything, that I can guarantee. He knew what was going on, and he had his finger on everything that was going on. And when you came to him with problems, he would solve them very quickly. He just didn't sit around and mull over it and sulk. He'd say, "Okay, let's have it go this way," and just change the whole direction of something.

DF: *You were handling the teen books and the humor books. Was Stan handling everything* else, or were there other associates like you?
AJ: Don Rico was handling some of the adventure stuff. Stan and Don Rico were in charge of all the adventure.

DF: *Now, going through history, and also your* **AE** *interview, it sounds like there were two downsizings, in '49, and again in '57. Did you leave and come back, or how did that work?*
AJ: I was downsized in mid-'49, and I don't know what happened with the '57 one, because I was freelance then. I came back to work for Timely after '49, but not on staff. I was doing ***Super Rabbit.*** Super Rabbit was... well, he was a superhero who was a rabbit. *[laughter]* I had a lot of fun with ***Super Rabbit***. And with ***Patsy Walker,*** which I was doing freelance. Stan said, "Do whatever you think is right and just bring in a completely finished book." Which I did. I did, on average, two complete books a month for about five years.

DF: *And those were edited directly by him?*
AJ: I brought them directly to him, and then we chatted and enjoyed each other's company for a while. But he didn't sit there and read my stuff. I guess it worked both ways. He trusted me, and I did the best I could, and he knew he didn't have to worry about anything I was doing. It was a very nice way for me to work, to not have to run back and forth and be edited on every panel. So I think it was good both ways. I enjoyed working with Stan. I felt that even though his position was much, much higher than mine, and his responsibilities and the way he carried them out were on a much higher level, still, I really thoroughly enjoyed working with him. He was very good to me, and I hope that I returned the same thing to him.

DF: *When you first started working there, he was so young. Was there ever a sense that anybody didn't take him seriously because of his youth, or was he able to rise above that?*
AJ: Not when he was 17, but when he was in his twenties, when I worked at Timely, there were a few people who didn't take being edited very easily, and they would grumble about this "young whippersnapper" kind of thing, "wet behind the ears, and what does he know?" "I know more about superheroes than he'll ever know," that kind of thing.

DF: *These guys were probably all of three years older than him.* [laughs]
AJ: They didn't challenge Stan, but because he solved problems very quickly, they felt he was cavalier about things. I'm not saying that there were a *lot* of people who felt that way, but there were a few.

DF: *Did you see any change in Stan over the years?*
AJ: Well, it's interesting. there were two Stan Lees, because one Stan Lee wrote little animal stories, but the Stan Lee that everyone has known for the last forty years or more at least is the co-creator of Spider-Man, the Hulk, and all of those other characters.

DF: *Was it two Stan Lees, or was it just two sides of the same person?*
AJ: Well, I think there were two Stan Lees because of the times that demanded a different Stan Lee. I mean, the Stan Lee of the 1940s was a guy who was doing a lot of Disney-like comic books. But his ultimate fame, of course, came from the superheroes.

DF: *Thanks, Al. I really appreciate this.*
AJ: Oh, you're very welcome.

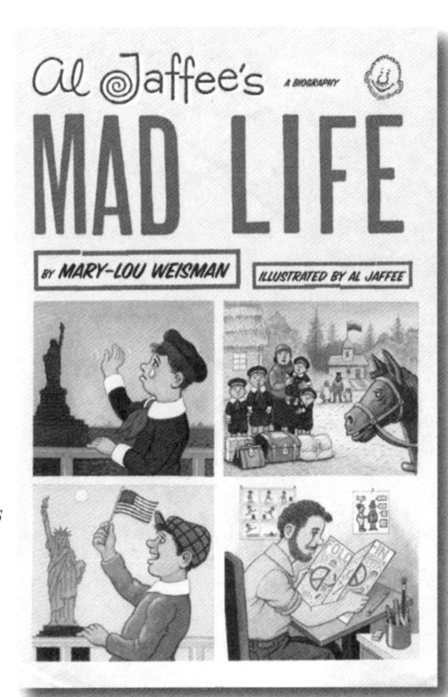

Al's years working with Stan are covered in his 2010 biography, ***Al Jaffee's Mad Life***, written by Mary-Lou Weisman, with 75 new illustrations by Al. [Book text ©2010 Mary-Lou Weisman. New Illustrations ©2010 Al Jaffee.]

Stan Goldberg

Few realize that humor illustrator supreme **Stan Goldberg** *is also the man responsible for picking the colors on the early Marvel Universe heroes and villains. He began his lengthy association with Stan by joining Timely Comics in 1949. During his long career, he illustrated* **Mille the Model** *for Atlas and Marvel, later did* **Binky** *for DC, and has been one of the most prolific Archie artists. Stan has recently done work for Bongo, DC, and Marvel, and in 2010, Schoolism Online (www.schoolism.com) released a* **Stan Goldberg Instructional Video.** *I spoke with "Stan G" via phone on January 29, 2008.*

—DF

Joe Sinnott, Larry Lieber, Stan Lee, and Stan Goldberg in 1995 at a Sotheby's comics-related auction in New York. Photo courtesy of Mark and Joe Sinnott.

DANNY FINGEROTH: *When did you start at Marvel, Stan?*
STAN GOLDBERG: In 1949, when I was 16, just about ready to turn 17. I got a job in the coloring department, and another year and a half went by, and the guy that was running it left, so it was a little department of three, sometimes four, and I became in charge of that. Eventually I started drawing little three-page stories that Stan would give me, little adventure stories. There were giants in that Bullpen, along with a proofreader or a letterer. There was Joe Maneely, and Bill Everett, and Carl Burgos, and Fred Kida, and John Severin.

DF: *Were there other editors besides Stan?*
SG: There was Stan Lee, and then there was Stan Lee. Gerta Gattel was there, and a woman named Bonnie Hano. They were more or less production people. Al Sulman was kind of an editor.

But everything had to go through Stan. I remember when I started doing the teenage books and ***Millie***, I would bring in these big pages of art, and Stan would turn the pages very quickly, but if there was something that was missing or wrong, there was his finger on it. "Do this, do that, do this." And Gerta would bring some books in that were ready to go to the printer, and he'd quickly go through the books, and if there was anything that had to be done, it would be done in the Bullpen.

When times got tough for the company. I left for a while, But Stan eventually called me back in because they were going to put out some comic books, and they needed to be colored.

DF: *And you came up with the colors for all the Marvel heroes?*
SG: For the superheroes and supervillains, for the first five or six years of all those characters that came out of Marvel, I was responsible for their colors. Stan says, "You do whatever you think will look best." He was too busy coming up with the ideas, and he trusted me in doing all that color stuff.

DF: *You wrote and drew* **Millie the Model,** *didn't you? 25 pages of story per issue?*
SG: There probably were, and then there were another five or six pages each issue—pinup pages, fashion pages—that I would design.

I think one of Stan's greatest contributions to comics was the idea of letting the artists come up with plots, and discussing them with the writer, of course. With me, it was, "Come up with some plots next week and tell me about it." And I would come in to him and give him a couple of plots, and he'd say, "Great. Give me 25 pages." That was the extent of it.

DF: *You wouldn't work it out scene-by-scene or anything?*
SG: No, and I think that was the best thing for me. You know, I was informed that ***Millie the Model*** was selling just as well as ***Spider-Man.*** It was quite a successful book, but after a while, when Stan was doing more work for the other books, putting more time and effort into the others, when I'd bring in pages, he didn't even have to see the breakdowns of how I was telling my story. This gave me an opportunity to tell a story, to come up with plots and ideas and locales that I felt like, and that I wanted to draw—not what a writer would tell me.

DF: *And Stan would do the dialogue when you would plot and pencil the stories?*
SG: Right. I put some along the side of the pages. And when I would bring the bunch of pages in for Stan, I would explain what was going on in them.

DF: *Did you ever have any of those plot conferences with him where he would jump up on a table and act out stories?*
SG: I remember one time when I told him I couldn't come up with a plot for a ***Millie*** adventure. He got very serious and said, "I don't want to ever hear you say you cannot come up with another plot." And just those words did something. I was always able to come up with plots after that. To have him as my editor in the first 10, 15 years of my career was the best thing any artist could ever have. And he is as important to the *industry* as he was to my career. Without him, I wouldn't have had this career, which I still enjoy tremendously.

DF: *Of his generation of editors, Stan is the one spoken most well of by people who worked with and for him. What do you think accounts for that?*
SG: I think it might have to do with the fact that Stan didn't come from another industry. He didn't come in when he was 30

years old after some other career. He really wanted to be a comic book writer and editor.

DF: *I know you would have lunch with Stan regularly, and go for walks with him, and he would drive you home. Any memories of conversations relating to craft—to plotting, scripting, drawing—from those meetings or those rides?*
SG: I would bring in my work on Friday, and he would drive me home, and we would go over the stuff. And before the drive, we would even take time to go out for lunch, and I would be there all day. But when he'd drive me home, before dropping me off, he'd say, "Do you have enough work for the weekend?" And I would say, "Stan, I just brought in so many pages." But he enjoyed working. Even when we would go to visit him at his and Joan's house in Hewlett Harbor, he would say, "Come on upstairs." That's where he worked. "Let's go over some new ideas that I have." These were ideas that we would try to submit for syndication.

DF: *That sounds like a partnership you had, kicking new ideas around? When he said, "I have an idea," would you two would build on it or something?*
SG: We would build on it and discuss it, "Let's change this, then change that." And sometimes we would work on something for weeks and weeks, and then he would come up with something, or I would see something different, and we would throw out what we did. I had envelopes full of these things. One was a single-panel gag strip, like ***The Lockhorns***. We called it ***Doc***. It was about a friendly little doctor, and nobody really is deathly sick or anything like that, but he was a funny character. But we couldn't sell it. There was another single-panel strip, it was about a lady of the evening. But we didn't designate her as a prostitute. Her name was "Lil Repute."

DF: *That has sort of a Mae West feel to it.*
SG: Yeah, exactly. And there was a character named "John Doe: Mr. Everyman," because that was that time of the movie ***The Man in the Gray Flannel Suit*** with Gregory Peck, so we came up with a character that was based on him.

DF: *Did you ever sell any of this stuff?*
SG: We were able to get rid of about 75% of the ***Doc*** material to medical journals.

DF: *Did you come close with any strips to anybody picking it up as a regular feature?*

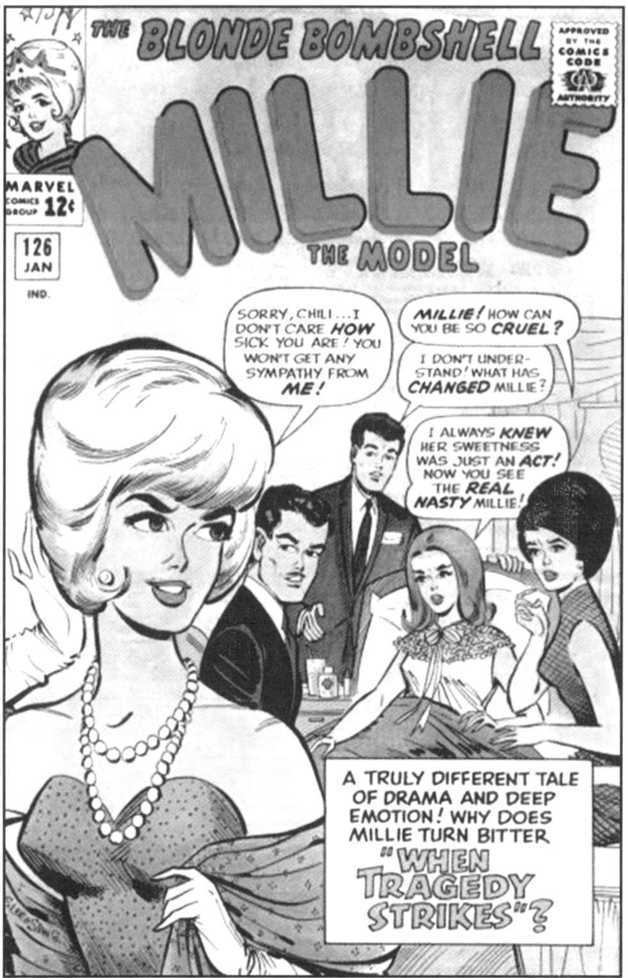

Cover to ***Millie the Model*** #126, January 1965, drawn by Stan G. [©2011 Marvel Characters, Inc.]

SG: Not with me, but Stan had a couple of successes that, one with Al Hartley, and one with Joe Maneely. The one with Joe was called ***Mrs. Lions' Cubs***, and then Joe died suddenly. And then there was ***Willie Lumpkin***, which Stan did with Dan DeCarlo. It was about a mailman, and it had a short run.

DF: *That was a name Stan used later for the Fantastic Four's mailman. It was actually his cameo character in the first* **FF** *movie.*
SG: We were just flying by the seat of our pants at that time.

DF: *This was great. Thanks so much, Stan.*
SG: It was my pleasure.

Jerry Robinson

Jerry Robinson *had just finished high school when he began assisting Bob Kane on the early exploits of Batman. He soon joined the DC staff as an artist and then went on to write and draw for other publishers, including Timely. After leaving comics, he produced comic strips and editorial cartoons, becoming one of the medium's foremost historians and educators. His* **Life With Robinson** *strip ran for many years. Among Jerry's numerous recent projects is a new edition of his classic* **The Comics: An Illustrated History of Comic Strip Art 1895-2010** *(from Dark Horse). I spoke with Jerry via phone on February 25, 2008.*

—DF

DANNY FINGEROTH: *When did you work with Stan, Jerry?*
JERRY ROBINSON: I worked with Stan mostly from '50 to '60. Just prior to the Marvel superheroes. We did all sorts of

Jerry Robinson penciled and inked this cover to the March 1953 ***Men's Adventures*** #19. [©2011 Marvel Characters, Inc.]

things—that was part of the fun of working with Stan. I'd do everything from romance, to crime, to science fiction, to mystery, to Westerns. So it was great variety. That's what I enjoyed most, coming off of so many years of just doing Batman.

DF: *How'd you meet him?*
JR: I think we met when I was teaching at the School of Visual Arts in New York. I taught there for ten years, roughly, in the '50s. I invited Stan to speak to my students. He was always very articulate and spoke very well. We kind of hit it off. And, I guess he must have know my work from Batman or elsewhere, because he said, "Gee, I'd love to work with you." So I decided, "Well, I'll do a few stories for him." So I wound up working for him. He enticed me back to comic books, since I wasn't interested in doing them at that time. He's a very nice guy. We got along very well. We had a very nice relationship for those years. And he was a very easy editor. I guess he had confidence in what I would do, so I didn't have to check anything with him.

DF: *When you worked with him, would you co-plot things, or would he just hand you a script?*
JR: Well, there was no "usual" with Stan. But a great deal of it was scripted in advance, some by him, and I would say, probably a lot by other people, such as Don Rico.

DF: *Did you ever write your own stuff for him?*
JR: Well, I would say I *re*wrote for him. *[laughter]* Stan trusted me to do what I wanted with his stories.

DF: *You must have been something of a celebrity coming over to Timely from* **Batman.**
JR: Well, it's not very humble of me to say this...

DF: *Don't worry about being humble. Please go on.*
JR: ... but in a documentary done about me for Brazilian TV, Stan said I was one of the best writers he ever had and that he was honored to have me. It was a nice speech.

DF: *That's a great compliment. Now, did you ink yourself on the stuff you did for Stan?*
JR: Yes. Most everything I did, complete.

DF: *Any memorable lunches, walks, or talks, with Stan?*
JR: Whenever I was down at the office, we'd try to get a lunch. Also, I remember going to the barber with him a couple of times, so we could talk while we were barbering. I didn't get in there that often, though. I'd mostly send my work in, but now and then it was always fun to go down there and talk with Stan. He was a very bright guy, very outgoing.

DF: *Thanks, Jerry. Great stuff.*
JR: Thank you, Danny.

Dick Ayers

Dick Ayers *entered comics in the late 1940s. He helped create the original* **Ghost Rider** *(published by Magazine Enterprises) and went on to pencil and ink in every genre. At Marvel, Dick inked much of Jack Kirby's '50s and '60s work. His penciling credits include* **Giant Man** *and a long stint on* **Sgt. Fury.** *Still active today, Dick has authored a three-volume memoir in comics form,* **The Dick Ayers Story: An Illustrated Autobiography**. *I spoke with him via phone on April 3, 2008.*

—DF

DANNY FINGEROTH: *How and when did you first meet Stan, Dick?*
DICK AYERS: One day, in 1951, I was near the Empire State Building, where Timely had its offices. I figured, maybe I'll go up and see if I can meet Stan Lee. I went up and sent in my portfolio, and back came a gal who said, "Stan wants to see

you." And sure enough, Stan said: "I'll have work for you." He came through after a couple of weeks and once he started, he kept me busy for a long, long time.

DF: *When he would give you a story, did you get the impression he was thinking, "This would be perfect for Dick," or that he was just giving you what was on the top of the pile?*
DA: No, he knew what he was giving me. At first Stan had me bring in the pencils to look at. Around the second or third story I did for him, he said, "You don't have to do that anymore, Dick, just deliver 'em."

DF: *Did Stan ever make you redraw anything?*
DA: Well, once I brought in a so-called "horror" story—I hate when people call them that, they were really surprise-ending stories—and it was about a ghost ship. He said, "This doesn't look like a ghost ship. Where are the cobwebs?" and where is this and where is that? "You take this story back and you add stuff to the ship so it looks like a ghost ship."

DF: *From the beginning, you were penciling and inking your work... ?*
DA: Right. Then, they were cutting down on production, and one day Stan said to me, "Dick, the ship is sinking." I went and got a job in the post office. Then I called Stan, and he said, "How about I try you inking somebody else's work?" So he sent me Kirby's pencils on a ***Wyatt Earp*** cover, because I was drawing the interiors. Stan liked that, and then he started sending me Kirby's monster stories.

DF: *When you worked with Stan directly, would he talk the plot out with you?*
DA: Early on he would write a plot synopsis—very short—and send it to me. Five or six paragraphs. But most of the time, we'd use the telephone. That happened pretty quickly with ***Sgt. Fury.*** Stan worked on it with me for my first twenty-some odd issues. I plotted, I think it was #23, the one I call "The Nun's Story," but that ended up being called "The Man Who Failed."

I'd call every other week to get a plot from Stan. But this time he said, "Dick, I haven't got an idea. *You've* got to think of one today." I couldn't sleep. My wife, Wendy, was upset. "Why can't you sleep?" "I can't think up this story," I tell her. So she thinks for a minute, and then she says, "Oh, this is easy. Have this nun coming out from behind the Japanese lines, and she's saving these kids." "Boy, I said, that's a good idea, but I don't think Stan'll go for it." Because this was the 1960s, and you couldn't really show religion in a comic. But Stan liked it. So I wrote the plot and Stan wrote the words.

I have this five-page story we did together, framed and on the wall. It's called "And Not a Word Was Spoken." *[From* **Two-Gun Kid** *#61.—DF]* It's all in pantomime, seven panels on a page. Stan described what should be going on in every panel.

DF: *How would you sum up working with Stan, Dick?*
DA: A really positive thing. I loved him. Still do.

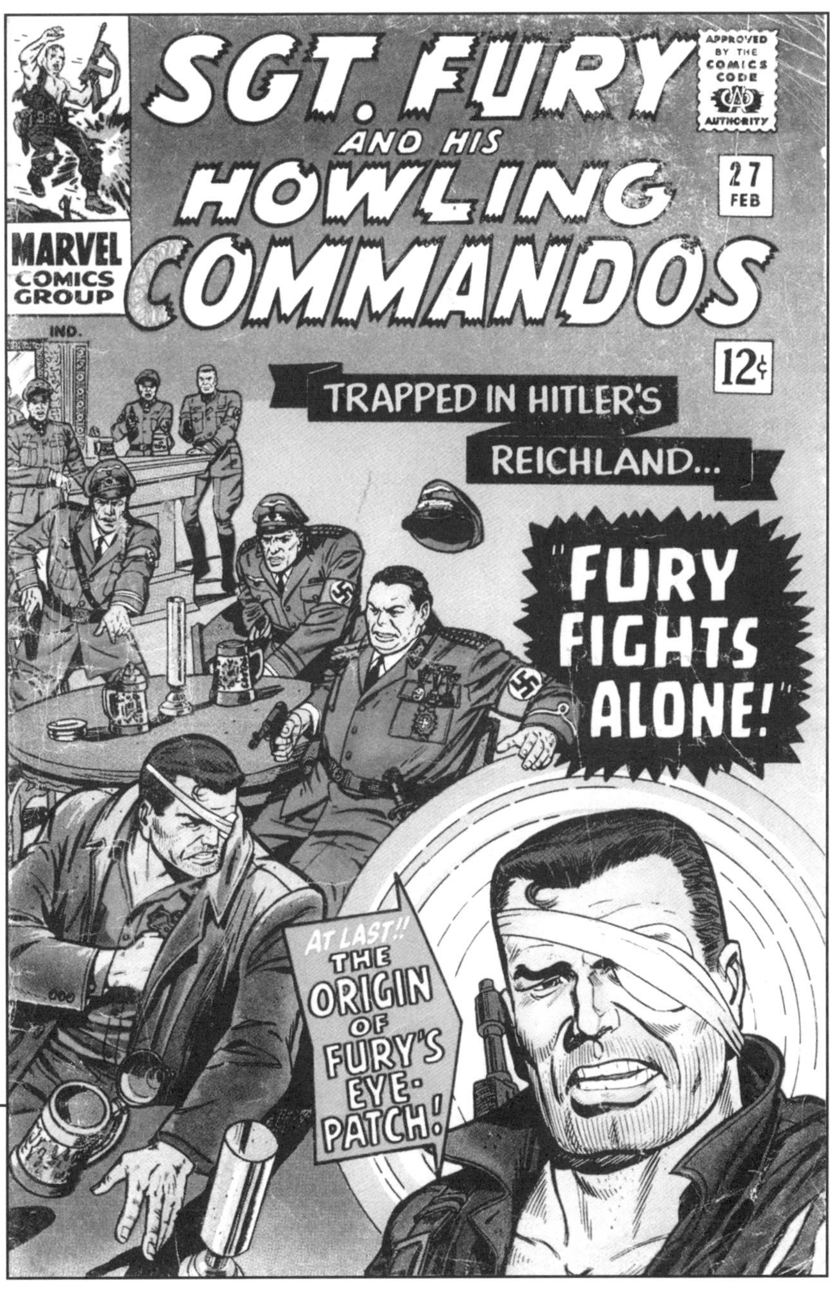

Dick penciled the cover and interiors to ***Sgt. Fury*** #27 (February 1966), written by Stan, in which readers found out how Nick Fury came to need an eye patch in his modern incarnation. Inks by John Tartaglione.

Flo Steinberg

*In the 1960s, "**Fabulous Flo**" **Steinberg** was the cheery face and voice of the Marvel Comics offices, greeting the freelancers and fans that made their way to the company's cramped quarters. She handled correspondence and worked as Stan Lee's secretary. Flo later went on to her own publishing efforts before returning to Marvel as a staff proofreader. I spoke with Flo via phone on February 11, 2008.*

—DF

In this panel from ***What If*** #11 (October 1978), Jack Kirby imagines "What If the Original Marvel Bullpen Had Become the Fantastic Four?" Here, we see Stan as Mr. Fantastic, Flo as the Invisible Girl, and Jack as The Thing. (In case you were wondering, Sol Brodsky became the Torch.) Script and pencils by Kirby, inks by Mike Royer. [©2011 Marvel Characters, Inc.]

***DF:** Flo, is there anything you remember about how Stan treated writers, and any tips you might have heard him give them, or any plot conferences you might have seen?*
FS: Well, I would not be in his office while Stan was having his writers conferences, but I could hear them. And people would go in, like Steve Ditko, or Jack Kirby, or Don Heck, or Dick Ayers, and Wally Wood, and so on. They would talk, and voices would get raised in excitement, and Stan would be acting out what he wanted the characters to be doing or saying, their actions, motivations. And there would be jumping around. And I don't know whether I imagined it or what, but I'm sure Stan was hopping up on the desk, on the chair. He was very physical, acting out the stuff, and he would run back and forth, and then—"boom-boom-boom"—the sound effects he wanted would come crashing through the walls.

DF:** When you went on to edit your own comics, in the mid-'70s,* ***Big Apple Comix, *did you apply things you learned from working with Stan?*
FS: Mostly to treat people with respect. And after ***Big Apple***, I worked for 12 years with this arts magazine where I did the editing, and printing, and really everything, because it was a small magazine. I always remembered the way Stan handled people—he did it so well.

Flo edited and published the 1975 one-shot ***Big Apple Comix***, which featured work by creators including Neal Adams, Archie Goodwin, Denny O'Neil, Al Williamson, and Wallace Wood. Cover art by Wood. [©2011 the copyright holders.]

He was so articulate. He was able to get across what he wanted, and to get it back from people. And, if he had to correct someone, he did so tactfully and gently. You know, he was a consummate professional.

***DF:** What did you do for Marvel's letters pages?*
FS: Well, zillions of letters came in, and there would be folders for each magazine. I would give them to Stan, and we would pick out ones that would go in the letters pages. And Stan would write the answers.

***DF:** And he would write all the announcements in the letters pages, too?*
FS: He would. It was all part of the job. He worked so hard, but he never got stressed, he was always pleasant to everybody, and always appreciated the work everybody did.

***DF:** Did he type all the stuff directly into the typewriter, or did he do it longhand first?*
FS: Directly on a typewriter. A manual typewriter. He would do his scripts right on the typewriter, too.

Stan was nothing but great. I love Stan. You know, one funny story: My cousin Jeffrey, who's a TV and movie writer out in L.A., was with a friend outside one of the big Jewish delis there. And Stan comes out, and Jeffrey goes over and says, "I'm sorry to bother you, but I just wanted to say that my cousin is Flo Steinberg, and I know if she knew I had run into you, she'd want me to say 'hi' for her." And when Jeffrey told me the story, I said to him, "I bet I know what Stan replied—it's what he always says when people mention my name." And Jeffrey told me that, sure enough, Stan smiled and said, "Flo—what a gal!"

Tell It To The Doctor

Stan's correspondence with comics fandom pioneer Dr. Jerry G. Bails

by Roy Thomas and Danny Fingeroth

Along with Roy Thomas, ***Jerry Bails, Ph.D.*** *was one of the founders of comics fandom, including, in 1961, founding* **Alter Ego** *magazine, which was later published by Roy. Jerry also became one of comics' greatest indexers, compiling the first* **Who's Who** *of comics creators. Here, from Roy's archives, are some letters Jerry exchanged with Stan in the early days of Marvel. They're a fascinating glimpse into the thought processes of both men. Sadly, Bails passed away in 2006 at age 73.*

MAGAZINE MANAGEMENT COMPANY
655 MADISON AVENUE, NEW YORK 21, N. Y. • TEmpleton 8-7900

SEP. 1 1961

8/29/61

Dear Jerry:

Enjoyed reading ALTER-EGO and the COMICOLLECTOR, and got a kick out of your little critique of THE FANTASTIC FOUR, written by Roy Thomas.

Just to correct a few small inaccuracies though, I'm not a "former" editor of Timely-- I've been editor and art director of that redoubtable institution for the past 21 years, and hope to continue ad infinitum. Also, it is doubtful that Mr. Thomas is the "only person who bought a copy" (although he said that humorously, of course) because judging by early sales reports, I think we have a winner on our hands!

As for the future of the F.F., we WILL have :
COSTUMES
A DIFFERENT TREATMENT (art-wise) OF THE TORCH
ADDITIONAL NEW CHARACTERS IN MONTHS TO COME
(Don't be too surprised to meet Sub-Mariner again, or Captain America! Who knows??)
AND A FEW MORE SURPRISES... so stay with us, pal!

Would be interested in your opinion of another new mag due to go on sale soon-- AMAZING ADULT FANTASY. We think it's a smash.

Regarding some of the various comments concerning the F.F., we have purposely refrained from letting invisible girl (oops, sorry!) Invisible Girl walk thru walls, and from giving TOO MUCH super powers to our characters, as we feel that effects like those are chiefly of appeal to the YOUNGER readers, and we are trying (perhaps vainly?) to reach a slightly older, more sophisticated group.

Enough for now- keep up the good work.

Regards,

Stan Lee

Dr. Jerry G. Bails in 1965
[courtesy interfan.org]

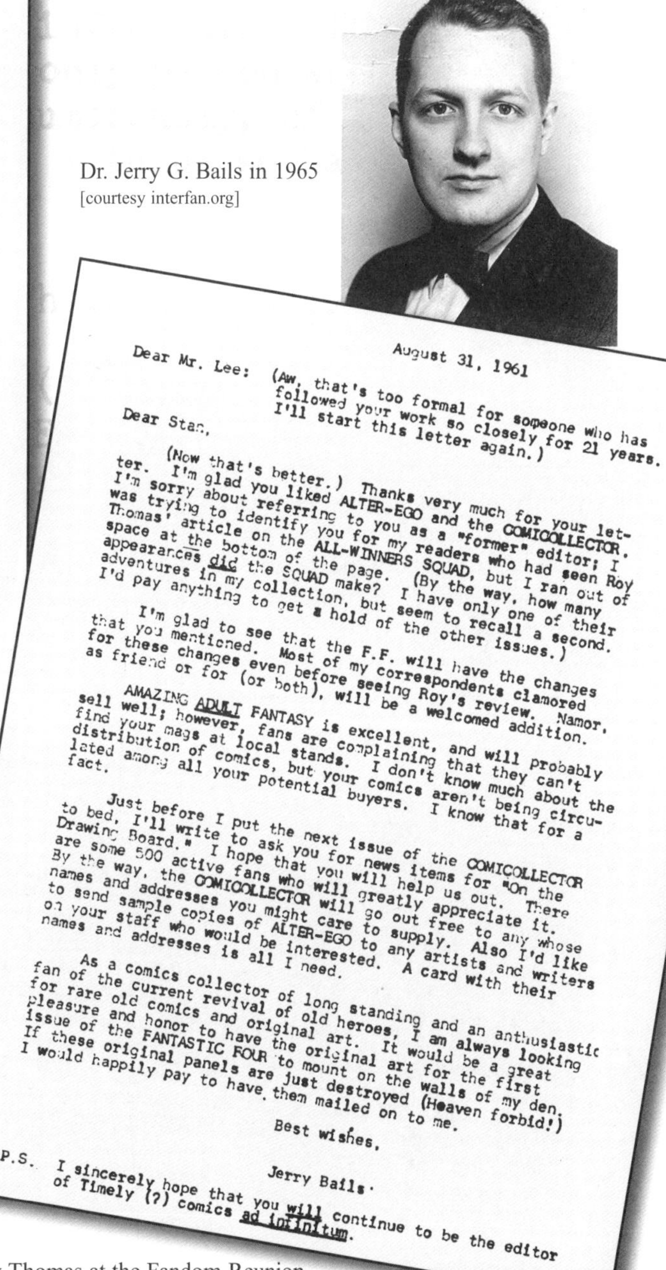

August 31, 1961

Dear Mr. Lee: (Aw, that's too formal for someone who has followed your work so closely for 21 years. I'll start this letter again.)

Dear Stan,

(Now that's better.) Thanks very much for your letter. I'm glad you liked ALTER-EGO and the COMICOLLECTOR. I'm sorry about referring to you as a "former" editor; I was trying to identify you for my readers who had seen Roy Thomas' article on the ALL-WINNERS SQUAD, but I ran out of space at the bottom of the page. (By the way, how many appearances did the SQUAD make? I have only one of their adventures in my collection, but seem to recall a second. I'd pay anything to get a hold of the other issues.)

I'm glad to see that the F.F. will have the changes that you mentioned. Most of my correspondents clamored for these changes even before seeing Roy's review. Namor, as friend or for (or both), will be a welcomed addition.

AMAZING ADULT FANTASY is excellent, and will probably sell well; however, fans are complaining that they can't find your mags at local stands. I don't know much about the distribution of comics, but your comics aren't being circulated among all your potential buyers. I know that for a fact.

Just before I put the next issue of the COMICOLLECTOR to bed, I'll write to ask you for news items for "On the Drawing Board." I hope that you will help us out. There are some 500 active fans who will greatly appreciate it. By the way, the COMICOLLECTOR will go out free to any whose names and addresses you might care to supply. Also I'd like to send sample copies of ALTER-EGO to any artists and writers on your staff who would be interested. A card with their names and addresses is all I need.

As a comics collector of long standing and an anthusiastic fan of the current revival of old heroes, I am always looking for rare old comics and original art. It would be a great pleasure and honor to have the original art for the first issue of the FANTASTIC FOUR to mount on the walls of my den. If these original panels are just destroyed (Heaven forbid!) I would happily pay to have them mailed on to me.

Best wishes,

Jerry Bails

P.S. I sincerely hope that you will continue to be the editor of Timely (?) comics ad infinitum.

Jerry Bails and Roy Thomas at the Fandom Reunion luncheon, Chicago, 1997. [©2002 Complex City]

THE TWO GREATEST NEW FANTASY MAGAZINES IN THE WORLD!

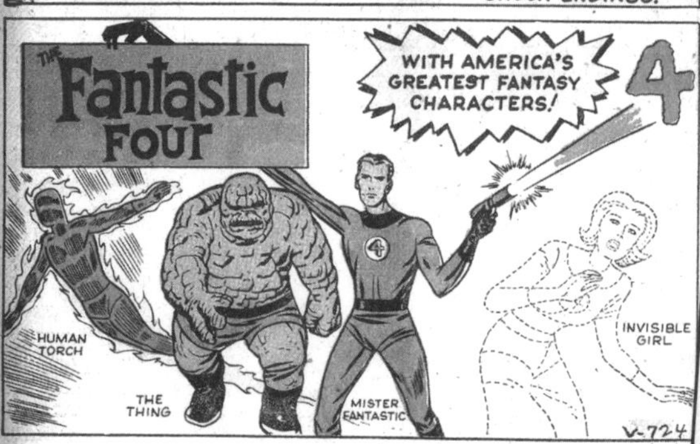

Jerry and Stan discuss *Amazing (Adult) Fantasy* and *Fantastic Four* in their correspondence. Above, a house ad for those then-new publications. [©2011 Marvel Characters, Inc.]

MAGAZINE MANAGEMENT COMPANY
655 MADISON AVENUE, NEW YORK 21, N. Y. • TEmpleton 8-7900

Dear Jerry: 1/8/62

Regarding your letter with request for info about the Fantastic Four, there's really not much I can say. We're playing it by ear, editing it mostly in accordance with the wishes of our readers who have been kind enough to send literally hundreds of letters with much constructive criticism.

I can say this, though. The mag has been better received than any other we've produced in a long time. And Jack Kirby and I have many ideas which we think are somewhat original for future issues. It seems pointless to mention them now, as it would probably spoil your enjoyment, as well as that of your readers, if you knew of them beforehand. My own theory is that surprise is one of the most important elements in a mag. (Which is why we try to make our characters somewhat unpredictable, and less stereotyped than some of our competitors'.) We follow the same formula in AMAZING ADULT, trying for surprise more than any other single element.

Unfortunately, we have a very small staff here- unlike National, and some other publishers. Your truly writes most of our mags, and edits them-- as well as doing the proof-reading, production, etc. We have a handful of artists who work steadily for us (on a free-lance basis) and I'm lucky if I even have time to see much of THEM during the week. That is the reason these letters are so few and far between. When I pause to write a letter like this, it means some script writing, editing, or some such chore, is being neglected. My dream is to some day be able to concentrate on one, or two, or even five mags, to the exclusion of everything else. Then, brother, you'd see some CLASSICS!

Anyway, I certainly do enjoy ALTER-EGO, and gave a copy to Kirby, Ditko, etc. Please understand that those guys are in the same boat as I-- always behind on deadlines, due to the press of work, and simply can't find time to write to you, although I will again suggest that they do if they can get a spare moment. One suggestion- if there are any specific questions you ever want answered, if you could jot them down, and leave a space for a yes or no answer, or some such thing, and send it to me- or to them in care of me, it might make it easier all around-- easier certainly than writing an entire letter.

One last bit of info- we're about to go on sale with a new title-- THE HULK. (Hits the stands the beginning of March). Like it or not, you'll have to admit it's gonna be real DIFFERENT. I'd be anxious to get your opinion, and that of your readers.

3/27/62

Dear Jerry:
Sorry you don't dig the HULK...But somewhere, out there in comic magland, there must be SOMEONE who likes nice mean ugly characters who don't wear brightly colored underwear in public! The next FF yarn in the works is called "PRISONERS OF KURRGO, THE SCOURGE OF PLANET X!" which should win a prize as the longest, if not the best title! Can't tell you what it's about because I haven't finished writing it yet. Some fun-- still writing the script, and the mag was due to go to engraver a week ago! Latest scoops: HUMAN TORCH will be featured in STRANGE TALES... ANT MAN featured in ASTONISH... THOR will be featured in JRNY INTO MYSTERY! And Stan Lee will be featured in the booby hatch if he can't crawl out from under these doggone deadlines!

All tha best-
Stan

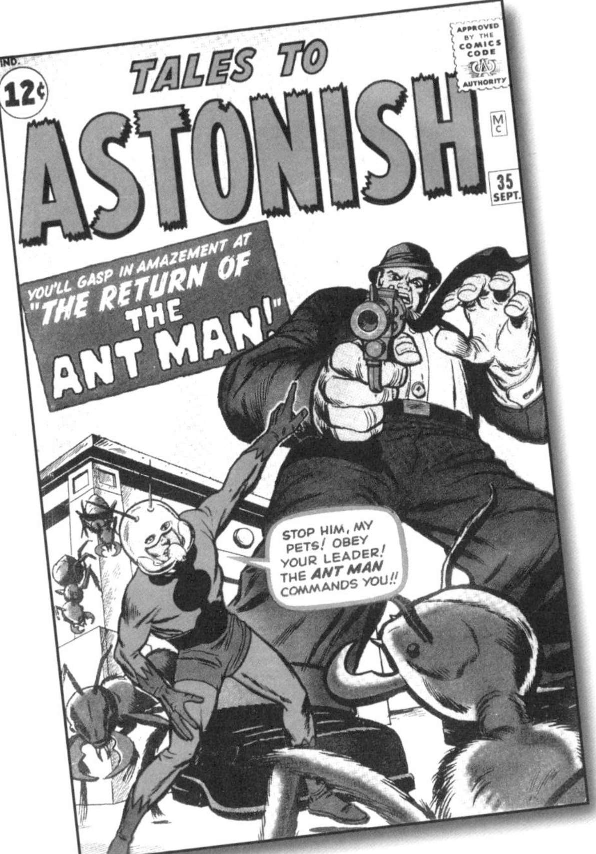

The cover spotlighting the second appearance of the Ant-Man—but his first in costume—from ***Tales to Astonish*** #35 (September 1962). Pencils by Jack Kirby, inks by Dick Ayers. [©2011 Marvel Characters, Inc.]

From ***Fantastic Four*** #7 (October 1962), a beautiful Lee-Kirby-Ayers full-page illustration.

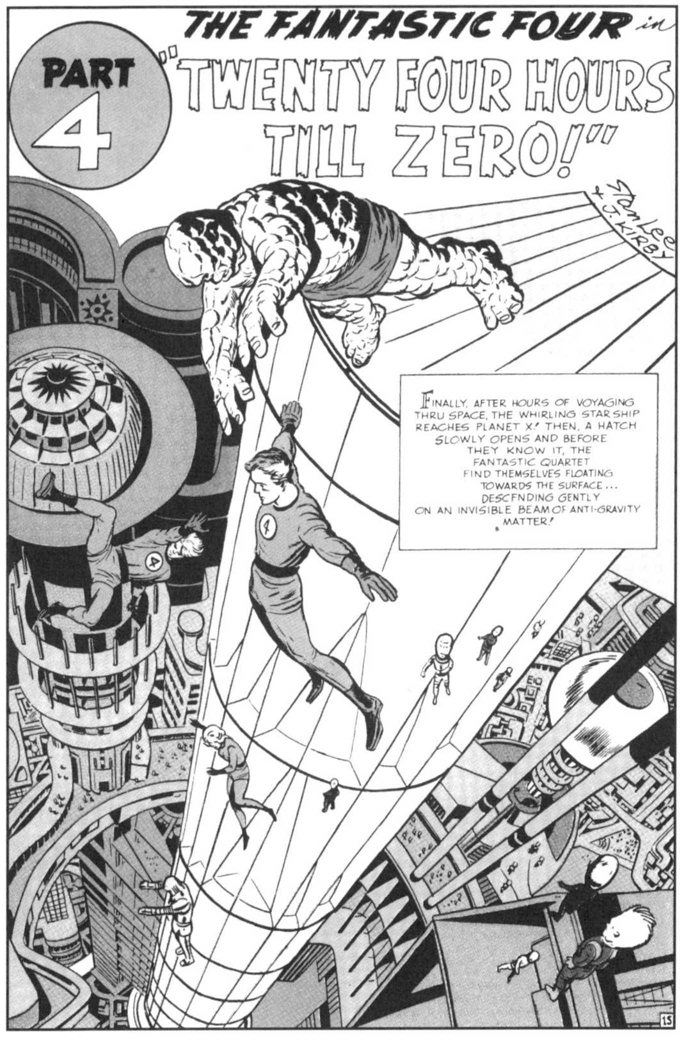

Here are some fascinating excerpts from a letter from Stan to Jerry dated January 9, 1963.

FF is easily our favorite book here at the Marvel bullpen. It's my baby and I love it. People have asked for original scripts- actually, we don't even HAVE any. I write the story plot- go over it with Jack- he draws it up based on our hasty conferences- then, with his drawings in front of me, I write the captions and dialogue, usually right on the original art work! It seems to work out well,

As for SPIDER-MAN, I wouldn't be surprised if he turns into a real winner, judging by the mail xxx we're receiving-- tremendous enthusiasm from the readers.

Mail-- that's my biggest problem. I take it too damn seriously- read each and every letter- wish I could answer 'em all- we get over a hundred a day- sometimes over 500!!! (after a long week-end). Can't keep up with it. Fans keep asking for MORE letters pages- wish we didn't have ANY! It's like a tiger by the tail- can't let go-

Are These Letters About Al Jaffee?

Stan's correspondence with "Alfred E. Neuman"

Al Jaffee, whose interview about his years working with Stan appears elsewhere in this book, went on, of course, to become one of the legendary stalwarts of ***Mad*** magazine, famous for his "Mad Fold-Ins" and "Snappy Answers to Stupid Questions." When the first book collection of "Snappy Answers" was being prepared, someone using the nom de plume of ***Mad's*** mascot "Alfred E. Neuman" (probably editor Jerry DeFuccio) sent out a call for tributes to Al. Herewith, "Neuman's" letter—and Stan's response, which was printed as part of 1968's ***Mad's Al Jaffee Spews Out Snappy Answers to Stupid Questions.***

MAD

485 MADISON AVENUE • NEW YORK N.Y. 10022 • PLAZA 2-7686

Dear Stan ___________,

Sinking to a new low, MAD plans to release a book entitled "MAD's Al Jaffee Spews Out Snappy Answers To Stupid Questions". This book was precipitated by reader response to a similarly entitled random article which appeared in MAD not long ago, as evidenced by the attached tearsheets. Incidentally, "reader response" constitutes two favorable letters on the same article as adjudged by the MAD editorial staff.

Obviously, some voice of protest should be raised to offset the incalculable damage the aforementioned book can do to our profession.

You, as a leading figure in this field, are therefore requested to stand up and be counted in this hour of dire need. A few paragraphs expressing your feelings about the artist and his (yecch) work will be of immeasurable value at this time. So let's have all your spleen, venom, hostility, disgust, rancor, and revulsion. In other words, let's have the truth!

There is, as usual, the one problem of deadline and in this instance, it is again yesterday. Of course, considering the great lengths I've gone to in writing you this touching personal letter, on expensive stationery, I expect a prompt and useful response.

So, drop everything and come out fighting for this worthy cause by August 15th.

MAD-ly yours,

Alfred

Alfred E. Neuman

8/9/67

Alfred Neuman, Esq.
MAD
485 Madison Ave.
NYC 10022

Al baby:

Having known Al Jaffee (as he is jovially referred to by his intimates) ever since those halcyon days when we produced countless, capricious comic books together, I can do naught but heap the most glowing praise upon his pointy little head.

This man, this creative titan, this Al Jaffee who walks among us, has a record which few can equal. Never, within human memory, has he precipitated a global war, committed genocide, or been incarcerated for jay-walking.

He also writes and draws funny stuff.

As ever,

Stan

Stan Lee

--Please send my check in a plain wrapper.

MAD's Al Jaffee SPEWS OUT SNAPPY ANSWERS to STUPID QUESTIONS

31330 IND. $1.75 94-409 WARNER BOOKS

What's the book about?

It's about moronic questions like that one . . . and clever answers like these:

It's about 7 inches tall, 4 inches wide and 192 pages thick!

It's about the most ridiculous idea for a book ever conceived!

It's about time that idiot out there stopped reading this cover and bought it.

Stan's letter to "Alfred E. Neuman" was printed as part of the introductory text to the 1968 ***Mad's Al Jaffee Spews Out Snappy Answers to Stupid Questions***, the first of many such compilations. Cover by Al. [©2011 E.C. Publications, Inc.]

Stan Lee correspondence with "Alfred E. Neuman," Stan Lee Collection, box 14, folder 8, American Heritage Center, University of Wyoming.

Stan the Man meets Conan (but not the Barbarian), 1968

Interview with Neal Conan, August 12, 1968

Transcribed by Steven Tice
Copyedited by Danny Fingeroth

FROM THE STAN LEE ARCHIVES

Neal Conan *is the award-winning host of* **Talk of the Nation,** *the national news-talk call-in show from National Public Radio News. Beginning his journalism career as a freelance reporter and writer in New York, Conan joined NPR in 1977, specializing in foreign affairs and national security issues. The network's* **All Things Considered** *won numerous awards during Conan's tenure as producer and executive producer, and he has received many personal awards as well. A comics fan, Conan has actually appeared as himself in Marvel's comics over the years.*

In 1968, very early in his career, Conan interviewed Stan Lee on New York's WBAI-FM. An audio copy of the interview was found in Stan's University of Wyoming archives, and we have transcribed and lightly edited it for presentation here.

When informed of our plans to run the interview, Conan was inspired to again interview Stan, which he did on October 27, 2010 on **Talk of the Nation.** *Introducing Stan, and referring to the '68 interview, Conan, tongue placed firmly in cheek, said:*

"Forty-two years ago, a devilishly handsome young man recorded one of his very first interviews with a legend in the comic book business... . In those days, I thought Stan Lee was old. Today, we all know he's immortal."

You can hear or read a transcript of the 2010 interview at this link:

http://www.npr.org/templates/story/story.php?storyId=130862700

But here in these pages, we present Neal Conan and Stan Lee on August 12, 1968...

NEAL CONAN: *My name is Neal Conan and I'm in the studio with Stan Lee, the single person most responsible for what many thousands of people call "the Marvel Age of comics." Stan, at this point you're the editor as well as writing several of the magazines yourself, isn't that right?*

STAN LEE: That's right, Neal. I think I'd rather you had said millions of people. We tell ourselves we have millions of readers.

NC: *What is your circulation?*

SL: Actually, it's sixty million a year. Now, I don't know that that's sixty million different people. There may be a couple of repeat sales there, but that's how many magazines we sell, approximately.

NC: *Does that make you number one in the field?*

SL: Oh, well, we think we'd be number one in the field if we sold two. No, from point of view of quantity, I think there's another company—who shall be nameless, as far as I'm concerned—that sells a few more, but they print a lot more. We sell more of what we print than anybody else.

A Marvel Universe version of Neal Conan has actually appeared in several comics. Here, we see Neal in ***Uncanny X-Men*** #226 (February 1988) in a story written by Chris Claremont, with art by Marc Silvestri and Dan Green. [©2011 Marvel Characters, Inc.]

1968 Stan Lee interview with Neal Conan on WBAI-FM, Stan Lee Collection, box 70, American Heritage Center, University of Wyoming.

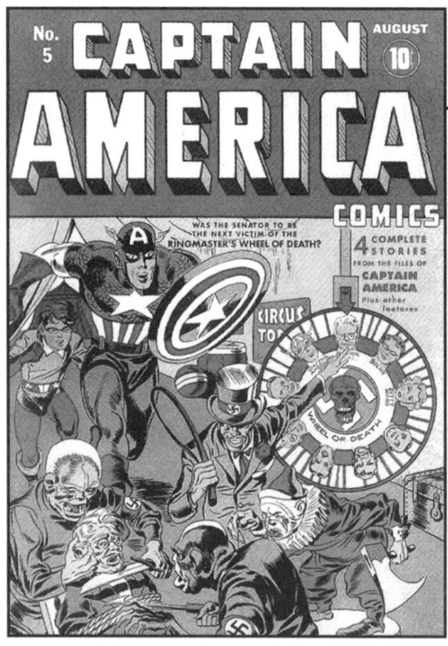

Stan's first Timely comic book (as opposed to prose) story, "Meet 'Headline' Hunter—Foreign Correspondent," appeared in ***Captain America*** #5 (August 1941). Here's the cover to the issue by Jack Kirby and Syd Shores. [©2011 Marvel Characters, Inc.]

NC: *In other words, magazine for magazine.*
SL: Mm-hm. I think ***Life*** may beat us.

NC: [laughs] *Okay, would you like to give us some of your background, and I guess incorporated in that would be the background of Marvel.*
SL: I'd like to think they're almost synonymous. *[laughs]* I'm just, I'm not terribly important as an individual. Everything I do seems to involve Marvel. One of the few native-born New Yorkers, I guess, extant, and I've been working at Marvel since I was about 17.

NC: *What were they publishing back in those days?*
SL: Comic magazines, too, but obviously I think they had Captain America, which was one of the biggest at the time, and they had ***Marvel Mystery Comics***, and ***Sub-Mariner***. ***Daring Comics*** and ***Mystic Comics***. Not too many others. It was a pretty small operation at the time. And I was there for a while, and, as a matter of fact, Jack Kirby, who is now just about our top artist, he was my boss at the time, he and Joe Simon, who had hired me. And after I was there a short time, Joe and Jack left, I was the only fellow remaining, and Martin Goodman, our publisher, asked if I would hold the job down until he could find somebody else on a permanent basis, because I could see he didn't relish a 17-year-old handling this entire, vast operation. And he's never told me that he found anybody else, but he never told me that he stopped looking, so, as far as I know, I'm still there on a temporary basis. *[laughs]*

NC: *What time do you really consider that the new age, or the Marvel Age, of comics really began?*
SL: It's probably one of the few questions you'll ask that I'll know the answer to, I would say, with the first issue of ***Fantastic Four***, which was about six or seven years ago. Until then, we had been turning out comic magazines just like everybody else, thinking of them as being for young children. And one of the reasons I even called myself "Stan Lee," which is just taking my first name, Stanley, and cutting it in two, was because I figured, "This is just a temporary job, and one day I'll quit, and write some Great American Novels, and I'll use my real name then." Well, after being there for about 25 years or whatever it was, I began to realize that I'm going to be doing this for a while, and it's about time to try to make something of these books.

So it took a little courage, I guess, on the part of Mr. Goodman, but he agreed to go along, and we decided to change the whole format and to do these magazines as though we're doing them for ourselves. If we were comic magazine readers, we said, what would we want to read? We certainly wouldn't want to read this stuff, you know? So we tried to inject all kinds of realism, as we call it, into the stories, and I say "as we call it" because, obviously, the stories are fairy tales, anyway. We think of them as fairy tales for grownups. And we take someone like Spider-Man and you have to accept the basic premise, which is that a fellow can be bitten by a radioactive spider and then be able to climb walls and so forth, which is, of course, nutty. But once (we hope) you've accepted that, then we try to make everything else very realistic. We say to ourselves, just because you have a superpower, that doesn't mean you might not have dandruff, or trouble with girls, or have trouble paying your bills. Well, this is what we started doing which was different than anybody, as far as I know, had ever done in comics before.

NC: *I've seen the first edition of* **The Silver Surfer***, and it was really beautiful.*
SL: We have very high hopes for that mag. I think it's probably

Here's the splash page to the "Headline Hunter" story that appeared in ***Captain America*** #8 (November 1941), "The Strange Riddle of the Plague of Death!" It was written by Stan, who signed it, but the art credits are unknown. [©2011 Marvel Characters, Inc.]

going to be one of the best comic magazines ever created.

NC: *The only thing that strikes me about the Silver Surfer is how Galactus ever was in on the surfing scene to name the Silver Surfer what he did.*
SL: I have a feeling, I've got the worst memory in the world, but I have a feeling, when Jack Kirby named him, he started out as a guest star in ***Fantastic Four.*** Jack and I can never really remember which of us came up with most names. He wasn't even supposed to be in the story. When I plotted it with Jack, it was just Galactus and so forth. And when I got the story from Jack to write the copy, he had drawn this fellow on the surfboard, and I think he called him "the Surfer" or "the Silver Surfer," and the name was certainly euphonious, and we decided to keep it. And we all fell in love with him. Well, you see, this is loosely translated. In his own language, obviously, he said something else.

NC: *Right. I've heard rumors that you are also asked to speak at colleges and whatnot. What do you say?*
SL: Well, it's more than a rumor. I've spoken at, I guess, just about every college in the East, and I've been asked to speak at almost every college and university in the free world, I guess. I don't do it because I haven't got the time to take these trips, much as I would love to. But I hate to make speeches, and it always turns into a question-and-answer period. I'll get up there and give a very long introduction, something like, "My name is Stan Lee, and I apologize." And that's about it. And then they start firing questions at me, and, as you can probably tell, one simple question and I go off on the deep end and forget the time. And, before you know it, two or three hours have gone by, and everybody's asleep, and that's the whole thing.

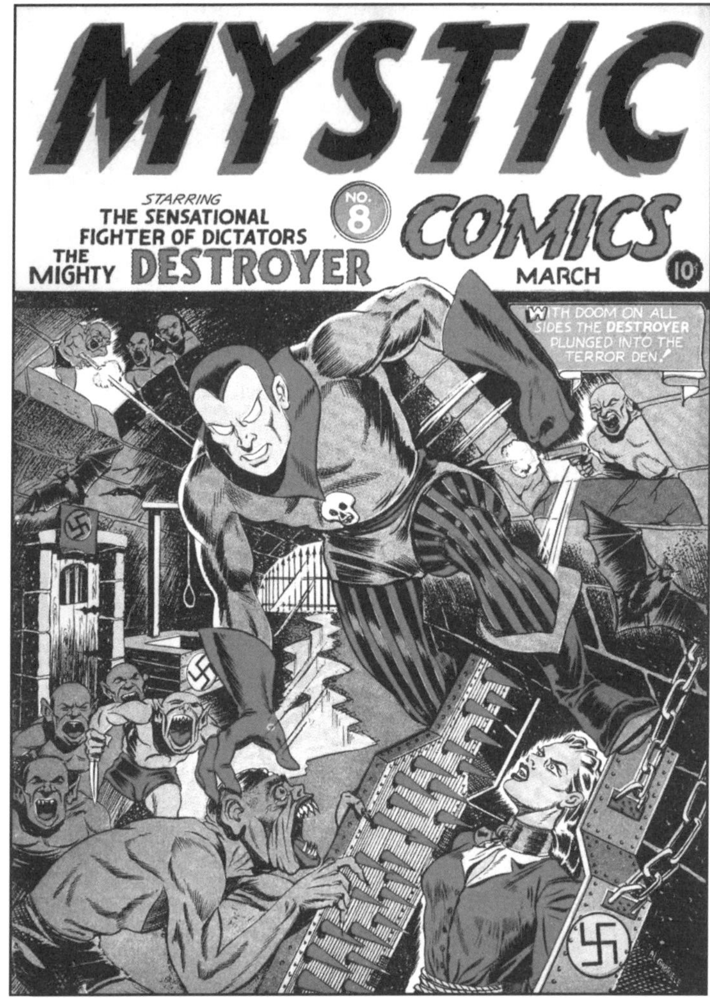

The first superhero Stan created for comics was the Destroyer, in ***Mystic Comics*** #6. The cover to the mag is penciled and inked by Alex Schomburg. Jack Binder did the art chores on the issue's Destroyer origin story. [©2011 Marvel Characters, Inc.]

NC: *Right. And you slink out.*
SL: Yeah. In defeat, as usual. But I love doing it, and these college kids are terrific. And I'm always amazed at the questions they ask, always on a philosophical plane. If they talk about Thor, let's say, who's our character who's the Norse god of thunder here on Earth, doing his good deeds, they won't say something as, well, you might expect the average comic fan would say, "Is Thor stronger than the Hulk?" or, "Can he run faster than Spider-Man?" or something. But I'll get something thrown at me like, "How do you equate Thor's position in the cosmos and his father Odin with our own God? How can you reconcile real religion and what you're trying to do in Thor, and isn't there a contradiction there?" And all of a sudden I've learned that I have to become something of an amateur philosopher, myself, in order to have these little lectures.

NC: *Well, I think, especially in* **Thor**, *you became something of an amateur philosopher writing the strip.*
SL: Oh, I guess I love philosophy, myself, and I think all of us at Marvel do, and it becomes so much more enjoyable when we can put what we consider to be a little meaning, and a little meat, and a little philosophy in the stories, instead of just making them action stories.

NC: *Well, I can remember trembling with anticipation waiting for the next* **Thor** *during the period when you had Id, the Living Planet, or Ego, the Living Planet. I think that was it.*
SL: Yeah. That was Jack's idea, too. I remember I said, "You've got to be kidding." He said, "No, let's get a living planet, a bioverse." Well, I didn't want him to think I was chicken. I said, "All right, you draw it, I'll write it." And, yeah, I think it turned out pretty good.

NC: *Is that how all your comics are done?*
SL: Yeah. Jack and I—well, in the beginning we spent a little more time on the plotting. Now we've gotten to work, I think, so well together, that our plotting session will be something like, "Hey, in the next ***Fantastic Four***, Jack, let's let the villain be Dr. Doom." "Okay, where does he come from? Where did we leave off with him?" And I'll say, "I don't know. Let's look it up for a second. Oh, yeah, he was fading off into another universe. Find some way to bring him back, Jack, and then we'll have him attack the Fantastic Four, and let's let the story with him running off and eloping with Sue Storm or something." And Jack'll say, "fine," and he goes off, and by the time he brings the artwork back, it might be that particular plot, or he might have changed fifty million things. And then I take it, and I try to write it and pull it all together. Whatever he has drawn, I try to tell it in my own way. So what happens, I

think, is the reader gets the benefit of the best artistic efforts of both the artist and the writer. The artist is uninhibited. He's not following an actual script, so he can go home and draw whatever he thinks are the most interesting, most dramatic pictures. Then the writer takes those drawing, and he's uninhibited by any real preconceived notions, and he just writes his dialogue to suit the drawings. So I'd like to feel, when we're all finished, it's rather a perfect marriage of art and script, you see.

NC: *Well, I find the basic difference between your magazines and "Brand Echh," as they're lovingly called, is that, in your magazines, the stories are tight, but you leave lots of loose ends. But in the other magazines, DC, everything is very tight. There's no loose ends, everything is taken care of almost, you know, anally. Is this because of a difference in editorial policy, or a difference in the way the magazines are put together?*

SL: I would imagine it's a difference in editorial policy, and also a personal difference. I'm not sure they're wrong and we're right. I think it's a matter of taste. I, myself, am not that interested in details. I'm interested in stark, sheer drama, and I guess I'm willing to sacrifice all sorts of things to get the most dramatic effect. It's not that we tend to purposely be careless or unconcerned, but we get so carried away with what might be the main point of the story that we may forget a few things that we've established earlier and possibly we should tie up neatly. Actually, what it amounts to is, as I say, it's a matter of particular preferences, too. I, myself, like to do a story where the mood, and the characterization, and the philosophy underlying what's going on, is the important thing.

Now, Brand Echh and a few other outfits, the editors there, and the writers, are terribly interested in details, and it always seems to me what they will do is spend all of their plotting time and creative time in saying, "We'll establish a little hangnail over here that nobody notices, but at the end of the story, that will be what unlocked the secret box which trapped the criminal, you see?" And then they'll write the whole story around that hangnail. Well, I'm bored with hangnails. See, I think what it boils down to is they like to write good detective type stories, and my preference is a Homeric type of Odyssey. I just want the scope, and I'm not that interested in tying everything up. If there are some things untied, we can always come back to them in a later issue. As a matter of fact, it might be the basis for a new plot, and it usually is.

Sidney "Paddy" Chayefsky is one of Stan's favorite writers. He wrote the Academy-award winning screenplays for ***Marty, Network***, and ***Hospital***. Interestingly, he and Stan were both 1939 graduates of the Bronx's DeWitt Clinton high school, although they didn't know each other there. [Chayefsky photo courtesy of Wisconsin Center for Film and Theater Research]

NC: *Well, speaking of that epic thing, one of my first critical evaluations of the* **Fantastic Four,** *in particular, was that it was the only possible forum of a modern epic. And it is a modern epic. I mean, the one thing that really astounded me was when Sue Storm and Reed were being married. The plot, the subplots, all those weird subplots twisting down there, never stopped. And it just goes on and on, and it's so great.*

SL: Well, I'm delighted to hear you say that. You know, one of the things that I got the biggest kick out of was, I was at some college, I think it was Princeton, and we had recently completed the stories with Galactus and the Silver Surfer, I think they were originally in three consecutive issues of ***The Fantastic Four***, and apparently they made a great impression on these students at Princeton who were interviewing me. And the first time they mentioned the three issues, they referred to them as "The Galactus Trilogy," you see? And they said, "Referring to the Galactus Trilogy, who did you originally," blah-blah-blah. Well, to me, these guys calling it the "Galactus Trilogy" and getting a lot of fan mail in which it was referred to that way, I remember saying to Jack and Martin Goodman, "I think we have finally made the first inroads in elevating the comics just a little bit. I think they're beginning to become a form of literature now, to some degree, and hopefully we'll continue on that path.

NC: *Right. I think a lot of people seriously underrate them.*

SL: Say, our own feeling is, I don't want to sound like a crusader, and certainly this is just a job, and we hope to be successful and all become very rich and buy ourselves a station like this one day. But even while trying to do good stories that people will like, I think the thing that's made everything at Marvel so much more exciting is we suddenly—and it happened accidentally, we didn't plan to do it, but we suddenly realized that we are doing something that hadn't been tried before, and certainly nobody would have thought it could succeed. We are convincing more and more people that there's no reason why comic books have to be worthless. There's nothing intrinsically bad about the comic book medium, because when you think of it, they consist of words and pictures telling a story. They're a form of communication. Now, certainly there is nothing wrong with television, which is words and moving pictures, or motion pictures. There's nothing wrong with a novel, which is merely words. We have the added virtue of pictures. It doesn't have to make the reader mentally lazy to look at a picture. He can still use his imagination in a million ways while reading the story.

The only thing bad about comics had been the fact that the people in the industry were usually the dregs. And certainly I don't mean this as an all-inclusive label, but, by and large, people who weren't good enough to write, to sell books, to sell radio shows, or TV shows, or something, could always somehow make sort of a living writing a comic book, because the editors weren't that particular. And it goes more for the writers than the artists. There always was a lot of really good talent in comics, but, because of the fact that they don't get paid very much per page, and that they have to do a lot of pages a day in order to eke out a living, or at least this was the case some years ago, the artists never had a chance to really show how good they are.

Another thing we're trying to do by increasing our sales is bring comics up to a level where they can pay more money to the creative people involved. We have some artists now, such as Jack Kirby, as we've mentioned, and new artist John Buscema—he's not new, he was with us years ago, then he left to get into advertising, and he's come back, John Buscema, who does ***The Silver Surfer***, and ***The Sub-Mariner***, and ***The Avengers***, and his artwork is just getting better and better. It's like looking at the most beautiful illustrations, especially in the originals, before they're inked. We have Gene Colan, who is both fast and terribly creative and imaginative. John Romita who does ***Spider-Man***, and he's magnificent as an artist. And we have so many others that I'm sure I'm going to catch hell for not remembering their names, such as Don Heck and Dick Ayers.

Hal Foster, the creator of the classic comic strip, ***Prince Valiant***, which Stan in this interview, compares to his and Jack Kirby's ***Thor.*** [©2011 the copyright holders]

NC: *Steranko.*
SL: Oh, and, of course, Jim Steranko. And he'd be the first guy to give me hell, too. Jim has started a whole new type of thing. He's tremendously inventive, and he's let his ability at design come to the fore, and he doesn't just draw a strip, but he designs every page, in every situation. And it's an amazing thing with Jim, he's only been in this particular business a little while, and yet we already find that many artists are using his layouts, and his interpretation, and his movie technique as examples, and are studying him and trying to work in that style, also. So, actually, our artists are terrific. The writers that we now have, I have some assistants, Roy Thomas, and Gary Friedrich, and Arnold Drake, and one or two others, and I think they're very capable writers, and they're doing a good job. And I think that it's just a matter of time before people realize that if you take a well-written script, and you take some sort of sincerity in the approach, and you take some beautiful artwork, and you put this together between two covers and sell it for twelve cents, why, this is one of the greatest bargains in the communications industry.

NC: *Not only great entertainment, but a lot of other little things thrown in, too.*
SL: Well, I'd like to think so.

NC: *Getting back to the epic thing, your magazines are really edited for the regular reader. I mean, someone picking up an issue of just about any magazine, it comes in in the middle of a story, and goes out, it's still in the middle of the story, and never really is conscious of what's going on.*
SL: Well, you know, it's a funny thing, Neal. I wondered, how is the public going to take this? You almost have to have been born as a Marvel reader in order to understand what's going on. And yet I find that it doesn't seem to make that much difference. It doesn't seem to turn anybody off who tackles us in the middle, and I can tell this by the fan mail. We get a lot of fan mail, literally hundreds of letters a day. We're probably in the same class as the Beatles in that respect, and I read just about all of it, or at least as much as I can, and I find that many of the letters will say, "Gee, to my lasting regret, I wasn't aware of Marvel until a month ago when my girlfriend told me," or, "my classmate told me," or something, "and I picked up the latest copy of thus-and-such, and I didn't understand most of it, but, boy, I can't wait to read it next month." Then we'll get some, "I've been reading your books for a few months and I finally know what's going on now, and I wouldn't miss an issue." If anything it seems to titillate them a little bit, and arouse their pique. I have the feeling, again, that people have been underestimating the intelligence of the public for so long.

Like one of our competitive outfits. They have sort of an editorial policy which I always thought was the nuttiest thing I ever heard. When a character's name is mentioned in the story, they letter the name in bold type. Now, to me, dialogue, what you read in the balloon is what the person is saying, and anything that's lettered in bold type, you assume the person is saying it extra loud and with more emphasis. Well, they'll put a name in bold type in a way where, in context, you wouldn't possibly be saying it loud or with emphasis, you see? But their thinking is, the reader is liable to forget what book he's reading unless we keep emphasizing the character's name, you see? And they would—well, I think, probably due to us, they've now resorted a little bit to using nicknames, you see, but they would never take any of their characters and cut the name short, or abridge it, or abbreviate it, or get an endearing term for it. It's always, "Blah-blah-blah man," and, boy, it could be his best friend talking to him, but it'll still say, "Blah-blah man."So I say, even a little thing like that, we have found that you don't have to say to yourself, "Gee, we can't continue this story because what if somebody buys the book for the first time next issue? They'll put it down, and they'll never like us again, and they'll never read us again." That's nonsense. Even a person who didn't read the first part, he'll be able to more or less figure out what it was, and if there's something he doesn't know, he'll ask somebody else who read it, or he'll keep reading the series until he gets the feel of it. And it's a little lesson we've learned, people are a heck of a lot smarter than we ever thought they were.

NC: *Well, one of the great things is, the longer you've been reading Marvel, the more of every magazine you'll understand, because there are references to battles with villains who disappeared ages ago, and all of a sudden somebody will say, "Well, in his battle with the original Vulture, Spider-Man... " And, of course, the original Vulture hasn't appeared in ninety issues or something.*
SL: I might add, he's coming back in the next ***Spider-Man***. That's a little plug, and I apologize.

NC: *That's okay. It'll be far too late by the time the program goes on, anyway.*
SL: Well, at least you said, "by the time." Usually people say, "*If* the program goes on." [chuckles] No, see, what we try to do, and I think we were probably the first at this, we try, even though they're different characters in different magazines, and possibly even living in different places, we try to make it all like one little world in which these characters all exist, the Marvel world, as much as you can do that in these magazines. It's one of the reasons many people have said it was, "Why do you have most of your characters living in New York?" Well, it makes it easier for us to have them meet. It also makes it easier for a fellow like myself, who hasn't traveled that extensively, and I do know New York, to write a story that has some degree of realism to it, because if I were basing a story on, I don't know, somewhere in Nevada that I haven't visited, it would be tough for me to do it realistically, you see. So that's one of the reasons that we keep our characters in New York. But we were the first to have characters from one book pop up just very casually in somebody else's book, and to take it for granted—well, why wouldn't Spider-Man bump into Daredevil, actually. Not as, "This is a special issue guest-star," and we bring it in out of left field, but just, there they are, and they happen to meet.

VAL SETS OUT FOR LLANTWIT TAKING WITH HIM AS GUIDES THE KNIGHTS WHO CLAIMED TO HAVE SEEN THESE MYTHOLOGICAL BEINGS. IN HIS ANXIETY FOR THE SAFETY OF HIS FAMILY HE HAS FORGOTTEN MERLIN'S TEACHING.

A classic page of Foster's ***Prince Valiant***.

NC: *I remember those two issues where Daredevil met Spider-Man were brilliant, just tremendous.*
SL: Thank you very much. We had a ***Fantastic Four*** story, I don't remember it exactly, but I think there was a football game involved, and Johnny Storm, who's just an ordinary teenager when he's not the Human Torch, was in the stands watching the game. And it just seemed to me that, why wouldn't Peter Parker be there, also, with his camera, you see, because he's a teenager, too, who's also Spider-Man, as you know, and he lives in the same city, and he's a professional photographer on a part time basis. So, in one of the panels, Jack had already drawn the panel, and it was just a crowd scene up in the stands, and we asked him to change one of the characters and make him Peter Parker recognizably, but we didn't make any mention of it at all in the story. We didn't have Johnny Storm turn around and say, "Aren't you Peter Parker?", anything like that. He just appeared in a panel. We must have had a thousand letters commenting about that. We do that a little bit whenever we can.

NC: *I remember one period when I was pretty isolated from the world at school and Marvel was about my only contact. I mean, if Spider-Man was having problems, oh, I'd just walk around in a daze, and sit and worry. I was terrible.*
SL: I would think that Spider-Man is the one we've had the most success with in keeping him true to character and never really deviating that much, and keeping him, oh, the kind of character, if somebody wanted to do a movie of him, you could almost take the scripts from the beginning and keep going.

Nothing has varied that much. Now, Jim Steranko, for instance, thinks that the layouts are rather dull. He says, "My gosh, why don't you really get far out with that stuff?" And John and I sometimes talk about it, ourselves, and we wonder, because it's sort of, it's calm and quiet, and the excitement comes in the story itself, and in the individual drawings, rather than in strange-looking page layouts, and we've had the book going so long, and it's sort of a wonder to us, and a puzzlement. He has been, is, and I'm sure will continue to be far and away our most popular character, and our best-selling character. And it sort of shows again that I think quality will out, without any tricks, and without any little padding, or gilding the lily, or anything like that. Just straight, good drawings, and hopefully good writing, and an interesting character, and you can just keep going with him.

As a matter of fact, I think that people would be surprised if they ever heard John and me discuss the plots on ***Spider-Man***. We sit and talk about this as if we were Paddy Chayefsky or Rod Serling planning some sort of involved movie, or Arthur Miller. We'll say, "Well, I don't know if this

Stan Has always loved to write Shakespearean-style dialogue for ***Thor*** comics. Here, we see Orson Welles (with Alan Webb) as Falstaff in his 1965 ***Chimes at Midnight***, a movie that combined the Falstaff pieces of five Shakespeare plays. One can't help but notice the resemblance between the Welles character and ***Thor*** cast member Volstagg, seen here in a page from ***Thor*** #143 (August, 1967). [Chimes ©2011 the copyright holders; Tales of Asgard ©2011 Marvel Characters, Inc.]

would be right. It would be out of character. Well, would he really do that? Well, would he relate in that matter? And is it significant?" And sometimes we find ourselves laughing and we say, "For crying out loud, this is a comic book we're talking about, y'know?" But we really get into it just about that deeply.

NC: *Yeah, well, I think your readers get into it that deeply, and I'm really pleased to see that you get into it that deeply.*

SL: Oh, we do. One thing I like, also, is the fact we try to do certain characters in different styles. Like Thor. The way Jack draws Thor I think is just magnificent, and if you could see the work in pencil before it's inked. No matter how good an inker is, there is so much more you can do in pencil, because you can get tones. You see, you can go light and so forth with the pencil, whereas with ink you've just got your black ink and your white paper, and it's going to be black or it's nothing. You can't really get grays. When Jack does his artwork in pencil, it is almost sinful to have to put ink over these drawings, because nobody, unless they've seen his originals, can ever really know how good this man is. I mean, they're magnificent illustrations. And his Thor is somewhat like Hal Foster's Prince Valiant except I think it has much more drive and power in the artwork. And I love writing it, because I'm a real Shakespeare buff, and I get a chance to be flowery and ornate, and have a lot of heavy drama, and so forth. It's completely different than, let's say, Spider-Man, and the Hulk is different than both of them, and we'd like to think that all of our characters have some sort of innate difference which keeps it interesting to us. We don't feel we're writing the same thing all the time.

NC: *It seems that every Marvel magazine, even though the characters are incredibly, wildly different they all have something in them, the same tone of the way they're done that seemingly no other magazine can capture or equal that tone. I remember, after you came out a few years ago, Charlton and Harvey came out with big things which more or less failed, and they just didn't have the same punch, somehow.*

SL: I think what happened, we really, I think, are pretty honest with the readers, and we try to give them our best effort, and I think a lot of these other companies still think of these as comic books for kids, and they may—see, for example, they may look at something like ***The Silver Surfer***, and they may say, "Gee, there's a guy who rides on a surfboard, and he's from outer space, and it's selling very well. Let's get a character and put him on a bicycle, a flying bicycle from the moon, and maybe that'll sell well." They don't take the trouble to really analyze it. Maybe they're not even able to comprehend what the Silver Surfer is, because he doesn't have to have that surfboard, and he doesn't have to be silver, and he could look different. The important thing is that he's a character who represents something, and stands for something, and reacts to things in a certain way. And there is a lot of philosophy, and a lot of moralizing, and there's something you can sink your teeth into if you like reading something with meat and possibly even with a message. Well, any embryonic competitor might read this, and they think they're copying us by, just as I say, getting a guy on a flying bicycle, but they're missing the entire shtick behind the whole thing, you see?

And that, I think, is what has happened with all our competitors. Now, I know the Nameless One, again, this nameless company—and, of course, we know almost everybody that works at that company—some of then are personal friends, just as many of our people are friends of their people. And we would really get a kick out of learning that they would have their conferences and wonder how to make their books a little more like ours, and they'd say things like, "Well, Marvel is using a lot of dialogue balloons on the covers now, so let's get a lot of dialogue balloons on the covers." Well, that had nothing to do with why our books were selling, so the minute we learned about that, we took our dialogue balloons off the covers. I never liked them, but they were something I had never even thought about one way or another. We had been doing it for years, and we kept doing it. And I'm very glad I learned that they thought that was one of the things about us, because the minute it entered our consciousness, we got rid of them.

Jim Steranko, he violates all the rules, and whenever he does, the job is beautiful. And I'm not even really an editor where he's concerned, because any cover he brings in—I mean, I might even look at it and think, "This is nutty! Forget it!" But the nuttier it is, the more I say, "Go ahead and do it." Only once did I make a change. Just recently he had one with no color at all, and it was kind of white. In fact, this may be the one you mean.

NC: *Yeah. It had no color whatsoever.*
SL: Did it have a red title?

NC: *Right.*

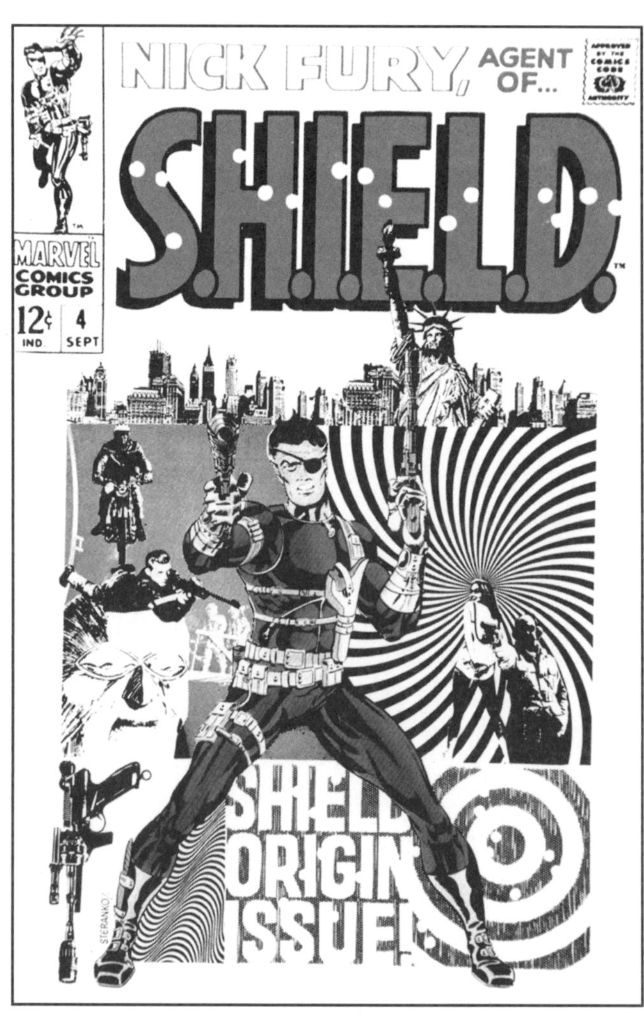

Writer/artist Jim Steranko originally wanted the cover of ***Nick Fury, Agent of S.H.I.E.L.D.*** #4 (September 1968) to be completely black-and-white but after, according to Stan, "three or four weeks of fighting and yelling and screaming," Jim was convinced by Stan to make the logo red for easier visibility on the racks. [©2011 Marvel Characters, Inc.]

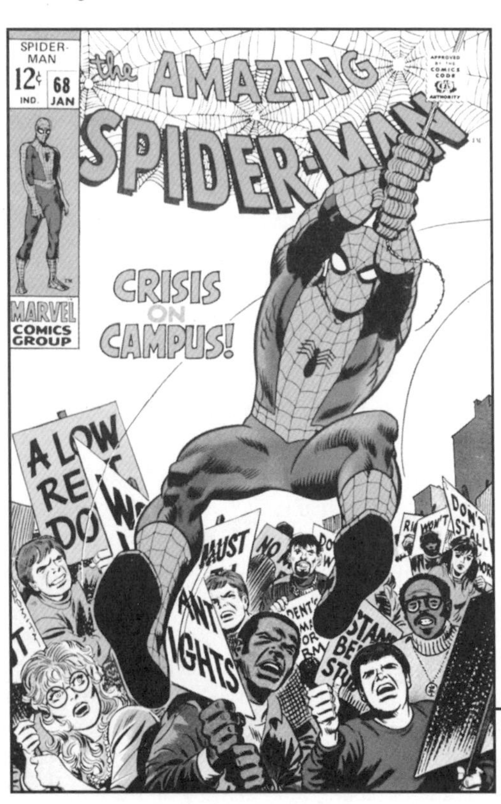

During the late 1960s, student demonstrations took place on college campuses nationwide. This campus unrest was reflected in John Romita Sr's cover to ***Amazing Spider-Man*** #68 (January 1969). [©2011 Marvel Characters, Inc.]

SL: Yeah. Well, you see, he submitted it first with no red in the title, and my only feeling was, it looked good aesthetically and artistically, but I thought nobody would see it on the newsstand. It would just be an empty space, you see. So we had, oh, maybe three or four weeks of fighting and yelling and screaming and threats, and finally he put the red in, and I think we both agreed, he agrees now that it does look pretty good. It didn't kill it aesthetically. But at least now, when it's on the newsstand, you see, and no matter how aesthetic we want to be, our first job is to be seen. We could have a beautiful magazine, but if nobody sees it, they're not going to buy it. We'd like to feel, that we can get a little bit crazy with the covers now because people, we hope, will start asking for our books, and will start looking for them. We're not as completely dependent upon one of our titles just catching the casual reader's eye.

NC: *Okay, I've been in the studio with Stan Lee, the editor of Marvel Comics, and we've been talking about Marvel and the comic industry. Thank you very much, Stan.*
SL: Thank you, Neal. It was a pleasure.

The Missouri Connection

Thomas, O'Neil, and Friedrich reflect on Stan

While Stan and most of the first Marvel staffers were New York area natives, the next wave of 1960s writers and editors to come knocking at the Bullpen's doors were from the "show me" state, Missouri. ***Roy Thomas****,* ***Dennis O'Neil****, and* ***Gary Friedrich*** *made the trip from the banks of the Mississippi to the shores of the Hudson, and comics history has been all the richer for it. On these pages, Roy, Denny, and Gary recount important things they learned about comics—and life—from working with Stan.*

[This article originally appeared in slightly different form in **Write Now!** *#18.]*

Stan Lee As Writer And Teacher

A Personal Recollection

by ROY THOMAS

ROY THOMAS *became Stan Lee's first Marvel-era assistant editor in 1965, and was soon writing many of Marvel's top titles, including* **The Avengers** *and* **The X-Men***. Innovating the* **Conan** *line of comics in 1970, Roy was the series' first and longest-reigning writer, and would also become Marvel editor-in-chief when Stan became publisher. Over the years, Roy has written for Marvel, DC, and other companies, and is the editor of the groundbreaking—and still running—***Alter Ego** *magazine, published by TwoMorrows.*

Any creative life—indeed, virtually any life at all—is bound to be filled with ironies.

One of Roy's most heralded early Marvel stories, in *Avengers* #57 (October 1968), introduced the 1960s version of the Vision. Pencils are by John Buscema. Inks by Buscema and/or George Klein. [©2011 Marvel Characters, Inc.]

One of many in my own is that I, who earned a B.S. in education in 1961 and had spent four years as a high school English teacher by the time I stumbled headlong into the comic book industry in 1965, cordially detested teaching and feel that, largely because of that attitude, I wasn't much good at it...

...while Stan Lee, who in an earlier day had no chance to go to college but went to work in the comics field in 1941 soon after graduating from high school, seemed to relish teaching others what he knew—and was an excellent teacher.

[Photo by Alan Waite.]

As I've related more times than anyone (including myself) cares to remember, I accepted a job Stan offered me as a "staff writer" for Marvel ten or fifteen minutes after we met one Friday, after he read the results of the "writer's test" I'd been given overnight by corresponding secretary Flo Steinberg, which consisted of writing dialogue for four pages of *Fantastic Four Annual* #2 from which all dialogue and captions had been omitted... and an hour later, having been unceremoniously ordered off the premises of DC Comics by my short-term boss, Superman editor Mort Weisinger, I was back in Stan's office starting my second job held within a period of two weeks.

The teaching, I suspect, began that very day.

Actually, I don't specifically recall Stan telling how to script the Stan Goldberg-penciled ***Modeling with Millie*** #44, the original art to which he handed me along with the assignment to write dialogue for its 18 story pages over the coming weekend. But he must have done so. After all, I was to indicate in pencil on tissue overlays taped to those pages where all captions and balloons were to be lettered—and how would I know what to do without having him explain his writing process to me that very day? He (or production manager Sol Brodsky) must also have given me a copy of one of his scripts, so I could imitate the style in terms of indentation, how to indicate bold words and thought balloon, etc., etc., etc. In fact, though it was probably well after 2:00 p.m. when I showed up on Marvel's doorstep for the second time that day, I have the distinct impression that Stan must have spent most of that afternoon with me, showing me the ropes... as well as introducing me to the bare handful of other staffers besides Sol: Flo Steinberg (whom I'd met on

Wednesday); production person Marie Severin (soon gone, but soon to return as an artist); a third woman, who was laboring on licensed comics... and Steve Skeates, a recent college grad who'd been working there as the other official "staff writer" for a week or two.

I can only assume that my mind was in such a discombobulated state due to quitting a job that was the fulfillment of a dream (working for DC) and taking one I hadn't even dreamed existed (writing for Marvel) that I draw a total blank as to the details of what happened the rest of that afternoon.

However, I do know that when I arrived in the office bright and early Monday morning, my real job—and education as a Marvel writer—began.

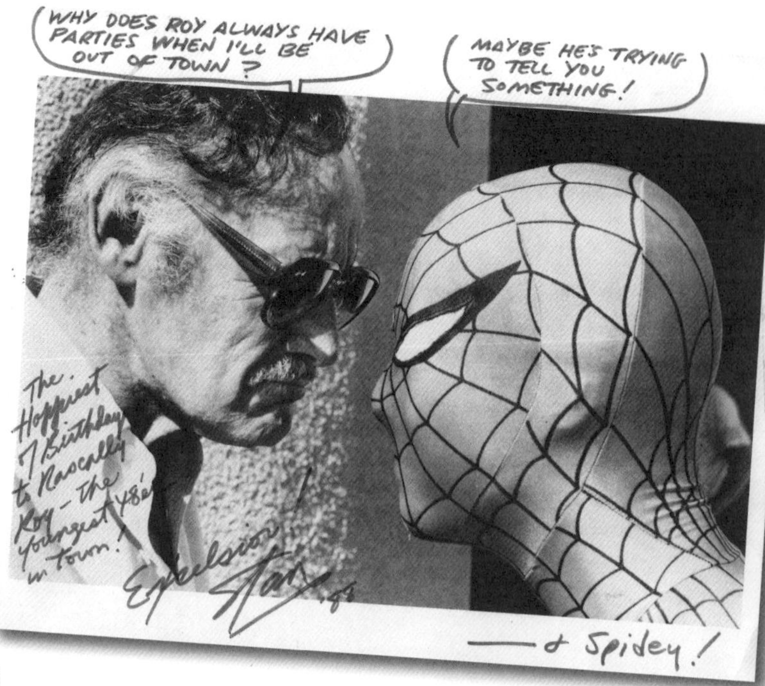

Stan personalized this classic "staredown" photo between him and Spider-Man (okay, an actor in a Spidey suit) for Roy's birthday in 1988.

Stan's routine was pretty consistent during those several years, and must've been followed that day, as well. He would call Sol and me into his office to go over what he'd brought in... often a combination of pages he had scripted and completed stories he had proofread on the original art. A policy was established right away of Sol standing on his right side, me on his left, as he (also standing, at a drawing board as I recall) went over the material, so that Sol could begin processing it. He soon took to joking about Sol being his "right-hand man," which made me his "left-hand man." He would go over most of the corrections he did on the completed stories, to make sure Sol understood what he wanted. The scripted pages, both his typed sheets and the original art (now marked up with balloon and caption placements), were handed over to Sol for mailing on to the letterer. On the splash pages, Stan invariably handwrote the dialogue in the captions and balloons, right on the original art, mostly because he wanted a feel for how much space they took up. All sound effects were lettered in roughly, too—and with very much the feel he wanted. Artie Simek was the better of the two main Marvel letterers of the day at rendering finished versions of those sound effects—but the famed "Artie Simek sound effects" were, in the end, at least as much Stan's as Artie's. Sam Rosen, though a wonderful letterer (I always liked him even better because he lettered a bit smaller!), tended not to get as much of the flare of Stan's effects into the finished versions, although I think only a few of them were ever altered after the fact.

Then, possibly while Sol was handling other things, he went over that ***Modeling with Millie*** script with me. (I don't recall Steve Skeates being in on these sessions, but he very well may have been, during that brief early period while he was still on staff.) If I had any dream that my work would be judged "perfect" right off the bat, it didn't last long. Stan changed quite a bit of the dialogue and captions—and I'm sure he went over every one of the 18 pages with me. He paid attention to everything—title (I think "Whom Shall I Turn To?" is mine, mostly taken from the Anthony Newley song); balloon placement (I was pretty good at it from the start, but Stan would find instances where he felt I should have done it differently); bold words (he wanted them to match speech patterns, except for a personal quirk or two which I don't think he noticed, but I did); sound effects (none in this story); *everything.* (The only thing that would be added later were the "fashion footnotes," crediting readers for the dresses the gals wore—though Flo Steinberg mostly faked those, just taking names from little girls' art submissions and occasionally little boys' letters and sticking them willy-nilly throughout the story.)

I wish I could remember specific things about that first story that Stan changed, but I don't—except that I believe most of the splash page was totally rewritten by Stan right on those tissue overlays. I'd like to think the name of a "designer," Jacques d'Eau, was mine... since "d'eau" means water and it was a sort of takeoff on "John Doe." But I'm not even 100% sure *that* was mine. But Stan did a thorough job—except that, because I hadn't known I was to write the creator credits, the story wound up without any. That can't have made artist "Stan G." happy—but maybe Stan figured that if he wasn't writing the book, it didn't need credits. Or maybe he just didn't notice till too late.

Stan can't have been totally happy with feeling he had to do so much rewriting, but he accepted the fact that a learning process was involved. (I don't know how much of this kind of thing he had done with Steve to date... nor am I aware of Steve's having written anything in that week or two before I arrived, or of knowing why he hadn't. I had my own stuff to worry about. I didn't get the sense that Stan was unhappy with Steve, or that the two of us were in competition. He wanted two staff writers/apprentices... and I was the second.)

Apparently the work was good enough that he intended to have me become the scripter of both ***Millie*** books: the 9-times-a-year ***Millie the Model*** and the 8-times-a-year ***Modeling with Millie***—and, in very short order, ***Patsy and Hedy.*** I remember that my second Millie-related assignment was ***MTM*** #134 (which, when published, would have a Jan. 1966 cover date).

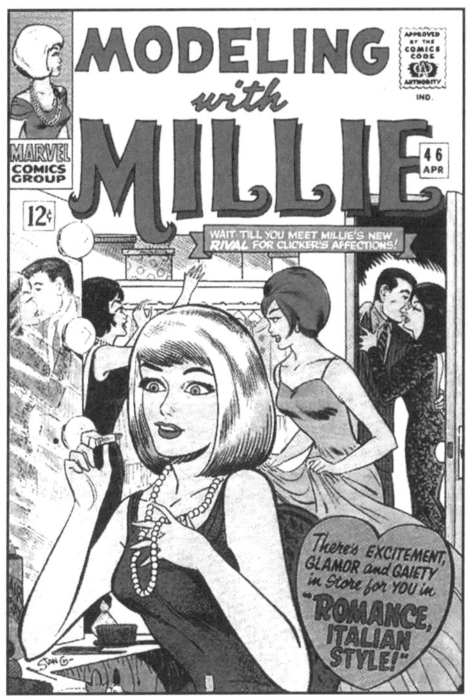

Roy's script for ***Modeling with Millie*** #46 (April 1966) was delayed by the blackout of '65. Denny O'Neil finished it. Cover art by Stan Goldberg. [© 2011 Marvel Characters, Inc.]

This, as I recall, went much better in terms of rewrites... even though, once again, all credits got left off. I recognize Sam Rosen's lettering on this one, and I liked it—the more so because all the dialogue I wrote could fit in the panels without covering up all the art. I don't know why Stan didn't tell me to write less... but he didn't. I do recall that I got a kick later out of a letter which a girl wrote after buying that particular issue. The gist of the letter—and I remember the phrasing of this sentence well—was, "I like the story very much. I have been reading it for a week and I am almost half through."

Naturally, though my writing the ***Millie*** and ***Patsy*** material would take a bit of the load off Stan and give him more time to spend on the more important superhero titles, he hadn't hired me to write ***Millie the Model*** for long. Within a few weeks of my being hired, he one day handed me Gene Colan's pencils to the "Iron Man" story for ***Tales of Suspense*** #73—the first episode of Ol' Shellhead that "Adam Austin" had drawn. I was thrilled, being a big admirer of Colan/"Austin's" work on "Sub-Mariner."

I was finding, though, that I couldn't get much work done on staff. Too many interruptions. Even though I'd been hired as a staff writer, Sol, no doubt with Stan's permission if not encouragement, was feeding me the original art of stories so I could check whether the "production department" (mostly Marie Severin, occasionally a freelance artist called in, or even Sol himself) had done the lettering and art corrections properly. I was working at a corrugated metal desk with a big old manual typewriter on it, but with room to do my proofreading by laying the art flat on the metal surface. At that angle, though, I had to lean down close to the work, which was horizontal to the floor. I wound up staying late, often an hour or so after everyone else left the offices; there was no problem about this in those days, and I would simply say goodbye to the guard downstairs as I left. I was, I believe, hand-lettering every single balloon roughly on the tissue overlays that I'd taped over the art... and then, when I was happy with what I had, I'd type it on the old manual.

Stan was less than thrilled with that "Iron Man" dialogue, as I detailed in ***Alter Ego's*** coverage of my work at Marvel during the 1960s, and he rewrote a lot of my dialogue and captions. The end result was about 50% my writing, and about 50% his. That's why there's no real writer credit as such on that story. The box on the splash, written entirely by Stan, says that just about everybody had a hand in this one. Even Marie (who colored it) and Flo (who answered the phone) were mentioned.

I also discovered, when I tried to put in vouchers for this story as I had for the "Millies," that the latter were to be counted as freelance work for which I'd be paid extra, but that "Iron Man" (and later my first "Dr. Strange" or so) were considered part of my staff work... even if I had stay after work to do them.

Not necessarily on that story, but on the next non-humor story I scripted—the Ditko plotted-and-drawn "Dr. Strange" ten-pager for ***Strange Tales*** #143, on which I worked from Steve's handwritten notes, seen in ***A/E*** #68—he had me rewrite my tissue overlays a time or two. That "written and rewritten by" before my name was no joke... not to me, not to Stan. And even at that, some of the lines were probably largely rewritten by Stan into the form in which they appeared in the published comic.

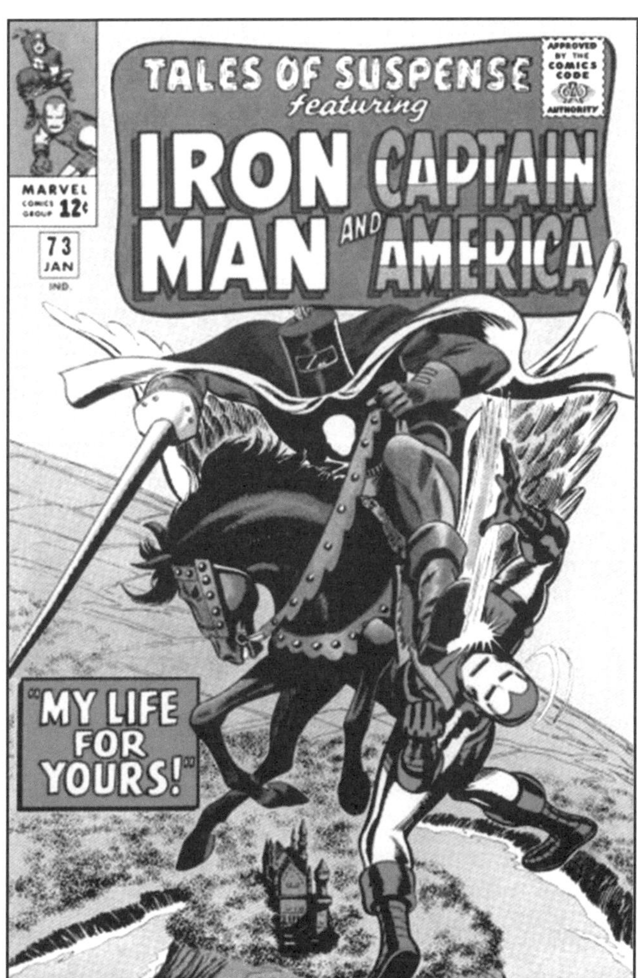

Roy's first pro superhero writing was in ***Tales of Suspense*** #73 (January 1966), for which he dialogued the Iron Man story. Cover by Gene Colan and Jack Abel. [© 2011 Marvel Characters, Inc.]

At some fairly early stage, though, Stan started having the stories I wrote lettered before he saw them, to save him time as I evidently improved somewhat. This proved a real headache for Sol Brodsky, because the fact that Stan hadn't seen the dialogue and captions before they were rendered in ink in no way inhibited him from making changes... often substantial changes. And while having me write and rewrite on tissue overlays slowed the process down somewhat, making copious changes after everything was lettered in ink was a production manager's nightmare. Sol would wince visibly as a story that needed to go out to the Comics Code and thence to the printers was marked by Stan with perhaps several hundred words of changes... which meant whiting out what was on the page, re-lettering it (and neither Marie nor Morrie Kuramoto, who soon began on staff as a letterer, was nearly as good a letterer as Simek or Rosen), and then proofing it again. Sol must have been complaining to Stan about this method of working all along... and I can't say I blame him.

Roy's second non-humor Marvel script was for the Steve Ditko-plotted-and-drawn Dr. Strange story in ***Strange Tales*** #143 (April 1966). [© 2011 Marvel Characters, Inc.]

Meanwhile, Steve Skeates was, not too long after I got there, relieved of his staff writer job. I don't recall anything Stan had him write—except one story for ***Kid Colt Outlaw*** #127, which would have a March 1966 cover date but must've been written in late summer or early fall of '65. Steve and I co-plotted it—though whether this was Stan's idea, or Steve's, I don't recall. I believe the assignment was Steve's, and that he asked me to co-plot it with him and generously added my name to the credits when I did, with him doing the dialogue for the tale, which involved the Western Dr. Doom type called Iron Mask.

Unfortunately, Steve and/or I had had the idea of starting not with an action scene but with two previously seen but relatively nondescript villains—Doctor Danger and the Fat Man—bumping into each other as they tried to enter a saloon at the same time. The next couple of pages involving them and a hypnotist named Bennington Brown were rather quiet—and even when Iron Mask enters on page four, he just walks down a flight of stairs.

Stan was most unhappy when he got this story in to proof. It had already been lettered and inked, so there wasn't a lot he could do about it without a lot of trouble, but he laced into Steve when the three of us were going over the tale in his office... one of the things that confirms me in my belief that the assignment had been basically Steve's. I do recall most vividly trying to put my 2¢ in to defend what Steve had done at some point with the dialogue (in which I had had no part)—only to have Stan turn to me with a withering look and say, ominously, "The less *you* say at this point, the better." I clammed up.

Whether Steve was already off staff by this time, or whether that soon followed, I really don't know. But I did feel sorry for him. He was clearly a talented guy—and he would prove it later at other companies, including DC—but he and Stan weren't on the same wavelength.

The same would be true of Denny O'Neil, whom I'd known briefly in Missouri and to whom I sent the same writer's test that had gotten me my job when Stan wanted to re-add a second staff writer. I don't believe there was anyone in between Steve and Denny. Denny, too, would go on to a sterling career at DC, and even spend significant time as a Marvel editor and writer... but again, somehow he and Stan were generally not on the same wavelength creatively in those days.

Why *I* should have "succeeded" in that area, I don't know. I didn't question. Stan knew what he wanted... and with all my flaws, he apparently felt that both as a writer and increasingly as an editorial assistant I was what he was looking for. It says nothing against Steve or Denny. In another time, another place, our situations could easily have been reversed.

But I do know that standing there at Stan Lee's left side, morning after morning for several years, was one of the great learning experiences of my life. Maybe I learned some bad habits along with good ones... maybe Stan should've kept on my case to write a bit more sparingly (he himself wrote rather copy-heavy text, but I exceeded his, I know)... but the fact that I've had some degree of success in the field these past 46 years owes, I feel, as much to Stan as it does to any native ability of my own.

He made it hard for me to work with other editors in later years, especially those who somehow felt they'd been divinely anointed as editorial geniuses the minute they got the job. Even Julius Schwartz at DC, my first editorial idol, found in the 1980s that I didn't knuckle under too easily to editorial control after my years of working with Stan. I felt I had worked with and for the best... and an editor had to convince me he knew what he was doing before I would have any respect for him. I did respect Julie, of course... but I wasn't willing to bend very much in order to do the kind of story, or write the kind of dialogue, that he wanted me to write.

I think the story I often tell about the big New York blackout of November 1965 probably sums up the way I feel about Stan Lee as a force of nature better than anything else.

Denny had been in town only a short time and was staying with freelance writer Dave Kaler and me at Dave's apartment on the Lower East Side. That afternoon around 5:30, Denny and I were trapped on a subway somewhere under the mid-30s in Manhattan when the lights and all power went out, and it was two, more like three, hours before a subway employee with a lantern came to lead us all up the dark track and onto the streets. We walked the 30-plus blocks to Dave's apartment, and the three of us went out to dine and talk at the Red Lantern, which was lit by candles. No thought of my finishing the dialoguing of ***Modeling with Millie*** #46, of which I had already done roughly the first half. New York had transformed into a special kind of nighttime festival, and we were young and had fun.

Next morning, I don't recall if the subways were running yet or not, but the two of us got into the Marvel offices and joined Stan and Sol in Stan's office. Stan apologized to Sol for not getting much done the previous night out at his Long Island home, but the blackout had hit there, too, of course. Stan then proceeded to pull out a number of pages he had scripted during the blackout. Stan (with wife Joan's help, I believe) had set up a "candle brigade" to give him ample light, and he had typed away with two fingers, as was his wont.

Sol, Denny, and I marveled at Stan that day.

I've been doing it ever since.

Dennis O'Neil

Dennis O'Neil *needs little introduction to comics readers. While most know him for his classic writing and editing work on* **Batman** *and* **Green Lantern,** *it all began with his passing the Marvel Writers Test in 1965 and learning about comics writing from Stan. Since then, Mr. O has become one of the most respected writers and editors in the field. Besides his comics achievements, he is also the author of many prose works, including the adaptation into novel form of the massive Batman storyline* ***Knightfall*** *and the* ***Batman Begins*** *and* ***The Dark Knight*** *films. I spoke with Dennis via phone on January 17, 2008.*

—DF

DANNY FINGEROTH: *You got to work at Marvel because you knew Roy, right, Dennis?*
DENNIS O'NEIL: I was working on a newspaper and had written a couple of articles about the resurgence of comics, and Roy's mother subscribed to the paper. They lived in Jackson, eight miles away from Cape Girardeau. Jackson, Missouri. Roy got in touch with me, and driving back from a St. Louis visit one Sunday afternoon, I stopped in to see him. He was teaching at Fox High School, and my poor girlfriend was bored out of her tree. She was a philosophy major. And I was just fascinated. Roy opened up this whole world of comic books and the subculture. He was at the time the editor of ***Alter Ego,*** which was, by a wide margin, the best fanzine around. That world was just getting started back then. And I had loved comics as a kid, but, y'know, just hadn't seen them for ten years.

DF: *So Roy wasn't yet at Marvel at this point, obviously.*
DO: No. This would have been 1965. Roy had accepted an offer from DC to actually come and work. So he was in a transition period, himself. He was about to leave Missouri and move to New York, but that wasn't going to happen for a month or so. And Roy started visiting this little shack-type place that I lived in. And that kind of deepened my interest. I started buying comics. Then he went to DC but

An early Dennis O'Neil script, over Stan's plot, appeared in ***Daredevil*** #18 (July 1966). Cover by John Romita, Sr. and Frank Giacoia. [© 2011 Marvel Characters, Inc.]

quickly switched to Marvel and sent me the Marvel Writers Test. That was right at the beginning of the Marvel explosion, and Stan needed more help yet, so, in the spirit of "there's no reason not to do this," I took the test, which was four pages of Kirby artwork without copy. And I did it in ten or fifteen minutes, not expecting anything would come of it, it was just kind of a novel little thing to do. I sent it back to Roy, and about a week later I got back to my newspaper office, and the phone rang. And it was Roy from New York offering me this staff job at Marvel. I took it, and when I got there, the first thing I had to do was buy a suit. It was a very different business back then. I was in a windowless office in the Madison and 59th office. It was a suit-and-tie business, pretty much. Roy went with me to Macy's. I remember I spent thirty bucks and got a suit.

Interior art from ***Daredevil*** #18, with Dennis's dialogue over Stan's plot and John Romita, Sr.'s pencils. Inks by Frank Giacoia.

DF: *You were a professional newspaper writer at this point, but who trained you in comics?*
DO: I learned an enormous amount from Stan. We all learned an enormous amount from him. People are still learning from him.

DF: *Did you learn directly from him?*
DO: He didn't do formal critiques. I remember him telling me about the need for a sense of a lot of things going on in a story, and the need for dramatic tension. I don't think he used words like that, but that's probably what it would translate out to. It was all very casual. I mean, the plots were two paragraphs long. A quick conversation Stan had with an artist in his office or in the hall. Slang had been a part of early comics, and then, by the '50s, it had kind of left the medium, probably because the companies were afraid of offending anybody. Well, Stan's characters talked in an interesting way. From that, you derived characters, so it was not the cookie cutter characters we were used to, where all the good guys had the same personality, and were totally unmotivated by anything other than they were the good guys.

DF: *Did you ever sit in on one of Stan's plot conferences?*
DO: One, where we did a long continuity for ***Nick Fury, Agent of SHIELD.*** It was Stan, Roy, and me, and I don't know who else. Anyway, I wrote the first story of that continuity, and after that, Stan took it over. But he had, getting back to the point I was making, he had shown us all not only a new way to write comics, but a new *attitude* toward them. Not the dry, solemn stuff that had been common in superheroes, but he would break the fourth wall, in effect, and *wink* at you. I considered myself quite sophisticated. I'd been in the Navy and I had a college degree. So I might have thought I was above comics, but Stan's little humorous asides and captions—the attitude was, he's not taking this seriously, so therefore I don't have to take it seriously. I think I was really responding, as much as anything, to the derring-do stories and the melodrama, but the attitude that Stan conveyed gave me permission to do that, and to pretend to myself that, well, this is just a goof. Stan was almost post-modern. He not only innovated in his use of language, but in the attitude that his books conveyed, all of which persists to this day. And, of course, that changed the way the other comics companies did business. At both Charlton and DC, the two that I was familiar with, Stan's influence was there. Stan had a very down-to-Earth, sane attitude toward the whole business of writing.

DF: *Now, when you say you would "script" something, say, that Stan had plotted, what did that mean? I know you said he either talked it out with the artist, or sometimes he would do a two-paragraph plot. So would you just get pencils?*
DO: Yeah, a lot of times, with the first bunch of jobs I did, I didn't plot the first Doc Strange. Probably Stan and Ditko plotted it. I think there were margin notes. I did ***Daredevil*** #18 because Stan got into a deadline bind. Romita had done the art and put notes in the margins, but Stan didn't have time to do the script.

DF: *Once you'd written the script, how would you place the balloons—on the original artwork?*
DO: On the art, in non-reproducible blue pencil. I have a story that may focus the Stan Lee of that era for you. The first big blackout was in '65. The city went dark. Both Roy and I had writing to do, but, come on, there was no light. We gave ourselves permission to goof off that night, and there was no harm done. But we got into the office the next day and here was Stan. He had done his work. It was a ***Daredevil*** story. The pages had *candle wax* dripped on them. He did not let a little thing like a huge blackout stop him from writing. I mean, he was just phenomenal. Incredible energy, incredible instincts. I think there were about seven years where Stan didn't make a single mistake. He just really was on an incredible roll, and everything worked for him.

DF: *Do you attribute that to anything in particular?*
DO: He had a long apprenticeship. He had his tool kit. I think he had always been a better writer than his pre-***Fantastic Four*** work might have indicated, and when the lid was taken off of the box, out he came. He suddenly had no false constraints. As his autobiography states, he had planned to quit, anyway, and he was thinking, at Joan's advice, "I might as well write comic books I would enjoy reading." There's a profound lesson for us all in there.

DF: *Any other observations about Stan?*

DO: Well, I am incredibly grateful to him, because, in tandem with Julie Schwartz, he revived comic books. They re-created the medium, they reinvented it, each in very different ways. They were very different guys, and it's one of the glories of my life that I worked for both of them. But that first year working for Marvel, my job was to, in effect, imitate Stan, because Stan's style really was Marvel. That's what it was at that time. It was not yet this big company. It was, like, three offices stuck at the end of a corridor that was taken up by men's magazines, and confession mags, and crossword puzzle mags. We all start out imitating somebody, and that was a very clear-cut pattern I had. "Okay, this is, in terms of this context, the right way to do it." And it was a great way to learn. I learned the basics. I learned the basics by imitating Stan, and he was, by a huge margin, the best guy to imitate back then. The best comic book writer in the world.

Gary Friedrich

Gary Friedrich, *one of the first writers to join post-***Fantastic Four** *Marvel after Roy Thomas, is best known for writing* **Sgt. Fury, Monster of Frankenstein,** *and* **Ghost Rider.** *As a member of the 1960s Bullpen, Gary was trained in the Marvel way of doing things by Stan himself. Here, he recalls some highlights of those days.*

Was I witness to any of Stan's plotting sessions? About a zillion, it seems. Most of the meetings I had with Stan, and frequently Roy Thomas as well, were about plotting. Either Stan would have an idea he'd want to bounce off us, or we'd have something we wanted him to approve. Or sometimes we'd just brainstorm about things in general and see what would come of it.

One of Gary's first writing jobs at Marvel was the story "The Avenging Son," in ***Kid Colt Outlaw*** #138 (January 1968). Here's the original art to the last page of the story. Pencils by Werner Roth, inks by Herb Trimpe. [© 2011 Marvel Characters, Inc.]

My memories of specific sessions are a little vague after all these years. We had the most meetings in my early days in the Bullpen, 1966-67, when both Roy and I were fairly new and Stan was feeling us out to see just what we could contribute, or at least I felt that's what he was doing. He'd throw an idea at us, then listen to our feedback. Then he'd let us know if he liked or disliked our ideas and why, which was helpful to me in getting a feel for what he expected.

I specifically remember the session we had to go over my writer's test. This consisted of three or four pages of ***Spider-Man*** artwork with the balloons whited out. As the one taking the test, I was expected to write captions and dialogues to fit the artwork. Even though I'd already been hired and was working on staff as an associate editor (or was I the assistant and Roy the associate? Whichever was lower on the totem pole, that was me), Stan still wanted me to do the test. In the early days, Stan had anyone and everyone interested in writing for Marvel take the test. Rumors have it that Mario Puzo and Bruce Jay Friedman, both of whom worked for the Magazine Management [Marvel's parent company] men's mag division, took the test at one time.

Anyway, I wrote the pages and then was called into Stan's office along with Roy. As when he was going over a finished story with us (more on that in a moment), Stan laid out the artwork and script on a drawing table in his office and had Roy and me stand on either side of him while he sat in front of the table between us. Then he'd begin to read the script, look at the balloon placement (not one of my strong-points) and make comments about same.

I hit the jackpot when Stan came to a balloon where I had Spidey say, "Hang loose, Herbie." Those were the magic words. Stan loved them, and we didn't talk any more about the test, just how phrases such as "hang loose" were exactly the type of hip language he was looking for. My test was never discussed again, but "hang loose" cropped up in all of our writing a lot from that day forward. One thing about Stan, he knew when he saw or heard something he liked.

[Historians note: Yeah, it's true I introduced "hang loose" to Stan. It was in my writing test. Stan doesn't remember this! Roy doesn't remember it, either, even though he was there when Stan went over the test with me. Funny thing is, I have no idea where I picked it up, though I'm sure it didn't originate with me. The expression just worked as something for Spidey to say in that particular panel I was writing. Actually, Spidey said "Hang loose, Herbie" to the villain. And Stan flipped out (in a good way) when he read it. All he could talk about in going over the rest of my test was that expression...and the rest is rock 'n' roll, or at least **Country Joe and the Fish**, who I invited up to the office to meet Stan one day. But that's another story.] [And it's a story told elsewhere in this book! —Danny & Roy.]

Plotting sessions went the same way. We'd get together to discuss a plot for, say, ***Sgt. Fury,*** and we almost always started out with the same question: "Who's the villain going to be?" I'd toss out a suggestion, say, Baron Strucker. Stan would want to know when he last appeared. Roy would have the answer. And if it had been long enough, Stan would okay him. If not, it was back to, "Who's the villain going to be?"

Once the villain was approved, we'd move into setting (the Howlers are secretly parachuted into Berlin), conflict (Strucker is wrapping up plans for the invasion of Britain and Howlers must stop him... but he's in a bunker surrounded by ten million Nazi storm troopers—if you're laughing, you didn't read ***Sgt. Fury***) and resolution (how the hell are the Howlers going to get through the ten million troops and stop Strucker?). This may seem an oversimplification, but that's basically how it worked. Of course, sessions for the superheroes were a little more complicated.

And yes, it's true, occasionally the artists would come in and be involved in these sessions, though I don't remember any specific plotting sessions with artists in which I was involved. I can recall Stan on more than one occasion doing his impressions of heroes. I particularly remember him stomping around, grimacing and otherwise acting in a Hulk-like manner for either Marie Severin or Herb Trimpe. I also saw him pose like the Vulture on the edge of his desk, although I don't recall the artist who was involved. It was hilarious, but also effective.

Those sessions didn't go on for long, as the company grew and more and more titles were added. Stan soon began to trust Roy and me more, and we'd just write our plot synopses and send them off to the artists without his approval. But at any rate, the plotting sessions became less and less frequent, which was good for artistic freedom but bad in that I got to missing them.

New characters, particularly villains, would often evolve from the plotting sessions as well. When we couldn't satisfactorily answer the "Who's the villain going to be?" question, we'd begin to kick around ideas for new villains, and soon one would be born.

He'd call us in and have us stand by him in front of the drawing table and go over the completed artwork of a story he'd written or one we'd written, and he'd edit it with us standing there, explaining any changes he'd made, why he put a balloon in a certain place, why he had a character say this rather than that, etc. One thing in particular I remember that he continually drove home was to always move the story forward. "Every word that's spoken should be for the purpose of moving the story along," he'd tell us again and again. I'd have been a better writer had I followed this advice more carefully.

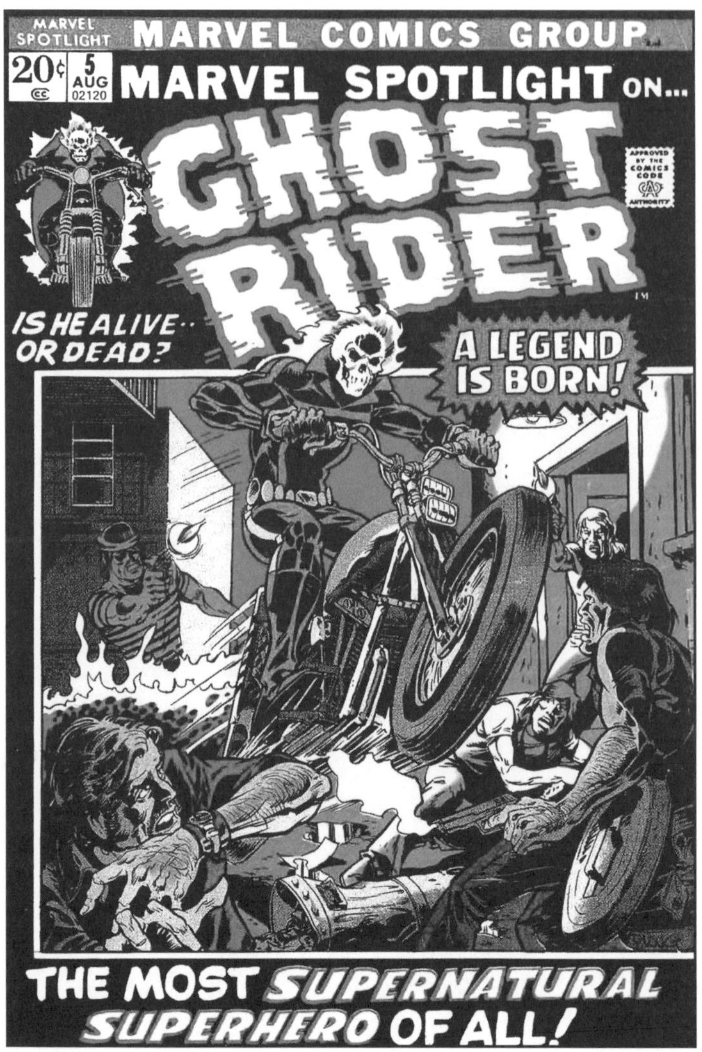

Cover to ***Marvel Spotlight*** #5 (August 1972), the origin and debut of the Johnny Blaze Ghost Rider, written by Gary. Cover art by Mike Ploog.

As for Stan's writing methods, I never actually watched him write anything, only rewrite as part of the editing process. But I believe he typed his scripts and drew the balloons directly on the artwork. I only recall him using overlays if major art changes needed to be suggested. Then he'd rough out the changes he wanted the artist to make on an overlay.

I think a couple of things made the Marvel Bullpen of the early '60s a remarkable place to work. One was the people who worked there. The other was the talent and drive of Stan Lee, which drove us to want to be better writers and artists. I know that, in my case, Stan made me want to be as good a writer as he was, and he did this primarily by continuing to write better and better stories himself.

From the first issue of ***Fantastic Four,*** comics were never the same... and neither was I. Stan's writing exerted a tremendous influence over the comics business and over my life. And I'll be forever grateful for both. Not to mention he was a great guy to work for, and a true friend as well as boss.

Letter to Stan from a future comics pro: Bob Rozakis

As a writer, **Bob Rozakis** is perhaps best known as the co-creator of ***'Mazing Man***, but his credits include more than 400 stories featuring Superman, Batman, and virtually every other DC character. He is also remembered as DC's Answer Man; using his vast knowledge of the company's history and characters, he responded to all sorts of readers' questions in a column that appeared in DC's books for a number of years. During his 17 years as head of DC's Production Department, Bob guided his staff (and, ultimately, the entire industry) into previously unexplored areas of computerized color separations and typesetting, electronic page preparation, and computer-to-plate printing. Bob's most recent comics-related work is "The Secret History of AA Comics," which was serialized in ***Alter Ego*** and ***Back Issue*** and will soon be collected into book form.

On this page is a letter Bob sent Stan in 1972.

In May, 2011, Bob had this to say about it:

"I was a junior at Hofstra when I wrote the letter and had met Stan when he spoke at nearby Nassau Community College. I believe that I got a response that enabled me to contact Michael Uslan, who was teaching a comics course at Indiana University. My efforts to establish one at Hofstra were shot down by the chairman of the English Department, who looked at my proposal and dismissively said, 'Are you trying to equate Superman with Shakespeare?' Amusingly, since graduating I have been invited to speak on the history of comics a number of times at HU, most recently as part of the university's 75th Anniversary celebration."

NEXUS 1972
HOFSTRA UNIVERSITY YEARBOOK
HEMPSTEAD, NEW YORK 11550
TELEPHONE 516 560-3323

February 15,1972

Dear Stan,

A group of us here at Hofstra are interested in setting up a course on comic books. However, one problem which confronts us is making up some sort of course outline to present for approval. I was wondering if you knew of any other schools which have courses like this because we would like to get in touch with them.

I would appreciate any information you might have on this and would be grateful if you would send it to me, either at the above address or to my home address

Thank you for you time and trouble.

Yours truly,

Bob Rozakis

Bob and Stephen DeStefano co-created the superhero spoof ***'Mazing Man***. Cover to issue #1 (January 1986) is penciled by DeStefano and inked by Karl Kesel. [© 2011 DC Comics]

Bob Rozakis in a recent photo. [©2011 Bob Rozakis]

1972 letter from Bob Rozakis, Stan Lee Collection, American Heritage Center, University of Wyoming.

Letter to Stan from a future comics pro:

Kevin Dooley

Kevin Dooley's impeccable credentials as a comics fan led him to a stint editing Fantagraphics' ***Amazing Heroes*** magazine in the 1980s. From there he went on to spend a decade as an editor at DC Comics, helming titles including ***Green Lantern*** and ***Aquaman***. These days, Kevin is still influencing minds as a schoolteacher.

Kevin j. dooley
[redacted]
~~March~~April 1, 1978

Marvel Comics Group
575 Madison Avenue
New York, N.Y. 10022
Dear Stan,

Tardy though this letter may be, I feel I must speak. Do not dismiss me as just another critic. I heard a certain character will get his own mag, and I'm sure it will be one of the biggest flops in comic history.

Let me tell you why. The premise for his powers is very weak. He isn't realistic at all. The plots and action can only hope to appeal to third grade reader mentality. You've had a multitude of great ideas, Stan, but this time you bummed out. A hero bitten by a radioactive spider, indeed.

People dislike spiders by nature. When parents see their kids reading about a gallivanting insect..well, the PTA will soon put a damper on that. Give it up. AMAZING FANTASY #15 was a good experiment, but a book devoted entirely to the exploits of this arachnid protagonist is a huge mistake.

Peter Piper, or whatever, isn't an identifiable character. If you insist on continuing, change his hair style and do away with the glasses...oh, and get rid of Aunt May - fast. Have Porker work at a newspaper or something. It has worked before, but I doubt if it will help. This is one Marvel mag that is definitely doomed to an early cancellation never to be remembered.

My surprise at Stan the Man, who brought us the Indelible Hulk and the Fantastic For, cannot be overstated. Next thing you know, you'll be giving us blind superheroes, magicians and platinum-coated surfboarders.

You really ought to take yourself to task on this one. Get out of the comic biz and do something practical and honorable, like shepherding. Otherwise you might find yourself putting out books with talking ducks in them.

Quite,

Kevin j dooley

P.S. Happy first of April, you silly fool.-Kd
Keep up the great work.

April 12, 1978

Mr. Kevin J. Dooley
[redacted]

Dear Kevin:

WOW! Your April fool letter surely had me going for a while.

It was a witty and clever epistle, Kevin. I enjoyed and appreciated it.

Excelsior!

Stan Lee

SL:mc

1978 letter from and letter to Kevin Dooley, Stan Lee Collection, American Heritage Center, University of Wyoming.

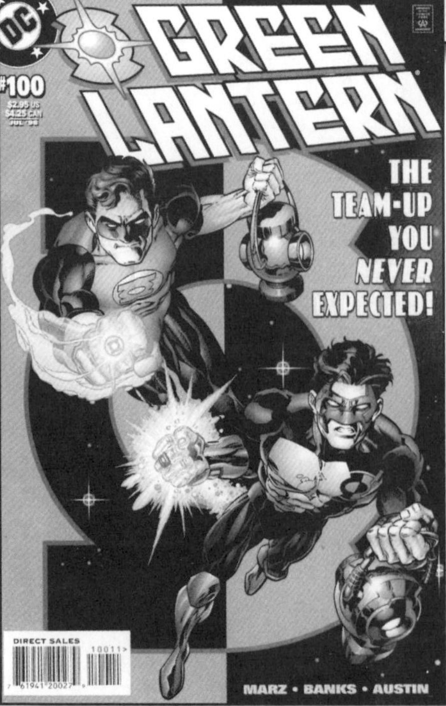

Among the many comics Kevin would go on to edit was ***Green Lantern*** #100 (July 1998). Cover art is by Daryl Banks and Terry Austin. [©2011 DC Comics]

Face-to-Face with Wertham's Partner!

Stan debates Dr. Hilde Mosse on the Barry Farber Show

WOR-AM Radio, November 12, 1968

Transcribed by Steven Tice

Copyedited by Danny Fingeroth

__Barry Farber__ was a prominent local New York late night radio host in 1968, when this program aired. Later, he would become, and remains, a national media figure. In this program, he brought Stan together with __Frederic Wertham's__ colleague, __Dr. Hilde Mosse__, a figure as controversial and prominent in American psychotherapy as was Wertham. Although the show, discovered on audiotape in Stan's Wyoming archives, takes place 14 years after the publication of Wertham's anti-comics tome, **Seduction of the Innocent**, *for Mosse, the issues are still the same as in the 1950s. Also on the broadcast are animation luminaries __Dennis Marks__ and __Barry Yellen__. The transcript has been edited to emphasize the dialogue of the primary "adversaries," Lee and Mosse. Some of Farber's, Marks's, and Yellen's comments have been deleted or shortened due to space limitations, as were commercials and station identifications. Also, while Mosse's syntax may seem a little odd, bear in mind that, as a refugee from Nazi Germany, she spoke in the manner of someone who, while highly intelligent and educated, was not a native English speaker. Hilde Mosse died in 1982, at age 70.*

Barry Farber has been a major radio personality for decades, and is still active today.

An undated photo of Hilde L. Mosse.

BARRY FARBER: I'm Barry Farber... Onward now into an argument. Not as big an argument as we would have had a couple years ago, but, who knows, in some aspects maybe a bigger one, about comic books, television cartoons, and movies for children. Hilde Mosse is a child psychiatrist. She's a medical doctor, of course. She's Assistant Clinical Professor of Psychiatry at New York Medical College, the School Bureau of Child Guidance. Let me get all the titles straight now so we don't crash on takeoff. You are School Psychiatrist at the Bureau of Child Guidance. Right?

HILDE MOSSE: That's right.

BF: In other words, you are as official a child psychiatrist as one can possibly be. You are just as official as Dr. Frederic Wertham. If he were to walk into this room, neither one of you would salute the other one. You are both equally competent in this argument, right?

HM: Yes, we worked together for years.

BF: Is your attitude the same as his?

HM: Yes, that's right.

BF: I've got to congratulate my assistants because we've got a great broadcast before we even begin. Dr. Wertham is famous for his comments about and, frankly, against most of the literature for children, including cartoons, comic books, and the like. I haven't heard a conciliatory remark from Dr. Wertham in ten years of Wertham-watching. Regardless of what's happened inside the industry, Dr. Wertham seems to maintain his anxiety and his powers of observation, and, in fact, his opposition to most of what's going on inside comic strips, and comic books, and television cartoons for children.

Here's Stan in the mid-1960s.

Barry Yellen is president of Childhood Productions. He has, before the age of 21, directed, produced, or written 582 different plays. Mr. Yellen, right now you are president of Childhood Productions, involved in all sorts of children's—.

BY: Children's films, motion pictures, theaters, and television. Primarily theaters.

Stan's wife Joan, here in a modeling pose, was with him at the talk show.

BF: Stan Lee is with us, and he came in with such a beautiful woman I almost said to myself, "Holy mackerel. I'm not going to to tell anybody, because who in the world has a right to walk into the studio with a woman that beautiful?" Well, Stan Lee does, because that's Mrs. Lee. And you know something? I made up my mind not to say a word if you come in with anybody. Before I even saw her, I was looking in the mirror. Look, it's not even a mirror, the glass right here, I could see her coming in and I just made up my mind I wasn't going to say a word, but I have a note in front of me that she's Mrs. Lee. So we're all going to live happily ever after for the duration of the broadcast.

STAN LEE: Hopefully, Barry.

BF: Dennis Marks is a TV writer. The last time Dennis Marks was on these microphones I said, "Let's see, now, you're a TV cartoonist." And I knew good and well that he wasn't a cartoonist. He wrote, he wrote the dialogue.

1968 *Barry Farber Show* on WOR-AM radio, with Stan Lee, Hilde Mosse, et al. Stan Lee Collection, box #71, American Heritage Center, University of Wyoming.

DM: And the stories.

BF: Has anybody got a flippant, light comment on comics and what's happened lately.

DM: TV cartoons are fun. That's my stand for the evening.

SL: Well, I'll say that comic magazines are great literature, which ought to get us into an argument about as fast as anything possibly could.

BF: Are you talking about all, or just you?

SL: Oh, no, I'm always referring just to mine, the Marvel Comics Group. You know, I might add that I actually don't know which side to be on, because, years ago, I was a very staunch fan of Dr. Wertham's, which is almost heresy for somebody in my field to say. When I was very much younger, I read a book, I think it was called ***Dark Legend***.

HM: That's right.

SL: A case history of a boy who killed his mother or some such thing?

HM: That's right, yes.

SL: It made a lasting impression on me, as a youth. It scared the life out of me, and I said to myself, "Gee whiz, anybody who would write this for young people, a book like this which would fall into young people's hands... " I was very surprised to find, years later, that he was crusading against violence, because I still find him a little bit frightening when I think of the title of that book, even. So I guess it just proves nothing at all, really.

BF: But I want to know what *this* proves, if anything. Reading now from page three of the CMAA. What does that mean, again?

SL: I think Comic Magazine Association, and the last "A" you've got me.

BF: Uh-huh. Here, Comics Magazine Association of America. Naturally. Listen to this. "During the recent election campaign in South Vietnam, candidates used more than two million comic books to win votes, ***Time Magazine*** reported."

SL: Even the losing candidates, which must say something for comics. No, the thing is, about comics, I think nobody will deny that there are good ones, and there are bad ones. But I think we had this discussion once before, Barry. Comics are a medium. They're a means of communication using pictures and words, and I don't think you can condemn them because of their format.

BF: No, you can't condemn them, but you can scrutinize them more than you can books. I'll tell you why nobody has ever done a show just on books. We may do a show on a specific book, but I don't know anybody who just said, "Tonight we're going to discuss books. In general." Because it's too big. Why discuss books? [But] we have the right to discuss comics in general for the simple reason that comic books have such power to propel, to pervert, to do anything they want to, that you deserve discussing.

SL: Well, do you think comic books have more power than a book or than a motion picture?

BF: *[whispers]* Definitely.

SL: Really? Why so, Barry?

BF: Because You're in a lower class mentality, either because of lower age, which is excusable, or because of normal middle age and lower mentality, which is less excusable, but you're in the much more impressionable group. But if I put [a message] in the medium of a compelling cartoon or comic book series, my audience is my marionette. My readership is my constituency. They're my toy, almost.

SL: Well, you're just really talking, then, about the audience, about the fact that any type of communication that's directed toward

Fredric Wertham in approximately 1955, responding in, well, shock to an issue of EC's ***Shock Illustrated***. [©2011 the copyright holders]

A clearer view of the comic Dr. Wertham is reading: ***Shock Illustrated*** #1 (September-October 1955). It was actually part of EC's post-horror-era "New Directions" line of comics with color covers and black-and-white interiors that had text and art, but no word balloons. Cover painting is by Jack Kamen. [©2011 EC Comics, Inc.]

younger people you feel will affect them more than some type that's directed toward older people, and I don't think you can argue that point. But, as far as comics being more influential, or having more impact, I don't think anything has more impact than a good, dramatic motion picture.

HM: Well, I would very much like to say something here, which I think is pertinent, about children swallowing fire-crackers. I know of cases which we are concerned about children playing on a vacant lot and getting into old iceboxes and then suffocating in them. And a friend of mine took that up in a class once, where there were about 35 to 40 children. And some children laughed at him, and snickered, and said, well— He said, "Why don't you take this seriously? Why don't you believe me?" Well, they say the Three Stooges and some other cartoon type film on television, they do it all the time, and they get out again, nothing happens to them. This makes an enormously deep impression on children, and of course it can be imitated.

I can give you a case I had the other day with my medical students, was a four-year-old child, was brought in by the mother because of fire-setting, and when we examined exactly what happened, the following had taken place. Mother was ironing, and the kids were watching television, and all of a sudden the four-year-old put out a scream, runs into the kitchen, and then the mother smells something funny, and she goes there, and the curtains are on fire. Apparently he had climbed up and had set fire in a manner which wasn't quite clear, but it had to do with the pilot light. Now, what they were watching, when we followed this story through, was, on a Saturday afternoon, they watched ***Road Runner***. And ***Road Runner*** very often has explosion and fire-setting in it. And you have to know, of course.

So this, and ***Speed Racer***, and many other programs. And you have to know how children react in order to know how it affects. And I'd like to say something that Mr. Lee says. You know, there's a tendency to confuse the issues completely. You cannot ever compare a book, which is scientific and artistic, like ***Dark Legend***, and compares the matricide committed by a New York boy with both Hamlet and Orestes with comic books, which consist only of pictures, which are directed specifically toward children, in which the story line is of the most primitive and simple outline. It's very easy to write them, because the majority of them now, and when we first started to be interested in them, of course, deal with these strong men type, whether it's Atomic Man or whether it is Spider-Man. It is a very primitive pictorial. Of course they make more of an impression, because by the time Wertham wrote his first book, a hundred million copies comic books were published a month, not a year, but a month, and they were the greatest publishing success in the history of known publishing. So this is something totally different from a book, which, if it's a bestseller, at that time had maybe 10,000 copies of less. So you cannot compare them.

Dennis Marks in the 1980s.

DM: That little kid who set fire after watching ***Road Runner.*** I just wanted to ask the good doctor, if there—well, strike that. She certainly doesn't have a provable case in court that, because ***Road Runner*** was on the air at that time, that that is what caused the kid to set fire to the drapes. Number one, I'm sure she will find in her records cases of twenty, thirty, I'll even give her a hundred kids who jumped off roofs with red capes saying, "I'm Superman." How many kids pushed their grandmother into the oven after reading ***Hansel and Gretel***?

HM: Wait a minute, you've said several different things I'd like to be able to answer. In the first place, there are proven cases, not only in this country, but all over the world, of direct imitative action, violent and otherwise, it doesn't have to be violent, following either film, or television show, or comic books.

You don't have to take my word for it. It's quite clear that imitation exists. Even imitation murders have been proven. Now, whatever that means, I would say, one way or other, it doesn't mean not necessarily you don't have to show murder on television. I mean, I don't jump to these conclusions.

DM: Well, where do you stop? That's what I want to ask?

HM: Wait a minute. We have to know exactly how children act. I am talking about children now, and that's the experience I have, because I examine children very carefully, and clinical examination, not any kind of speculation or anything like that, shows that this exists.

SL: Dr. Mosse, aren't children affected by everything that they hear and say?

HM: Of course they are.

SL: And you'd almost have to segregate them from the world itself if you don't want them to be adversely affected by things. I mean, what do you do about a war? Now, they're exposed to the headlines about a war. They're exposed to newspaper crime news.

HM: Well, unfortunately, there's nothing I can do about it. But I'd like

the author of THE SHOW OF VIOLENCE and DARK LEGEND

SEDUCTION OF THE INNOCENT

Fredric Wertham, M. D.

the influence of comic books on today's youth

Seduction of the Innocent was Wertham's 1954 book that attacked comic books and contributed to the severe constriction of the industry and the loss of income by many talented writers and artists. [©1954 Rinehart and Co.]

to protect children from harmful influences.

SL: But isn't the purpose of psychiatry and psychology, doesn't it deal with mental health, or at least with trying to attain some sort of mental health? And is it mentally healthy, is it even rational, to pick one very small area in a world which has so many more serious maladies, and to be continually harping on it? Now, I feel, for the past twenty years, I have heard this particular speech. I have heard the same arguments, and the same answers. Dr. Wertham and his followers, or disciples, or whatever, have never been convinced, and have never swayed, from their point of view. I don't think the people of my persuasion have, either. Nor do I like to sound like the heavy. I'm not in favor of causing children to do terrible things. I think we all have the same objective. The only point is that, I think that you were quite right a moment ago when you said, "Well, what about ***Hansel and Gretel?***" I mean, where do you stop? You don't let them read the Bible because there are horrible things there? Fairy tales, newspapers? Why pick on certain things? There must be a more rational type of thing to do, and there must be something that is more applicable to solution. Obviously, what you're trying to do, if you had your way completely, it would not be a healthier world, and that is where I think Dr. Wertham's philosophy is completely ridiculous, because if everything he wanted came to pass, if there were no comic books, and if every television show with crime, and with action, and with violence, were taken off the air, I do not believe the mental climate in this country would be improved one iota, because all that would happen is the other things, which are far more serious, would then affect the children even more, and there'd be no relief in fantasy.

Dark Legend: A Study in Murder was a 1941 book by Wertham that Stan admired. It was an exploration of the mind of a real-life teenaged killer. [©1941, Duell, Sloan and Pearce.]

HM: Well, first, I think it's very interesting that you're right away on the defensive. I haven't attacked anybody. I've just stated what our findings are. I haven't said anything about program content except that this is the way children are affected. I think it's very interesting that you right away feel that you are attacked. I examine children. I am a scientist, I am a doctor. I examine children who are brought to me.

SL: But will you admit that Dr. Wertham does attack persons?

HM: I don't admit anything, because you haven't even let me finish. You can only understand this as you can only understand any other social phenomenon if you know its history. Now, when we first examined the affect of mass media on children, there was no television. Dr. Wertham, and a group, and myself, we started the first mental hygiene clinic that was ever started in Harlem, and we examined children there, and I was in the school system, etc., and in private practice, and we found that these children, the majority of them, were very much preoccupied with certain picture stories which they carried around with them, and which we found were comic books.

Then we started to study the comic books, which at that time nobody but us absolutely nobody had done. And in the process of researching the reactions of our children not in relation to comic books, but examining them thoroughly the way we do as doctors, examine the entire inner and outer life, their conscious, their unconscious, their behavior at home, in school, and anywhere, we came to the conclusion it took us very many years to come to that these comic books made a very deep impression on children. Whether or not it was positive or negative, that was really beside the point. But we found we're the first ones to say publicly there is a factor here totally new in history, a mass media directed to children specifically, which influences them deeply. And in the process of examining them, we found that one aspect of the negative influence that this mass media had was wherever it dealt with portraying crime and violence. Now, this, of course, research has been expand very much since then. At that time we also found that, right away, anybody that had anything to do with the comic book industry reacted exactly the way you're doing, they become the defensive right away.

SL: Well, I feel you're defending your point of view right now, Dr. Mosse. And, I might add, I might add—

HM: I'm not defending anything. I am stating what I find—

SL: I guess I mightn't add.

HM: —I find as a doctor when I examine children. That's all.

SL: Well, let me just say that we could have saved you a heck of a lot of time and trouble, because if it took you years of intensive study and research to learn that children were affected by these millions of comic books and were influenced by them, I think we could have told you that after about ten minutes. I wonder why it's necessary for such profound people to have to devote so much time to exploring and discovering the obvious.

DM: Stand at the corner newsstand and watch them buy it.

HM: Well, you can't have it both ways. You can't say on one side it's obvious, and on the other side say that it does not affect children.

SL: I never said it doesn't affect children.

HM: You see, what we found—

SL: I said everything affects children, and everything affects adults.

DM: I don't think Mr. Lee or I ever said we don't have a responsibility. Of course, we do.

SL: You know, something, Barry? I mentioned before I hate to sound like the heavy, and, unfortunately, as Dr. Mosse said, and very rightfully so, it always sounds as if we're being defensive, as if we're the publishers of some sort of—contemptible literature, and we get on the air and we try to defend this horrible thing we're doing. Now, I tried to mention before, I really think we're as responsible as the various medical people who so often condemn us, and so often unjustly condemn us, and I'll be happy to give reasons why I say that. I might also add that, unless it provable, there are just as many people with medical credentials who have taken the opposite viewpoint, completely, from Dr. Wertham, and Dr. Mosse, and the others of their ilk. I do feel that our responsible, and our feeling of responsibility, is very great. We try to turn out the best product we can, and I think we're doing a good job. I think, in many respects, the job we're doing is a lot better, and is a lot more honest, than the job that some of our detractors are doing.

In this program, Stan recalls attending a lecture by "a man who had worked with Wertham" who referred to a children's comic Stan had edited as being an example of "vulgarity." It's likely Stan is referring to Gershon Legman, author of ***Love and Death: A Study in Censorship*** (1949, Breaking Point) whose views on media and sexuality were controversial, to say the least.

BF: I think, not just a right, but a duty, to stand back and review once in a while. I was first interested in this because I wonder how I survived my earlier children's films. We had something they don't have anymore. Too bad, there's so much they don't have anymore. We used to have [movie and radio] serials.

HM: They don't need them because the kids watch the television set. Saturday is the most violent morning in the history of the United States as far as murderous programs being presented—.

DM: [There's also the] seven o'clock news every evening.

HM: And I will tell you that television industry themselves, after the murder on Senator Robert Kennedy said, we are going to take the violence out of the Saturday shows, and they are going to change the Saturday shows.

DM: Have they?

HM: Yes, they have.

DM: We did it before that.

HM: Because there are very, very many people who connect the violence that we are witnessing right now, and you know perfectly well you can't walk any streets in any city in the United States without being fear of attacked—

DM: I'm hearing nonsense.

HM: —and with the fact that violence now is committed by ever younger and younger children with the mass media. Now, that's not the only factor—

DM: Thank you.

HM: —but it is one, and a very important, factor. And I think it's totally irresponsible to sit here and say it has nothing to do with it.

DM: We never said it had nothing to do with it!

HM: Children watch television many more hours than they go to school.

SL: I think the thing that worries me, Dr. Mosse, when you talk about things being irresponsible, I think of myself, really, as rather a scholarly person, and I try to take the scientific—

BF: We all are, or we wouldn't be welcome in this chamber.

SL: And I'm sure that's so, Dr. Farber. And I try to take a scientific approach to things and not leap to hasty conclusions, and when these various psychologists years ago were up in arms against the comics, and then later the TV shows, and so forth, I was really on their side, because at first I began to think, well, there must be some reason why all these terrible things are happening, and maybe they're right. And I looked into it, and I studied it, and I went to lectures, and I

For some historical context, this November 1968 Farber show with Stan took place a week after Richard Nixon was elected President for the first time, narrowly defeating Hubert Humphrey. Here's a look at the political scene three-and-a-half years later, when Nixon was running for re-election, by Stan and John Romita, Sr., from ***The New York Times Magazine*** of April 16, 1972. [Spider-Man ©2011 Marvel Characters, inc.]

remember going to a lecture that an assistant of Dr. Wertham had given, a man who worked with him or for him, I don't know, and I won't mention his name because maybe what I'm going to say is sueable. I don't know, but I remember at this lecture he held up a magazine, and it happened to be a magazine that I had been the editor of, for little children. It wasn't a violent magazine, it was a funny animals type of magazine, like a Mickey Mouse type of thing. And we had a gag on the cover, and it had a giraffe. And I remember when we did this cover, we thought, "Well, we've done everything else, what could we do?" And we wanted a simple, decorative cover that might appeal to a five-year-old. And we took this giraffe, and put him in a cage, and cut a hole in the top of the cage, and the giraffe's head was sticking through, munching an apple or something off a tree above. And we thought it was charming, and we published it, and that was the end of it. Well, imagine my consternation, and, really, my shock, when a few months later, this associate of the good doctor's held this magazine up and said, "It should be painfully apparent to everyone in the room what these horrible publishers were getting at, the phallic symbolism and the vulgarity."

HM: I can assure you that was never anybody who worked with Dr. Wertham—

SL: I can give you his name when we're off the microphone.

HM: We never, never had said anything about the sexual aspects.

SL: No, he worked with him because he was at a class with Dr. Wertham at NYU that I attended, Professor. At the time I saw this at class, I said to myself, and I've been thinking about it a lot since, because I think there are some very genuine problems in the world today which are deserving of analysis, and hopefully of solution, and I said to myself, if some of the finest psychological brains in the world can be this ridiculous, and can go off the deep end this way, and can be this far divorced from anything reasonable or rational, what do you believe in? Who is really going to save us? And I've found, since that day, I have lost such confidence in people who come armed to a debate like this with folders, with statistics, with things to show, and everything they say, in and of itself, makes a lot of sense until you sit back and think about it, and you say, this is like a scene from ***Alice in Wonderland***. What they're saying just isn't valid.

BF: How many comic books does [Marvel put out] in all?

SL: Oh, I guess about twenty a month, Barry.

BF: Dr. Mosse, I've told you about my exaggerated experience where, as an intelligent eight-, nine-year-old, I was literally about to jump off a roof because I had seen it done, not in a cartoon series, but in a serial. I didn't, and I've got to tell you, I don't know anybody else in the neighborhood who did, but I just remember wanting to, and being about to.

HM: Yes, well, this is a very frequent occurrence, and that's another thing that adults very frequently know nothing about. See, I teach medical students, and we always discuss this fact, we always discuss mass media, because, after all, they belong to the comic book, and now television, generation. And out of a group of seventeen, between sixteen and seventeen, there always three or four, always, who start to snicker, and to giggle, and to say, yes, that's exactly what they did as a kid. They try to fly, and there's always one, or sometimes two, who had a broken ankle or a broken arm and said, "Look, we always said it's an accident. We never told our parents what really happened because we were ashamed of it." And it's a rather frequent occurrence, which only shows that children are deeply impressed by what they see. And, you see, you cannot see this imitation with a mice. They think mice can light fires, that's totally unimportant. What children do, and if you have your own, you don't have to take my word for it, watch them. They go and play with their mice or not. They imitate exactly what they see, especially on the television screen. It makes much more deep impression on them than comic books, and I want to say, of course, they reinforce each other, now, because many comic books call themselves now TV comics, because you can get them in comic books and then television. What little children do is that first they act it out in play. Now, if you show them something that is potentially dangerous and violent, then they act it out. And any teacher will be able to tell you that anybody who knows anything about children, kindergarten children, the type of play that they play is formed by whatever they have seen on television or seen in comic books. So this is not a matter of debate, this is a matter of just exactly what happened.

DM: This is not good or bad, that's just the way it is.

SL: Doc, if you were the queen of the world and could do whatever you wanted, what would you do about the scene in ***Peter Pan*** where the children fly?

HM: Well, that's a fairy tale, you know. The comic book publisher, they always have the same arguments. They always want to get people who listen away from the real issue. Violence is a very serious issue.

DM: That wasn't the real issue. You said children imitate.

HM: It has absolutely nothing to do with it.

SL: Why is it what I say has nothing to do with it?

HM: Wait a minute, let me finish. The ***Peter Pan*** show is on maybe once a year, twice a year.

SL: Oh, but it's a book that's read all the time. Comics are never on the air.

HM: Look, of course Spider-Man is on the air. Don't tell a lie, an outright lie, here.

SL: We have some that aren't.

HM: Yeah, but many of them are.

SL: Well, Spider-Man doesn't fly.

HM: But I'm talking about one aspect of this that's flying. Children imitate other aspects, too. That's totally beside the point.

DM: No, it's not beside the point. It is exactly the same.

SL: [So what we say is] besides the point, and what you say is germane?

HM: Let me describe how children experience this, and how they identify with it. I give you a quote from children. I mean, I'm not, whatever they see might affect them in this way, and my only concern, by golly, is violence. I have no other concern. I don't want to discuss any other aspects, because the violent aspect, that's what does the harm. Nothing else does the harm.

SL: Well, see, when I say something, you say that people who have my point of view always give the same answers. Of course, I might say, I think with great justification, that I have heard the same attacks from you for the past 25 years, so I don't think it's fair to say we say the same thing when you're saying the same thing all the time. Now, what I'm asking you is, and let's forget ***Peter Pan*** if you don't feel you want to answer that. What I'm asking you is, if you were in charge of all the media, what would you do? Would you say there are to be no comic magazines and no children's cartoons? Or would you say, "Let me decide which cartoons are good, and which are bad?" And at what point would you stop? I'm sure you should also decide which regular shows are good and bad, because there's always apt to be some child who will watch a normal—some child might watch ***The Flying Nun*** and decide to fly, so obviously that should be taken off the air.

HM: You know perfectly well that that's not my point. What I would say is—

SL: I don't know perfectly well *what* your point is.

HM: I talk about violence, I don't talk about—

DM: No, you talked about imitative action.

BY: —that most children realize very quickly is not possible.

DM: Very quickly.

HM: Well, you asked me specifically what I would suggest. The only suggestion I would have is that it would be, that one would not have a condition where a child now that has grown up between the age of about five and fourteen can watch about 12,000 murders committed in the mass media on television screen. I don't know whether I would reduce that number to 2,000.

SL: Well, you wouldn't see 12,000 in any given viewing period, I don't believe.

HM: Oh, yes, you would during that time of his life.

Here's Dr. Wertham in a 1967 appearance on the syndicated ***Mike Douglas*** TV show, promoting his then recent book, ***A Sign for Cain: An Exploration of Human Violence.*** That's Douglas on the left. [*A Sign for Cain*, 1966, MacMillan Publishing Company]

SL: Oh, during the time of his life. I see.

HM: Of course. Now, there is a relationship between fictional violence, and fictional murder, and what people think, their fantasies, especially in children, and the way they find solutions to conflict that is it creates a readiness to commit violent acts. Now, what I would suggest, and I'm not the only one, that there would be less violent action portrayed in all the mass media. I don't care whether it's the comic book, television, or film.

SL: I think that's a noteworthy suggestion. Noteworthy.

HM: I'm not suggesting how it is to be done. How it is to be done is not up to me. As a doctor, I say this is a harmful part of the mass media.

SL: That's like me saying, "I would suggest, in all sincerity, there should be no war, and there should be no crime, but for goodness sake, don't ask me how to do it. I mean, I made the suggestion. Now, let the rest of the human race abolish the war." I'm with you, Doc. I think there shouldn't be as much violence. I wish the children only saw things that did them a lot of good. I wish there was nothing negative, and I wish there was nothing harmful put in front of young, or old, people. I would love to be in the forefront of those who are going to participate in this crusade. I'm still waiting for somebody to say how to do it. We think our books are good. We think our shows are pretty darned amusing and don't have one iota of harm in them. Now, there may be people who disagree, and there may be people who feel the ***Peter Pan*** flying scene is bad. I don't know, but I would like somebody to say, specifically, unless this is just a conversation to kill some time and sell some products, and that's not a bad objective, either, I would like somebody to say, specifically, what should we do, and how should we do it?

HM: Well, it's very, very simple. Everybody knows what violence is.

SL: Well, but nobody will agree on that.

HM: Well, if we all agree on it, then why don't you and Marvel comic books and the Marvel television shows do something about that?

SL: No, I say *nobody* agrees on what's violent.

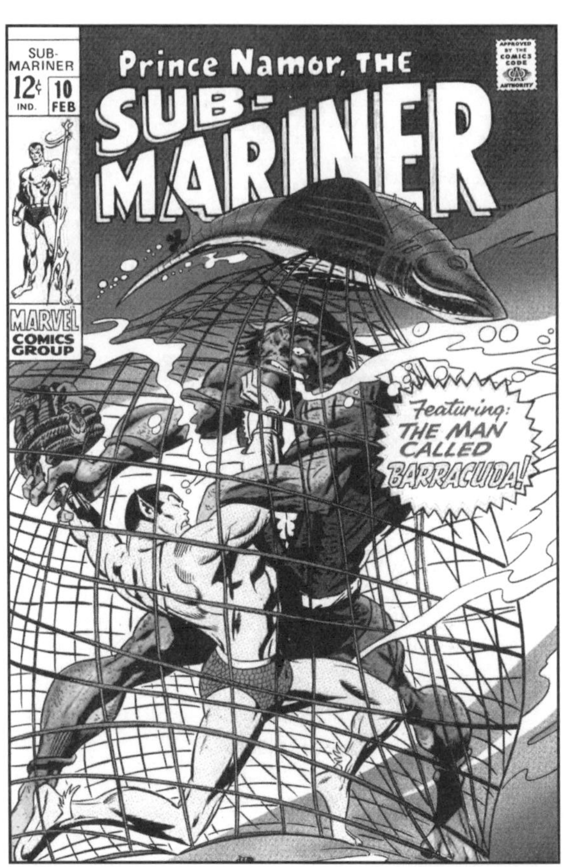

You have to give Dr. Mosse credit for knowing the name "Sub-Mariner," even if she and Stan can't agree on how to pronounce it. Here's the cover to the February 1969 ***Prince Namor, the Sub-Mariner*** #10, on sale around the time of this Farber show. Cover penciled and inked by Gene Colan. [©2011 Marvel Characters, Inc.]

HM: Characters like Hulk, characters like the Atomic Man.

SL: Atomic Man isn't ours. Superman isn't ours. The Hulk, our lovable green giant, is ours.

HM: Well, I don't care whether it's yours, it's all the exact same—

SL: Oh, no! Oh, goodness!

HM: —comic book story.

SL: You see, now, that proves you don't read them. They're not the same at all.

HM: I watched them, they are completely the same, because there's only one—

SL: Do you read them?

HM: Will you let me finish, please?

SL: But, you see, you say things that aren't true, but I can't stop you at that point, and you say, "Let me finish," and then you've finished and I've forgotten, and we're on to another subject, and it really sounds as though everything you're saying is very valid, and this is what so many of you people do. You speak with such authority, and you're not factual. If somebody tries to say, "Wait a minute, that's wrong," you say, "Let me finish." Well, okay, go ahead and finish.

HM: Okay. The Hulk, the Sub-Mar-EE-ner, Spider-Man—

SL: Sub-MAR-in-er.

HM: Sub-MAR-in-er.

SL: Thank you.

HM: I don't care how you pronounce it. Spider-Man, Superman, Batman, they are all the same, psychologically the exact same type of character.

SL: Well, you will forgive me if I disagree.

HM: Will you let me finish?

SL: Yes, yes.

HM: They are the very powerful muscle-type men, heroes, who solve every problem by physical violence or weaponry. Modern weaponry plays an enormous role. Organized society, as an organization, the law does not exist because they take it in their own hand to solve whatever conflict they are on. They are the antithesis of democracy, because they are the muscle Superman, they are the adoration of physical violence and power. They are exactly, exactly what anybody who knows anything about what the fascism stands for, what Nazism stood for, they are the ideal that people had in the Hitler era.

The Superman people tried to put your ***Superman*** in Germany after Hitler, that was in the '40s and '50s, and I know people in Germany who were appalled by the comic books and especially, of course, by ***Superman*** that was sent over there and promoted over there. Now, I gave a talk about that in 1954. I'm quite pleased that ***Superman*** from then on was not published in the German language anymore, because there were too many people in West Germany who were appalled by it, and the reaction against it was so strong that it alarmed Jews, because they certainly know what type of mentality is promoted with all these superheroes. I don't care what you call it.

SL: You know, it's an incredible thing. I would imagine many, many people listening to this show right now, who don't read comics, and don't watch the cartoons on television, are very impressed with what Dr. Mosse said. And I know, of course, that anybody who does read the books is just dumbfounded, because obviously these characters are not all the same, they're not psychologically motivated in the same way—

BF: Stan Lee, would you care, at this time, to embrace your allies in the comics and denounce your enemies so that they'll be off in a side pocket and we can just talk about the good guys and the bad guys, agreeing who's who?

SL: Well, first of all, let me just say to answer you that I'm not on a different side than Dr. Mosse. I would love there to be less violence. As I said before, I would love all the stories to be good and to have nothing but all sorts of assets for the readers. I'm just waiting for somebody to tell me how to go about doing this. I gather by what she said about Superman in Germany and so forth, and I never thought, forgive me, from ever being here defending Superman, who is a competitor, but I gather that she feels that Superman is harmful and therefore there shouldn't be a Superman, because the whole psychology behind it as wrong. So it would seem to me, to carry it a step further, that these books should, there just shouldn't be superheroes. Now, of course, in legend, and, of course, in classics, there are all sorts of superheroes. I would imagine that would be next, because where does the good doctor go after the comics have been wiped out, and after the cartoons have been wiped out, and there is still crime and violence? We're going to have to attack something else. I would imagine there'll be quite a sterile world in another few generations, but as far as delineating—

HM: If you think that the only creative element in man is his propensity for violence, I think we are on totally opposite sides of this.

SL: I never said that. I never said that.

HM: Well, it sounds like that.

SL: I never said that. I'm waiting for somebody to tell me what is violence, and how to eliminate it, in the stories? In other words, it would seem to me that every story is based on conflict, every story is based on a problem that must be solved. Now, children want stories in which the conflict is somewhat physical. A child won't read a story, and this is the reason for the success of a ***Treasure Island*** or something like that, won't read a story in which there isn't physical conflict. Now, I'm quite sure one could take your premises and say, and point to a thousand things in ***Treasure Island*** which are very harmful, and, well, we go right back to the same argument. I could take every classic in the world, and, as I say, we could take the Bible, which is the most harmful, I'm sorry, the most violent bit of literature probably ever published— The thing is so sophistic, and it's so ridiculous, that I, myself, feel like a fool sitting here trying to speak articulately about something where there should be a conclusion to be reached, but you're not even trying to find the solution, you're just trying to propose an argument.

TREASURE ISLAND

During the heated conversation, Stan favorably compares action-adventure comics to books like Robert Louis Stevenson's classic, ***Treasure Island.*** Mosse doesn't agree. Here's the cover to a 1924 edition of the book.

BF: Maybe Dr. Mosse's solution is do away with comics.

HM: Well, wait a minute, please give me a chance to answer. In the first place, it depends entirely on how you portray violence. That's one aspect.

SL: That's what I'd like to know. How?

HM: The second aspect, I want to make very, very clear that it's totally impossible for anybody who looks at it to compare comic book stories to the Bible, or Sophocles, or any of the other stories of fairy tales. Because, just by looking at the pictures, you can tell that the fact of the stories, one fistful in the head, in the stomach, or in the eyes, especially after the others, it's one violent image in one after the other. The violent image, the physical violence is the story. There are some exceptions. Spider-Man is a little bit more sophisticated, where some very intelligent young men like it very much. But, by and large, that is the story. There is nothing else to it. We must make a difference between comic books, please, and television, because it's very, it's wrong, scientifically, to lump things together. Now, to my mind, comic books are not even a legitimate medium. They are just based on the fact that there is a cheap way—

SL: Listen—

HM: Wait a minute. To produce very many of these comic book types because there were new colored presses invented so that many, many could be printed at one time. Television is something totally new, a new invention of mankind, and one of the greatest inventions that exists. Without comic books, mankind would be just as well off. But that's different.

SL: Do you think it's possible that it may be good to scare the kids with things like the queen in ***Snow White*** changing into a witch? Maybe that makes them able to bear the traumas of reading about things in Vietnam, and reading about Buchenwald, and so forth? Maybe if we didn't have stories like that, which are fantasy and fiction, maybe these kids would be a lot sicker and in a lot more trouble.

BF: You give rise to a very interesting question. [Describes seeing boring German comics.] Does it, or does it not, say something to you when a country that wantonly committed the most monumental violence in history had completely antiseptic, sterile, weak comics for kids?

HM: It has nothing to do—one has nothing to do with the other.

SL: She does have a way of saying that when you bring up a—.

HM: Absolutely nothing to do, the children were indoctrinated. I know exactly how they were indoctrinated. Look, I went to school with kids who were National Socialists. I mean, their parents were. My parents were very liberal. My father was the publisher of a very important newspaper in Germany, and very democratic, and he wouldn't believe what I told him about what the theories the kids were talking. But this has nothing to do with comic books at all.

SL: But, Dr. Mosse, may I say something without you telling me that it has nothing to do with it? Maybe Barry posed his question too clearly, and too articulately, and possibly if one were more obtuse and tried to circumvent the whole thing, does the absolute contradiction of this, does the insanity of this, not even register, where you're saying that we should reduce violence in the comics, or possibly eliminate comics, because the world is a little too violent and unhealthy and this is going to hope, Barry brought out what I think is a fairly good point. Here is a country which was probably guilty of the most heinous crime upon mankind in the history of the world, a nation which had tame comic books, which virtually had no comics books, where the children were tightly regimented, where they didn't go to movies until a certain age, and they were controlled by their parents. Now, doesn't this at least make you stop and think, and possible, for a moment, question the validity of your premise?

HM: Do you mean if the comic books and television had existed in Germany, you say fascism wouldn't have come to pass?

During the Farber show, Stan remarks: "The thing I fear is a fanatical do-gooder... the person who says, 'That's bad because I say so.'" He had expressed a similar concern in ***X-Men*** #16 (January 1966) where, at the end of the mutants' epic battle with the Sentinels, the Lee-written story warns, "Beware the fanatic! Too often his cure is deadlier by far than evil he denounces!" Layouts by Jack Kirby, pencils by Werner Roth, inks by Dick Ayers. [©2011 Marvel Characters, inc.]

SL: No, but I say that the comics might have been a first line of defense. It's very possible, had the comics been published and written in a creative and a free atmosphere, the children might not have listened, or heeded, their adults as much. They might not have followed Hitler as blindly. They might have seen the insanity. They might have recognized the harmful violence. They might have been able to recognize the hero and the villain. They might have been able to tell them apart. It seems to me, and I'm not just espousing comic books, I mean, it could be anything. But it seems to me, and I've never thought of this before, but possibly one function of literature and art is it makes us recognize things in the world about us. It gives us a better perspective.

The thing that I fear is a fanatical do-gooder. I fear that terribly. I fear the person who knows what's right and wrong for my child. I fear the person who, when I write a story that I think is amusing and entertaining, and I really think I'm as good a judge as anybody else, and I know I'm not a villain, I fear the person who says, "That's bad because I say so." And then I say, well, look. Here's a nation that didn't have things like this, and they're much worse than we are, or ever will be, or ever were, and then this person says, "Yes, but that has nothing to do with it. And I'm not even, I'm not all for comics. If I had a kid who just read comics, I'd be pretty worried. The college kids who read and love our books don't just read our comics, for goodness sake. And I don't think I'd read them if I weren't in the business.

BY: It seems to me that your argument reminds me of the arguments against gun control.

SL: Which I'm in favor of, by the way.

BY: The question then is, can we just do whatever we want, because there are other things outside? Just as the people who are against gun control said, "Well, there will be murders even if you do control the sales of guns." That doesn't mean that we should not control the sale of guns, which maybe is one step that we can take.

SL: You know, I've got to tell you this, as a fellow who's in comics—and, again, I can't speak for the rest of the industry—if you knew how little attention we pay to violence, if you knew how we try to keep it out of our books, if you knew how we just include an absolute minimum because we get so much mail from our younger readers who say, "That last story didn't have enough action," and obviously we don't want to use the younger readers. If you knew that we spend all of our time playing up the satirical angle, playing up the psychological angle, playing up the sociological angle, playing up the characterizational hang-ups of our various characters, playing up the subtle subplots and the—. In fact, I feel ridiculous talking about this. You don't expect somebody to talk about a comic magazine this way. But this is what we concentrate on.

BY: No. This, to me, is a much more intelligent argument, not to argue that violence doesn't do any harm.

SL: But I don't argue that violence doesn't do harm. What I argue about, and I'm afraid I must not be making the clear. I wonder if anybody, and I don't think Dr. Mosse can, she certainly hasn't, can give me a guideline which I would be happy to follow. Now, the Comics Magazine Code office has a guideline. We follow that. If somebody could give me a guideline as to what constitutes harmful violence. If somebody would tell me what's harmful violence, we will eliminate it, and you have my promise. Nobody ever has. People just say it's like let's abolish crime, and let's abolish war. How?

HM: No, that's absolutely not true that I said that you can eliminate all violence. That's ridiculous. There is a way of portraying violence in such a way that it has an anti-violence effect.

SL: Oh, I'd love to know how.

HM: If you read very good literature, my God, Dostoevsky's ***The Brothers Karamazov***, for instance, has quite a bit violence in there, but it's a statement against violence. There was a marvelous episode, for instance, in what is it? ***Ironside***, isn't it? That's a television show. There was a marvelous story there where there was a violence committed where, in the end, unquestionably, you had the feeling not only—. It was not only not the right thing to do, but it was the tragic accident occurred, that really violence is not only not a solution, but it is something that creates more violence. I want to mention an absolutely marvelous film which I think you should all see if you have a chance to. It's a French film, ***The Cousins***, which was an incredibly marvelous film, which has a lot of violence and corruption in it. But if it leaves you with anything in the end, it is the tragedy that anybody who has a gun will use it, and that the reality of violence is there, but you go away with a feeling where this is a horrible thing that happens to people, and maybe something should be done so that we can avoid this from happening. I'm making it much too crude, but you are an artist. You know how to do it. I'm not an artist.

Dr. Mosse likes Dostoevsky's ***The Brothers Karamazov***, despite its violence. She gives no indication, though, of how she feels about the 1958 movie version, directed by Richard Brooks, whose cast included Yul Brynner, Maria Schell, Claire Bloom, and (in tiny letters) William Shatner.

SL: Doc, let me ask you something. What is the last issue of ***Spider-Man*** you've read?

HM: I have one here dated November.

SL: Did you read it?

HM: Yes! Sure, I read it.

SL: Now, what feeling did that give you, that violence is something desirable?

HM: Of course, it's the *only* thing that's exciting, to have the power and strength of—.

DM: Doctor, I'd like to agree with you on one particular thing.

Unnecessary violence, and ways to portray violence, and I'm talking specifically now about television, animated cartoons.

SL: Well, I think what you're saying, there are things which are in good taste and things which any rational person would know, "This is not in good taste."

DM: That is correct.

SL: I claim that most of the things that we do I think are in good taste. I think that there's no argument here.

BF: I don't habitually watch the childhood comics on Saturday morning on television, but I did one morning, and after that morning I couldn't understand how a single younger brother or younger sister in America survives. This was not violence; this was psychedelic, cataclysmic violence... Either a mouse would have a house fall on him, or get cut in two and get back together again—

SL: You didn't have to watch that on television, that was being done in the movie cartoons ever since they started. See, I don't think those things are harmful, Barry. I think they're harmful only in one sense. I think they're so completely uneducational. I think they have so little value of any sort, and I think they're boring.

DM: You know that the people who create, not only for the mass media but for artistic purposes not so broad as t elevision, do not write for sick people. They write for the norm, they write for an audience, and if bad people or sick people take offense and do, pervert the words, pervert the actions that they see to bad purposes, that is not the fault of the writer.

SL: The other day I saw ***Barbarella***, and I kind of got a kick out of it. I haven't been to a movie in years. And the first thing I thought for a while, I said, gee, I used to see things like this in formen-only type of things, and at stags. I mean, I didn't know you could go and see a perfectly naked girl in a theater where anybody could go. This was a whole new world opening up for me in a motion picture. When you talk about the motion picture categories and classifications, and if you read the ads in the ***Times***, I mean, anybody who's going to start saying that motion pictures are beyond reproach, why, it's just ridiculous.

BY: No, no, nobody is saying that. But what I am saying is that the motion picture industry has now taken a step, not in the way of censorship, but in the way of classification, saying, well, the children will not be permitted to see this.

SL: Fine. And I'm not saying there's anything bad about it, because I don't know that anything is really, provably bad as far as nudity, or as far as violence, in the kind of stories we're talking about.

BY: What we're talking about in this fact is that the adults can say and choose, but the parents should know what they're choosing for their children to go and see.

SL: I was brought up on Mickey Mouse and Donald Duck, and maybe I'm unique. I never for a moment—I was brought up on the Harold Lloyd movies and things like that—I never tried to balance on a ledge in a building. I watched ***Jekyll and Hyde***. I enjoyed ***Frankenstein***. I didn't try to create a monster. Now, it would seem to me that a youngster who was sick can be adversely affected by an advertisement in the paper, by seeing somebody walk down the street, by anything on God's Earth, and to try to protect—. You see, I have ambivalent feelings about this.

BF: I have different experiences. No, I really do. I remember not trying anything like this, but some friends of mine said they did. You're talking about, shall we say the age group ten to fourteen?

SL: I mean, I wasn't thinking of a specific group. I don't think that there's any point in classifying the group.

HM: It's very important to classify the group.

SL: Well, what group are we talking about?

HM: Children of different ages react quite differently. And you find much more out from girls, because the girls are, of course, the victims, and that's one thing that we haven't discussed at all, that most of these superhero types are strictly written for boys. For instance, I've made my own, you know, I asked the girls. They don't like to watch ***Batman***, they don't like to watch ***The Hulk.*** The women

The Roger Vadim-directed 1968 film ***Barbarella*** got an "M"—for "mature"—rating (in the days before the current movie-rating system), which enabled Stan and Hilde to discuss it without raising their voices. [Copyright 1968 Dino de Laurentiis Cinematografica]

in all these stories are the victims. Look at it sometimes. The women are bandied about. They are just things.

SL: But that's not why the girls don't—

HM: Either they're gun molls, they're—

DM: And how many times have you seen a cowgirl hero?

SL: They're not gun molls at all, doctor.

HM: They're in a horrible and sadistic position in practically all comic books and television shows. Look at it sometime.

SL: They're the hero's girlfriends, that's what they are. They're not gun molls. And the heroes are the good guys.

HM: They're the hero's girlfriends.

SL: I mean, Superman, what's Superman's girlfriend's name?

DM: Lois Lane.

SL: She's not a gun moll. Spider-Man's girlfriend isn't a gun moll.

HM: They have no girls that a girl can even admire or want to be like.

SL: Well, girls play with dolls, and boys and—

HM: Wonder Woman is a very sadistic sort of a woman to be want to emulate. That's about the only one in the comic books.

BF: I have in front of me a copy of the Code of the Comics Magazine Association of America, Inc. Bear with me while I read from it: "Crime shall never be presented in such a way as to create sympathy for the criminal, to promote distrust of the forces of law and justice, or to inspire others with the desire to imitate criminals. No comic shall explicitly present the unique details and methods of a crime."

I think that's great, because I'm sure that one charge against comics throughout history that hasn't been brought up or which I'm sure will be quickly admitted is that the details, the details. The criminal may have gotten punished, but the real-life delinquent copied his technique, nonetheless.

SL: Can you give an example for the past ten years, Barry?

BF: Not right now, but if you'll come back...

SL: You see, the kind of crimes we show are Dr. Doom wants to take over the Earth, so he invents a ray that will hypnotize everybody on Earth, and then he gets a rocket ship and goes over to the moon where he won't be affected. Now, I'll admit, that's pretty easy for kids to emulate, and maybe we shouldn't have done that story, because I can see these kids building these rays and going off to the moon so they won't be affected, and I'll be the first one to plead guilty to this. I am terribly sorry for these dangerous plots that we come up with. I believe the purpose is it shouldn't seem as though we're glamorizing crime. Now, I don't think Dr. Mosse would object to or take umbrage in anything you've read so far.

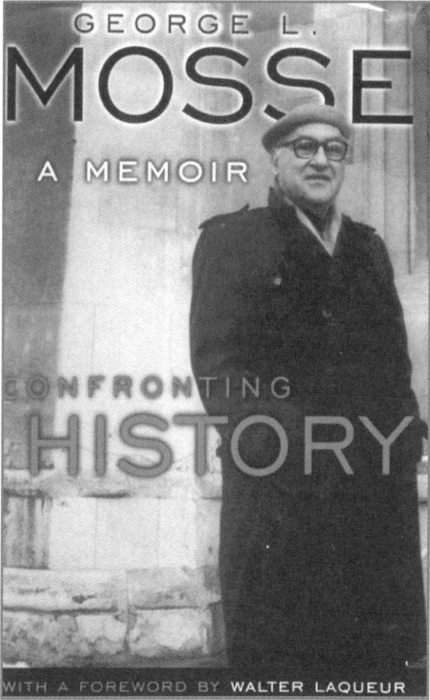

Hilde Mosse's brother, George, was a prominent historian. Here, the cover to his memoir, ***Confronting History***. [©2000 The Board of Regents of the University of Wisconsin System. All rights reserved.]

HM: But you have to know the history of this code. This code is a reaction to Dr. Wertham's book in 1954, ***Seduction of the Innocent***, and the fact that parents all over the country took action against the portrayal of crime just the way it said, we are not going to do this, because that's exactly what they were doing. I did a study several years later for the magazine of the ***New York Herald Tribune*** where I wrote "Comic Books Revisited," and I studied that. And the result of this code, and the result of the action of parents all over the country, was two-fold. One is that a large number of comic book publishers went out of business, that the comic books from a hundred million a month went down to thirty million a month. They have risen again. And that "crime" disappeared from the title. That was one of the result of concerted, I might say democratic, grassroots action. And this code was sort of a publicity stunt of the comic book publishers in order to deceive the public, make believe that something was being done.

SL: Do you see how difficult it is to satisfy the crusaders? When they object to something, and when people who are in the position of producing the product that has been objected to, make a very, a most serious effort to correct the ills that have been pointed out, and they do something such as the code Barry read, which I'll admit it sounds, it's kind of tough to read it, but, at the same time, it was a very honest effort. I think it was as good an effort as could have been made. I think it almost adhered to the letter to what Dr. Wertham had wanted because at that time we figured, well, by God, he's a psychiatrist, and if he says so, and we'll go along with it. We don't want to do anything bad. So we did the code exactly as asked. Then this lady comes to the table and says, "Look at this obvious cover-up." I simply submit to you, what would you have us do? If we do what you ask and you call it a cover-up, what should we do?

HM: I'll tell you exactly what it did. "Crime" disappeared from the titles. The blood pools, of which there were very, very many, disappeared from the content of the comic books. But crime was portrayed just the same.

SL: Well, that isn't true at all! That's, you're just saying something that is patently untrue, doctor. Now, I wish I could get the audience to read every book on sale now.

HM: Well, why don't they just go and buy a bunch of comic books and see for themselves? That's all.

SL: Oh, that's a great idea. I would love it.

HM: Get them from their kids. That's all.

SL: You know, it's funny. But, as I say, the kids listening in who read the books, Barry, you are going to be so showered with mail—. As a matter of fact, did you ever see our book, ***The Silver Surfer***?

HM: No, I've never seen it.

SL: Now, we've tried to do one book where we were going to go a step above comics. I would say the Silver Surfer is the closest thing to a Biblical analogy in comic form. This man is all goodness. There is virtually no violence at all in it, and he is a person who philosophizes, who worries about the state of the world today. He's from outer space, and he can't understand the seemingly insane things that are happening on Earth today. And he's persecuted, himself, because he's so darned good that nobody understands him. I mention this book because there was a young man here in the studio a few minutes ago who, upon leaving, whispered, "Why don't you mention the Silver Surfer if Dr. Mosse is still talking about violence?"

And it occurs to me it might be worthy of mention. We are trying desperately to do good things. I have a daughter, myself. I have a wife, and I live in a community. We all do, in this business. We are, honest to gosh, we're fairly respectable people. I think we're fairly well-motivated. We don't want to do anything that's bad. We know we're not doing anything that's harmful, and we bend over backwards, when people criticize, we bend over backwards to do what we can to take care of the criticism. If there's even a chance that there's any validity to the criticism, we're more than anxious to take care of that. I really do resent when people then say, "Yes, they did what we asked, but it was a cover-up." In that case, possibly we should do more than is asked. And, as I've said before, if somebody will give us some specific suggestions other than saying, "Just stop publishing your books," we'll be glad to go along with it.

BF: I want to read a little bit about this code, and particularly since we have Dr. Mosse with us, who is a psychiatrist. "All scenes of horror, excessive bloodshed, gory or gruesome crimes, depravity, lust, sadism, masochism, shall not be permitted." My question is, what went on before? What prompted such an extreme provision of a code for comic books for children? What in the world were they up to?

HM: Well, I'll tell you, there was nothing they would not show in comic books, and the Kefauver Committee *[the Senate committee that investigated comics in 1954.—DF & RT]* brought that off very well. There was cannibalism. There was the famous story that one of the comic book publishers, there was a woman shown, or a man holding up a woman's head by the hair, it's a famous picture now, with the head cut off and the blood dripping down in the bathroom.

A couple of years after investigating the comic book industry, Senator Estes Kefauver was featured on this 1956 cover of ***Time Magazine*** during his second unsuccessful bid for the presidency. [©2011 Time Inc.]

SL: I might add, Dr. Wertham made it famous.

HM: Incidentally [Otto] Larsen has a book out, ***Television and Violence,*** which is an excellent book, and if anybody is interested they can read it, and they have the picture in there, even. *[Dr. Mosse is probably referring to Larsen's 1968* **Violence and Mass Media**.*—DF & RT]* It's a paperback. And they have the whole testimony about this kind of comic book. Anyhow, they showed, I don't know, relations with corpses, things you couldn't even mention over the air, in a certain type of comic books, eerie and gory. You all know that.

SL: Our company didn't publish things—

HM: So, anyway, that disappeared. You see that disappeared.

SL: I want to say there was nothing that Dr. Mosse is talking about that [was published that] couldn't be mentioned over the air. And I'm not trying to defend it. We didn't publish those books.

HM: No, you didn't.

SL: I used to see those books because, as a competitor, I tried to see what was going on. When you say "relationships with corpses," there were stories, but these were so-called "horror" magazines, and some stories took place in a graveyard, and somebody would open up a coffin or something. They weren't my taste, but they certainly could be mentioned over the air. I do think you have a way of making these things sound worse than they are, or worse than they were.

[The broadcast continued into the night, but the archived tape ends here.]

“A Comeback for Comic Books”

Roger Ebert on the state of comics, Marvel, and Stan Lee in 1966

From *Midwest Magazine* of the *Chicago Sun-Times*

December 18, 1966

***Roger Ebert** has been the film critic of the **Chicago Sun-Times** since 1967 and his reviews are syndicated in more than 200 newspapers around the world. He won the Pulitzer Prize for criticism in 1975.*

*The following year, Roger and Gene Siskel began a long run of reviewing movies on TV with **Sneak Previews,** which was followed by **At the Movies** and **Siskel & Ebert.** After Siskel's death in 1999, he was joined by Richard Roeper on **Ebert & Roeper** until illness deprived him of the ability to speak. He and his wife Chaz now produce **Ebert Presents: At the Movies,** which is syndicated on PBS stations nationwide.*

*Ebert is the author of more than 20 books, including the 2002 best-seller **The Great Movies, Awake in the Dark: The Best of Roger Ebert,** annual volumes of **Roger Ebert's Movie Yearbook, Scorsese by Ebert,** and **I Hated, Hated, HATED This Movie.** His memoir, **Life Itself** (from Grand Central Publishing) was recently released.*

Ebert is the only film critic honored with a star on the Hollywood Walk of Fame.

Scorsese by Ebert, featuring Roger's articles about and interviews with the famed director, spans a period of four decades. [Published by the University of Chicago Press. ©2008 by The University of Chicago.]

*Early in his career as a pop-culture critic, Ebert wrote this article about the 1960s surge in popularity of of superhero comics that starts on the next page. Although apparently spurred by the success of the **Batman** TV series—where visual sound effects such as those in the article's title, “Sock!” and “Pop!” (the latter probably also a reference to comics as “pop art”) were prominent graphic elements of the show—the article deals largely with Stan Lee and Marvel Comics.*

*Special thanks to Roger Ebert and **The Chicago Sun-Times** for permission to use this article.*

—DF & RT

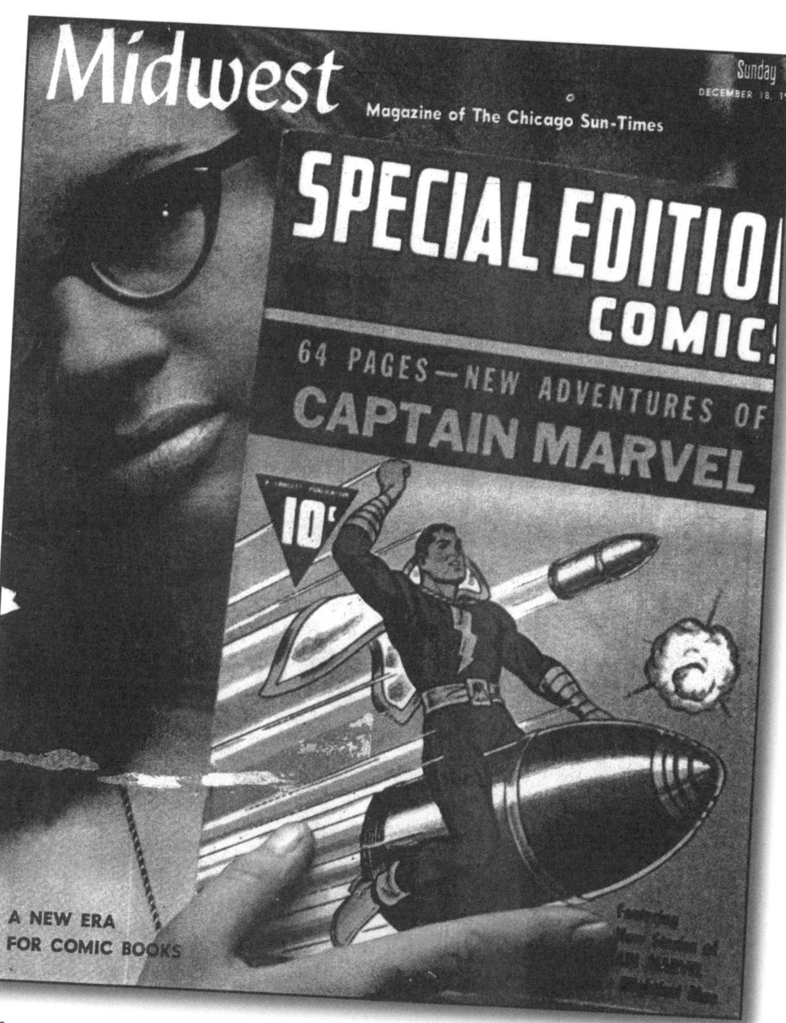

Cover to ***Midwest Magazine*** of December 18, 1966 , featuring P.A. (Sam) La Chapelle holding a copy of 1941's ***Special Edition Comics*** #1, published by Fawcett. [Special Edition Comics ©2011 DC Comics. Midwest Magazine © Copyright 2011 Sun-Times Media, LLC.]

“A Comeback for Comic Books,” Chicago Sun-Times, MidWest Magazine, December 18, 1966, Stan Lee Collection, box #3, folder #1, American Heritage Center, University of Wyoming.

A Comeback For Comic

But the old superheroes are gone, replaced by a new breed of bogeymen created for—and bought by—adults

By Roger Ebert

Miss P. A. (Sam) La Chapelle is a comicologist. A comicologist? "Sure, a *comicologist*. Why not?" asks Sam, an attractive blond who can quote you Batman's genesis quicker than most people can name his television sponsor. "To be honest, I got into it as a business, but it's a fun business. And, let's face it, I like comic books."

So do lots of other people, who in their everyday identities are mild mannered businessmen, college students, bus drivers and (naturally) reporters. Once inside the Acme Book Store at 414 N. Clark, however, they turn into vicarious Spider-Men, fearlessly scaling the heights of inflated comic book prices to capture items for their collections.

Chicago film critics Gene Siskel and Roger Ebert, hosts of the movie review programs ***Sneak Previews, At the Movies***, and ***Siskel & Ebert***. The duo made famous the "thumbs up/thumbs down" movie evaluation system. [© 2011, rogerebert.com]

Like several other used book and magazine shops on N. Clark, Acme is a speciality house, catering to collectors rather than the general reading public. Veteran book seller Noel Roy, the proprietor, considers hobbyists his mainstay, and the shelves are classified according to subject: the circus, railroads, photography, Chicago lore, occult, flying saucers, Americana, Big Little Books, movie posters, Edgar Rice Burroughs, monsters and, of course, the comics.

"Comic books have reached some sort of high point today," said Miss LaChapelle, Acme's resident comicologist and Roy's partner in the business. "There are two things happening at once. The collector's market is growing, and at the same time people are reading new comic books who wouldn't have been caught dead with a comic five years ago."She attributed this renaissance to the appearance in 1961 of the Fantastic Four, a group of improbable characters created by the venerable Marvel Comics group out of sheer boredom with run of the paper mill superheroes.

"But you can't understand the Marvel thing without knowing a little comics history," Miss LaChapelle said, patiently tutoring a Clark Kent type who had only read the things, not pondered them. Comic books were unknowingly in a golden era during World War II and early postwar years, she explained. Superheroes multiplied by the dozens, coined in imitation of Superman (first appearance in ***Action Comics*** no. 1, June 1938) and Batman (a few months later). From the beginning, knowledgeable readers preferred National Comics (Batman, Wonder Woman, Superman, etc.) and the Marvel Group, owners of Captain America, the Human Torch and Sub Mariner.

Fawcett's Captain Marvel (no relation to the Marvel Group) also scored a brief success before he was successfully sued by Superman, whose copyright owners charged plagiarism. "Cap's days were numbered anyway," Sam sighed. "He was undoubtedly the stupidest superhero in history. And toward the end be was so musclebound he looked like a great big red cheese." The comic book industry went into a slump after the war ended. Out of work superheroes, shorn of their roles as saviors of the Allies, twiddled their superthumbs as circulation dropped. ***Captain America***, the last of a breed, gound to a halt in 1949, his wartime heroism forgotten.

Comic book writers and editors, desperate for plots, turned to the eternal themes of sex and horror, but the 1954 Comics Code rang down the curtain on that ploy, and comicdom entered its Dark Ages. "But always there was Stan Lee, doing fine things," Miss La Chapelle sighed in the tone ordinarily reserved for descriptions of Scott Fitzgerald's last days in Hollywood. Impressed by her admiration, we contacted the great man himself.

Lee, editor of the Marvel Group, began writing comics in 1941. But it was not until. he and his artists created the Fantastic Four two decades later that his unsung labor was rewarded. "Name any period you want after the war, and comics people would rather forget it," Lee said, wincing at the memory. "The late '40s, the early '50s, the late '50s–we were starving. The industry was in a turmoil. For a while, Westerns would sell, and

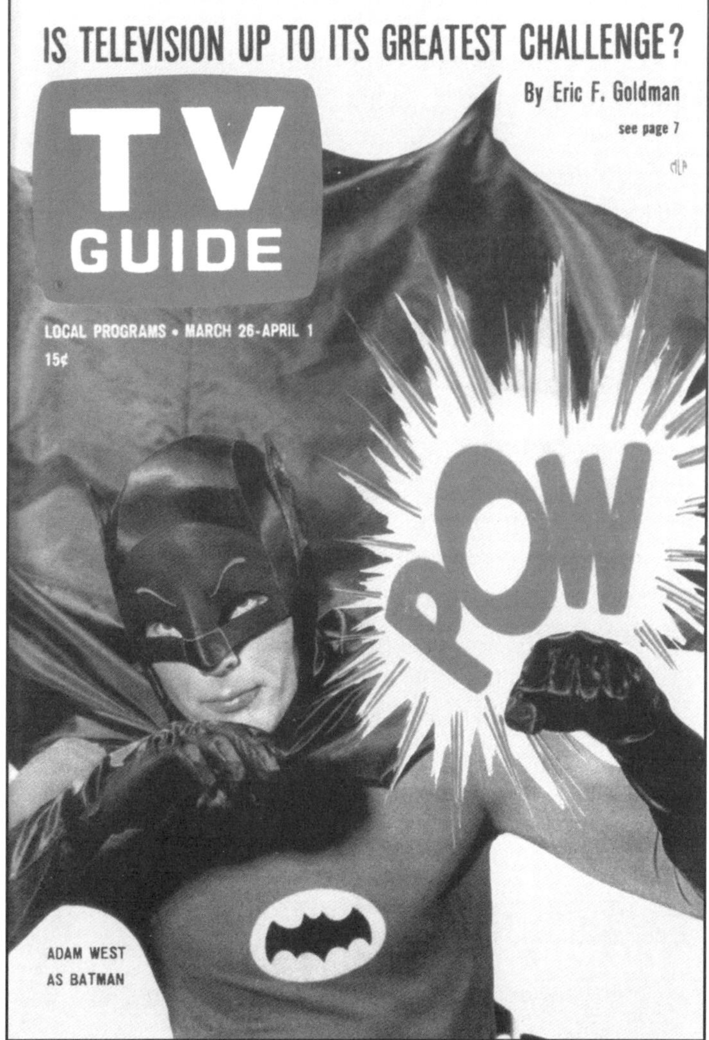

IS TELEVISION UP TO ITS GREATEST CHALLENGE?
By Eric F. Goldman
see page 7
TV GUIDE
LOCAL PROGRAMS • MARCH 26-APRIL 1
15¢
POW
ADAM WEST
AS BATMAN

This 1966 issue of ***TV Guide*** features Adam West as the not-so-dark knight, wielding a sound-effect producing punch, which was a regular feature of the 1960s hit ***Batman*** TV show. [Batman TV series © 1966 20th Century Fox Television, Greenway Productions, ABC, and DC Comics. TV Guide ©2011 the copyright holders.]

[Caption from the original article:] UNLIKE earlier superheroes, Lee's characters have personal problems and fits of depression. This sequence shows Peter Parker (secret identity Spider-Man) pondering an offer to join the Avengers, top Marvel superhero team.

[Comic panels 1-6 from *Amazing Spider-Man Annual* #3, 1966, by Lee, Romita, Sr., Heck & Esposito. Pan. 7 from *Amazing Spider-Man* #43, Dec. 1966, by Lee & Romita, Sr.]

everybody would turn out Westerns. Then it would be love stories for six months. Nobody knew where they were going."

Then, in the monumental month of November 1961, ***Fantastic Four*** (by its own admission "The World's Greatest Comic Magazine") appeared on the stands. "For years we had been producing comics for kids, because they were supposed to be the market," Lee explained. "One day, out of sheer boredom, we said—let's do something we would like. So we tried to get rid of the old clichés. Comics were too predictable. Why not accept the premise that the superhero has his superpower, and then keep everything else as realistic as possible? If I were Spiderman, for example, wouldn't I still have romantic problems, financial problems, sinus attacks and fits of inscurity? Wouldn't I be a little embarrassed about appearing in public in a costume? We decided to let our superheroes live in the real world."

[Caption from the original article:] MARVEL'S gimmick is placing superheroes in the real world. Here, Iron Man performs on television for President Johnson and Secretary of Defense McNamara. Some say it's serious, some say it's satire. Writer–editor Lee smiles and won't say.

 [Comic panel from *Tales of Suspense* #83, Nov. 1966, by Lee, Colan, and Abel.]

The formula clicked, and Marvel developed a stable of superheroes. Some of them, like Spider-Man, the Fantastic Four and the Incredible Hulk, were new. Others, like Captain America and the Human

Chicago and Comics: 1966

For a little background on the state of collectible comics retailing in Chicago circa 1966—and "Sam" LaChapelle's role in it—here's what George Hagenauer said in his obituary for legendary Chicago comics retailer Joe Sarno in ***The Comic Buyer's Guide*** website (cbgxtra.com) on March 19, 2010:

> "Comics collecting in Chicago started on Skid Row. The city at that time had three of them on the near north, south, and west sides. It would have had one on the east, except for the presence of the lake there. The north Skid Row along Clark Street had four used book and magazine stores, run by what may have been the most eccentric group of book dealers ever known. At age 10, when my father introduced me to where he had bought most of the used children's books that I had read, I had to step over passed-out drunks in order to buy early Silver Age ***Flash*** and ***Green Lanterns*** for 5¢.
>
> "The collectors who prowled these seedy haunts were divided into two camps: the young guys in their teens and the 'old' guys in their upper 20s and early 30s. (Sorry about the 'guy' reference; [***CBG*** editor] Maggie Thompson may have been the only woman I knew in fandom, with the exception of red-haired, voluptuous Sam La Chapelle, who sat behind the counter at Acme Books on North Clark Street: a veritable Blaze Starr of used paper.)"

And if you're wondering who Blaze Starr is... that's a story beyond the scope of this book.

—DF & RT

A recent shot of the now-gentrified Chicago neighborhood where Acme Books had been located in 1966. The Starbucks is at 430 N. Clark St. Acme was at 414.

Torch, were resurrected. All were given problems: Daredevil is blind, Spider-Man is a college student who feels inadequate to handle personal relationships, and the Thing is in love but feels insecure because he looks . . . well, like a Thing.

"What we were doing," Lee said, "was creating fairy tales for adults. I think we were the ones really responsible for the pop art bit. College students started reading our books back in 1961, and eventually the word got around that comic books were popular again. But the average newspaper feature writer didn't read comic books, and so what books did hc think of? ***Batman*** and ***Superman***. But only kids read ***Batman*** and ***Superman***. Marvels are for intelligent people."

If writing intelligent comics qualifies as an industry first, so do some other Marvel breakthroughs. Lee was the first comics editor to integrate his books, and now Negro superheroes like Gabriel Jones and the Black Panther stalk wrongdoers in partnership with old established firms like the Avengers, X-Men, and the Fantastic Four. The bad guys in Marvel Comics have also taken on a contemporary tinge. Cigar-smoking hoods and prehensile Nazis, the stock enemies of the war era, have been replaced by organizations like the Serpents, whose members spout a far right-wing line and want to rid America of "foreigners."

Identifying with Lee's approach, some 50,000 college students have sent in $1 to become card carrying members of the Merry Marvel Marching Society. Marchers receive an insider's newsletter describing the doings of Marvel's bullpen, and can also order sweat shirts and T-shirts with their favorite superheroes on them (top sellers: the Hulk and the Thing). Five of the Marvel characters now have their own TV show on Ch. 9 and some 50 other stations.

For the past three years, the Marvel superheroes have been hot sellers on campuses. One Hyde Park bookstore, which doesn't sell any other comics, advertises in the ***Chicago Maroon*** that all 10 Marvel titles are available each month as a $1.20 package deal, sold in a plain brown wrapper. As the author of all the Marvel plots, Lee himself has become something of a campus folk hero. He has spoken at New York University, Princeton, Bard, Columbia and Vassar, and next April 27 he will speak at the University of Chicago.

All of which is music to the ears of Miss LaChapelle and her fellow comicologists. "The comic book business is booming right now," she said. "I'll give you an example. Almost any title published before 1944 is rare, because nobody thought of saving comics and the wartime scrap par drives consumed millions of issues. As a result, four years ago the first appearance of Batman in ***Detective Comics*** no. 27 brought $25 in mint condition, and that was a good price. Today, it's worth $100 to $125 and you can't find anybody who will sell." Recently, a Chicago area collector paid Acme $200 for the first five issues of ***Batman***. Issues 6 through 10 are still in the company vault.

THERE'S NO REASON FOR THE BLACK PANTHER'S CAREER TO COME TO AN END! THE WORLD WILL ALWAYS HAVE NEED OF A DEDICATED, POWERFUL FIGHTER AGAINST INJUSTICE!
REED'S RIGHT, FELLA! THE WAY THINGS ARE GOING TODAY, YOU NEVER HEAR OF A SUPER-HERO BEING OUT OF WORK!
ANYWAY, WITH A COSTUME LIKE THAT, YA CAN ALWAYS BECOME A RASSLER, OR A NEW KINDA FOLK SINGER!
I SHALL DO IT! I PLEDGE MY FORTUNE, MY POWERS--MY VERY LIFE --TO THE SERVICE OF ALL MANKIND!

[Caption from the original article:] UNDER Lee's editorship, Marvel was the first comics group to integrate. The Black Panther was the original Negro superhero. Pats on back come from the Thing.

Stan Lee: Speaker Man!

The bell-bottomed cure for "same-old-speaker" syndrome

This 1970s promotional brochure from the American Program Bureau, produced during Stan's college lecturing days, presented him this way:

> "If your lecture program is in danger of being mired in a cultural wasteland, if students on your campus are tired of the same old speakers, then this is a job for Speaker-Man!"

The brochure/comic, as it should, speaks for itself. The artists are unknown, although the Stan-faces look as if they may have been touched up Marie Severin.

Speaker-Man comic-brochure, Stan Lee Collection, American Heritage Center, University of Wyoming.

FROM THE STAN LEE ARCHIVES

Legend meets Legend

Stan Lee interviewed by Jud Hurd of Cartoonist PROfiles magazine

From *Cartoonist PROfiles* #4, November 1969

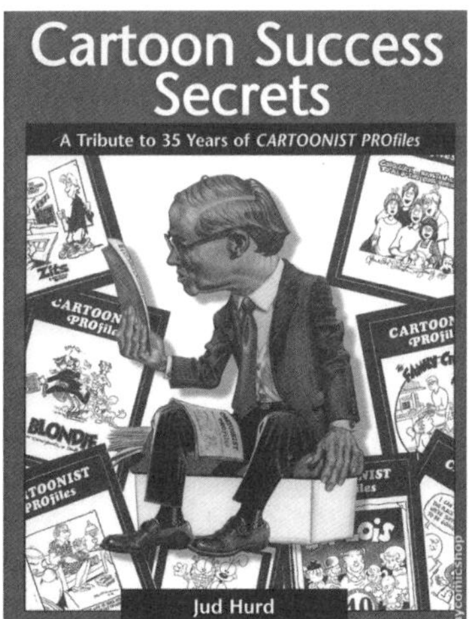

[Copyright ©2004 Jud Hurd and Copyright ©2007 Philip J. Hurd]

*According to **Jud Hurd's** 2004 book, **Cartoon Success Secrets: A Tribute To 35 Years Of Cartoonist Profiles:** "Author Jud Hurd may tell friends that he's been 'in the cartooning business since year one,' but it only seems like it. The venerable cartooning editor actually began in 1925. In 1969, he founded **Cartoonist PROfiles**, which has been providing an insider's perspective on the cartooning industry ever since."*

Hurd passed away in 2005, and with his death, the magazine ceased publication.

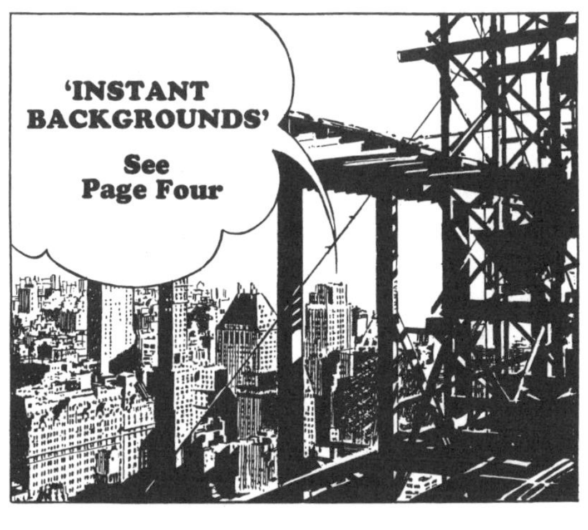

CARTOONIST PROfiles

A unique quarterly magazine for the professional, the cartoon buff, the student, and all who enjoy cartoons.

Issue No. 4 — November 1969 $2.50

[Cartoonist PROfiles Interview and cover copyright ©2004 Jud Hurd and copyright ©2007 Philip J. Hurd.]

***Stan Lee**, the very articulate editor of Marvel Comics, is always an articulate man to talk to. **Cartoonist PROfiles** readers can listen in here on a conversation we had with him on a recent afternoon.*

***Q:** Are you anxious to receive scripts or drawings from people who want to get into the comic book field.*

A: Not really. If somebody who's absolutely fantastic should be available, we would try to make a spot for him, but we have about all the people we need at the moment. We've been very lucky since you and I talked several years ago. By trying hard for years, and combing the nation, and calling everybody we knew, or ever had known, and trying to develop new talent, we now have reached the point where we have what I think is about the best comic magazine art staff ever assembled. We can always use a good writer, but I'm even reluctant to say that, because our demands are so difficult that even a good writer might not be able to write for us. There's so much else, besides being a good writer, that enters into doing the type of material we need.

***Q:** In the past, many young artists who first worked for the comic books have later switched over to doing syndicated newspaper comic strips. Does the answer you have just given mean that young people can no longer look forward to this?*

A: Well, any answer that I give you is only true for this particular moment in time—now next week we may decide to put out a few new magazines, in which case I'll be looking for people again. I look at the samples of anyone who comes up to the office, and if the fellow's good and we can't use him, I'll of course take his name anyway because we never know what will develop. Here's one problem that an editor or an art director always has. Suppose somebody came up right now with samples and he's better than the men I have now. Let's say that I don't have a book to accommodate him—the only thing I could do is to fire somebody who's working for me now. Now I would owe that to our company, if this new man is better, to get rid of one of those men now working for me. But, as a human being, how do you react to a situation like this? It's a difficult problem. In the comic magazine field, it seems that we always have too

As a kid, Stan liked to copy the art from comic strips such as Chester Gould's ***Dick Tracy***. [©2011 Tribune Media Services.]

1969 interview with Stan Lee in *Cartoonist PROfiles* #4, Stan Lee Collection, box #31, folder #3, American Heritage Center, University of Wyoming.

Young Stan also imitated the art style of ***Milton Caniff***, who's seen here in a self-portrait. [©2011 the copyright holders]

many artists or we don't have enough—we never reach a plateau. If you're at a point where you have just the right number, within a week someone else who's good will come along, and then what do you do? So this is something we live with all the time.

Q: *Do you pay a lot of attention to the many fanzines which are produced by comic book buffs and collectors?*

A: Yes—I pay attention to the fanzines in the sense that I believe in brain–picking and I'll pay attention to anybody or anything that wants to voice a comment about comic magazines. Most of the fanzines are highly repetitive—a lot of them are just interested in peddling their own wares—they'll have their own drawings and their own little stories. But very often the things I enjoy are their criticisms—and I don't mind it even if they're very derogatory; I like to know what they hate about the books that I edit—I don't always agree, however. They may criticize things without a full knowledge of why the things are done that way, but I still want to know why anybody who's interested in comics likes or doesn't like something that we're doing or something that a competitor is doing. I learn by reading their opinions.

Q: *Letters from readers of your magazines reach your desk in piles, don't they?*

A: Yes, and they are a much better source of opinions than the fanzines. These opinions are more typical because the fanzines generally express the opinions of the fanatical fans while the mail expresses the opinion of the average fan. Actually, I read all the mail given to me and I read all the fanzines that cross my desk. I used to have wonderful eyesight before I started this job and now I'm going blind. My biggest beef with many fanzines is that they are produced with letters one-millionth of an inch high and they're usually mimeographed without enough ink, etc. When reading them, I wear my strongest glasses plus a magnifying glass; But I read every page—it's like a compulsion with me. And I read every letter.

Q: *You write a great many of the Marvel Comic Magazines. Can you tell me how you go about that?*

A: Well, we work differently than any other company. In most other companies, a writer will write a script—more than likely he'll discuss the plot with the editor or submit a plot to the editor, and if it's O.K., he goes home and writes a script. Then he gives it to the artist who draws the strip. We find that it's faster and more palatable and seems to give us a better result to have the writer discuss the plot with the artist. The artist then draws the strip with no script at all—just a knowledge of what the plot is. So the artist is part writer—he's breaking the story down as he sees it—his only limitation is that he must know how many pages the story is. I, or Roy Thomas, or whatever writer discusses the plot with the artist, will say, for instance, that this is a 20–page story so the artist knows he's got that many pages to fill.

And here's one of Caniff's most famous creations, ***Terry and the Pirates***, which debuted in 1934. This Harvey Publications comic—of which Caniff's cover to the June 1947 issue #4 is shown—was comprised for the most part of collected daily and Sunday ***Terry*** strips, but also contained new material by creators such as Joe Simon, Jack Kirby, and Jack Keeler. [©2011 Tribune Media Services.]

Q: *Are these sessions between writer and artist verbal or written?*

A: They can be either way. I verbalize them myself—I don't have the time or the interest—I'm too bored to write the plot out and I have the kind of relationship with the artist where we sit and talk for five minutes about it. Later on, while the artist is making his drawings, he puts little notes on the side of the pages indicating what the hell he's drawing, just to help me know what he's doing in the various panels. Here's an idea as to how I work with several of our artists: In the case of Gene Colan, I'll write maybe a page of notes for myself, including all the things I want to discuss. Then I will phone Gene and he puts his tape recorder against the phone and I discuss the story with him sort of reading the page I've written. In the case of Jack Kirby, I will merely phone him, or he will phone me, as

As a kid, Stan was also a fan of George Herriman's ***Krazy Kat*** strip. [© King Features Syndicate, Inc.]

he did about two hours ago, and say, "Stan, I'm ready for the next story." He's calling from California and we both start cold. I'll say, "What book are you talking about?" And he says, "***Thor***—is that the one we need next?" "Yeah." And so the conversation goes back and forth. "What do you think we ought to do?" "Well, let's bring back that girl he used to be in love with; that's a good idea." "Suppose he tries to save her but he doesn't want her to know it's him saving her and at the end she figures, "Gee, it's funny; Thor never did come to help me"—not knowing it was really him who saved her." "Great idea, but what do we save her from?" "Oh, that's right—we need a villain." "Well, let's see—who haven't we used or should we make up a new one?" "How about this crook who wants to use a transplant—he's old and he's dying and he's very rich, and he doesn't want to die, and he wants to transplant his brain in a healthy body—great!" "Hey, Stan, how about the body he wants to use being Thor?" "Perfect, O.K., Jack, you got it?" At this point I don't know what the heck the story is going to be—this is basically the thread—the skeleton outline—that's all that I discussed with Jack. He will send back 20 pages drawn as he sees it.

I will then write the copy. Then in pencil I indicate where the balloons go on the artwork, I number each balloon, and then on a sheet of paper I type the dialogue with numbers corresponding to the balloons I've indicated. I don't letter in the dialogue myself in the strip. The letterers don't have the remotest idea where to put these balloons—when the writer indicates the balloons, he can design the page nicely and complement the art work. I know that if a panel has a lot of beautiful artwork, I'll keep the dialogue sparse—if there's a dull panel, I'll write a lot of dialogue to fill up the panel. This is the reason I said a while ago that even a good writer may not be able to write comics—because this is something that no writer even thinks he has to contend with. There are so many of those little things involved. The artists don't even think much about the balloons—they're so good that they automatically-subconsciously—they'll leave enough space on top. The writer, of course, has to have a sense of knowing about how many words will fit into the space which has been allowed for the balloon. Next the script and the artwork go to the lettering man—he puts the dialogue in and then the strip goes to the inker. The inker could be the man who penciled the strip or it could be a different inker. In our case, it's usually a different inker.

Part of a photo of the crew at the 1975 San Diego Comic-Con Inkpot Awards Ceremony at the El Cortez hotel, about six years after Stan's interview with Jon Hurd. Left to right: Gil Kane, Jack Kirby, Stan Lee, Jim Steranko, Will Eisner and Jerry Siegel. [Photo by Jackie Estrada]

Q: *Weren't you saying something about how you evolved this Marvel Comics system of doing stories?*

A: Years ago when I was writing all the books, I just couldn't write fast enough—it took me 12 minutes to type a page, so if I was doing 20 pages, it would take 4 hours to type a story. And there might be an artist waiting for one story while I was finishing another—and I couldn't afford to let that man sit around doing nothing. So in desperation I would say to him, "Look, I don't have time to write your script but your story is going to deal with Doctor Doom who comes to town, etc., why don't you start drawing it and I'll put the dialogue in later." With this method, the artist was kept busy while I was typing the script. After a while I realized that this was a great way to do it. The artist could now create; he wasn't just blindly following what the writer did. And the artist could envision this better than the writer. The artist could play up what he considered pictorially interesting. Then the writer could be inspired by the artist's drawing. For instance, it's easier for me to write copy looking at a drawing than it is to write copy looking at a sheet of blank paper. No other companies want to work this way—although I think it's wonderful. The other editors feel that they would lose control, and many other artists feel that they don't want to do the writer's job, etc.

Q: *You have written a tremendous number of stories, haven't you?*

A: Well, somebody said to me, "You know, Stan, I'll bet you have written more stories that have been published than any professional writer who's ever lived." I would add, "Certainly not better stories, but more, probably." For 30 years I have never written less than two complete comic magazines a week—sometimes three or four in that length of time. Even Walter Winchell with all his columns never totaled that much. I think this is what I'll rest my case on—as far as my claim to glory is concerned.

Q: *How much of a staff do you have?*

A: Well, our staff is very small—there's myself, then I have Roy Thomas, who's my associate editor—I'm the head writer and he's the next writer. I write about 10 books a month, he writes 4 or 5 or so. Roy and I do the bulk of the writing. Archie Goodwin and Gary Friedrich do some additional scripts. Occasionally another writer will try out. In some cases the writer doesn't have to discuss the plot of an upcoming story with the artist over the telephone as I mentioned earlier. John Romita, who draws ***Spider-Man***, is on salary right here in the office, for instance, so he comes into my office and we discuss the plot face-to-face. The one thing I don't like to do is waste an artist's time—if a man is a freelancer, his time is money. Take the case of Jim Steranko, who lives in Pennsylvania. I hate to ask him to come to New York if our business can be handled on the phone, and I'm not going to ask Jack Kirby to fly in from the Coast. And I won't even ask an artist to come in from uptown Manhattan if we can get together on the phone.

Q: *Can you say a little about how you got into the comic magazine business?*

Joe Simon (top) and Jack Kirby (editor in chief and art director, respectively of Timely Comics) around the time they first met Stan, who came to work as their assistant in 1940. [Copyright ©2011 the copyright holders].

A: Well, I never thought of being a writer. I thought I would be an artist. As a young kid I was able to draw ***Dick Tracy*** better than Chester Gould, I copied Milton Caniff, ***Krazy Kat***, etc. I was always pretty good at writing in school, however, and during high school days, ***The New York Herald Tribune*** had a contest called "The Biggest News of the Week." Students were invited to write essays on this topic and it happened that I won this contest three weeks running. The editor called me and asked me to stop entering the contest, and he said, "By the way, if you haven't thought of what you want to do when you get out of high school, you'd better become a writer. You'd be pretty good at it."

I still didn't want to become a writer, although I was a voracious reader—I loved Shakespeare and Mark Twain and Sherlock Holmes, science fiction, etc. But the thing I really wanted to be was an actor. I had belonged to the WPA Federal Theater—I liked Shakespeare because I like things that are exaggerated—I would have loved silent movies. Everything Shakespeare wrote was done on the grand scale and I try to get this in our comics—everything is over-emotional—if a man is scared, he's terrified. I wanted to be an actor but I had to eat and the world wasn't saying, "Here's a million dollar contract, Stan." So when I graduated from school, I had to make a living fast. I heard that there was an opening here—it was then called Timely Comics and Joe Simon and Jack Kirby were here on staff. It was practically a two–man staff. They hired me to be a copywriter, an errand boy, to sharpen the pencils and correct scripts and proofread, to be a boy of all trades for $12 a week or whatever it was. I did it, and I loved it, and I wrote a Captain America story and I was thrilled—I was about 17 years old at the time. After a while, Joe and Jack left and I was the only guy here. Martin Goodman, the publisher, said, "Stan, do you think you can hold down the job until I can find somebody permanent?" At the time, because of my age, he obviously didn't think of me as a permanent employee. Well, I tried, and I've been here, ever since. It's gotten to be a joke now, but he never told me that I'd gotten the job permanently, so, as far as I know, he's still looking for that other editor.

I changed my name from Stanley Lieber to Stan Lee, thinking that I didn't want to use my real name for comics. I felt that when I wrote the great American novel or became a famous playwright or an actor or something that I'd use my real name, but as it is now nobody even knows me as Lieber. I've never changed it officially though. After I'd started comic magazine work, I always did other things on the side—I did some advertising work, I did some radio work, I've been involved on the periphery of television, etc. But I was always so busy with this work that I never could get involved in the things that I've always dreamed of doing. So it's been a little bit of a frustration. Finally, about seven years ago, my wife said to me, "You know you're a nut, Stan—you're obviously going to be in comics most of your life—why don't you stop thinking of these other things and tearing yourself in two—just concentrate on making a mark in comics." And that's when I decided to really give it the old school try, and I forgot everything else for a while. We came out with a new line of Marvel Comics and I tried to make them as well-written, and as sophisticated as I could, and I'm happy to say they really caught on. Until this point, about seven years ago, we were just doing what had been done before—I think we did it as well as anybody—but they were cliché comics. We were the first, undoubtedly, to break out of that mold.

Q: *Does your publisher, Martin Goodman, decide when you will drop books that aren't selling and when you will start new ones?*

A: I think I could say it this way—he's about the greatest guy in the world to work for, because when things are going well, I don't see him or hear from him and I'm the complete boss as far as the creative policy of these books is concerned. When the sales will start slipping, he will enter the picture, as is very natural, and we go over things very carefully. He's a magnificent analyst, a magnificent editor, and he will very often see things much clearer and much faster than I will because I'm so close to it. For instance, he might say, "Gee, Stan, do you realize that when you started with ***Spider-Man*** you had a good policy, but you've been trying so hard to be original that now you've gotten away from the thing that made it good." Suddenly I'll say, "My gosh, you're right—I didn't even realize that!" He's invaluable –whenever I'm concerned about something, I'll ask his advice, etc. But the publisher concerns himself mostly with distribution and sales, etc.

Q: *Do you have any other thoughts about the business that you'd like to express here?*

A: Well, let's say that there have been a lot of articles written about Marvel which give us our due, but most people who don't know the business lump all comic magazines together, which is something that always annoys me a bit. Because I think I can truthfully say that Marvel comics are popular on campus—and other comics are not.

Stan the Self-Publishin' Man

Mr. Lee blazes another trail

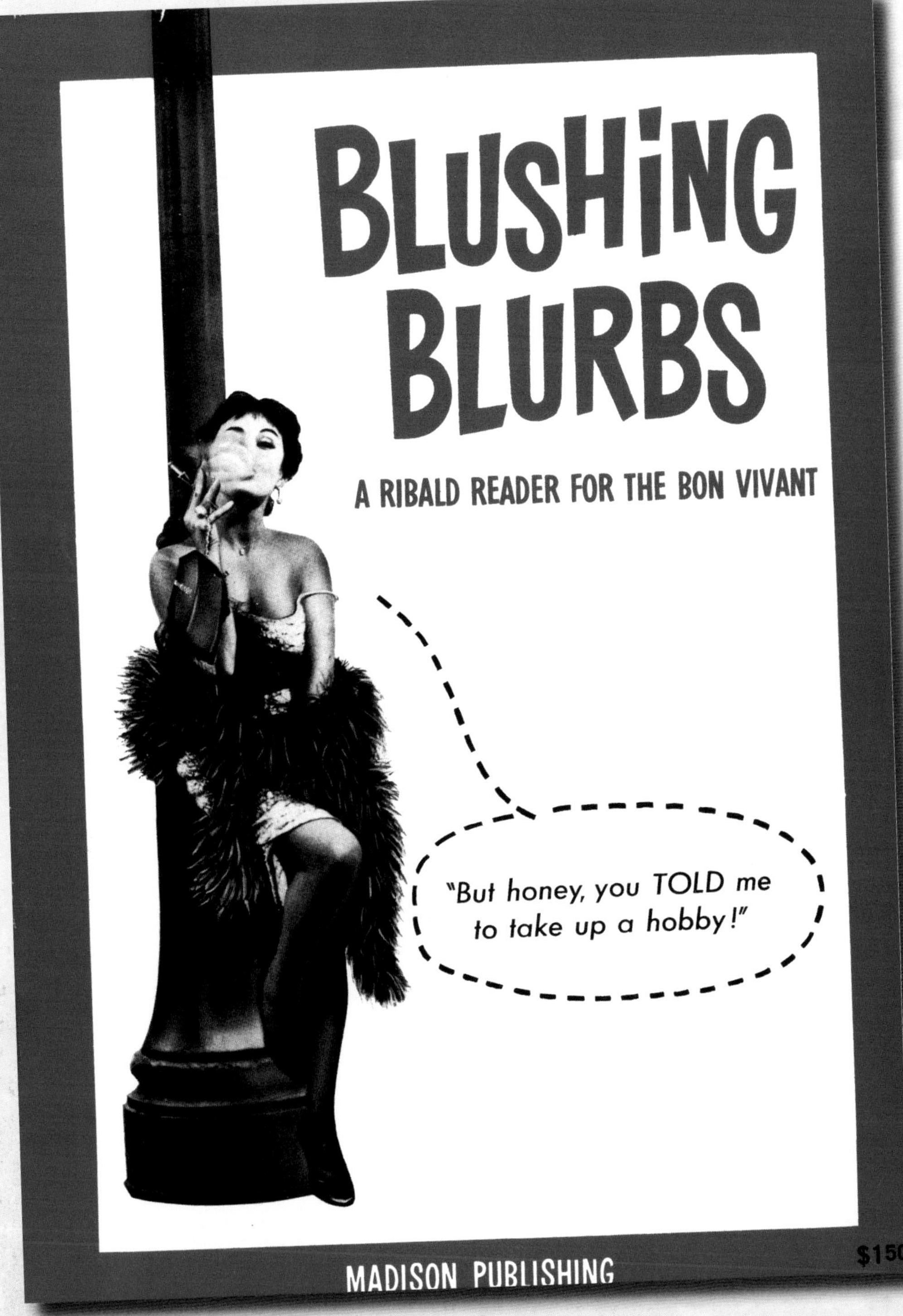

BLUSHING BLURBS
A RIBALD READER FOR THE BON VIVANT
"But honey, you TOLD me to take up a hobby!"
MADISON PUBLISHING
$150

While Stan's recent non-Marvel efforts for his Pow! Entertainment company have gotten a lot of attention, he was ahead of the curve in producing books (via his own Madison Publishing) that were his and his alone. These included 1947's ***Secrets Behind the Comics***, 1961's ***Golfers Anonymous***, and the 1960 photo-funny book, ***Blushing Blurbs***, featuring none other than his wife Joan, done up à la Sophia Loren for the cover.

Stan Lee's Top Ten Tips For Writers

The Man shares his most closely guarded secrets!

This article's title pretty much says it all. Proudly, we present the ten things Stan thinks it's most important for writers, aspiring or established, to know. Take it away, Mr. Lee...

First of all, lemme say that I don't normally spend my time dreaming up tips for writers. Mainly because I don't feel I'm any more of an authority than the next guy who tickles a keyboard or pushes a pen. Also, who needs extra competition?

However, Dynamic Danny Fingeroth can be very persuasive, or maybe threatening would be a better word, so just to get him off my back, I'll try to dream up ten tips, in no particular order, for those of you who dwell on such things, and let the chips fall where they may.

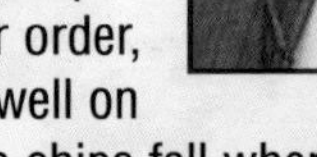

1

Write about things you know. If you don't know, Google the stuff and start learning. Or else, be so vague that no one can pin you down—like when I dreamed up Bruce Banner becoming the Hulk due to a gamma bomb. I don't know any more about gamma bombs than I do about brain surgery, but I didn't try to explain how it worked. I just said that he became the Hulk because of gamma radiation. Hey, who can find fault with that? At least it sounds scientific. So, to summarize—be totally factual, or else be so vague that you can get away with knowing nothing about your subject. But whatever you do, don't try to fake it.

When Bruce Banner first became the Hulk, Stan said the cause was "gamma radiation." That vague reference sounded scientific and worked for the story. Cover to ***The Incredible Hulk*** #1 (May 1962) is by Jack Kirby and George Roussos.

[This article originally appeared in slightly different form in ***Write Now!*** #18.]

2

When you're reading a comic book or watching a movie or TV show, don't just get caught up in the story and sit there like a couch potato. Try to analyze everything that's on the page or screen. Why did the writer add that bit of dialogue? Was it more dramatic for the hero to say nothing in that particular scene? Why didn't the writer introduce that important story element until fifteen minutes into the film, or until five pages into the story? Why did (or didn't) the writer have such an enigmatic ending? Why, in that movie, was Act Three so much shorter than Act Two? Why, in the comic book, did the writer use so many captions on pages 3 and 4 and no captions at all on the next six pages? Why so many long shots—or close-ups? Would it have been more interesting the other way around? Etc. Etc. You should be able to learn something new about writing every time you read a comic book or watch a film—if you remember to analyze everything you see.

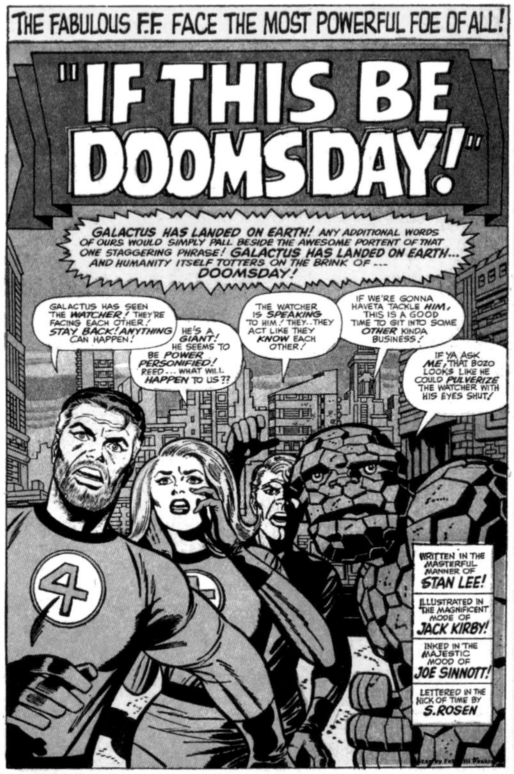

As Stan advises in tip #8, "try to give every character a different way of speaking." In the splash page to ***Fantastic Four*** #49 (April 1966), Stan has given each team member—as well as the omniscient narrator—a distinctive speech pattern. The art is by Jack Kirby and Joe Sinnott. [©2011 Marvel Characters Inc.]

3

Keep writing. I figure writing is like any other activity, like swimming, or jogging, or sex. The more you do, the more you'll enjoy it, the easier it becomes and the more you'll improve. If you find yourself getting bored writing, or tired of it, there's only one answer. Find another career.

4

Write about things that interest you. If you write about subjects that bore you, thinking they're what the market wants, you'll just end up writing boring pages. The more interested you are in your subject, the better chance you have of making your subject more interesting, too.

5

Try to write at the same time every day. Writing can be a habit, like anything else. If you stick to a schedule, it makes it easier to turn pages out like a pro.

6

Stop writing if you find yourself getting tired or bored. Take a nap or a short walk to wake yourself up. You can only do your best writing when you're mentally alert and interested in what you're doing.

7

When you've finished with your script, proofread it carefully. Don't read it as if it's your baby and you love every word of it. Pretend you're the world's toughest editor, looking for every fault you can find in story structure, dialogue, characterization and motivation. Be as tough on yourself as humanly possible—because that's how your editor will be. And keep rewriting until your script is as good as you can possibly make it.

8

In writing dialogue, try to give every character a different way of speaking. In any script, it's boring to have the characters all speaking the same way. Think of people you know—think how they speak; think of their verbal idiosyncrasies and mannerisms. Remember, nobody speaks exactly the same as anyone else. When listening to people conversing, train yourself to pick up all the subtle nuances of dialogue and use those varied nuances in your writing.

9

Make your characters interesting. Sounds obvious, doesn't it? Sounds easy, doesn't it? Well, failing to do that is one of the main reasons so many scripts are rejected. Reading a script is like visiting people—the people in the story. You wouldn't want to visit dull, colorless people, would you? You wouldn't wanna spend time with bores. The characters you write about must be interesting, colorful and unique in some special way. They must have problems we'll care about—and solutions to those problems that we can't wait to see.

10

DON'T GET DISCOURAGED! Lots of really good, successful writers didn't make their first sale until long after they started writing. Of course, if you've been unable to sell anything for years and years and are now starving and homeless, you might start thinking of another vocation. But short of that, stay with it—tomorrow may be your lucky day!

Okay, that's it. If, after reading the wondrous words above, you suddenly become a fantastically successful and wealthy writer, don't forget my commission!

Excelsior!

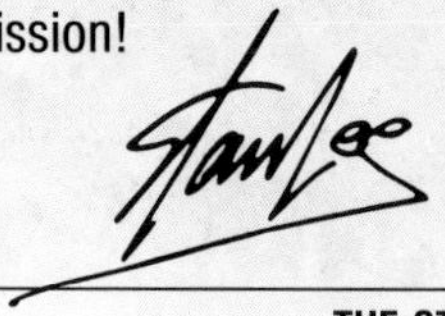

Stan Lee

Stan the Rock 'n' Roll Man

Stan's fans include rockers from the 1960s to today

While Stan's tastes in pop music run more toward the Sinatra end of the spectrum—or why else would he have nicknamed artist John Romita "Ring-a-Ding," taken from the title of a Sinatra album?—Lee's Marvel comics have always been of interest to rock 'n' rollers. More than a few of them made a point of meeting The Man over the years, and Stan talked about many of those encounters in the Bullpen Bulletins. In the Stan's Soapbox section of the Bullpen Bulletins for September 1968, Stan closed out by saying:

"And now we've gotta cut out—Country Joe and the Fish just arrived to visit us—and we don't wanna keep 'em out of the water too long!"

Now that may not have been their first visit to the Bullpen, or it may have been a message that was delayed in being published, but in any case, we found, in Stan's Wyoming archives, the 1967 correspondence on this page between Stan and his "Piscatorial Pals."

Country Joe & theFish
P. O. Box 2233
Berkeley, Calif.

May 19, 1967

Stan Lee
Marvel Comics Group
625 Madison Ave.
New York, N. Y.

Dear Stan,

No doubt you'll be pleased to know that your creations have so entered the consciousness of the generation that they emerge, yes actually emerge, in the folk music of the times. If you listen carefullyto this record on your office stero (every office has an office stero, in New York, right?) you'll hear and see two actual figments.

Quite naturally we read your comics alla time here instead of working because our beloved leader J. E. Hoover said that our kind always did read comic books.

So we thought after you listened to the record we could make a deal. Here'e the deal: you let us join the MMMS for freebies, and we'll let you join the Intergalactic Fish Fan Club for freebies. And then we can trade posters, and then. . . why the world is the limit. That's our deal, and I sure hope you dig it 'cause we dig you!

peace and joy,

Country Joe & the Fish

CJF/nf

5/26/67

Hi, Piscatorial Pals!

Never mind your record! What I wanna know is-- why types your letters? He, she, or it is great!

Anyway, we're deliciously delighted that our somewhat forensic fame has reached as far as the hallowed harmonious halls of Berkeley-- and penetrated, howe'er insidiously, the liltin' lyrics of thine own rollickin' record!

What I'm trying to say, guys, is-- enjoyed your tintinnabulatin' tunes-- got a kick out of our mention-- and ame glad to dub thee-- one and all-- Merry Marchers in Perpetuity!

Your membership goodies are herewith dispatched. Any group that can come with a name like Country Joe and the Fish can't be all bad!

Hang loose, gang-- you're our type of heroes.

'Nuff said!

Stan

1967 correspondence between Stan Lee and Country Joe and the Fish, Stan Lee Collection, box #14, folder #8, American Heritage Center, University of Wyoming.

Country Joe at Woodstock, 1969. [© 2009 Warner Bros. Entertainment Inc.]

For those of you who weren't around back then, "Country Joe" McDonald is probably best known for leading the crowd at 1969's Woodstock Music Festival in an off-color cheer, which is featured in the 1970 ***Woodstock*** movie. But if that's all you know of his and the Fish's music, it's worth checking out what else they've done, as a band and individually. Certainly you might find their song "Superbird" of interest, because it namechecks some Marvel superheroes.

***Gary Friedrich** alluded to the band's 1967 Bullpen visit earlier in this book, and here's his full account of it, as recalled in 2008.*

WHEN COUNTRY JOE MET CITY STAN

It was the summer of '67 when Fish band member David Cohen dropped by Marvel. It was sometimes my job to go out and speak to fans in the lobby.

I went out. David introduced himself, and I was star-struck. I was a big fan of the group. Funny thing is, he was a little star-struck, as well. He told me he and the rest of the band were huge Marvel fans and would love to meet Stan while they were in town for a concert. (Their song "Superbird" was filled with Marvel references.)

Naturally, I wanted to accommodate the band. But "audiences" with Stan were not easily arranged in those days. Stan was only in the office three days a week (he was home, writing, the other days), and he liked to spend that time working. He wasn't really turned on by meeting celebrities.

I gathered up my courage to propose the meeting to Stan. I'd been working at Marvel less than a year, so my solo meetings with Stan had been few and far between.

Anyway, I went in and asked Stan if he could spare a few minutes in the next couple of days to meet CJ and the Fish, to which he responded with something like, "Country Who and the Whats?" He wasn't a big rock fan, to say the least. But after some arm-twisting on my part, mainly buttressed by my pointing out the value of mentioning the meeting in the Bullpen Bulletins, he relented, and a meeting was arranged.

A couple of days later, David showed up with Joe, Barry, and the rest of the band. While they waited in the lobby, word leaked out around the office that this strange group of hippies was visiting, and the Bullpenners began to march in and out of the lobby for a peek. If you recall, the boys in the band were something of a sight, and most non-musicians hadn't adopted the '60s style of dress yet.

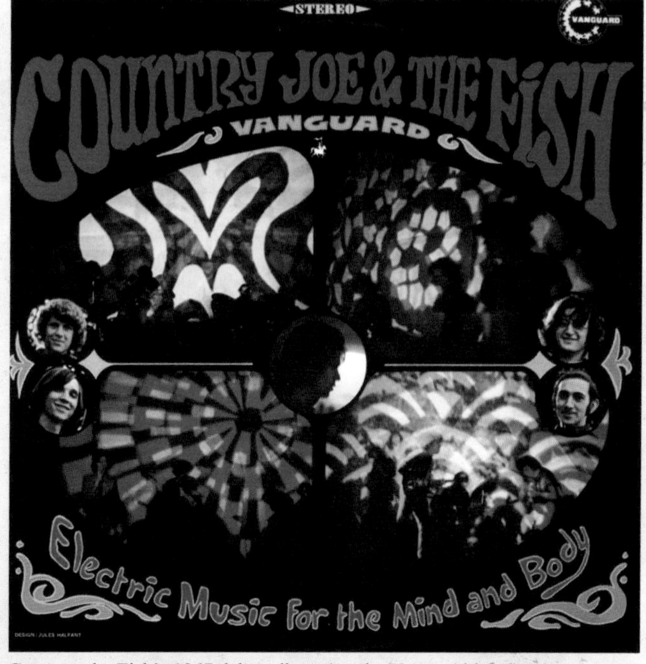

Cover to the Fish's 1967 debut album (on the Vanguard label) ***Electric Music for the Mind and Body,*** containing the song "Superbird," which references the Fantastic Four and Dr. Strange (as well as Superman). [All songs copyright © 1967 renewed 1996 by Joyful Wisdom, BMI]

I escorted the band into the inner sanctum and we were greeted by the ever-smiling Stan. He was very cordial, as always, and passed around his infamous sourballs. The meeting didn't last long. Joe asked Stan a few questions. I don't remember what, specifically. But the band was somewhat awe-struck. I think Stan, as always, just wanted to get back to work, though he'd never have let his guests know that.

After a few minutes, Stan very graciously broke it all up, shook hands all around, and the big meeting was over. Wish there were some funny stories to relate, but that's about it. Stan would light up the room with his smile for guests, make them feel perfectly at home and that they could spend the day if they wanted. Then, in no time flat, he'd wrap it up, shake their hands and move them out so he could get back to work. And I never talked with one of Stan's guests after one of these meetings who didn't feel they'd been treated royally and that this had been one of the highlights of their lives. It was the same with CJ and the Fish.

After the band left, Stan called me in and said, "So that's where you get your fashion ideas?" I never was quite sure whether he thought my hippie dress was cool or horrifying.

—GF

Country Joe and the Fish in 1967. Left to right: Barry Melton, David Bennett Cohen, Bruce Barthol, Joe McDonald, Gary "Chicken" Hirsh. [Photo: Jim Marshall]

Flash forward to August 2010, when Danny spoke with two members of the Fish who were at that fateful meeting. Here's what they had to say:

DAVID BENNETT COHEN

keyboardist and guitarist with the Fish

Cover to David Bennett Cohen's 2007 album, ***Cookin' with Cohen***. Photo by Manuel Elias [Album ©2007, Rich Hen Music, BMI]

"I was the one who instigated the visit, I called Marvel Comic Books to thank them for their comics. There was just something about Marvel's comics. They were grown-up comics. It wasn't like teenage stuff, or kid stuff. Of course, it was fantasy, and it was beyond the realm of reality, but it had a maturity about it.

"You know, when you're on the road, there's a few things you can do. You can sleep, you can read, you can get into trouble. I used to read comic books. And it was really a way of passing time when there's nothing going on, traveling, or sitting in the van. So I called the office to thank them, and told them I wanted to come up and meet them. I told them I was from Country Joe and the Fish, and I thanked them, and I think somebody may have invited me up.

"I remember when I walked in, I thought it was [band member] Chicken Hirsch, but it may have been Barry. And we walked in, and the receptionist screamed. You know, like a Beatles fan scream. And that was the first time that ever happened. I mean, that happened every now and then, that when we get on stage people would get excited, but not like that. That was the first time, and that really endeared her to me.

Country Joe at Woodstock and in a recent photo.
[Woodstock photo by Jim Marshall. Modern photo copyright © Positive Productions. All rights reserved.]

"Stan Lee made an impression in my *life*. Meeting him was almost anticlimactic, because, you know, those comics really sustained us a lot of times."

***David Bennett Cohen** has been a professional musician for more than 40 years. Best known for his innovative keyboard playing as an original member of the '60's rock band, Country Joe and the Fish, he is an equally accomplished guitar player who has been involved in numerous music scenes throughout his varied career. Over the years, he has played and/or recorded with The Blues Project, Elvin Bishop, Jimi Hendrix, Johnny Winter, Buddy Miles, Huey Lewis, Michael Bloomfield, Bob Weir, Jimmy Vivino and many others. His website is: www.davidbennettcohen.com.*

BARRY MELTON

co-founder, guitarist and singer with the Fish

"Of course I remember meeting Stan—I could never forget meeting one of the greatest creative minds and inspirational human beings of my generation.

"We were fans, just straight out. As the band rose up the success ladder, we got to meet a lot of musicians that I had always hoped to meet, B.B. King and people like that. But we didn't get to meet a whole lot of people in other media. And meeting Stan Lee was just like meeting Pablo Picasso.

"Dr. Strange and the Silver Surfer, and, to some degree, the Fantastic Four, were just part of our subculture in San Francisco, which ultimately became the subculture of the country's young people. As we went out on the road during the Sixties, we went to visit the islands of youth culture that were emulating what we were doing in San Francisco, and, for some reason or another, and I can't explain it, there was a direct link in that subculture to Marvel Comics in New York.

"I remember Stan being really encouraging. I thought he must be an old beatnik or something because he wore dark glasses. Maybe he knew he was 'on stage,' but he was just really animated, really encouraging. He said 'What you guys are doing is great. We gotta do some work together.' We came up with ideas. I think we talked about making an album about the Silver Surfer.

"I don't think kids today understand how limited our channels were for youth culture. Music assumed a huge importance back in those days on radio, and rock music was one of the few channels for kids to express themselves. Similarly, Marvel Comics was part of that picture. Marvel Comics, sociologically, was part of the youth movement of the Sixties.

"We were definitely right in the heart of the audience.

I can't express to you how much, particularly characters like Dr. Strange and the Silver Surfer, were right down the middle of that counterculture consciousness of the Sixties.

"I am totally enamored of Stan Lee and the impact he's had on our culture. I mean, the guy was truly a giant."

*In 1965, **Barry Melton** co-founded Country Joe and the Fish, and began his career as a guitarist and singer, recording and touring with "Country Joe" McDonald as a duo and with various bands, with his own bands, and as a solo artist under the name Barry "The Fish" Melton. In 1982, Barry was admitted to practice law before all courts of the State of California and before the U.S. District Court for the Northern District of California. He recently retired as Public Defender of Yolo County, California and is a past President of the California Public Defenders Association [CPDA].*

Barry has continued to play music during the course of his legal career, including a long stint with Dinosaurs, a band of '60s veterans that has at various times included Peter Albin and David Getz (Big Brother and the Holding Company), John Cipollina and Greg Elmore (Quicksilver Messenger Service), Papa John Creech (Hot Tuna and Jefferson Starship), Spencer Dryden (Jefferson Airplane and New Riders of the Purple Sage), Robert Hunter (Grateful Dead lyricist), and Merl Saunders.

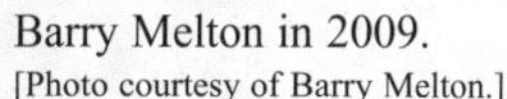

Barry Melton in 2009.
[Photo courtesy of Barry Melton.]

For more info about Barry, you can check out his website: http://www.counterculture.net/thefish/index.html

The Fish appeared in ***Nick Fury, Agent of SHIELD* #15** (November 1969), courtesy of writer Gary Friedrich and artists Herb Trimpe, Dick Ayers, and Sam Grainger.

KEEP ON ROCKIN' IN THE STAN LEE UNIVERSE!

The Fish weren't the only rock stars fascinated with Stan and Marvel. Here are some other examples from over the years:

R&B singer-songwriter, record producer and actor Ne-Yo's 2010 album ***Libra Scale*** was packaged with a comic of the same name, starring Ne-Yo as a superhero, produced by Stan's Pow! Entertainment.

Here's Stan with the legendary Beatle Ringo Starr as they plan Ringo's Pow! comic.

The band X Japan's Yoshiki will be collaborating with Stan and Todd McFarlane on a comics project.

Kiss starred in 1977's ***Marvel Super Special***. Here, the band members pose with Stan, as well as writer Steve Gerber and artist Alan Weiss. Cover art by Weiss and Gray Morrow.

Stan's Night at the Museum

"Stan Lee: A Retrospective" —a comprehensive look at Stan's career— ran from February 23-August 6, 2007 at New York's Museum of Comic and Cartoon Art (MoCCA)

by Danny Fingeroth
Exhibition curated by Ken Wong and Peter Sanderson
Photos by Gary Dunaier

Here's how this amazing exhibit was described on the on the museum's website (www.moccany.org):

The exhibition will address Stan's contributions as a writer, artist, art director, editor, promoter, and leader of the "Marvel Revolution" during which Stan—along with artists Jack Kirby, Steve Ditko, and others in the fabled "Marvel Bullpen"—introduced a host of novel, complex, humanized superheroes that have since become world-famous, blockbuster movie/television/entertainment franchises.

*MoCCA's **Stan Lee: A Retrospective** exhibition... will include examples of Lee's early work in comics, address Lee's crucial role in the famed "Marvel Revolution" (including aspects such as the "Marvel Method" of writing, Lee's cultivation of comics fandom, and of course, Lee's role as co-creator of now world-famous characters such as The Fantastic Four, Spider-Man, The Hulk, Thor, Dr. Strange, Daredevil, and more) that took place during the Silver Age of superhero comics, and remind viewers of the ever-pioneering work that Lee is still doing today through recent projects at DC Comics, Dark Horse Comics, and POW! Entertainment. The exhibition is the first ever at MoCCA devoted to a comics writer rather than an artist—that is, a comics creator who is not (also) an illustrator.*

[Characters ©2011 Marvel Characters, Inc. Painting by Arnold Sawyer.]

Above and below: Portions of the ***Stan Lee: A Retrospective*** exhibition, featuring original art (by Jack Kirby, John Romita, Sr., and others) from stories written and edited by Stan, as well as artifacts from the course of his seven decade career.

There was a gala opening celebration for the exhibit on February 23rd. Despite having spent the entire day at the New York Comic Con, Stan came to the party—and stuck around for a couple of hours, leading the lucky attendees on a tour of just about every item in the show!

In this photo and the one just below, Stan animatedly discusses the work on the museum walls. In the second shot, one can imagine him explaining the secret origin of the succinct but expressive phrase, "WA-HOOO!"

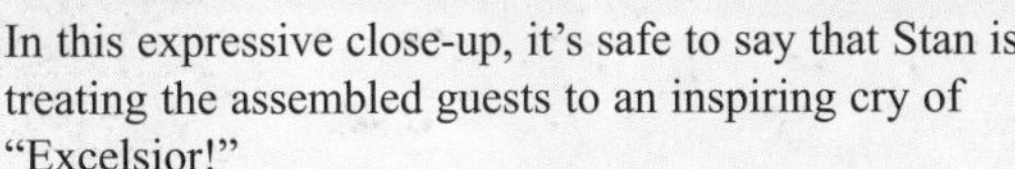

In this expressive close-up, it's safe to say that Stan is treating the assembled guests to an inspiring cry of "Excelsior!"

Among the attendees at the opening were Danny Fingeroth and Jim Salicrup, who have both worked with Stan for many years.

"Stan Lee: A Retrospective" photographs © Gary Dunaier.

To Hollywood and Beyond

Stan and the movie *auteurs*

by Danny Fingeroth

FROM THE STAN LEE ARCHIVES

From the dawn of the Marvel Age of Comics, Stan has known and worked with the best and brightest directors of several generations.

ALAIN RESNAIS

In the March 1970 Stan's Soapbox, Stan announced that he and **Alain Resnais,** the noted "French film genius" spent "many pleasant hours rappin' about movies, comic mags, and the arts in general. According to Alain, Marvel Comics are definitely the 'in' thing in the arty circles of Europe today."

Stan and Resnais developed a close friendship and even worked on two proposed films together (See part of Stan's screenplay for one, ***The Monster Maker***, elsewhere in this very book.)

April 9, '80

Mes Cher Amis,

I've got only a minute to dash off this short note--

Just wanted to tell you that THE HOLLYWOOD REPORTER, dated April 8th, wrote: "Favorites among French films selected for Cannes this year are: "Mon Oncle d'Amerique" by Alain Resnais," etc. Yours was the FIRST mentioned, and they mentioned 3 others, by Tavernier, Allio, and Jean-Luc Godard. Very impressive. I'm not sending you the clipping itself because I'm saving it to show to people here in Los Anggles-- and I don't have a Xerox machine easily available.

NEWS: We didn't buy a house here yet, because I haven't yet sold our apartment. Mortgage interest rates are so high it likes like we'll never sell the apartment! I didn't sign my new contract yet because we're still negotiating and I'm listening to other offers. (I'm very nervous about it!) I've been speaking to Henry Winkler about playing SPIDER-MAN as a big budget movie-- he's excited about it. It all depends upon whether he and Marvel can come to terms. (He's the guy who plays Fonzie in the hit tv series HAPPY DAYS). I even told him I'd love it if we could convince you to direct the movie- he thought it might be a great idea. Well, we'll see. I'm learning (as you've always said) nothing is ever definate out here, and it takes forever to come to any agreement on anything between any two parties.

Have to rush now-- the usual meetings and conferences. Write me when MON ONCLE is finished-- and let me know when you're coming to the US again. Hope all is wonderful with you both.

Excelsior!

-- and love from
both Joanies to
the two of you.

5/23/79

Dear Flo and Alain,

Here's a brief Lee news update...

I LOVE Los Angeles. Joanie loves Los Angeles. (Not as much as I do-- but almost). In case I forgot to send it to you, our address is:

10701 Wilshire Blvd.
Los Angeles, Ca. 90024
(213) 474-1180

We're returning to New York May 31st. (We've been here in L.A. since April 15th) Joanie will stay in New York long enough to try to sell the house in Remsenburg and our daughter's apartment. Then, she'll rejoin me in L.A. I'll be returning to California in a week or two, and spend most of the remainder of the year here.

A few days ago we learned our New York apartment had been robbed!!! Every bit of jewelry Joanie owned was stolen. And-- we're not insured! It's a very big loss, both financially and sentimentally. We try not to think about it, but it's the most depressing and distressing thing imaginable. It's one of the reasons we'd like to pull up stakes and come out to Los Angeles permanently, if we can.

I've met a lot of people here and hope to meet lots more. With luck, I may be able to infiltrate into the tv and movie business yet. Will write again, in a few weeks, after I return to L.A., to give you an more complete report about what's happening business-wise. The one big item right now, and I can't remember if I told you or not, is that Lee Kramer, Olivia Newton-John's manager and boy friend, wants to do a big-budget Silver Surfer movie with me-- and it looks like he will. I'll serve as consultant and some sort of associate producer. Hanna-Barbera may do Kid Colt- same arrangement.

Hope all is well with you and your film. When are you returning to the U.S.? Can you come to L.A.? Anything new and exciting? Lock up your jewelry!

And now, through the tears, Joanie and I say--

Excelsior!

1979 and 1980 letters from Stan Lee to Alain Resnais, box #14, Stan Lee Collection, American Heritage Center, University of Wyoming.

A recent photo of Resnais. [Cineuropa]

Resnais ***(Night and Fog, Hiroshima Mon Amour, Last Year at Marienbad)*** sought out and worked with Stan. In a 2007 article about Resnais by Frederic Tulen, the author writes that Resnais "lights up when I ask him if he has been in recent contact with Stan Lee, the great comic book artist who also had a role [narrating] in ***The Year '01.*** 'Not for some while,' he says, but they are and shall always remain friends. He recalls working on a film script with Lee in New York... 'It was wonderful being in New York in those days and to see Stan Lee every morning, to talk with him and to see him smile.'"

In Stan's Wyoming archives, we found these letters from Stan to Resnais and his then-wife, Flo, including one describing a burglary at the Lees' Manhattan apartment. (In the first letter, "both Joanies" refers to Stan's wife and his daughter, who have the same first name.)

JAMES CAMERON

Although **James Cameron** didn't get to direct the ***Spider-Man*** movie for which he wrote a "scriptment," he's done all right for himself with movies like ***Terminator*** and ***Avatar***. Here's a handwritten note he sent Stan in 1991.

Stan,

Merry Christmas and what a thrilling prospect for the New Year and beyond to work with one of my great childhood idols on the film version of his greatest creation — Spidey.

All the best!

Jim

Peace on Earth

James Cameron

OLIVER STONE

Here's a copy of a 1973 letter, found in Stan's Wyoming archives, sent in response to **Oliver Stone** when he was a relative unknown. Hence, he received a polite response from Stan to an inquiry, but the letter was sent from Stan's secretary. Stone, of course, would go on to direct ***Platoon*** and ***JFK***, among many other films.

Marvel Comics Group

575 Madison Avenue New York, New York 10022 212 TEmpleton 8-7900

A DIVISION OF
Cadence Industries Corporation

August 9, 1973

Mr. Oliver Stone
C/O Euro-American Pictures, Ltd.
319 East 50th Street
New York, New York 10022

Dear Mr. Stone:

Stan asked me to give your letter and script to our Editor, Roy Thomas, and you will be hearing from him shortly.

Thank you for letting us see your material.

MARVEL COMICS GROUP

Fran Lyons
Fran Lyons
Secretary to Stan Lee

fl

1973 letter from Fran Lyons to Oliver Stone, Stan Lee Collection, box #12, folder #4, American Heritage Center, University of Wyoming.

FEDERICO FELLINI

In November 1965, Italian filmmaker **Federico Fellini** ***(La Strada, 8 1/2)*** came to visit Stan at the Marvel offices. Stan recalled it this way in a 1987 interview with Pat Jankeiwicz in ***The Chaffey College Mountain Breeze:***

"Federico Fellini came to see me in New York! I couldn't believe it. The secretary said, 'There's a "Mr. Felony" or something, here to see you... ' I said, 'Okay, show him in,' and sure enough, Federico!

"I wanted to talk to him about his movies, and all he wanted to talk about was our comics! I was so flattered! We became a little bit friendly for a few years, writing letters to each other... "

KEVIN SMITH

Stan and **Kevin Smith** (who directed Stan in ***MallRats***) "thwip" Spidey-style on the set of the **Scott Zakarin**-directed ***Stan Lee's Mutants, Monsters, and Marvels***, a 2002 feature-length interview of Stan by Kevin. [©2002 creative Light Video. All rights reserved.]

JON FAVREAU

An emotional moment at the 2007 Comic-Con in San Diego with ***Iron Man*** and ***Iron Man 2*** director **Jon Favreau** beaming as Stan is hugged by **Robert Downey, Jr.**, who starred in both movies. [© 2011 the copyright holders]

KENNETH BRANAGH

Stan and ***Thor*** director **Kenneth Branagh**, at the May 2, 2011 L.A. premiere of the movie. [©Paramount Pictures.]

TIM STORY

Here's Stan conferring with **Tim Story**, director of the 2005 ***Fantastic Four*** movie and its sequel, 2007's ***Fantastic Four: Rise of the Silver Surfer.*** [© 2011 the copyright holders]

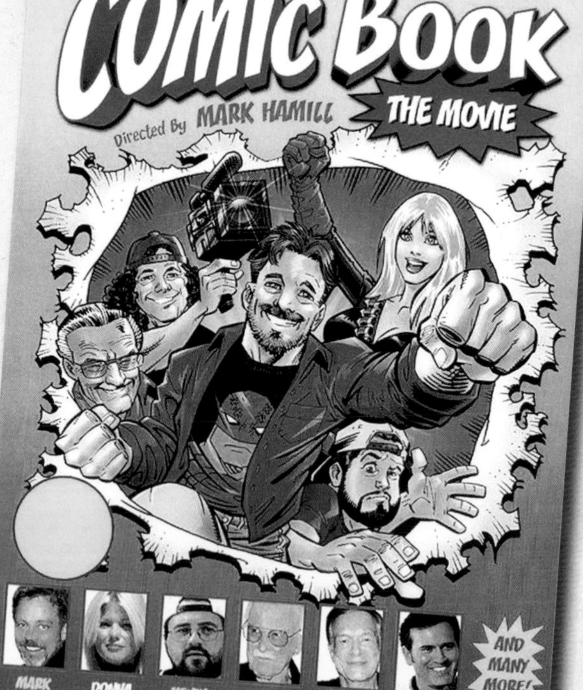

Mark Hamill directed the 2004 ***Comic Book: The Movie***, in which Stan appeared as himself. [©2011 Miramax.]

"This Generation's Homer"

Stan and Marvel take the college crowd by storm

by Danny Fingeroth

FROM THE STAN LEE ARCHIVES

Trenton Sunday Times Advertiser
TRENTON, N. J.
SUN. 79,720

MAR 1 3 1966

Whigs Call Editor Today's Homer

By Jonathan Wax
Times Advertiser Special Writer

PRINCETON — The comic hero of the Merry Marvel Marching Society found himself the topic of discussion in the not-so-hallowed halls of the nation's oldest college debating society.

Stan Lee, writer-editor of Marvel Comic Books, was the guest of Princeton University's Whig - Cliosophic Society this weekend and was hailed as "this generation's Homer" by one studnet.

"Thank you, literature fans," Lee opened his tongue-in-cheek speech. For the past 20 years, he has been "temporary editor" of the firm which publishes such epic serials as "The Fantastic Four," "The Incredible Hulk," "Dr. Strange's Spider-Man" and "Captain America."

"Our secret is realism, noted the man who sells 45 million comic books a year. "Five years ago we switched to superheroes, bot not like other superheroes.

"We asked ourselves what would anyone do if he suddenly gained superpowers. So we have heroes with human problems. The Spider-Man's girl hates superheroes, for example."

Lee writes much of the cloud - captions for the 20 titles published by Marvel Comics. "I really like to do 'The Mighty Thor,'" he said. "His language is really flamboyant and I pretend I'm Shakespeare."

The 50 Princeton undergraduates who march along with the Marvel Society were full of praise for the man behind their heroes and what he offers.

"I've always felt my education was founded on comics," exclaimed one Princeton English major. Another came forth and decried, "We think of Marvel Comics as the Twentieth Century mythology and you as this generation's Homer."

In the mid-'60s, Marvel Comics started to have a large following among college students. This 1965 article by Jonathan Wax, from the ***Trenton Sunday Times Advertiser***, was the source of the quote that Stan was that generation's Homer.

A more in-depth view of Marvel's popularity among college students was presented in a September 1966 article in ***Esquire*** magazine. Here's the title of the original article:

O.K., You've Passed the 2-S Test—Now You're Smart Enough for Comic Books

("2-S" was the Selective Service—draft board—designation for "student deferment." During the then-raging Vietnam War, that designation could be, literally, a matter of life or death.)

Jack Kirby did new art especially for the 1966 *Esquire* article.

Among those quoted in the **Esquire** *article was* ***Richard "Rick" Weingroff****, a college student at the time, who was active in comics fandom, including writing the "Rocketship Gossip" column for* **The Rocket's Blast Comic Collector** *fanzine.*

Here, Weingroff recalls the era and the article from the perspective of more than four decades later...

ESQUIRE AND ME

by Richard F. Weingroff

My 15 minutes of fame came two years before Andy Warhol claimed in 1968 that "everyone will be world-famous for 15 minutes." I wish I had known about that when I appeared in the September 1966 issue of ***Esquire*** ("The Magazine for Men") explaining the significance of Marvel Comics within the limits of a word balloon. As far as I can recall, my post-publication fame was limited to my family and a few friends at the University of Maryland, who quickly forgot about it. If anyone else in the world was aware of my fame, they neglected to mention it.

Richard F. Weingroff
University of Maryland

"Spidey [Spider-Man] is comicdom's Hamlet, comicdom's Raskolnikov. The uninitiated have disagreed about this of course—but we don't feel we should hastily appraise Hamlet and Raskolnikov just because they are from literature."

Richard Weingroff as he appeared in ***Esquire***. The Kirby-drawn Spider-Man above his head seems to be, Hamlet-like, pondering mortality, or else considering a career in dentistry. [Spider-Man ©2011 Marvel Characters, Inc. Photo ©the copyright holders.]

The September 1966 issue was the magazine's sixth annual college issue, a yearly bestseller. Articles of interest to college students included one on how to beat the draft by staying in college and a series based on the idea that college students were "digging" comic books, especially those by Stan Lee's Marvel Comics. To illustrate this point, the short lead article said that Lee had addressed the Princeton Debating Society, Columbia, and Bard "where he drew a bigger audience than President Eisenhower." Over 50,000 college students had joined Merry Marvel Marching Societies, while letters poured into Marvel's offices from more than 225 colleges. The article quoted an unnamed Ivy Leaguer as telling Lee, "We think of Marvel Comics as the twentieth-century mythology and you as this generation's Homer."

The article added, "At this stage of the game it is not yet clear whether the profound impact of Marvel Comics on the campus reveals more about the comics or the campus."

This was a remarkable change for a medium that had always relied on younger readers who stopped buying comics by their mid-teens. This popularity with an older, presumably educated crowd was not only newsworthy, but a culture shock. For years, after all, movies and TV shows had depicted adult characters reading comic books as a shorthand way of portraying their low intelligence, limited social skills, and possible criminal tendencies.

I don't recall how the magazine contacted me or what it said it was looking for, but I agreed to participate. With a comics-reading friend along to snap the historic photo, I sat on a tree stump on the university's College Park campus trying to reproduce the pose of Rodin's "The Thinker" while reading the June 1966 issue of ***Fantasy Masterpieces*** with Captain America on the cover. (I don't recall why I chose a comic that reprinted stories from the 1940s to illustrate my comment about the 1960s Marvel revolution. Maybe I chose it to demonstrate that I was sufficiently knowledgeable about the past to talk about the present. Or maybe that comic book just happened to be on the top of the pile when we went out to take the picture.) A word balloon contained my quote:

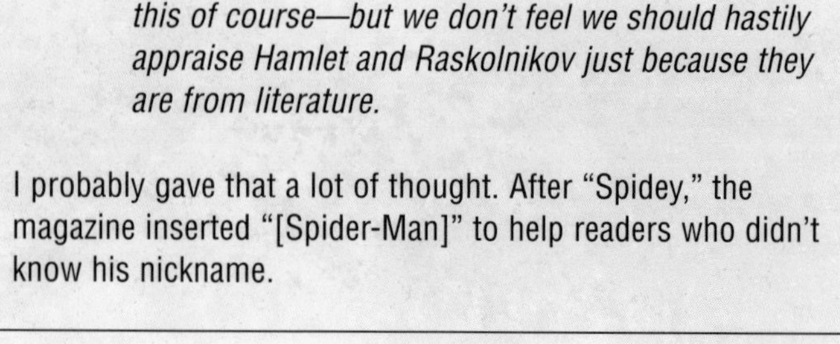

> *Spidey is comicdom's Hamlet, comicdom's Raskolnikov. The uninitiated have disagreed about this of course—but we don't feel we should hastily appraise Hamlet and Raskolnikov just because they are from literature.*

I probably gave that a lot of thought. After "Spidey," the magazine inserted "[Spider-Man]" to help readers who didn't know his nickname.

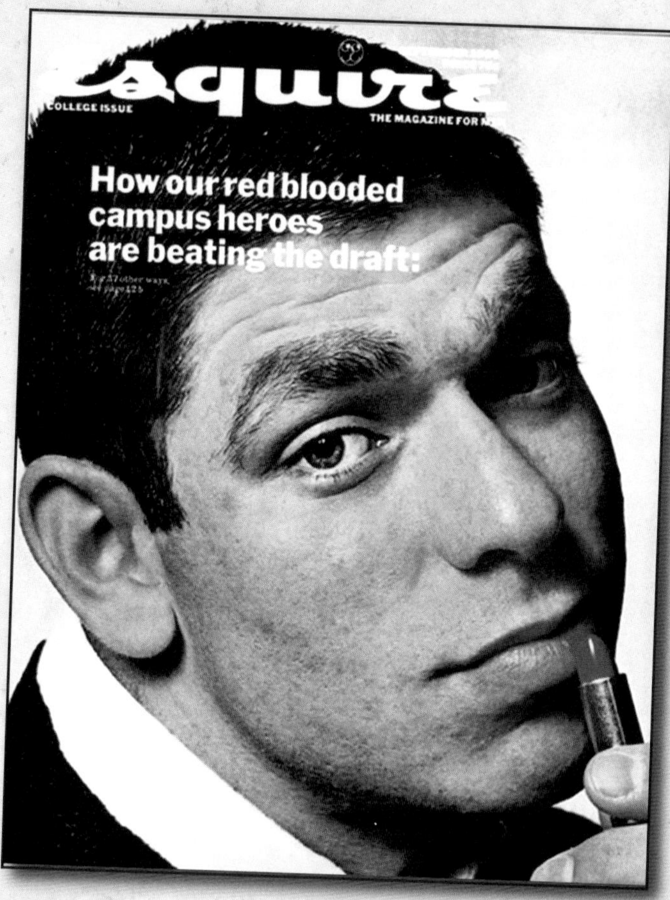

Cover to the September 1966 ***Esquire***. It was their sixth annual college issue. While the cover seems designed to appeal to students anxious about the draft, it also satirized students' efforts to avoid being called to serve, even, perhaps, tossing a barb at campus antiwar demonstrators. Is the magazine laughing at or with students? Possibly both, in order to appeal to the widest possible demographic. [©2011 Hearst Magazines Division, Hearst Communications, Inc.]

When the magazine came out, I showed the article to a few mildly interested friends at college and family members, who were glad that I finally had something to show for all the time, effort, and money I'd put into comic books. Eventually, after showing it to everybody who could possibly be willing to look, and some who weren't, I put the magazine away and didn't look at it again for decades.

As I sat on that tree stump, what I didn't know is that a year later, I would stop reading comic books, leave comic fandom, and sell my collection.

In 1961, Marvel introduced the ***Fantastic Four***, its first new superhero story in years. Although the new team reflected what would become the Marvel style, I don't recall thinking, "Wow, this transforms comics." The introduction of Spider-Man by Stan Lee and Steve Ditko in 1962 proved to be the dividing line between the past and the future. Spider-Man had nearly as big an impact on the industry as the introduction of Superman in ***Action Comics*** #1. Marvel quickly introduced more superheroes who had personal problems, issues with each other, and a ready supply of snappy comebacks. DC Comics, content with its #1 position in the industry, took a while to react, but eventually, its characters began questioning their powers, their identities, and their role in the world.

I don't recall my first superhero comic book in the 1950s. Perhaps it was a ***Superman*** comic—I was a fan of the TV series ***Adventures of Superman***, so that seems likely. Whatever it was, I soon abandoned my favorite Disney and Archie comics to spend my allowance on the latest DC Comics products and a few of the Wild West, monster, and astonishing tales comics from Atlas, Marvel's predecessor company.

With the DC Comics late '50s superhero revival and the Marvel revolution, I was one of the Baby Boomers who wanted the larger culture to take comic books seriously—and readers not to give up on them in their mid-teens. When reasonably large numbers of teens continued reading comic books in college, the media saw it as a trend worth reporting, if not entirely seriously. The *Esquire* feature is an example of coverage that reported on the phenomenon, but with a tone of adult amusement that suggests the trend might have been the latest in a long line of silly fads among college students who no longer swallowed goldfish or competed to get as many of themselves as possible into a telephone booth.

Looking back on my quote four decades later, I see that I

As a child, Weingroff was a fan of the 1950s ***Adventures of Superman*** TV show. Here, Noel Neill (who played Lois Lane on the show and in the 1948 and 1950 Superman movie serials) and series star George Reeves. [©DC Comics and Warner Bros. Entertainment Inc., All rights reserved.]

wasn't trying to be serious. I didn't think that Spider-Man was equal to Hamlet or should be read as if he were a character in a novel by Dostoyevsky. I was exaggerating to make my point in a theoretically humorous way that Marvel had changed the superhero stereotype and deserved to be taken a little more seriously than society usually did. The quotes in ***Esquire*** from the other college-age fans reflected this same serious-with-tongue-in-cheek viewpoint.

For a notable example, Jack Marchese of Stanford (arms raised like Spidey leaping off a building) said he liked the Marvel heroes and villains because "they are real" in their emotions and ideas. "Spider-Man exemplifies the poor college student, beset by woes, money problems, and the question of existence. In short, he is one of us." That may be the closest any of us came in the two-page photo spread to explaining what Marvel had done by giving its new line of characters the flaws we nonsuper mortals all share—as opposed to worrying about which color kryptonite is being thrust our way.

In a Publisher's Page commentary, Arnold Gingrich assured readers that the theme articles in ***Esquire***'s September 1966 issue were "tantamount to required reading for any sort of glimmer of light as to where we may all be headed." Like the Marvel fans in the two-page spread, Gingrich probably wasn't entirely serious. Forty years later, I know where we went, but I'm not sure these quotes or the other college-themed articles proved to be arrows pointing the way.

One thing was certain: By revitalizing the superhero concept, Lee and his fellow creators allowed Marvel's comics to retain their appeal as readers grew older. In response, DC Comics took its characters on a similar journey of change with the times.

As for me, I quit fandom and comic books in 1967 during my junior year at the University of Maryland. As Roy Thomas and a few other fans began moving into the creative side of the industry, I knew I would never follow them. I was an English major who wanted to write novels. I needed the time I had spent reading and writing about comics to focus on my goal. In abandoning a medium that had been part of my identity for half my life, I didn't experience the agony of cold turkey withdrawal I might have expected, but maybe I was too busy with school work and writing the first of several unpublished novels. Or perhaps I've simply forgotten how hard it was.

As it turned out, I wasn't successful as a novelist, but my experience as a writer in comic fandom proved to be good training for my career as a writer and "unofficial historian" with the Federal Highway Administration, which I joined in 1973 after graduation and 4 years in the Air Force. I look back on my years in comic fandom as an entirely positive part of my life.

Richard Weingroff in 2011, with the magazine that gave him what he thinks of as his Warholian "15 minutes of fame." By the way, that's *not* him on the cover. [©2011 Richard Weingroff]

I still don't read comic books, but I occasionally read a superhero graphic novel or collection. The characters are different than I remember, the storytelling is less linear, and the artwork less inhibited than in the days of the Comics Code Authority. But I didn't keep up with the crises and multiverses and other overlapping. At the same time, I enjoy the idea of superheroes. I'm happy to see how the characters have become part of our shared culture.

During the 1960s, I attended two comic book conventions in New York City where I met some of the writers and artists I had long admired. At the 1966 convention, I met Stan Lee as he was entering the meeting area with his "gal Friday" Flo Steinberg. When we shook hands, I was amazed that he knew who I was and recalled one of my articles. It was one of the high points of my years in comic fandom, and remains a moment I still recall fondly whenever I see him in a film cameo or TV appearance.

Or at least, that's how I remember it.

Stan Lee: The Marvel Bard

An interview conducted by Mike Bourne, 1970

This conversation is reprinted from **Changes** *magazine for April 15, 1970, and was located for us by* ***Barry Pearl****, Fearless Front Facer (a '60s Marvel designation of high fan achievement). It is reprinted with permission of Mike Bourne.[The interview also appeared in* **Alter Ego** *#74.]*

Marvel Comics spring from modest Madison Avenue offices randomly decorated by oversize drawings, copy, and other assorted fanciful diversions. In several small cubicles, like freaky monks, a staff of artists variously evoke the next month's adventures in all-brilliant color and style. While in his office, his complete Shakespeare close at hand, editor Stan Lee smiles broadly behind his cigar and beckons me enter his head.

The cover of the April 15, 1970, issue of ***Changes*** tabloid magazine—as preserved by Barry Pearl, FFF. [Art ©2011 Marvel Characters, Inc.; other art ©2011 the respective copyright holders.]

MIKE BOURNE: *With which superhero do you personally most identify?*
STAN LEE: Probably Homer the Happy Ghost. You know, I honestly don't identify with *any* of them. Or maybe I identify with *all* of them. But I've never thought of it. I've been asked this question before and I never know how to answer it, because I think I identify with whichever one I'm writing at the moment. If I'm writing ***Thor***, I'm a Norse god at that moment. If I'm writing ***The Hulk***, I have green skin and everyone hates me. And when I stop writing them, they're sort of out of my mind. I'm not identifying with anyone.

MB: *You're like an actor when you write.*
LEE: Yeah, I think more than anything. In fact, when I was young I thought I would be an actor, and I did act. And when I write now, my wife always makes fun of me. She says: "Stan, what did you say?" I say: "Nothing, I'm writing." She says: "Well, you talk to yourself." And I find very often I'm saying the lines out loud. And I'm acting! You know: "Take that, you rat!"

MB: *Asking a writer where he gets his ideas is like asking an actor how he learned all those lines, but Marvel is known as the House of Ideas.*
LEE: Only because I originally *said* we were the House of Ideas.

MB: *All right, but obviously you have mythological influences. And Jim Steranko's "House of Ravenlock" for* ***S.H.I.E.L.D.*** *was very much from the Gothic novel. But what are your primary sources, or your favorite sources for material? Just out of your head, or where?*
LEE: Mostly. I think it all has to do with things I read and learned and observed when I was young, because I don't do as much reading or movie-going or anything now as I would like. I'm so busy writing all the time. But I was a voracious reader when I was a teenager. And actually, I think my biggest influence was Shakespeare, who was my god. I mean, I loved Shakespeare because when he was dramatic; no one was more dramatic than he was. When he was humorous, the humor was so earthy and rich. To me he was the complete writer. I was just telling somebody this morning who was up here to try to do some writing for us to get as close to Shakespeare as possible. Because whatever Shakespeare did, he did it in the extreme. It's almost like the Yiddish theatre. When they act, they act! Or the old silent movies where everything was exaggerated so the audience

In this interview, Stan speaks of being influenced by "old silent movies where everything was exaggerated so the audience would know what the mood was." Here, Charles Chaplin in his 1925 silent classic, ***The Gold Rush***. [©2011 the copyright holders]

would know what the mood was because they couldn't hear the voices. So, actually, as I say, I used to read Shakespeare. I love the rhythm of words. I've always been in love with the way words sound. Sometimes I'll use words just because of the sound of one playing upon the other. And I know comic book writers aren't supposed to talk this way. But I like to think I'm really writing when I write a comic, and not just putting a few balloons on a page.

MB: *Do you consciously strive to catch the tenor of the times? You've covered campus protest in* **Spider-Man**. *But what about other issues? Do you feel that it's your responsibility as an artist—and I won't say "comics" artist here, but obviously we can accept you as an artist with other kinds of artists—is it your duty to take a stand on issues?*
LEE: I think it's your duty to yourself, really, more than to the public. See, this is a very difficult field. For years my hands were tied. We thought we were just writing for kids, and we weren't supposed to do anything to disturb them or upset their parents, or violate the Comics Code, and so forth. But over the years as I realized more and more adults were reading our books and people of college age (which is tremendously gratifying to me), I felt that now I can finally start saying some of the things I would like to say. And I don't consciously try to keep up with the tempo or the temper of the times. What I try to do is say the things I'm interested in. I would love to be writing about drugs and about crime and about Vietnam and about colleges and about things that mean something. At least I can put a little of that in the stories. As I say, though, I'm really doing it for myself, not the reader. But everybody wants to say what he thinks. And if you're in the arts, you want to show what you believe. I think that's pretty natural.

MB: *What do you consider your responsibility as a comics artist, then?*
LEE: To entertain. I think comic books are basically an entertainment medium, and primarily people read them for escapist enjoyment. And I think the minute they stop being enjoyable they lose all their value. Now hopefully I can make them enjoyable and also beneficial in some way. This is a difficult trick, but I try within the limits of my own talent.

MB: *Several years ago,* **Esquire** *published a collage of the "28 Who Count" on the Berkeley campus, and included were the Hulk and Spider-Man. What's this great appeal of Marvel Comics to college students?*
LEE: I don't know. I would think the fact that there's a sort of serendipity, there is surprise. You don't expect to find a comic book being written as well as we try to write Marvel. You don't expect to find a comic book that's aimed at anyone above twelve years old. And I think a college kid might pick up a Marvel comic just to idly leaf through it and then a big word catches his eye. Or a flowery phrase or an interesting concept. And before he knows it, not every college kid, but a good many of them are hooked. And I think it's the fact that here is something which has always been thought of as a children's type of diversion. And they realize: "My God! I can enjoy this now!" This is kind of unusual.

MB: *It's like the end of the one* **Avengers** *story when you used [Percy Shelley's poem] "Ozymandias" to reinforce the villain's downfall.*
LEE: Wasn't that great? That was Roy Thomas' idea, one of the best he's ever had. Beautiful ending that way.

MB: *I've always wondered that perhaps the appeal is the catalog of neuroses in the superheroes. That they're all into the numbers people are going through now. Human fallibility, altruism, identity crises, these sorts of things. Even your arch-fiends like Dr. Doom and The Mandarin and Galactus are not really all bad. They've all been forced to be bad, to be misanthropes, by force of circumstances. But when's sex going to come into Marvel Comics?*
LEE: Unfortunately not until we get rid of the Comics Code, or put out a line strictly for adults (which I've been wanting to do). But I just haven't been able to convince the powers-that-be that the world is ready for them yet.

MB: *Well, obviously you've broken some barriers by having heroes married and having children.*
LEE: Hopefully, someday we'll be able to put out a line—not that we want to do dirty books—but something that's really significant and really on the level of the older reader.

MB: *I recall one thing that wigged me in that regard: the beginning of a* **Nick Fury** *story where it was morning with a subtle hint of the previous night's activities.*
LEE: Oh yes, that was Jim Steranko's. Wasn't that great? I was very pleased that it got past the Code. Well, actually you had to

be smart enough to grasp that. But that's part of these stories. I think it's utterly ridiculous to shield our readers from things in comic books which they see all around them.

MB: *Where are you going on the race issues? I read, of course, where the Black Panther character pooped out because of the real Black Panthers emerging.*
LEE: Yeah, that was very unfortunate. I made up the name Black Panther before I was conscious that there is a militant group called the Black Panthers. And I didn't want to make it seem that we were espousing any particular cause. And because of that we're not able to push the Panther as much, although we're still using him.

MB: *Well, also it would have been strange to have a black superhero who is also the richest man in the world.*
LEE: Yeah, so the whole idea was a little bit off. I told Roy Thomas what I'd like to do with him is have Roy write the Panther so he teaches underprivileged children in the ghetto and uses his own knowledge and his own force and leadership to help these kids.

MB: *How about the Falcon as a black superhero?*
LEE: Now I think we have a better chance with The Falcon. We've used him in three stories, then we dropped him, and I want to wait and see how the mail comes in. I'm hoping it'll be good and I'd like to give him his own book. I'd like to just make him a guy from the ghetto who is like Captain America or Daredevil. No great super-power, but athletic and heroic. And let him fight for the cause that will benefit his own people. I would have done this years ago, but again the powers-that-be are very cautious about things and I can't go leaping.

MB: *How serious or how deep is the religious allegory in* **The Silver Surfer***?*
LEE: I think pretty unconsciously. I'm really just trying to write something kind of poetic and kind of pretty and kind of mystical sounding. I think you can read a lot into it. In fact, when I discussed the character with John Buscema before he started drawing the book, John said: "Well, how do you want me to think of him? You know, what kind of guy?" And I said: "The closer you come to Jesus Christ, the better." He has that kind of a personality. He's almost totally good, unlike most of our heroes, and I'm enjoying doing ***The Silver Surfer***.

MB: *But why "Surfer"?*
LEE: Actually, we're stuck with the name, because when he first appeared, he appeared as an incidental character in a ***Fantastic Four*** story. Jack Kirby just threw him in—I think the name was Jack's—and called him The Silver Surfer. I thought it sounded good and used him. Had I known that we would end up doing with him what we're doing today, I would have taken more pains to get a name that was more applicable. But actually, nobody else seems to mind the name. It's easy to remember and it's almost a put-on. And I haven't had any complaints about it. [**NOTE:** *As I've written before, Ye Co-Editor, who was in the Marvel offices the day Kirby's pencils for* ***FF*** *#48 came in, is nearly 100% certain that the name Jack gave the character in his margin notes was simply "The Surfer," and that it was Stan who christened him "The Silver Surfer." –RT]*

MB: *My walls and ceiling are papered with Marvel Comics covers, and one cat came in one day and said, "This is the most violent wall I've ever seen!" What about violence in Marvel Comics?*
LEE: I don't know. What the hell is violence? I don't think our books are violent at all. I think our books are the exact opposite of violence. I don't like to say this because it's become a cliché by now, but real life is violent. I mean crime, Vietnam, poverty, and bigotry are violent. There's nothing violent in our books: good guys trying to save the world from bad guys. If somebody punches somebody in a story, we throw it in because the kids wouldn't buy the book unless we did. Frankly, it's our concession to the younger readers. There has to be a fight scene somewhere. Just like you're not going to get any young kids to go to

Stan cut his eyeteeth writing "Shakespearean" (and related King James Bible/Arthurian) style in the first issue of ***Black Knight*** (May 1955), drawn by Joe Maneely. [©2011 Marvel Characters, Inc.]

a Western movie unless there's one or two shootings. But compared to the problems of the world today, I don't consider a punch in the jaw really violent as we do it. Even there it isn't a normal punch in the jaw. It's usually one invincible human being hitting an indestructible creature of some sort. You don't even get the feeling anyone's jaw is getting broken as it might happen in real life. It's all so totally fictitious and so totally fanciful that it isn't what my conception is of violence. I would call it exciting and fast-moving and imaginative. But I really wouldn't call it violent.

MB: *How do you feel about the gory publications that exploit violence? Those where you see spikes through young girls and blood spurting all over?*
LEE: Well, that's what killed comics years ago. We don't do anything like that. It doesn't particularly bother me. I think it's in bad taste. There's so much to be said and there's so many ideas to be brought forth that you just don't need all that gruesome stuff. And you don't need all the dirty stuff. It almost dilutes the message. Nothing wrong with good horror stories, but you just don't need the things that are in such bad taste that you don't even appreciate that maybe the story was good beyond that.

MB: *Do you feel that you romanticize war in* **Sgt. Fury***?*
LEE: It is possible. I haven't written ***Sgt. Fury*** for years now. I wrote the first few. And in the beginning I did not try to make war look glamorous at all. I don't think the people who are writing the book now are trying to make war look glamorous. But, of course, it can always come across that way. It's not our intention. If it does come across that way, it means we've slipped. We are certainly not pro-war, not pro any kind of war. And we try, even in those books, to point out little morals. We try to speak out against bigotry and other things. But any story you do that's a war story, no matter how carefully you do it, it's going to seem as if you're romanticizing war. Maybe if we did nothing but that one book and took the greatest care and spent a whole month creating a plot and making sure we plugged all the loopholes, we could let the book stand as a tremendous indictment. But in order to make the book an indictment against war and to make it as horrible as it would have to be, we wouldn't be able to get past the Code office. Because we'd have to show the horrors of war. So we're kind-of stuck there. We can't show violent deaths or anything like that. And ***Sgt. Fury*** is just something we publish and some people buy it and I don't think it's really doing any harm. And I try not to think about it too much.

MB: *Another thing I've noticed that might explain Marvel's kind of appeal is all our contemporary fears of annihilation, from one thing or another. Almost every month your world is about to be destroyed, or at least it's in peril some way. But we always know it's going to be saved and thus tension is relieved. Except that we know in real life there's no superhero to save us.*
LEE: Well, I think we all like to think that there are superheroes in real life. I think we all wanted to think that John Kennedy was a superhero. Franklin Roosevelt before him. Maybe Bobby Kennedy. For a short time we hoped that [Senator Eugene] McCarthy would be a superhero. I think that the human race needs superheroes, and whether they're fictional or not—obviously a real live one would be more satisfactory—I think if we don't have them, we're almost forced to create them. Because I think we're all consciously or unconsciously aware that the problems that beset us are just too big and too grave to be solved by ourselves. And we can either throw up our hands and figure that nothing is going to help, or we can

THE WORLD'S GREATEST COMIC MAGAZINE! APPROVED BY THE COMICS CODE AUTHORITY
Fantastic Four 52 JULY 12¢
MARVEL COMICS GROUP
Introducing: THE SENSATIONAL BLACK PANTHER!

Current events caught up with Marvel when a controversial organization of the 1960s used the same name as the Black Panther character introduced in the July 1966 cover-dated *Fantastic Four* #52. [©2011 Marvel Characters, Inc.]

figure that somehow somewhere someone knows more than we.

MB: *What's the power of comic books?*
LEE: Your guess is as good as mine. That's the thing, the one thing I'm not an authority about, is anything that happens after the book leaves this office. It's the power of anything that influences the people who read it. Human beings are influenced by everything they see, hear, touch, taste, smell. We sell about 60,000,000 copies a year. And if millions of kids and adults read these books every year, then they must have some power to influence them, to shape their thoughts a little bit. It's like saying what's the power of movies, or what's the power of anything.

MB: *But you do have this fanciful medium which would be perfect for moralizing.*
LEE: I try to moralize as much as possible. I'm always a little nervous and hope I'm not overdoing it and turning people off. But maybe I'm naturally half a preacher at heart. I find I enjoy it. And it's funny, because it seems that people enjoy it. Like I used one phrase in a ***Fantastic Four*** story once: "In all the universe there is only being who is all powerful." Somebody was talking about this all-powerful character having a great weapon. And I think it was The Watcher answered by saying there is only one who is truly all-powerful and his greatest power is love. I must have gotten 500,000,000 letters about that, saying how great that was and how it brought a tear to their eye and a lump to their throat and why isn't there more of that stuff in the comics. I may become the Lawrence Welk or, more probably, the Billy Graham of the comic book business.

MB: *Can you think of particular elements that mark Marvel comics more than typical escape literature? I suppose it's all these things we've been talking about.*
LEE: Well, I hope it is. And if it is, I would think—in music you might call it soul. [*When asked about the new wave of underground comix.*] I know there are reasons why these things are done. But I think what a damn shame it is that all that talent isn't used on something that doesn't have to be quite so vulgar, which is the only word for it. I sometimes think, as with the underground newspapers, too, that they very often use vulgarity in place of quality, in place of something meaningful. And I know it is all done for the shock value and there are millions of reasons. But I know that after the first flush of the underground surge is over, then I think these papers and these strips will begin to take their rightful place and really show the talent that's behind them, which I think is kind-of hard to find in many cases now.

The famous love scene from ***Nick Fury, Agent of SHIELD*** #2, July 1968, written and drawn by Jim Steranko. [©2011 Marvel Characters, Inc.]

MB: *How big a business is Marvel Comics?*
LEE: Well, our subscriptions are high, and we lose money on them. It costs too much to process them and mail them out. As far as how big it is, as I say, we sell about 60,000,000 copies a year, and that's pretty big.

MB: *What age figures are your major consumers?*
LEE: Rough guess: about 60% of our readers are under 16 and about 40% are over 16. We have an adult audience of a magnitude that comics have never had before. I've lectured at a dozen colleges. And I've been invited to over a hundred colleges, but I just don't have the time to go. And I don't say that every college is hipped to Marvel. But in every college there is a nucleus of students who are big Marvel buffs, which is great.

MB: *Before I came, I interviewed a Marvel freak, who had been a Marvel freak at Berkeley. And he's become very disillusioned with you lately and says that a lot of the Berkeley radicals who first went into Marvel Comics are becoming very disillusioned for several reasons. For one, he thinks you've lost the simplicity that you had at one time,* *that you've become so complex you're taking yourself too seriously. And he mentioned like the Sandman changing from the polo shirt to a more exotic outfit. And Paste-Pot Pete no longer the sort of funny character he was, but now The Trapster. He figures they've lost the easy identification.*

LEE: Well, it's a funny thing. We only did that last for one reason. We didn't sell enough copies when we used Paste-Pot Pete. I made up the name and loved it. I thought: there's never been a villain called Paste-Pot Pete. It was great, and it didn't take itself seriously. It was all tongue-in-cheek. Whoever had a Paste Gun? But the older readers loved it and the little kids—it wasn't dramatic enough for them. So, we're still a business. It doesn't do us any good to put out stuff we like if the books don't sell. And The Trapster attracted the younger kids, sounded more dramatic. I don't like it as much. We had a story once in ***Fantastic Four*** called "The Impossible Man." He was a funny little guy from the Planet Poppup, and he could do anything. He could turn himself into a buzz saw, and he gave the FF one of their hardest fights. And I loved him, and he was humorous and really far out, and the older readers were crazy about him. And that was the worst-selling *Fantastic Four* we've ever had. Because he was too unusual and too frivolous for the very young kids, and it made me realize, unfortunately, that I can't get too far out on these stories, or we just don't sell enough copies.

Paste-Pot Pete wasn't taken seriously by readers until he changed his codename to "the Trapster," although Stan preferred the original name. Here's the splash to Pete's debut in ***Strange Tales*** #104 (January 1963), plotted by Stan, scripted by Larry Lieber, penciled by Jack Kirby and inked by Dick Ayers. [©2011 Marvel Characters, Inc.]

MB: *The second objection was that he accused you of selling out to kids.*

LEE: Well, I try not to. But I would gain nothing by not doing the things to reach the kids, because I would lose my job and we'd go out of business.

MB: *So where are you now heading?*

LEE: I don't know where we're heading. Each day I get a new idea or somebody has a new suggestion. We have trouble just keeping our balance and meeting all our deadlines. It's a mad scramble. I'm sitting here looking, I imagine, rather relaxed now. But you've no idea. It's just panic all day long. We don't know from day to day what we're gonna do tomorrow. It's just whatever hits us. I would like to think we could come up with a million new ideas. I hate to sit still. And we have been sitting still too long. The only reason we're putting out these kids' books and things like that right now is that business has gotten a little soft. There's a little bit of a slump, and those are a little more inexpensive to put out. So it brings the whole overhead down a little by turning those out and enables us to continue the good stuff.

MB: *I've asked you where you're heading. So, where have you been? What do you feel you have achieved as an artist in your career? The most satisfying aspect?*

LEE: I don't know. I guess maybe the single most satisfying thing may be that I've been somewhat responsible for elevating—I hope I've been—for elevating comics a little and taking them out of the realm of reading matter that was deemed to be just for little kids. And making comics reach the point where somebody like you would be interviewing me about it. I think that's a hell of an accomplishment. Because it wasn't an easy thing to do. I think there's probably a lot more I could have done and I hope I'll live long enough to do a lot more. I don't think I've really done that much. This is like the guy on the moon: it's a first step.

MB: *Obviously you have lifted a popular diversion to not only a major business but also a very widespread influential art form. But what is the legacy of Stan Lee?*

LEE: I don't know. The only thing that bothers me about the question is that it makes it sound like the story is over. I have a couple of more years to go. A lot of people think I've started a certain style of writing, and when new writers come up here they say, "I think I could write in your style." I don't know what the hell my style is. I think I write in a lot of different styles, depending upon what book I'm writing. And, you see, there's another funny thing: people lose interest very quickly the minute something becomes too successful. People look for something new. And I think we're entering a phase where we've got to start coming up with new things. Because, otherwise, Marvel's had it. I mean, there was a time that it was very clever and very "in" to discover Marvel. Now everybody knows about Marvel, so now people are looking for something else to discover. I would like to keep moving with that crest, but in a slightly different area for them to keep discovering us. So I don't think we can ever stop. I hope we'll have all kinds of surprises for you in the next year or two, next time you come.

And just as I packed up my recorder, a plot crisis with Roy Thomas sent Smilin' Stan once again into the search for our future Marvels.

Endorsed by Stan Lee

Stan's salesmanship on display

Stan has always enjoyed being involved with ad campaigns, and used advertising strategies to help make the world aware of Marvel's comics. Here, a 1970s print ad with the ever-dapper Lee extolling the virtues of a popular brand of shirts.
[©2011 the copyright holders.]

Stan had been involved in a different kind of shirt ad a decade or so earlier, announcing one of the first Marvel apparel items to be offered to the public [©2011 Marvel Characters, Inc.]

Stan Lee Hathaway Shirts ad, Stan Lee Collection, box #7, folder #12, American Heritage Center, University of Wyoming.

Another sensational Stan-dorsement

The Coming of... Personna Man!

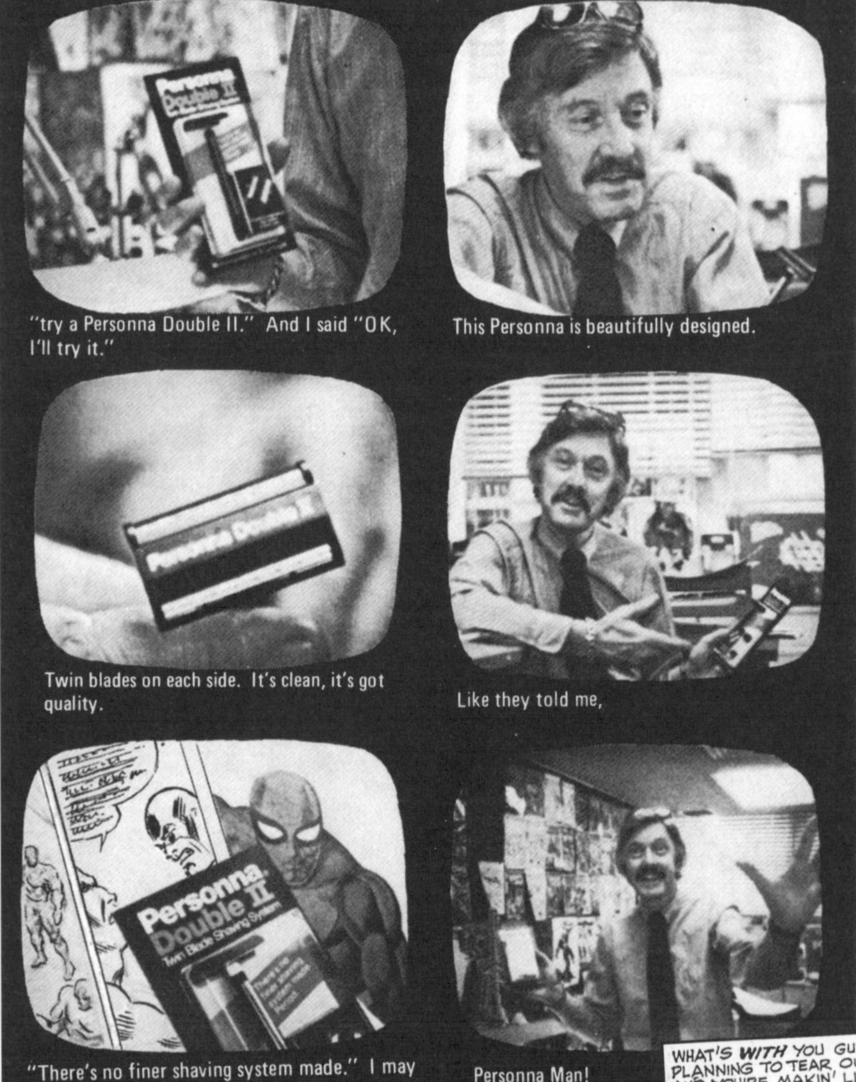

"try a Personna Double II." And I said "OK, I'll try it."
This Personna is beautifully designed.
Twin blades on each side. It's clean, it's got quality.
Like they told me,
"There's no finer shaving system made." I may create a whole new character . . .
Personna Man!

In 1976, Stan starred in a TV commercial for Personna razor blades. These screen shots from the commercial were run in ***FOOM*** #17. [©2011 the copyright holders.]

WHAT'S *WITH* YOU GUYS?? GALACTUS IS PLANNING TO TEAR OUR PLANET APART, AND YOU'RE MAKIN' LIKE A *TV SHAVING COMMERCIAL!!!*
RELAX, JOHNNY! WE BEEN TRYIN' TO COOK UP A *PLAN!*
NO HARM IN TIDYING UP WHILE WE'RE THINKING, IS THERE, LAD? *YOU* COULD USE A SHOWER YOURSELF!
NUTS! YOU'RE JUST *GIVING UP*, THAT'S ALL! *ADMIT IT!*

Apparently, Stan had been thinking about "TV shaving commercials" for a good long while before he made the Personna spot. Here, Reed Richards tidies up before facing off with Galactus in ***Fantastic Four*** #49 (April 1966). Script by Stan, art by Jack Kirby and Joe Sinnott. [©2011 Marvel Characters, Inc.]

The Man and the Work

Creators from the '70s to the present talk about Stan as writer, editor and art director

Over his career, Stan has worked with hundreds of outstanding creative talents in comics alone. We've heard from Golden and Silver Age luminaries, as well as the Missouri-spawned folks who helped Stan move the Marvel Age into high gear. Now, here are recollections of, and reflections on, Stan from comics pros from the 1970s to today.

[This article first appeared in slightly different form in **Write Now** *#18.]*

Marv Wolfman

Marv Wolfman *has written extensively for Marvel and DC, including runs on* **Spider-Man,** *and* **Fantastic Four,** *and the landmark* **Crisis on Infinite Earths** *maxi-series. Co-creator of* **The New Teen *Titans,*** *Marv also had a memorable run with Gene Colan and Tom Palmer on* **Tomb of Dracula***, and served as Marvel's editor-in-chief. Currently writing novels, animation, and video games, Marv is also the author of the recent award-winning non-fiction graphic novel,* **Homeland: The Illustrated History of the State of Israel.**

Here, Marv recalls what he learned from working with Stan.

—DF & RT

Stan wasn't writing quite as much by the time I was working at Marvel, and he was off to California later on, so I wasn't in any of those fabled plot sessions. But I did work with him directly on writing and editing of the books I controlled. He was a good teacher, although he probably never realized he was teaching. He'd point out character and story problems, show how art should be manipulated to fix things, understood what was important and what wasn't. He took a very relaxed view of the work, never going insane over it as many of us did. I think he knew this wasn't brain surgery or rocket science. If we did a bad book, nobody would die. But despite this, he was very firm about the books being the best they could be. He would often jump up and demonstrate how panels needed to be the most exciting moment of each action. He would get excited about the work, talk about the pacing and show us how to place balloons so they moved the story forward without covering the art. He actually was incredible about that. I'd often bring him a cover where I couldn't figure out the balloon placement and he'd solve it in a second.

Stan would extensively mark up copies of the book after they came out with all his thoughts, notations, etc. He would let us do what we thought was right, and rather than stop us before we tried something, he would let us know afterward where there might have been mistakes, or where things worked. I thought that was a great way of doing it; he encouraged our own individual voices, never asked us to write like him and actually preferred we didn't. But he firmly understood the characters and wouldn't hesitate to guide us in that department. He also very much cared about quality, and insisted the top books had to have the top talent. Stan also had a style that would enable him to tell you if your story was awful, yet somehow he wouldn't make you feel bad about it. I don't know how he did that, but you came out of a meeting with him understanding what the problem was and you'd work harder next time because you weren't being put down. It's just your story that needed improvement, not you. I guess one of his strongest points is that he didn't make the work personal, so you didn't feel awful if something you did failed to work.

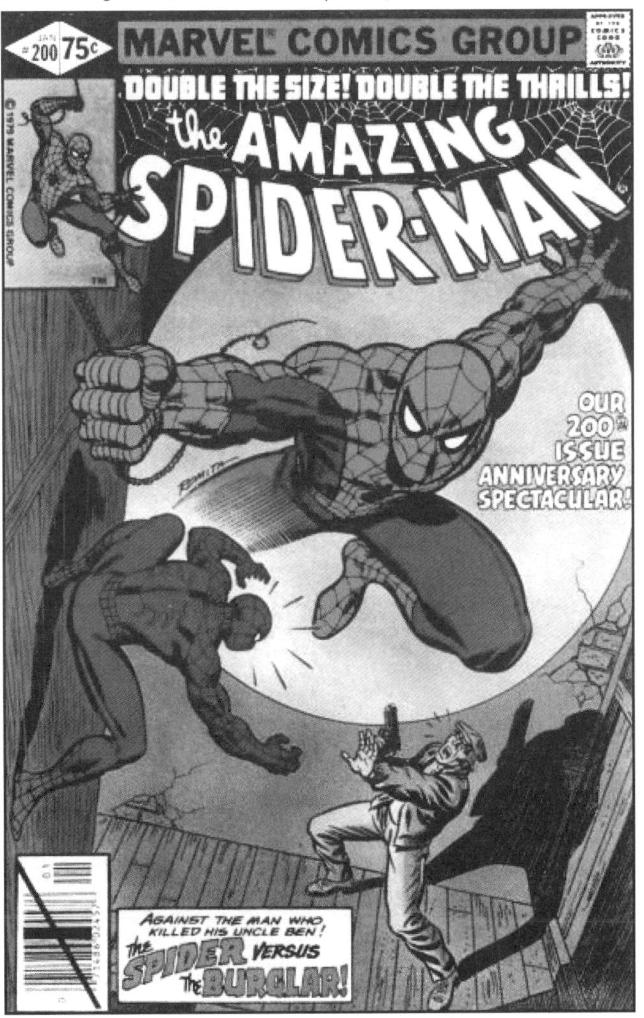

In ***Amazing Spider-Man*** #200 (January 1980), Marv developed plot-points first laid down by Stan in Spidey's first appearance. Cover art is by John Romita, Sr. [© 2011 Marvel Characters, Inc.]

Herb Trimpe

***Herb Trimpe** worked for Marvel Comics over a 30-year period, drawing many of the company's top characters. He read his first Marvel Comic while spending a year in the Central Highlands of Vietnam with the 1st Air Cav, and although he didn't know Stan Lee from Adam, wound up working for him shortly after his departure from the USAF in 1966.*

Especially known for his eight-year stint on **The Incredible Hulk,** *including stories co-created with Stan, Trimpe also introduced the Wolverine character of X-Men fame in the legendary issues #180 and particularly #181 of* **The Incredible Hulk**. *Other titles of note produced by Trimpe were* **Godzilla, Shogun Warriors, Defenders** *(those three all at once),* **G.I. Joe: Special Missions, Transformers,** *and* **Fantastic Four Unlimited.** *Trimpe lives in Rhinebeck, New York, and does commission work as well as the occasional freelance job. Check out his website at www.herbtrimpe.com. He can be reached at trimpdog@hotmail.com.*

Herb looks back for us on working with Stan.

—DF & RT

It's funny, but I think everything I remember is standard Stan stuff. Never saw him jump up on a desktop to illustrate a scene. He did do most of the talking, however, at least with me, but would take suggestions if he thought they were good. I'd go into his office and he'd ask, "Okay, what did we do last issue?" Then, we'd sort through some villains and pick one that wasn't being used by somebody else. Then he'd say something like, "Why don't we have the Hulk doing...," and he'd go on to lay out the premise of the story. Somewhere along the line he might have Flo Steinberg order his lunch, a grilled cheese sandwich. He always ate grilled cheese on toast.

The stories were simple and were quickly worked out. I'd leave the office and write down a short paragraph or two on what we talked about, and lay the story out from that. I got to fill in a lot of the details, shtick, and he hardly ever had a problem with that except the time I lettered "Mattel" on the side of a submarine in a Hulk/Subby story. He chewed me out on that one, free advertisement and all that, but Stan never really ever got mad or held a grudge. Not with me, anyway.

I think he hired me because I could tell a story, but he mentioned a couple of times that I "couldn't draw." True enough, at least not in the Marvel/Kirby way, and I was brought into the bullpen surrounded by some mega-talents.

He once took me to Philadelphia with him to appear on a local TV show, and we rode Amtrak out of New York. He was a riot—outgoing with other people and maybe a little bit of a flirt with the ladies. The safe kind, not something that would offend his wife Joan. He was fun to hang out with, but never talked serious opinions about this or that—not politics or religion or what was going on in the news or any of that stuff.

I was living in England when he appeared, I believe, at Royal Albert Hall in London (I may be wrong on that). Anyway, he invited me to appear with him and I did drawings on an overhead projector while he talked to the audience. He charmed the hell out of them.

As far as lessons go, I got a big one right up front. One time, in the beginning of my penciling career, I was working on a story, and after I laid out a few pages, Stan give them the once-over. It could have been a one-time once-over, the last one, because the work wound up in the wastebasket. That was my doing. He hated those pages, they were a little like EC comics of which I had been a big fan, lots of small panels. Stan got Frank Giacoia to show me how it was supposed to be done. Next issue, I thought my life in comics was hanging in the balance,

Herb Trimpe's cover to ***Rolling Stone*** #91, featuring future ***Sopranos*** writer and executive producer Robin Green's article about Marvel. [Hulk ©2011 Marvel Characters, Inc.] [Magazine © 1971, Rolling Stone]

and when Stan silently scrutinized my work, he nodded, handed them back, and told me to finish the job. From then on, no problems.

As far as the nuts and bolts of producing a story went, I think Stan indicated balloon placement on the pages themselves. I think if you look at old work, you might find evidence of that. How he wrote the script, I have no idea. That happened after the art was finished. Never saw one. I would occasionally put notes in the borders to clarify something, which was iffy, because it might indicate I could have laid out more clearly. Remember, Stan's genius (besides everything else), was that he had the artist tell the story, realizing that the medium was primarily visual. The words would supplement the pictures, not repeat them. It also gave the writer freedom to really have some fun offsetting the pictures with the dialogue or captions that was clever and witty. It's a shame that is a thing of the past, because it's what made Marvel great and it made comics exciting.

Gerry Conway

***Gerry Conway** wrote some of the most famous Marvel stories of the 1970s, including the always-controversial "Death of Gwen Stacy" storyline in* **Amazing Spider-Man.** *Gerry has written and edited at various times for DC as well as Marvel, and served as Marvel's Editor-in-Chief in 1976. Among his many credits, Gerry was writer and executive producer of the TV phenomenon* **Law & Order: Special Victims Unit.**

—DF & RT

In my first stint at Marvel, I didn't have much direct contact with Stan before I eventually went to work for DC. When I returned a year later to become Marvel's editor-in-chief, I worked more directly with Stan, who stood up for me when several freelancers threatened to quit after I demanded they start meeting deadlines in a timely manner.

As writer, Stan had a great impact on my life. It was his work, scripting the early ***Fantastic Four*** and ***Spider-Man,*** that inspired me to become a comic book writer. Especially during my first run at Marvel, I consciously sought to emulate Stan's style and approach to storytelling. Whether that was a good or bad thing, I'm not sure, but at the time I couldn't imagine a greater compliment than to be told I wrote like Stan Lee.

The final page of the Conway-written ***Amazing Spider-Man*** #121 (June 1973), penciled by Gil Kane and inked by John Romita, is one of the most stunning cliffhangers in all of Marvel's history. [© 2011 Marvel Characters, Inc.]

Sal Buscema

***Sal Buscema** may be the younger brother to industry legend **John Buscema,** but his work as a penciler on* **Avengers** *and* **Incredible Hulk** *earned him his own place the comics pantheon. Reinventing himself in the '80s and '90s, Sal's work on* **New Mutants** *and* **Spectacular Spider-Man** *was some of the best of his career. "Retired," he's doing plenty of inking, including on DC's* **Superman Beyond** *#0.*

His work with Stan ranged across the entire Marvel Universe and his efforts as either penciler or inker were always well received. (A word to the wise: Don't ever play pool with Sal for money.)

We spoke via phone on January 30, 2008.

—DF

***DANNY FINGEROTH:** You originally worked primarily as an inker, right, Sal? When did you start?*

SAL BUSCEMA: I started inking for Marvel in 1968. But I made the "mistake" of working up about a half dozen penciled pages and sent them up to Stan. I hadn't done any penciling, professionally, before that. When he got them, he wanted to see me, so I went up to New York. I had to commute from Virginia, so it was an all-day thing for me.

***DF:** Did your brother suggest you submit penciling samples?*

SB: Yeah, we talked about it, and John was a help, because he told me what they were looking for.

***DF:** What was the age difference between you guys?*

SB: Eight years. John would have been 80 in December, had he made it. Anyway, I went up to talk to Stan, because he was very impressed with the samples. I had done a six-page Hulk story, a very simple story I made up, about a mad scientist trying to take over the world. I didn't have any dialogue or anything. I just tried to show some continuity, that I could do the storytelling, and so on. I did very tight pencils.

The next thing I know, Stan is showing me some of Herb Trimpe's ***Hulk*** pencils. He wanted to show me the beauty of Herb's graphic storytelling. I looked at it, and I listened to what Stan had to say, and before I knew what was happening, the guy is leaping around the room, and he literally jumped up on his chair, and on his desk, to visually and physically show me the kind of drama that he wanted to get across in each panel. And, I'm telling you, I was terrified. *[laughs]* But I'm looking at this man, and I think, "My God, I hope he doesn't jump out the window, because we're pretty high up here." But it was a lot of fun.

DF: *How would you sum up Stan's approach to comics art, Sal?*

SB: I think I can describe it best in what John Romita said at Stan's roast in Chicago, where he said his experience with Stan was, he wanted you to just go all out, and do what you thought would knock the reader dead with the pictures that you were drawing—and then, before you showed them to Stan, think about it as not being enough, and go even beyond that. You're sitting down and you're thinking about a page, and you want this page to just come flying up and hit the reader right between the eyes. But then, when you've decided this is what you're going to do, then scrap it and go even beyond that.

Sal penciled the cover and interiors to the Stan-edited, Roy-written ***Avengers*** #71 (December 1969). Inks by Sam Grainger. [© 2011 Marvel Characters, Inc.]

John Romita, Jr.

John Romita, Jr. *long ago established his own reputation separate and unique from his legendary father's. Starting with* **Iron Man** *in the 1970s through runs on* **Spider-Man, Daredevil,** *and* **The X-Men,** *JRJR has become known as one of the top artists in the comics field today. He finally got to draw a Stan Lee-written adventure in* **The Last Fantastic Four Story.**

—DF

DANNY FINGEROTH: *You've known Stan since you were how old, John?*

JOHN ROMITA, JR: I met Stan when I was a young teenager, just growing up as a fan geek with my father. I first worked with him professionally when I was 18 or 19, in 1976. But we never did a story together until recently.

DF: *So let me just backtrack a little. It doesn't sound like you were ever in any of the plot conferences with your father or any of those famous car rides out to Long Island or anything?*

JRJR: No, but I did hang out with my father in car rides after his plotting sessions with Stan. I was getting the grumps and the groans and the anxiety over those plotting sessions, so it was pretty much second-hand plotting angst. "Oh, God, I didn't write any of this down, how am I gonna remember all of this stuff? Stan gave it to me verbally, and I can't remember what he said! How am I gonna fill all this stuff in?"

Page from 2007's ***The Last Fantastic Four Story***. Written by Stan, the story is penciled by John Romita, Jr., and inked by Scott Hanna. [© 2011 Marvel Characters, Inc.].

DF: *Didn't he figure out after the first couple of times that maybe he should write it down?*

JRJR: I think Stan would sneak up on him. "Johnny! I've got to speak to you." And nobody knew shorthand back then, let alone my father, and there were no such things as mini-recorders, so it was dependent on my father's memory.

DF: *So Stan never, as far as you know, gave your dad anything in writing?*

JRJR: If he did, it wasn't early on, and I would have firsthand information from my father when he would come home and start talking about it out loud to anybody in general. "I can't believe I've painted myself into a plot corner. How am I going to get out of this?" And then, of course, my brother and I would come running and listen. I don't know if we ever helped out, but we certainly were there as punching bags.

DF: This must have been when you were a little kid?
JRJR: Oh, yeah, when we were little kids. Well, '65 was when he started working for Stan again—he'd worked at Timely in the '50s. I was eight. And a couple of years after, when he was first getting used to Stan, and I suppose before Stan would give him written plots, those were the times that we, as young kids, would listen to him.

DF: Did Stan later give him written plots?
JRJR: I think so. I don't think my father could have kept doing it without that. He would have to have said, "Stan please, write something down!" Now, that being said, Stan might have given him three words.

DF: Didn't you come up with the Spider-Man character, the Prowler?
JRJR: Yeah. After I started getting interested in comics, as a kid, I started doodling and creating characters, like every young kid does. And one of the characters, amidst the trash that I was throwing at my father, was named "the Prowler." He had a standard costume. But, for some reason, I convinced my father to show it to Stan. Stan liked the name, and used it as one of Spider-Man's villains. I was given credit for it. This was 1969. So I actually got my name in a comic book, at age 12 or 13.

DF: Was your design used for the character?
JRJR: It wasn't even close. My dad redesigned it. He said, "The costume's gotta go, but the name is great."
DF: How did **The Last FF Story** *come about?*
JRJR: Tom Brevoort, the editor, said, "Listen, I've got this plot from Stan on the end of the FF. You've got to work on it." I definitely wanted to work on it. It was a chance to work with Stan.

DF: Any closing thoughts on Stan?
JRJR: I'm glad I was able to work with Stan at this stage of my life, because if it had happened when I was starting out, I may not have done any justice to his story. It was as much fun to work on because it was Stan as it was working on the FF. I had so much fun on it. This was full circle—me working with him after my dad had for so long.

Todd McFarlane

Todd McFarlane *revolutionized comics in the 1990s on both the creative and business sides. After a wildly successful run on* **Spider-Man,** *Todd went on to co-found Image Comics, for which he created* **Spawn** *(comic, movie, animated series), and from there went on to more great success with the McFarlane Toys division of Todd McFarlane Productions. I spoke to Todd via phone on May 30, 2007.*

—DF

DANNY FINGEROTH: *How would you describe Stan's legacy, Todd?*

TODD McFARLANE: Stan's legacy goes back so much further than just the inception of what people think of as the "Silver Age" of Marvel comic books in the early '60s. He paid his dues, he didn't just magically appear out of nowhere. He had a couple of decades under his belt by the time he made his mark. And then he found his niche. We were just coming from the Dr. Wertham witch-hunts, and Stan was smart enough to just go, "Okay, this is the way the world is now going to move forward."

Instead of fighting against the Comics Code, *per se,* whether it was right or wrong, he just went, "Okay, they want a more sort of polished, sanitized version of this

The cover to the January 1990 *Amazing Spider-Man* #328 (from the Hulk's grey period) features Todd's take on two of Stan's most famous co-creations. [© 2011 Marvel Characters, Inc.]

stuff, I'll give it to them." Or maybe, from his point of view, it might have just been going back to a version of the early Superman type of stuff, you know? "Okay, that seemed to work and didn't get people in trouble. What's the new 1960s version of this stuff?" And then he was able to grab some tremendously talented artists that would help give the pictures to all of it.

To this day, I think his greatest trait is that he's been able to keep the little boy alive inside of him for 85 years. He hasn't let the boy go away. Forty-five years ago, at 40, he was just being boyish and stuff, going, "I want the Fantastic Four to fight somebody big! What's the biggest stuff we can come up with? We've just gotta go large here. And let's get it universal, and let's get it infinite!" With Thor, he just made it big, and it just seemed so grand. And you went for a ride with it.

Dan DiDio

***Dan DiDio** is Co-Publisher of DC Comics. He also has an extensive background in animation, where he was Sr. VP, Creative Affairs at Mainframe Entertainment, where he was active in creating series such as* **ReBoot,** *and* **Gatecrasher.** *Dan's also an accomplished TV and comics writer, and an avid student of Stan Lee's writing techniques. Here, Dan discusses a couple of the many things he learned through careful reading of Stan's oeuvre.*

—DF & RT

When you look at some of Stan's early Marvel material, say the original ***Hulk*** series, which only lasted six issues, you can see that every issue, Stan was trying to figure out what direction, what attitude, for the book to take, and there was a different dynamic to the character every issue, until they finally figured it out in issue #6, but by then it was canceled. Another example was with ***Thor.*** At a certain point early on, Stan developed a strong, clear direction on what Thor should be, but it took a while and interpretations by several writers and artists before he got to that..

Something I always use as an example when discussing the use of themes in comics, is how Stan would use similarly-themed stories across the Marvel line. In other words, you have Mole Man, who lives underground and was a Fantastic Four villain. Then you had the Avengers vs. the Lava Men, Iron Man vs. Kala, and Hulk vs. Tyrannus. Each one of those stories takes place against the background of an underground civilization. But each one of those villains was unique, and played against the weaknesses of each of the heroes. Kala played to Iron Man's weakness with women. The Mole Man's ugliness paralleled the Thing's feeling of ostracization in the FF, and so on.

In today's comics, we'd probably have one character that played against all four books, and I think that weakens the stories, ultimately. Stan had one theme, but he found a way to enhance and grow the characters because he and his artists found ways to make the villains unique to each one of the heroes, so therefore they were able to exploit the heroes' weaknesses, which would make for much stronger stories. It's extremely interesting to see things like that, and you watch how the Marvel world builds slowly outward. It seemed there was an organic growth to the Marvel Universe.

In ***The Incredible Hulk*** #5 (January 1963), the Hulk fought Tyrannus, who ruled an underground civilization. Around the same time, other Marvel heroes also went up against subterranean menaces, but, Dan observes, "Stan... found a way to enhance and grow the characters because he and his artists found ways to make the villains unique to each one of the heroes." Art by Kirby & Ayers. [©2011 Marvel Characters, Inc.]

Paul Ryan

***Paul Ryan** has been drawing comics since the 1980s. Best known for long runs on* **Fantastic Four** *and* **DP7,** *Paul was the penciler on Stan's* **Ravage 2099** *series. Currently, he pencils and inks* **The Phantom** *newspaper strip for King Features Syndicate.*

Here, Paul recalls working with Stan...

—DF & RT

The year was 1968. I was eighteen years old and a junior at the Massachusetts College of Art. I was also a diehard Marvel fan. Along with some friends, I was going to make my first trip to NYC. New York, the home of Marvel Comics and my hero, Stan Lee. I wrote to Stan weeks prior to the trip, introduced myself as an art student, a Marvel fan, and asked if I could meet him when I got to New York. The reply I received was in the form of a standard reply card. "Sounds great, True Believer, but I'm just too busy. Good luck! Excelsior!" Signed: Stan Lee.

I did get my foot in the door on that trip thanks to a young man named Allyn Brodsky. Alas, no meeting with The Man. He really was too busy and out of the office that day.

Flash-forward twenty years to a comic convention in Edmonton, Alberta, Canada. I am one of several Marvel artists invited to attend the con. I was there with my then-girlfriend Linda (now my wife). To my delight, the main attraction at the con was Stan Lee. We met at the pre-con party. I was working on ***The Avengers*** at the time, and apparently Stan was familiar with my work. I never mentioned my failed attempt to meet him in '68. Linda and I had dinner with Stan one night during the con and he discussed his plans for a new project at Marvel. It projected the Marvel Universe one hundred years into the future. He would launch this new line of comics with a graphic novel. He was working with John Byrne, and Stan was very excited about the collaboration and his new direction for the House of Ideas.

As I mentioned, I was working on ***The Avengers*** at the time. John Byrne was the writer. I was the penciler. John kept me appraised of his project with Stan. John and Stan experienced creative differences over the project. John didn't agree with Stan's approach and just did his own thing. Eventually John took his work, which bore no relation to Stan's vision, from Marvel and shopped it around, eventually publishing it as ***John Byrne's 2112.***

I called Editor-in-Chief Tom DeFalco and asked him if Stan was still going forward with his project. Tom said he was indeed. I told Tom that I would be happy to help out in any way.

I was working on ***Avengers*** and ***Avengers West Coast*** at the time. Penciling two team books a month was plenty of work to keep me busy. Tom called a few days later and offered me the penciling assignment on Stan's book, ***Ravage 2099.*** There is no false modesty in the following statement: I didn't feel worthy, at that stage of my career, to work with Stan Lee. I asked Tom to clear it with Stan first. He did. Stan was happy to have me on board. So I kept ***The Avengers*** and quit the ***AWC*** to work with Stan.

Stan was fun to work with. I remember that he put a lot of story into the early issues of ***Ravage.*** I took parts of the first plot and turned the one story into a two-issue story arc. Issue #4 was based on a couple of paragraphs from the plot for issue #3. Stan was happy with the results.

Paul's cover for ***Ravage 2099*** #1 (December 1992), the first issue of the series written by Stan and drawn by Paul. [© 2011 Marvel Characters, Inc.]

Not long after we starting working together (and you have no idea how cool that was for me) Stan asked me if I'd like to pencil the ***Spider-Man*** Sunday strip. I was very professional in my response, stating that I would be happy to help out on the strip. Of course, as soon as I hung up the phone I started bouncing off the walls of my studio.

I'll always treasure our time together. Thanks, Stan. *Excelsior!*

Some ***Ravage 2099*** penciled concept art by Paul. [© 2011 Marvel Characters, Inc.]

Clifford Meth

Clifford Meth's *writings have been teamed with such artists as Neal Adams, Jim Steranko, Gene Colan, and Dave Cockrum, and been optioned for Hollywood films. His recent work includes* **Meth, Colan & Other Theologians** *(Aardwolf Publishing) and* **Billboards***(IDW Publishing), which featured an introduction by science-fiction legend Robert Silverberg. Here, some of Clifford's thoughts on Stan...*

—DF & RT

I can only imagine how many young writers have turned to Stan for advice or a blurb or, worse yet, an introduction to their book. It sounds like a full-time job for two people just keeping his fans satisfied. Nevertheless, as a young writer (and even as a middle-aged one) I benefited enormously from Stan's generous spirit. He is not only eager to help, but he returns calls and e-mails faster than most people's secretaries. Despite the showmanship, the charm, the shtick, Stan is one of the most genuine, down-to-earth, and consistently generous individuals I have known in this or any other industry.

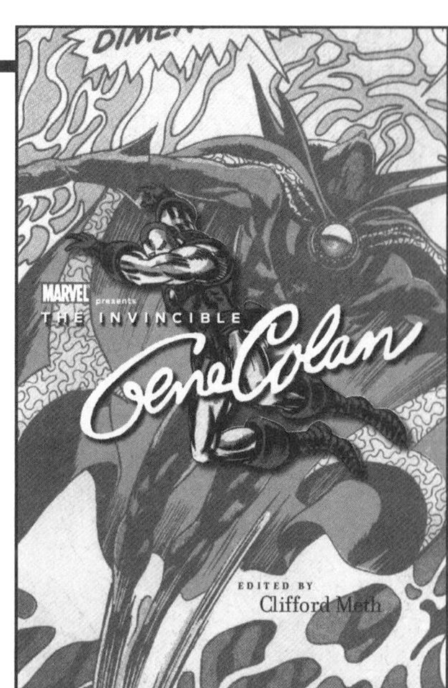

Stan contributed thoughts on Gene to the 2010 Meth-edited ***The Invincible Gene Colan***. [Iron Man ©2011 Marvel Characters, Inc. Book ©2011 the copyright holders.]

Arie Kaplan

Arie Kaplan *writes for comics, film, TV, animation, video games, magazines, and the Web. He also writes books. In whatever time he has left over, he draws cartoons and lecture all over the country. Recently, Arie wrote the story and dialogue for Legacy Interactive's* **House M.D.** *licensed video game, based on the popular TV drama. Here, Arie tells us how Stan has inspired him.*

—DF & RT

The first time I interviewed Stan Lee—for ***Masters of the Comic Book Universe Revealed***—I found him giving me the ordinary, softball answers that he'd usually give to most other journalists. This really frustrated me, until I realized I was asking him the ordinary, softball questions he was used to fielding.

So I went home and buried myself in obscure Stan Lee lore. I watched Stan the Writer mutate from workmanlike comics scribe in the 1940s to one of the greatest writers in comic books. I watched Stan emerge as the Walt Disney of Marvel, the public face of the company he helped shape since its infancy. Then I interviewed him again. This time, he opened up more. A lot more. We talked about such things as his work with the Federal Theater Project. And he shared stories about working on ***Ziggy Pig and Silly Seal*** comics in the '40s with Al Jaffee.

When I interviewed him for ***From Krakow to Krypton,*** he pointed out how selective memory is. We remember things in a certain light, but that doesn't mean they really happened that way. I pointed out that many comics historians are now saying that Jack Kirby based Ben Grimm on himself. Stan says that he based Ben on Jimmy Durante. I figure they're both right.

A huge inspiration for my ***Speed Racer*** miniseries was the Lee/Ditko ***Spider-Man***. I "Peter Parkerized" Speed Racer, and I'm forever indebted to Stan for showing me the way. With Spider-Man and the rest, Stan made perhaps his greatest contribution to comics: creating conflicted heroes with feet of clay. Without Stan, there'd be no ***Watchmen, Buffy the Vampire Slayer,*** or ***Heroes.*** When I interviewed him for ***Masters,*** he had this to say about Buffy: "She could be Peter Parker's sister!"

In 2005, I wrote a piece for the ***National Lampoon*** website titled, "Other Superheroes Who Got Hit By Radiation (But Weren't As Well-Publicized As The Fantastic Four)." One of the superheroes was "Secret Victoria," whose underwear can turn invisible—but only when she's wearing other clothing on top of it. As soon as that piece went online, I got an e-mail from Stan: "Congratulations, Arie, I got a real chuckle outta 'Other Superheroes Who Got Hit—etc.' Glad you weren't around when I was writing that kind'a stuff—I wouldn't have welcomed the competition!"

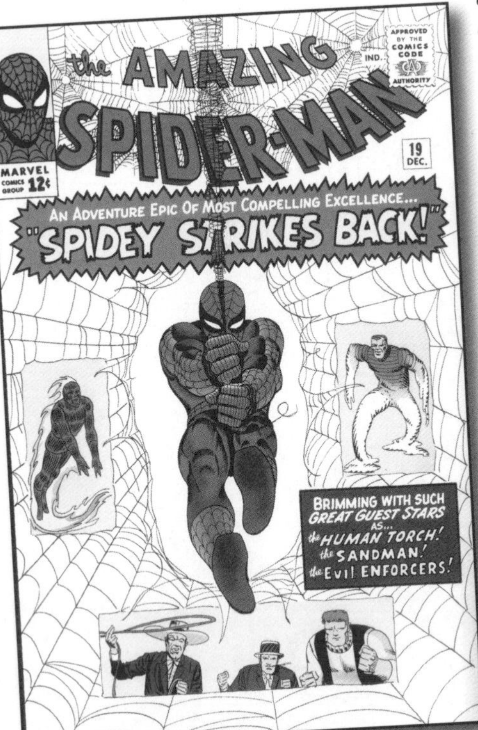

The Stan Lee-Steve Ditko run on ***Amazing Spider-Man*** was a big inspiration to Arie. Here, Ditko's cover to the December 1964 issue #19. [© 2011 Marvel Characters, Inc.]

Stan the (Family) Man

Photos from the Lees' personal collection

The Sept. 9, 2007, Sunday edition of ***The New York Times Real Estate Magazine***, of all things, spotlighted a major feature on Marvel's creative head honcho, with rare photos supplied by Stan and Joan Lee. Thanks to Stan & Joan for permission to print them here, and to Bob Bailey for sending us the scans. For more photos from the Lees' personal life, pick up a copy of Stan's autobiography ***Excelsior! The Amazing Life of Stan Lee***, co-authored by George Mair and published by Fireside Books in 2002.

[This article also appeared in ***Alter Ego*** #74.]

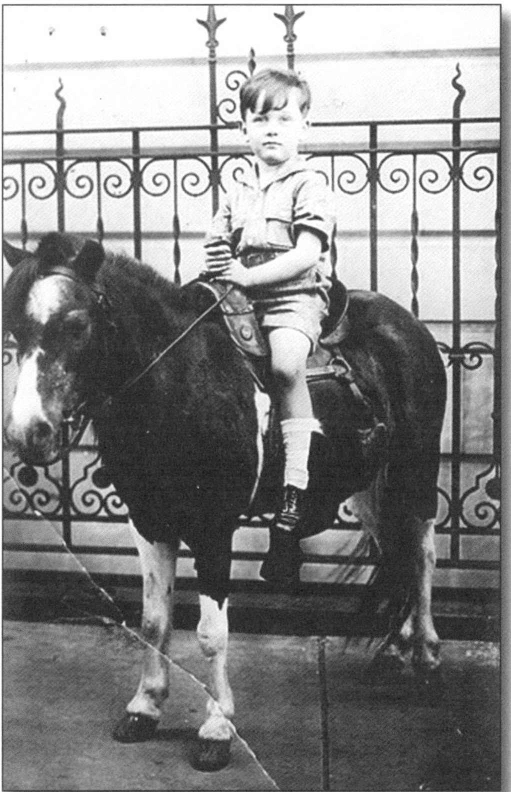

Young Stan on a pony. Any chance that its name was Marvel?

When Stan was 16, the Lieber family lived in this apartment house at 1729 University Avenue in the Bronx. Years later, future comics writer and editor Len Wein would spend part of his childhood in the same building.

Stan and Joan Lee as newlyweds in their one-bedroom apartment in Manhattan's East 90s, circa 1947-48. Stan married Joan Clayton Boocock on Dec. 5, 1947, just two weeks before his 25th birthday. In his autobiography, Stan's co-writer scribes: "Stan always thought she was the best birthday or Christmas present he ever got."

Stan prepares to carry Joan across the threshold of their new 3-bedroom home at 1084 W. Broadway, Woodmere, NY. The date on this picture is a rather vague "1949-52," but we really doubt if it took Stan three years to carry her inside.

Stan, Joan, and daughter Joan Cecelia in their new home on Long Island, in a pic dated "1951."

Here's the little family group circa 1953-54, in front of the same house, whose address is given as 226 Richards Lane, Hewlett Harbor, NY.

Stan liked to write outside, weather permitting—which gave him plenty of room for his two-finger typing style! This snapshot of a bearded Stan banging out a script at home is dated "1955-60," though since Stan probably typed out the note that says he was "about 30" when it was taken, that would make it closer to the early 1950s. The note says: "Always wrote standing up—good for the figure—and always faced the sun—good for the suntan!"

Stan, Joan (standing), and Joan Cecilia in the 1970s, in their Hewlett Harbor home.

Once in a while, though, a fella's just got to get out with the boys! Here's Stan with a couple of unidentified pals, reportedly at 220 E. 63rd Street in Manhattan, circa 1975-80.

Projects that Weren't

Ideas from comics greats Will Eisner and Richard Corben that never saw print

by Danny Fingeroth

FROM THE STAN LEE ARCHIVES

Even top creators have projects that never see the light of day for all sorts of reasons. In Stan's Wyoming archives is some early 1970s correspondence between Stan—by then Marvel's publisher—and two acknowledged comics titans, ***Will Eisner*** *and* ***Richard Corben****, relating to projects that never got off the ground.*

A classic Will Eisner *Spirit* splash—this one from October 2, 1949. [©2011 Will Eisner Studios]

Will Eisner

Will Eisner in the 1960s. [©2011 Will Eisner Studios]

Will Eisner *(1917-2005) was raised in the tenement Bronx of the Great Depression. He was a pioneer in the creation of comics of the "Golden Age" of the 1930s and '40s, achieving immortality with his noir crime-sighting hero, the Spirit, the first character to star in a comics insert distributed in newspapers. At one time or another, just about every comics great of his own and succeeding generations worked with and for Eisner, including Jules Feiffer, Wallace Wood, Jack Kirby, Al Jaffee and Mike Ploog. When* **The Spirit** *ceased publication in 1952, Eisner devoted himself to producing educational and instructional comics. Then, in 1978, Eisner reinvented himself—and the medium—with his graphic novel,* **A Contract with God**. *Other notable Eisner graphic novels included* **To The Heart of the Storm, A Life Force,** *and* **The Name of the Game.**

In 1973, Eisner, probably at Marvel's request, submitted ideas for a humor magazine. Eisner was no stranger to humor, using it often in ***The Spirit*** and in his instructional comics work, as well as in publications.

M E M O

TO: Stan Lee
Roy Thomas
FROM: Will Eisner

RE: Editorial Conference 2/12/73

The following is a general (tentative) plan for issue #1 of the new satire magazine, subject, of course, to second thoughts and quality of submissions.

FEATURES: (4 pages)

Review of the best ofthe underground-- write to: Print Mint, Rip-off Press, Krupp Comic.

WORST MOVIES OF THE SEASON: (4 pages)

Use actual stills if possible. Maybe Gene Shallit to review it. If not him we'll fake a review.

SECRET PAPERS FOR SALE: (2 pages)

Introductory page-- visual showing a display of papers (imagined) and facing it a page showing a Marboro-type advertisement. List a whole set of way-out documents.

PLANNING THE NEXT WAR (8 pages)

Make this the lead feature. Open with a meeting at the pentagon with general staff.

Things are very slow. We've got to plan a New War. The question of who comes up. The suggestion is two small countries in Africa. They run that through the computers. Plan it all out like Viet Nam. They send "advisors", etc. The "advisors" start calling for money. Russia gets involved. President ecstatic. He would get a third term. In the end, the deal is blown because the two countries have a Pepsi-Cola contract which, if a war starts, will be blown. The Pepsi-Cola people stop it.

Wind up with the general staff trying to think up another country...

THE OCCULT: (4 pages)

A visit to a Sabbat. Photo article, maybe people being changed into another thing. Maybe a Jewish-type mother serving food...ala Goodbye Columbus.

Will's Memo about "Editorial Conference 2/12/73" gives his overview of the points discussed on that day. [©2011 the copyright holders.]

Memos from Will Eisner re: 2/12/73 editorial conference and ideas for proposed humor magazine, Stan Lee Collection, box #7, folder #1, American Heritage Center, University of Wyoming.

Here's what this book's co-editor, Roy Thomas, who was Marvel editor-in-chief at the time, and was cc'd on Will's proposal, has to say about the project's development:

"I suspect the Eisner notes (probably written by Will, not by Stan, and I'm sure I didn't) is a follow-up after the lunch Will and I had about his doing a magazine for Marvel that would've been somewhere between ***Mad*** and ***The National Lampoon*** (because not as outrageous in terms of sex, language, and probably attitude as the latter). I don't remember much about the luncheon, except that we kicked around a general approach... the lunch might even have been after the notes were written, but I don't recall the notes at all."

In any case, for whatever reasons, the proposed humor magazine never came to be. Later in 1973, Marvel would put out ***Crazy*** magazine, edited by Marv Wolfman, which counted among its contributors... Will Eisner!

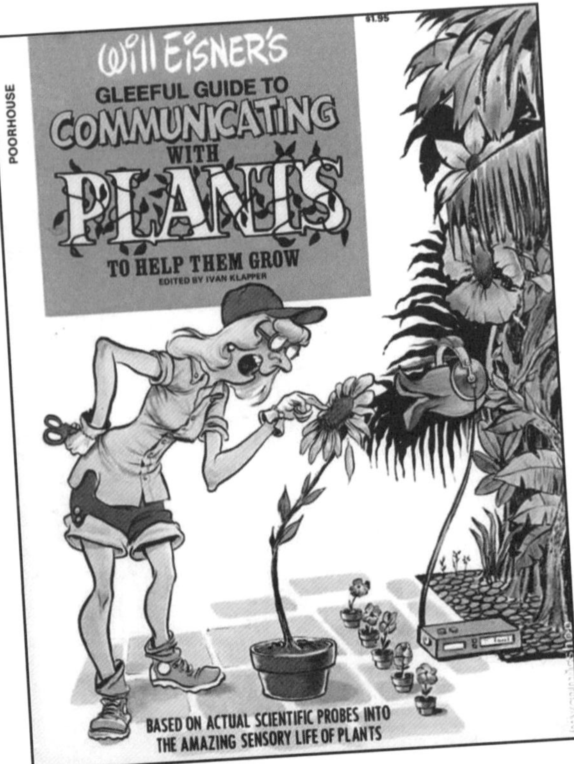

Eisner often used humor in his work, including ***The Spirit***. Here, his cover to the 1974 ***Will Eisner's Gleeful Guide to Communicating with Plants to Help Them Grow***, lampooning a then-popular theory. [©2011 Poorhouse Press]

Page 2
Memo: Will Eisner
Re: Editorial Conf. 2/12/73

SPORTS: (4 pages)

Football announcing-- what if the announcer were to tell the truth about each player.

THE MOTHER: (4 pages)

Series of cartoons on the mothers today-- perhaps a school for mothers.

INTEGRATION OF WOMEN IN ARMY (4 pages)

Done in Beetle Baily style, or maybe Sad Sack style-- try Baker (Harvey) he's in California.

SATIRE ON "NATIONAL SPITOON": (8 pages)

Emphasis on tasteles humor and the censorship. Maybe a censored version.

INTERVIEW: (3 pages)

Layout should show about 20 spot photos of the man being interviewed.
Candidates: Woody Allen
Gene Shallit
Steinberg
Cosby
Al Capp
Rock Star

FAMILY BIT IN COMMUNE: (3 pages)

Maybe father & son talk. Or, how about a series of spot cartoons on life in commune.

GUN CONTROL: (4 pages)

Display of weapons that shoulc be controlled. Maybe several senators and public figures (visual article) discussing their ideas in a press conference.

Then do a control arsenal (Avis-- or Herz) who will have a rent-a-weapon system.

THE AMERICAN DREAM MACHINE: (3 pages)

Try to get the T.V. show to let us run a photo article on them. Maybe do a playback.

A humor piece by Will appeared in Marvel's ***Crazy*** #10 (April 1975). Cover art is by Nick Cardy. [©2011 Marvel Characters, Inc.]

Page 3
Memo: Will Eisner
Re: Editorial Conf. 2/12/73

BOOK REVIEWS

Underground selections. The best of the Recent crop of underground. Run short sequences selected. Clean stuff.

GREAT GURUS: (2 pages)

Do a feature on a current guru and his philosophy. Really rip him off.

SUGGESTED SUBJECTS AND POSSIBLE TREATMENT OF POTENTIAL ARTICLES

SUBJECT — TREATMENT CARTOON/NARRATION/ARTICLE

THE MAFIA:

Who are the new types? Do they still talk with an Italian accent? Are they now using big corporation techniques. Are they all College men? What's the future? Sinatra has been seen with Agnew often...Sinatra is supposed to have Mafioso connections... What if...(Oh my God!!!) What if Agnew is a captive of the Mafioso-- Or how the Mafioso can put a president in office.

THE INTERNATIONAL DRUG TRAFFIC: PHOTO ESSAY

A guide to drugs and what they can do for you. Map of the world showing routes (suggested routes). A photo article showing people coming into LaGuardia and Kennedy, Rome, Marsailles, using balloons or quotations to satirize the scene.
The Poppy Crop In Turkey...A big year. TYPESET WITH PIX/GRAPHS Treated as a financial page article...Say, with graphs and charts-- like an economic report. Interviews with Turkish farmers and "distributors", "Heroin manufacturer in Marsailles."
Perhaps a funny bit about the farmer who is getting very rich by not planting poppies. Maybe do something with the fact that World War Veterans sold poppies for years (they no longer do it) to get funds for disabled Veterans.

HIJACKING...THE CURRENT STATE OF THE ART

Do a three pager which satirizes the present state of the art of airport search and detection-- bit about the effect of magnetic fields which recently caused someone's watch to stop. How about guy with magnetic bomb under his coat which is exploded by the detection devices Run several ads throughout advertising hijacking kits-- advertisement by tourist bureaus of poor countries who can't get tourists any other way-- "Come to beautiful Conga, we have accomodations...Hijack your next plane to our country--"etc.. signed by minister of tourism.

WARS AROUND THE WORLD: Cartoon or News Article/with illustrations

It may not have made the headlines and we may not have heard of it yet-- but somewhere in the world there's a war-- small war maybe. Perhaps a scene in headquaters where they're considering how to get the U.S. involved.

EXPATRIATES:

What about Eldridge Cleaver in Casablanca? What about the hippie colonies of Americans in various sun-spots. Like, the scenes on some of the Greek Islands that have drop-outs.

In this document, Will elaborates on some of the ideas from the earlier memo. The knowledge of what parts of these concepts were his, Stan's or Roy's contributions is lost to the sands of time.

PAGE 2

BLACK COUNTRIES WITH ANTI-WHITE POLICIES:

Funny sequence about whites (British maybe?) in a sort of white ghetto. The whole program bit in reverse.

THE CAMPUS: One scene/ big double page spread

Nobody on campus is in full agreement on anything except Vietnam. The campus scene panarama. The New Protests treated as a bird's eye view.

MOTHERHOOD:

First it was Philip Wylie's Momism-- then it was Sophie Portnoy. What's the New mother like. How about a school for mothers. How about licensing mothers?

FATHERS: Comic strip sequence

What about American fathers. Under the new marriage concepts-- what is the New father's role? This needs a parody-- perhaps a confession sequence showing the role of the father in each of the past 5 major eras.

MISSING PERSONS: One-pager/spots

Lots of people have dropped out of the news, some real, some imagined.

HEALTH FOOD: Display page

Layout-- display of the well known foods and what they're supposed to do for you.

SHALL WE LEGALIZE MARAJUANA? Ads, sequence feature

It seems almost here. Recently a Connecticut state legislator proposed that we legalize the sale of pot and sell it via state-controlled stores like, liquir stores. This is a fair subject for satire.

PAGE 3

THE SUBCULTURES, U.S.A.: 4 Comic Pages

A parody on the subculture. In fact a parody on proposed U.S. subcultures would be very interesting and could be funny.

PRISON REFORM: Display

Let's take different segments of society and envision what they (each of them) would create or design for a prison system.

FOOTBALL ANNOUNCING: Television satire

The announcers are always most complimentary of the player, what if they told the truth. For example-- ..."That last play was broken up by Pete Wozneack No. 43...Pete is one of the worst players in the league. He's dissolute and the coach would bench him for the season except all his other line backers are in the hospital.

EARTHQUAKES:

San Francisco is doomed, so certain forcasters predict.
How about a set of anti-earthquake homes.
How about a fantasy showing what would happen if the West Coast were separated from continental United States by a deep chasm. Would there be an attempt to start a new country? Would Reagan become king or president?

ACCIDENTS OF FATE:

What if Billy Graham was a door-to-door salesman.

More Eisner humor on the cover of the 1955 *PS Magazine* #32. [©2011 the copyright holders.]

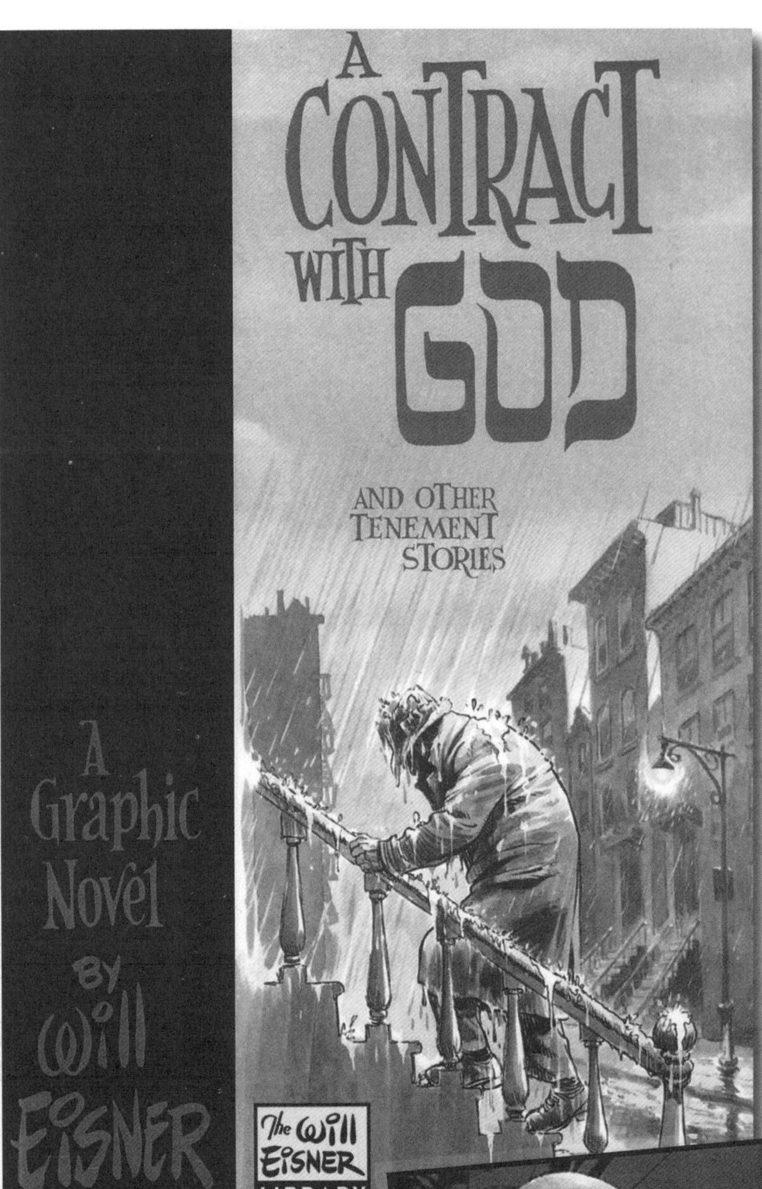

In 1978, Will revolutionized comics with his pioneering graphic novel (actually, four short novellas), ***A Contract With God.*** [©2011 Will Eisner Studios, Inc.]

Although the proposed humor magazine never saw the light of day, Will, Stan and Roy all, of course, went on to many other successful creative endeavors. As anyone who's ever tried to start a project from scratch knows, lots of good ideas get left of the proverbial cutting room floor.

Eisner's 1991 ***To the Heart of the Storm*** was an epic-length autobiographical work. [©1991 Will Eisner Studios.]

In the early 1990s, Stan hosted ***The Comic Book Greats***, a series of video interviews with prominent comics creators. On one episode, he spoke at length with Will. [©2011 Heritage Comics Auctions.]

Now, let's take a look at another proposed project from another top-notch talent... .

Richard Corben

Richard Corben grew up in Kansas City, where he studied at the Kansas City Art Institute. In 1970 he published his own underground comic book, ***Fantagor***. Afterwards he worked on the underground magazines **Slow Death** and **Skull**. Also in the '70s, Corben was a regular artist for **Eerie, Creepy** and ***Vampirella*** magazines. He also did groundbreaking work for France's ***Métal Hurlant***, known as ***Heavy Metal*** in the US. Currently Corben draws for Marvel, DC and Dark Horse Comics. In 2005 he worked with Rob Zombie and Steve Niles on the independent comic, ***Bigfoot***, for IDW Publishing.

In August 1972, Corben sent a letter and proposal to Stan...

August 28, 1972

[redacted]
Kansas City, Missouri

Stan Lee
Publisher, Marvel Comics Group
625 Madison Avenue
New York, New York 10022

Dear Stan,

I did like you said and thought very much about what you said on the phone August 17. I'm sending along my thoughts about a new comic which I could do and be published by Marvel. It would be sort of a "missing link" between regular comics and underground comics. It would be for mature readers and look completely different from anything you've ever published. I've gathered my ideas under several subject headings, such as Physical Description, Editorial Control, Advertising, Production Schedule, and Ownership. I bet you thought I merely wanted control over the story and art content. As editor, I have something to say about every aspect of my books. Most of what I discuss concerns the 1st issue of one title.

I seem to remember we agreed that my remote location ruled out the possibility of me editing a whole line of books. Also, such a step would be premature since we are comparitively unknown to each other. Undoubtedly, the following pages will discourage your ideas about working with me, but at least you'll know where I stand. I've found that the planning of this tenative book has helped me in finding what my goals really are concerning comic books, and I thank you for the motivation.

Sincerely,

Richard V. Corben

Richard V. Corben

After the cover letter came the proposal itself...

Richard Corben's eerie cover to January 1971's *Eerie* #31. [©2011 Warren Publishing Co.]

August 28, 1972 cover letter and proposal from Richard Corben, Stan Lee Collection, box #12, folder #1, American Heritage Center, University of Wyoming.

Exploring the Possibilities of a Corben-Marvel Book

The following paragraphs discuss several aspects of a proposed comic book to be done by Richard Corben and published by Marvel Comics Group. Although it would be related to the established comic form and the underground comics, I want it to look and be different in some ways. It would be aimed at an audience of young adults over 16. To borrow the movie rating system, it would contain material ranging from PG to X but done in accordance with my ideas of good taste. It would carry the "Adults Only" disclaimer on the cover. It would be competing somewhat with undergrounds and not at all with regular comics. I wish to create as attractive a package as possible and sell in the 50¢ to a dollar range. The book will also be related to the Warren hybrid because I want to have slick, high quality covers and printing.

1. A Physical Description
This book will be regular comic book size, 7"x10", and 36 pages counting covers. The covers will be on ~~slick coated paper~~ and I want the highest quality printing possible here. It will be my choice of 4 color process or hand made color separations and will have 150 line screens. The interior paper has to be a finer grade than you are using now. Even the underground comics beat you on interior printing quality. They regularly use zipatone screens reduced to an equivalent of 85 to 120 lines per inch. I also have seen ads printed on a finer grade of newsprint in 4 color process using 133 line screens. The result is brilliant compared to the average color comic. So, I require high quality color printing on the interior of the new book with at least 85 line screens. The interior color will be all hand made color separations done by me. I've had some experience with this kind of color work in the underground comics. I'll send you a copy of FANTAGOR 3 when it comes out to give you an idea of how I work with color.

2. Editorial Control and Direction
I wish to have control or a voice in all aspects of the book's contents and production. Of the 1st issue, I'll do the covers, create a host, write the stories or get a writer of my choice, do all the art (with the possible exception of the lettering), and limit the number and placement of advertising pages. I'll do all hand color separations and allow you to provide color separations of my full color art in the case of 4 color process. The host will be compatible to the books theme and will probably be semi humorous. The host will introduce the book; he may or may not introduce, narrate or make comments on the stories. If there happened to be a second issue, I might want to invite another contributor to be in the book and there might be a page for letters. You would make no changes in the art or writing without consulting me. Examples of people I would invite are Vaughn Bode, Jeff Jones, Greg Irons, Jaxon, Wally Wood, Alex Toth and many more.

The book's theme will be a mixture of fantasy, horror, and science fiction. Stories may be straight, humorous, ironic or satirical. I'd like to do adaptions of short stories of known writers such as Ray Bradbury, Phil Farmer, Robert Heinlien, Harlan Ellison, H. P. Lovecraft, C. A. Smith, R. Block, etc. This would be a big plus factor with our mature audience. I would do the adaptions and decide the length of the stories. I'm trying to push my book, FANTAGOR, in this direction too; so there would probably be a family resemblance between FANTAGOR and this new book. The difference between them would be better paper, better printing and better distribution on the side of the new book.

On the cover, I'd strive for a better organized uncluttered look in contrast to kids comics. There would be a strong title logo, a full bleed illustration taken from an interior story scene, the issue number, the price, the "Adults Only" disclaimer, a publishers seal, and that's all. No balloons, no captions, no repeat of the title in the corner, and everything but the title and illustration would be subdued and designed so that the emphasis is where it belongs.

It occurred to me that some of the most important points in this pre-proposal concern the extremness of adult material and how far removed will this book be from the comics code acceptance; so, I've gone over the code and I generally approve of it for children's books. The book we are contemplating is <u>not</u> a children's book and won't be subject to the Comics Code. I reserve the right to show complete nudity and suggest sexual activity. I probably won't show "intercourse of organs" as Warren once put it. There will be slang and profanity where necessary. I'll have no restrictions on violence or gore and I'll make my moral points regardless of respected institutions.

3. Advertising
The front cover, the back cover, and the inside covers will not have advertising. There will be no more than 4 pages of interior advertising. The choice of advertisers should be compatible with the book's mature content and audience. Uncluttered good design should be encouraged in the ads and their placement will not interrupt the stories but be inbetween the stories.

4. The Production Schedule
Production will be started after we agree on all other conditions. I'll decide on the deadline and it will un-

Richard didn't skimp on detail in his proposal. He had a vision of how he wanted comics to be. Unfortunately, it wasn't a vision that the comics world—at least Marvel's part of it—was ready for in 1972.

1971 Richard Corben art from his own ***Anomaly*** #3. [© 2011 Richard Corben.]

doubtedly be longer than any you're used to. I'll write or control the writing myself. The first things you'll get from me are the rough story breakdowns which will include panels, dialog and captions. Included with this will be sketches for the covers and inside covers. After you approve of these, I'll proceed with the final art. In the course of production, I'll have some camera work done on the covers and a sampling of the interior pages. Color key proofs will be make and sent to you with all the final art. After you accept the art, I'll expect payment for the book. You won't do any editing or story switching or break up the book in any way. You will schedule the book for the earliest possible publication. All artwork will be my property and returned to me after publication. The art will be copyrighted in my name. In the case of a contributor other than me, the copyright will be in their name. All characters and names invented by me for the book will be mine. The books title will be copyrighted jointly by Marvel and me with an agreement that neither will use the title without permission of the other.

In the event that this outline is completely unacceptable, ~~you wish~~ to go ahead with your own adult comic book, and you want a contribution from me, I'd like to know what your book's stand is on each of the subjects I've touched.

Richard V. Corben

Here's Stan's reply (reproduced from a carbon copy of the original letter) to Richard's proposal. Corben's ideas were more suited to what would, years later, become the independent publishing world. Story content aside, his business ideas weren't concepts any mainstream comics publisher was set up to handle in the early 1970s.

September 7, 1972

Mr. Richard V. Corben
Kansas City, Mo.

Dear Dick,

I appreciate the letter you sent me with all its information, terms, conditions and miscellaneous in-depth data. I've read it a few times, studied it carefully and unfortunately-- as I'm sure you expected-- can't find any realistic basis on which we can proceed any further.

While we try to give as much freedom of expression as possible to the people who work for us, we have always felt that the ultimate responsibility and authority for what is done under the banner of Marvel can only rest with Marvel's publisher.

I'm still as much of an admirer of your work as ever and I would like to close with the hope that we might be able to come to terms sometime in the future.

Cordially,

Stan Lee
Publisher
MARVEL COMICS

SL:cj

Again, despite the fact that Corben's proposal was rejected, he has been an extremely successful and popular artist over the decades since, including doing a substantial quantity of work for Marvel.

Corben's cover to Marvel's ***Epic Illustrated*** #2 (summer 1980) helped propel that magazine to a long, successful run.

September 7, 1972 letter to Richard Corben, Stan Lee Collection, box #12, folder #2, American Heritage Center, University of Wyoming.

Stan Lee: 1974

Re-presenting a classic conversation with Marvel's master

From *Comics Feature* magazine
Interview conducted by Jay Maeder

Comics Feature *was a professional magazine published for several years by the fabled Schuster brothers, Hal and Jack. This is a neglected Stan Lee interview from* **CF**, *located by* ***Barry Pearl,*** *who contacted interviewer* ***Jay Maeder****. It is reprinted by permission, for which we thank Jay profusely. And thanks to Barry for finding it in the first place. [This interview also appeared, in different form, in* **Alter Ego** *#74.]*

—DF & RT

JAY MAEDER: *There are probably worse things to be than the wildly celebrated king of the comics. I imagine you rather enjoy being Stan Lee.*

STAN LEE: It wasn't always this way, I must admit. In the first fifteen years or so that I was the head writer and editor at Timely and Atlas, I remember, my wife and I would go to cocktail parties and somebody would say, "What do you do?" and I'd say, "Oh, I'm a writer." "Really? What do you write?" And I'd start getting a little nervous and I'd say, "Uh, magazine stories." "Really? What magazine?" And I knew there was no way of avoiding it, and I'd end up saying, "Comic books," and suddenly the person's expression would change... "Oh, isn't that nice," and they'd walk away, you know, looking for some television or radio or novelist celebrity. That's all changed now. I go to places and I'm held up as one of the more interesting celebrities... and people go over to the playwrights, you know, and say "Hey, I want you to meet Stan Lee, he's the head of Marvel Comics, he made up Spider-Man."

And I must say I'm very happy that this has happened. It's like achieving one of my goals, because I remember I wrote an editorial, it must have been a good fifteen years ago, and I said one of our main objectives would be bringing some additional measure of respect to comics, that I would consider myself and our company successful if we found a way before we were through this vale of tears to elevate comics in the minds of the public. So that if somebody said, I write comics, or I draw for comics, people would say, "Hey, really? Tell us about it." And not say, "A grown man like you?" You know what I mean? So from that point of view I'm very happy now.

JM: *How did you get where you are?*

SL: Sheer accident. I never wanted to be a writer particularly. As a kid I joined the WPA Federal Theatre. I wanted to be an actor. But there wasn't enough money... and I always loved advertising, and the closest I could get to it was, I found a job writing copy for a news service, and then I started writing obituaries for people who were still alive, and I was writing publicity releases for the National Jewish Tuberculosis Hospital in Denver. All of which was pretty depressing. A million things, you know. I was an office boy for a trousers company, I was an usher at the Rivoli Theatre. Anyway, they had a contest at the *Herald-Tribune* [newspaper], an essay contest, which I won three weeks running, and whoever the editor was at the time called me and asked me to stop entering the contest. And he asked me what I intended to be. I was just out of high school, you know, and I said, well, I don't know, an advertising man or an actor or a lawyer or something, and he said why don't you be a writer?

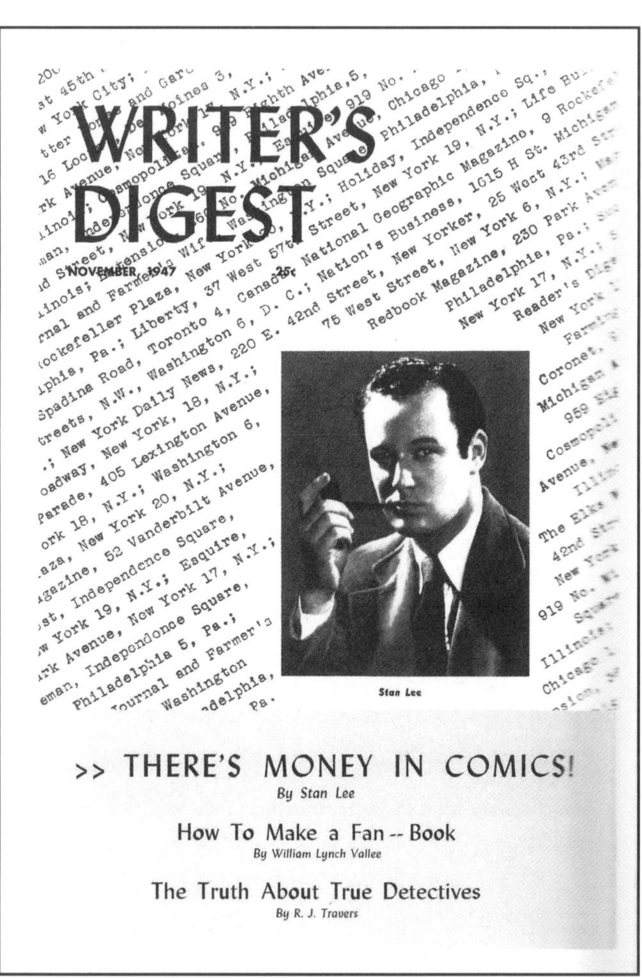

Despite having his picture on the cover of the November 1947 issue of ***Writer's Digest***, it wasn't until years later that, as he tells Jay Maeder, people at cocktail parties would start to be interested in what Stan did for a living. [Writer's Digest © 2011 F+W Media, Inc. Article © 2011 the copyright holders.]

Coincidentally, I learned of a job that was opening up at Timely

Comics. They needed a gofer. Timely Comics then had Joe Simon and Jack Kirby, and they had just sort-of created Captain America, and they were doing "The Human Torch" and "Sub-Mariner," and I came in, and before I knew it, they had me writing "Captain America" and they had me doing some editing. Shortly thereafter, Joe and Jack left, and I was like the only guy there and the publisher asked me if I could fill in as editor until he found someone else. And he never found anyone and I've been there ever since.

I never thought of it as a permanent job. I never particularly wanted to be in the comic book business and I always figured, hey, this is great, I'll stay here a year or two or three until I make some money and then I'll write the Great American Novel. And for years and years I stayed in the job, never thinking of it as my permanent career. For years this went on. And I was too dumb to realize, hey, this is what you're doing, Stan, this is it. I always had this feeling of temporariness.

And business got bad and we had to fire a lot of people... I was left with a skeleton crew, which consisted mostly of me. And we were living at Timely under the conditions where every few years there was a new trend. We'd be very big in Westerns and suddenly the Western field dried up and we had to find a new trend, and we'd be doing a lot of superheroes and then there was a lack of interest in superheroes so we had to find a new trend... and we'd do romances or mysteries or funny animals. Whatever. And there was no... I mean, I'd write one as well, or as badly, as another. It never made a difference to me what type of thing we were doing. The [Comics] Code was no problem to me. We never put out books that I felt were too violent or objectionable. They certainly weren't sexy. I never had trouble putting out books that would be acceptable to whoever had to accept them. So when this period came around, *it* was just like another new trend. Okay, we've got to drop the so-called horror stories and now we've go to find something else to do. And we did. We came out with... I don't even remember what we came out with, but I assume we found something.

JM:*The whole Atlas thing... this was not the greatest period the comics have ever known...*

SL: Yeah.

JM: *Atlas is into the journey into unknown world thing, you know, you and Kirby and Ditko are doing variations on the Japanese monster film, Fin Fang Foom and all this... and somewhere in here you start dreaming about a whole different approach, and what I'm asking is this: was this an accidental thing or did you guys sit down and very deliberately create a revolution.* [**NOTE:** Actually, Maeder is referring to the post-Atlas period of the late 1950s and very early '60s. —DF & RT]

SL: Both. It was accidental *and* I did it deliberately. What happened was, like I say, I'd been thinking it was a temporary job, you know, I'm waiting till I've saved up enough money so I can quit and go do something else. And my wife said to me one day, "Stan, when are you gonna realize this is permanent? And instead of looking to do something sensational in some other field, why don't you make something sensational about what you're doing? I mean, you're writing, you are creating... do something really good."

Well, of course, up until then I had always done mostly what the publisher wanted. As you mentioned, it was not a glorious period for the comics. Certainly not for our company. And our publisher, who also published other types of books—movie books and crossword puzzle books and so on, the slicks—by this time he had left the comics pretty much in my hands. He didn't have any tremendous interest. They weren't doing all that well and he wasn't that much concerned, I suspect. And coincidentally my publisher walks in one day and he says, "You know, Stan, I just realized, I was looking at some sales figures, and I see that National Comics' *Justice League* seems to be selling pretty good. That's a bunch of superheroes, Stan, maybe we ought to form a team of superheroes. Maybe there's a market for that now."

So all three things came together: my wife telling me why don't you do something good, the fact that I was able to do almost anything because the publisher wasn't that much on top of what we were doing, and the fact that he wanted a superhero team.

So I figured okay, I'll do it as I've always done it, I will do as

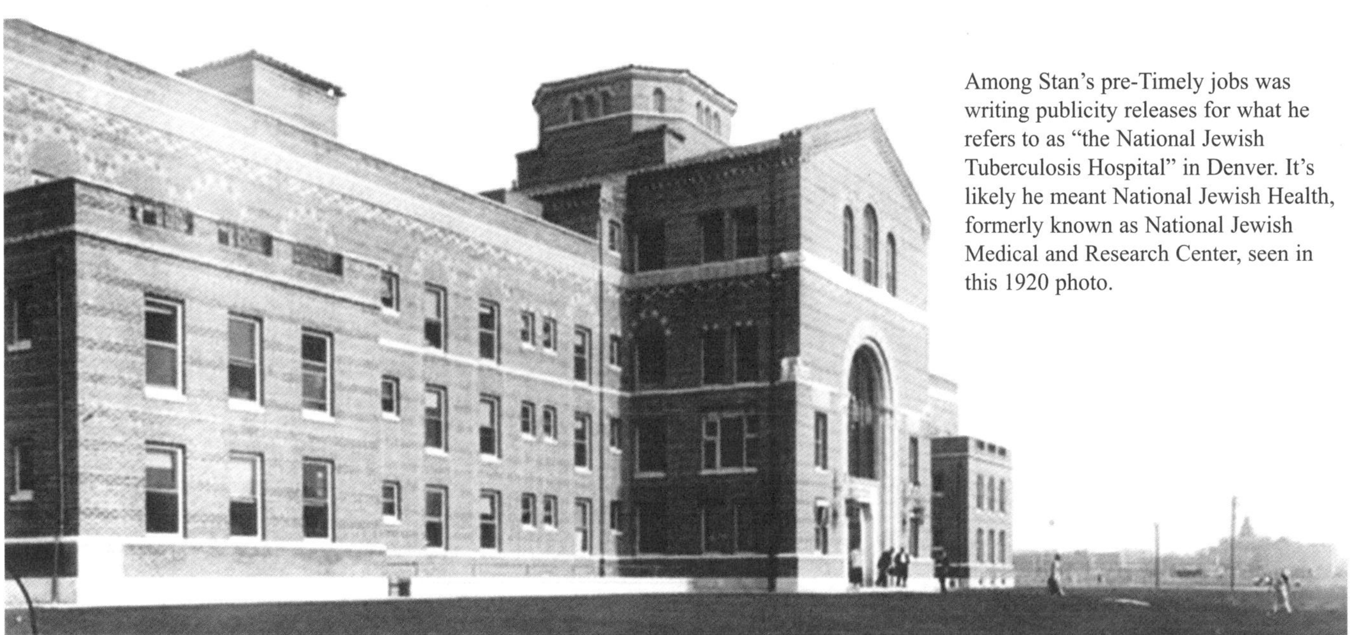

Among Stan's pre-Timely jobs was writing publicity releases for what he refers to as "the National Jewish Tuberculosis Hospital" in Denver. It's likely he meant National Jewish Health, formerly known as National Jewish Medical and Research Center, seen in this 1920 photo.

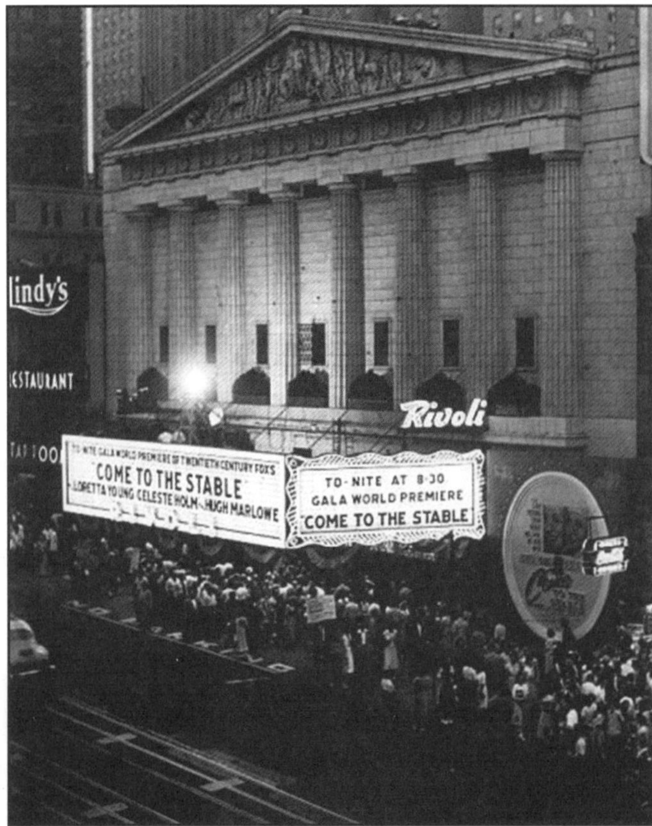

Another of Stan's pre-Timely jobs was at the Rivoli Theater on Broadway in New York. [Joe Coco Collection, THSA American Theatre Architecture Archive]

he says and give him a superhero team. Only this time I'm going to make it totally different from anything before. As different as I could make it. I figured, I'm sick of stories where the hero always wins and he's always 100% good and the villain is 100% bad and all that sort of thing. So I figured, this time I'm going to get a team of characters who don't hew to the mold. Fighting amongst themselves... the Torch wants to quit because he's not making enough money. The Thing wants to get out because he's not getting enough glory and he thinks Reed Richards is hogging all the headlines. Occasionally a crook gets away or beats them up. They're evicted from their skyscraper because they can't pay the rent because Reed Richards invests all their reward money in stocks and the market takes a nosedive... I tried to do everything I could to take these super-powered characters and in some way to make them realistic and human. To have them react the way normal men might react if those normal men happened to have superhero powers.

And then I carried it forth with Spider-Man. So he's got the proportionate power of a spider, or whatever. Isn't it still conceivable that he might have halitosis or fallen arches or dandruff or acne? Mightn't he have problems with money? Does it follow that just because he's Spider-Man all the girls are gonna love him?

I tried to figure how many fallible features I could give Spider-Man. Almost all of our characters. Iron Man with his weak heart, and the fact that he's a munitions maker and a capitalist and people hate him and think he's a fascist. And Captain America, who felt he was an anachronism because here he is a big patriotic figure at a time when patriotism really isn't in vogue...

And I suddenly realized I was enjoying what I was doing. I could have been writing movies: I was worrying about characterization, I was worrying about dialogue... When I wrote Thor I had him speaking in a semi-Shakespearean manner. Everybody told me I was crazy. They told me that no little kid is going to read stories whose characters say thing like "Get thee hence, varlet!" And I said the hell they won't. Well, Thor became one of our most popular characters, and I used to get letters from college kids who'd say I've been reading *Thor* and I've just noticed that you're actually writing in blank verse, the meter is perfect, it scans, and they started discussing it in class and so forth... and I'd get letters from kids who were doing term papers on the origins of Dr. Strange's incantations and they'd say, "Well, it's obvious from my research that you're basing this on old Druid writings." Which was nice to know, considering I'd never read old Druid writings... So I felt I was doing things that hadn't been done before. I was able to get away with it because nobody was really paying very much attention.

I tried to introduce style. Heretofore, nearly all the stories had been done, ours and the competition's, in the same style... the caption would say "therefore" or "the next day" or "meanwhile"... that was the extent of the captions. I tried to write captions that said something. I tried to develop an informal, breezy method of communicating with the reader. We inaugurated the Bullpen Bulletins Page, kind of a club page, where we brought the reader into our little circle and made him a friend rather than just a fan or a reader...

JM: *Your instincts are in advertising and promotion...*
SL: Funny you should say that, I was just thinking about that the other night. Thinking back, the whole thing was treated like an advertising campaign. The catch phrases, like "Make Mine Marvel" and "Face Front" and "Excelsior"... I did it unconsciously, but it all was in the direction as though, I guess, as though I was building a product. I wanted to make Marvel Comics a product that people... would love.

JM: *It probably has a lot to do with the general frame of mind of the industry in that doldrums period... because, you know, you're telling me that your wife is saying to you, well... look, Stan, how come you don't try to do something good. Because the implication here is that this is something that just never occurred to you.*

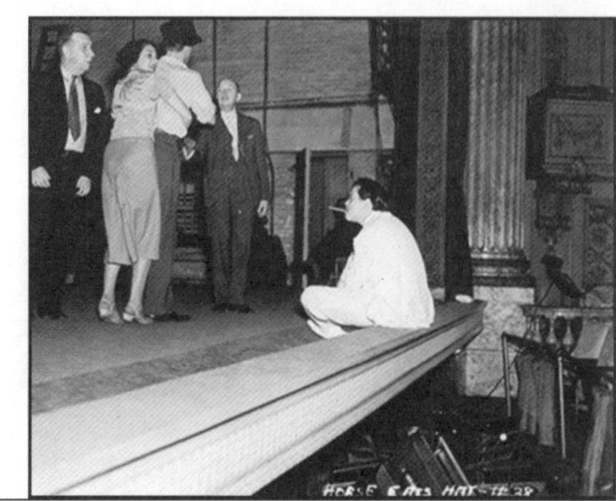

Pre-Timely, Stan worked briefly for the Works Progress Administration (WPA) Theater Project, though he never got to work with Orson Welles, here seen, seated, directing a rehearsal of 1936's ***Horse Eats Hat*** for the Project. [Federal Theatre Project Collection, Music Division, Library of Congress.]

SL: Well, that's right. See, I was always thinking that the good things I did would be done outside of comics. Because what the hell good can you do in comics? You know.

So if I'd get an idea for a story, I'd never say this would be great for ***Captain America***, I'd say, hey, wouldn't this make a great movie, I'm gonna make a lot on it. Someday when I have a chance I'll do a screenplay. So finally she said do something good in comics. And that really had *not* occurred to me.

Luckily and coincidentally, it began to happen at a period of time when a spirit of informality was pervading society...

JM: *Yeah, Marvel did to comics, I think, pretty much what the Beatles did to music, and of course we're talking about approximately the same period of time. It was a pretty creative period in general. You must have felt really swollen with fertility.*

SL: Yeah. It's true. It was a very exciting period. And the best thing about it, it hasn't ended. I think I have the same feeling of excitement at this moment that I had fifteen years ago.

JM: *Just how much have things changed? What are your current readers expecting from Marvel?*

SL: They're expecting us to be in the forefront. If there are innovations they expect Marvel to come up with them. We try not to let them down... I think there's a feeling of quality. We've sort-of become known as the Rolls-Royce of the comic book industry. They expect our artwork to be a little better, our stories to be a little better... I don't know that we always succeed, but we're surely always trying.

The change in our position now... the only problem is our own success has made it difficult to continue the way we're going, because we're putting out so many books... And a lot of it is a personal problem of mine: it's hard for me to turn down... if we have an idea for a book that I think is good, it's hard for me to say, well, look, we don't have the time to do it, we don't have enough men to do it, let's forget it. Because I figure, no, it's a good idea, and the time is right, we'll find a way to do it, we'll get another artist... And we have such a tremendous workload now that, unlike other people in other fields, our problems are never knowing what to do. We know the stories to do, we know the artwork we should be using, we know what the reader wants. We never have the problem of, my God, what if they stop liking our stories, what if we're doing the wrong things... We think we know the right thing to do, but it's hard to find the time to do it.

Joe Maneely's cover to ***Western Kid*** #2, dated February 1955, from Timely/Atlas's Western comics heyday.

JM: *And this is a recurring criticism of the Marvel Group is some segments of the fan press. That it spreads itself too thin.*

SL: And they're right. But for every one that criticizes us for that, there are fifty others who say, why don't you guys put out more science-fiction, why don't you guys give us more... anything, you know. And we always try to satisfy them and we always try to satisfy our own enthusiasm.

What we should do as we add new books is drop old ones, but from a business point of view, even our worst-selling books are making fairly good money. And you simply cannot drop a property that is making money, when other companies are just looking for anything that will show a profit.

JM: *Who is your market? Who reads Marvel?*

SL: Our market is not the same as our competition's. There are books for younger kids, like the Archie group and the Harvey group... Our closest competition, the DC line, has pretty much our market, but I don't believe, and they might deny this, I can't speak for them—I think we have far and away the largest older audience, and by older I mean of college age and in many cases older than college age. I do a lot of lecturing on campuses, probably a minimum of twice a month, and I usually lecture to very large and enthusiastic audiences. In fact, I would say I'm probably one of the most in-demand college lecturers today.

The incredible thing about it is here we are one form of media that not only seems to appeal to older people, but we still have as many younger readers as any other comic book group, if not more. We seem to have luckily found the way to produce a product that can be enthusiastically enjoyed by kids from the age of six to twelve and also enjoyed and appreciated by one of the most sophisticated and hardest-to-please groups in the world, which is the high school and college kids. So I'm very proud of that. I would think that's one of our biggest successes.

Well, I don't want to sound smug. Sure, I have great feelings of satisfaction, but there's a lot that I think we're doing wrong. I've been trapped into, as I say, I think I made a mistake somewhere by having so many books, and I don't know what the

Thor speaking in "a semi-Shakespearean manner." Script by Stan, art by Jack Kirby and Bill Everett, from ***Thor*** #143 (August 1967). [©2011 Marvel Characters, Inc.]

answer is to that. It's frustrating. I don't have time to personally supervise every one the way I did years ago. You remember I told you this company published other magazines as well, the slicks—well, I've been made publisher of those, too. I don't have a minute to turn around. And I wish there were more hours in the day, because some things aren't being handled as meticulous as I would like to do them...

JM: *Which brings us to something that is bound to be a fairly big item in the fan press. A couple of years back you moved out of the editor's chair, and it was widely believed at the time that Roy Thomas was your heir apparent.*
SL: Yeah.

JM: *He isn't in that editor's chair anymore, and apparently you will be devoting more of your energies to the day-to-day editorial product, more so than you have been in the last couple of years.*
SL: Right.

JM: *What's going on up there?*
SL: Well. Roy... who I think is just one of the most talented guys that... we have been so lucky to have had him all of these years... he's made it possible for me to go on to somewhat other duties and still feel secure for the comics. But, for one reason or another, Roy felt that he'd rather spend more time writing. I think Roy... I don't know how you're going to write this, and I don't know how to word it so it will sound right... as you move higher in the executive level here, it involves getting more involved the business area. And there are certain decisions made in business that sometimes go against the grain creatively but which have to be lived with. And I'm aware of these things, and Roy... would fight them. Quite a bit.

And I just felt there was getting to be almost a political problem. Not between Roy and me. But just, I felt Roy was spending—I think Roy felt this, too—he was spending so much time having to worry about conflicts between the business end and the creative end. And so forth. We sort-of decided that it might be better if Roy just... he's going to still be an editor, he'll still edit the books he's doing. And he'll be editor emeritus, so to speak.

And I felt also, maybe it is better for me to get back into this as much as possible, because Marvel in the beginning had been so much a—well, I don't want to say a one-man operation, but... I just think maybe it's easier if I'm a little closer on top of everything.

And I have a feeling I've said this wrong and I'm going to hate the way you write it.

JM: *Well, corporation politics are interesting... I'm not sure to what extent, though, that...*
SL: Please don't make it sound like I'm knocking the corporation.

JM: *Yeah, I understand that you're not. I think we're going to need to deal bluntly with the circumstances of the resignation. Was it entirely voluntary on his* part*?*
SL: I think it was, yes. I mean, Roy and I are very friendly. He's going to be working exclusively for us. It's just... he'll be able to devote himself purely to the creative end. He'll not have to be bothered with all the matters of company policy, you know, at the business level.

JM: *Because it's been common* rumor *in the fan press for a while that Lee simply hasn't been very happy with the directions the line had taken. The thing with, you know, there was a story about Stan Lee picking up a copy of* **Thor** *after not having seen it for months, and...*
SL: You know, you're faced with these things, and what can you do? I don't have time to write refutations. I had picked up a magazine, that was one instance out of thousands of instances, I'm always picking up the magazines, and I was usually always saying, hey Roy, Jesus, I just looked at the *FF*, what a great story, you never-told me about that plot, it's sensational... I just picked up this, where did you get this artist, he's the best one I've seen... One day I picked up a ***Thor*** and I said, hey, you know, a few of these words, the sentence structure seems to be a little bit different... I don't even remember what I disagreed about. I said, "I have the feeling he's a little off the track here, and I wanted to mention it"... we spoke to the writer and... I mean, it was an absolutely nothing incident.

JM: *Would it be fair to say that, inasmuch as you are planning to return to closer control of the day-to-day product, that there was, to one degree or another, a feeling on your part that things were off the track?*
SL: No, I just feel that it needs somebody... it probably needs one person who would be able to have the... correct *overview.* And I think, at the moment, I'm the logical person.

You see, we had so many books it was virtually becoming impossible for Roy to edit them. If you're producing fifty books a month, how the hell can you edit them if you're one person?

There ain't even time to *read* them. After a while an editor becomes almost a traffic manager. I really don't think that editorially we had gotten off the track. And I'm not saying this politically. Don't forget, I was always in editorial control, I was always determining what books we would put out and what the style would be. I would oversee the covers. And Roy would discuss with me any major policy changes if the storylines were going to take unusual directions.

But I left the actual editing and art direction to Roy. And I was perfectly happy, the books were absolutely in the direction I wanted them to be. Had they not been, I would have changed them. Because it's much too important a business, and too personal a business, for me to allow the books not to be the way I feel they should be.

At the time of this interview, Marvel's vampire comics were surging in popularity. Here, the cover to ***Tomb of Dracula*** #24, September 1974. Art by Gil Kane and Tom Palmer.

JM: *In any case, you're going to be taking a firmer stance at the helm, and the question is what's going to happen* now *at Marvel in ways that the Marvelite will find apparent?*

SL: I don't think there's going to be much difference. We have some very good other editors. We have Marv Wolfman who'll be devoting himself to the black-&-white books mostly. We have Len Wein, who will be devoting himself to the color comics mostly. We have John Romita, who I'm going to be working with closely.

And we still have Roy, who's going to be writing most of our important books and who's going to be available to consult with me just about all the time. He'll be doing *Conan*, probably the *Fantastic Four*, *Dracula*... it will be his choice, whatever books he wants to do. I'll give him that option, certainly.

JM: *Will you be doing any writing at all?*

SL: I would love to, but at the moment it doesn't look as though I'm going to have time. The one book I've been wanting to bring back, *The Silver Surfer*... I keep delaying it, because it's one character I don't want to bring back unless I can write him myself. And... I don't know, it looks like I just get busier and busier. There are screenplays I'm supposed to be writing, that I've committed myself to, and I keep putting those off because I don't have time. And I have a feeling we'll have to do a sequel to the book *The Origin of Marvel Comics*, and I don't know when I'm going to write that.

JM: *What are Marvel's top-selling titles today?*

SL: Spider-Man is still our biggest character. And Conan is very big. The so-called vampire, werewolf, that particular field, whatever you call it, that's doing well. The kung fu has done fantastically well. The beautiful thing is that the difference between our top-selling books and our just regular books isn't very great. Virtually everything we're doing is doing well. I have the feeling that Cadence Industries is really totally delighted with the progress of Marvel.

JM: *The success you've had with the vampire material is interesting in its own right, because it wasn't so many years ago that you couldn't produce something like that. Do you think the Code will loosen up any more?*

SL: Not really that much more. You know, we're still always conscious that we're producing a lot of books for very young kids. I don't see how it can loosen up much more. But by the same token the Code has to be reasonable. If any little kid six years of age can go to movies and see pictures that are just one

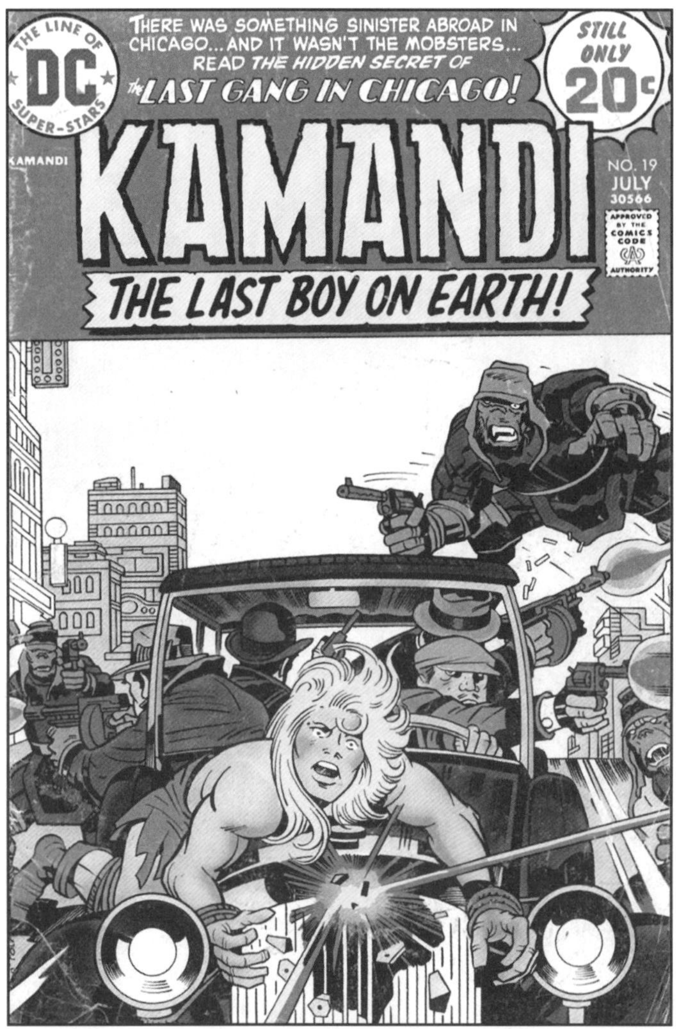

THE LINE OF DC SUPER-STARS
THERE WAS SOMETHING SINISTER ABROAD IN CHICAGO... AND IT WASN'T THE MOBSTERS... READ THE HIDDEN SECRET OF THE LAST GANG IN CHICAGO!
STILL ONLY 20¢
KAMANDI
KAMANDI
NO. 19 JULY 30566
THE LAST BOY ON EARTH!

Around the time of this interview, with Stan discussing the possibility of Jack Kirby's returning to Marvel, Kirby was writing, penciling and editing titles including ***Kamandi, the Last Boy on Earth*** for DC Comics. Here's the cover to issue #19, cover dated July 1974, the same year as the Maeder-Lee conversation. (Kirby would indeed return, with an announcement about it the following summer, and his first new Marvel titles debuting in early 1976.) [©2011 DC Comics, Inc.]

bloodbath after another and can watch things of that sort on television hour after hour... apparently it's the feeling of the Code that it's very silly not to allow even the mention of the name "vampire"... but I think that, compared to most of the other things that kids are exposed to, our books are still rather tame.

JM: *Why did Jack Kirby leave Marvel?*
SL: Oh... I don't even know the real reason. I suspect that Jack just felt maybe like I felt after all those years, I wanted to do something different... that he wanted to do his own thing. The first few years of his career, so many things said "by Joe Simon and Jack Kirby"... I suspect he woke up one morning and said, "Gee, all these years everything has said 'by Stan Lee and Jack Kirby,'" and he probably wanted to prove how good he is on his own.

I know we never had a fight. We got along beautifully. I have the utmost respect for his ability and I wish he'd come back.

JM: *There was talk, at the time the [DC Fourth World] trilogy folded, that he was in fact returning to Marvel.*
SL: Yes. I'd met Jack once or twice and told him I'd like to have him back and he seemed very interested. But the last time... I don't know. Jack is a rather personal person. He keeps things to himself. I don't know what his plans are at this point.

JM: *What's your competition doing that you enjoy?*
SL: I don't want to sound like the kind of guy who isn't up on what's happening in the field, but I simply, in the past six months, haven't had time to look at their books. I look at the type of books they're putting out... the 60¢ books and the 20¢ books and so forth, but I haven't really read anything of theirs.

JM: *And I wonder what predictions you might have on what effect the new Goodman [Atlas/Seaboard] line will have on the market.*
SL: Oh, I'd be very surprised if it has much of an effect. I think it's reached the point where there isn't much that can happen. We're by far the biggest-selling company now and have been for quite a while. The only thing that could really hurt us would be ourselves. If we start slackening in our own efforts to produce good material. If we start getting careless. But it would be unlikely that any external source could affect things too much.

JM: *The last area I'd like to discuss is the economy. Publishers, like everyone else, are caught up in the inflationary spiral... just how bad are things? What is the outlook? How will Marvel deal with the problems that there are?*
SL: I think that we're really in a pretty good position. The biggest problem, of course, is the increase in the price of paper, the price of printing. When we get a printing raise, in one fell swoop that means a quarter of a million dollars more or somewhere in that neighborhood... . But basically I think we're in a pretty good spot. We have our audience, we think we know what our audience wants, we seem to have the staff to provide it, and we hope that we're bright enough and alert enough to move with the times. We're always trying to anticipate problems. We try to build cushions into our budgets to provide for them.

I worry a little. I wonder, after a while, if the economy itself goes sour, how long people will be able to afford to spend money on the higher- and higher-priced publications, not only comics but all of them.

However, I must say that so far there seems to be no diminution of sales. And I really don't expect that the comic book field will change that radically, because I think there's always going to be a market for color comics. Because they're still one of the cheapest and apparently most satisfying forms of entertainment. Luckily, even in a recession, people want to be entertained, they want to take their minds off things. And one of the things that Marvel gives them is entertainment. Just sheer basic entertainment.

And I'm rather hoping that people will always have a quarter or a half dollar or whatever in their pockets for a few hours of entertainment.

Stan Keeps a Promise—
25 Years Later!

by Stan Lee
SECRETS BEHIND THE COMICS
PRICE $1

In his self-published (as "Famous Enterprises") 1947 book, ***Secrets Behind the Comics***, the 24-year-old Stan Lee promised readers that if they sent him a dollar, he would critique their artwork. 25 years later, in 1972, Russell Maheras took Stan up on that offer, to which, amazingly, Stan responded with the promised critique—of Maheras's "Souperman"—as seen in the letter on this page.

Marvel Comics Group

575 Madison Avenue New York, New York 10022 212 TEmpleton 8-7900

A DIVISION OF
Cadence Industries Corporation

STAN LEE
EDITORIAL DIRECTOR
AND PUBLISHER

December 7, 1972

Mr. Russell Maheras
950 North Laramie
Chicago, Illinois 60651

Dear Russ:

Okay, never let it be said that sweet ol' Stan ever reneged on an offer (even if it was made 25 years ago!) A promise is a promise! And besides, I can use the two bucks.

However, rates have gone up in 25 years, so all your buck and the buck for postage will buy you is a footnote! Hence footnote--

Do you have talent? Yeah, it seems that way. Have you a sense of humor? Apparently. Is your artwork of professional caliber? Not yet. Why not? Glad you asked--

Your anatomy is still weak-- practice it, study it, work on it. Don't worry too much about inking yet. That can come later. The pencilling is the important thing to begin with. Your layouts are good. You seem to have the ability to tell a story pictorially-- which is important in comics, obviously. But, if you really wanna become a pro, you're kidding around too much. Nobody's impressed with "Souperman" takeoffs now. We were doing them 30 years ago. Do real serious stuff. For example, pick a character you think you could handle-- HULK for example. Then do a serious, no-kidding story about him-- using your own drawings and layouts (no swipes). That's the only way to really tell if you have the stuff or not. When you think your work is as good as what's already appearing in the mags, send it in to us-- or DC, or anybody. Till then, keep studying.

Worth $2.00?

Stan
Excelsior!

P.S.-- Your backgrounds are pretty good, too.

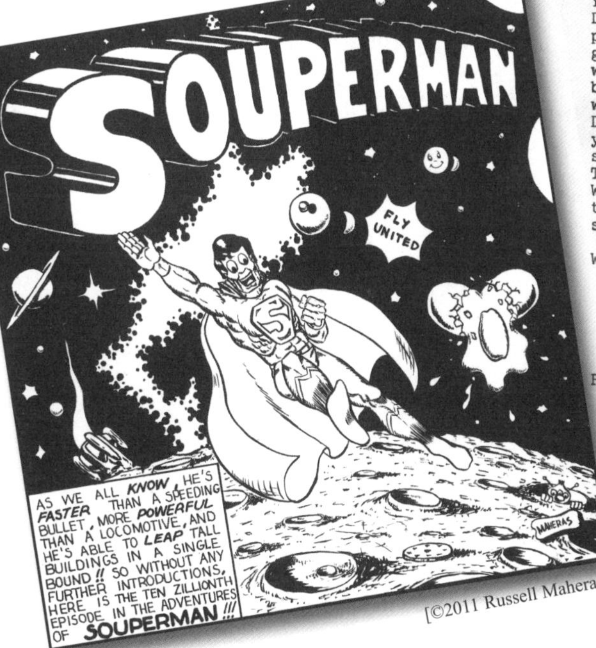

Asked if he had a copy of the original letter he wrote to Stan, Maheras told Danny Fingeroth in March 2011:

"No, I don't have the letter I sent Stan. At that stage of my life it was no doubt hand-written (with no carbon copy) and impulsively dashed off. What's crazy about back in 1972 is that when one sent a portfolio, one basically sent all one's original art via snail mail, and prayed it didn't get lost or damaged, and that it was eventually returned. Artists like me had no money for printers' stats, and, as I recall, copiers (if you could find one) were still very crude, relatively expensive, didn't reduce, and thus couldn't handle large-sized work. The fact that I got my originals back even though I only gave Stan an extra buck for postage shows just how nice about the whole deal he was."

Finding Marvel's Voice

An appreciation of Stan Lee's Bullpen Bulletins and Soapboxes

by David Kasakove

Most people don't realize how long Stan personally wrote all the Marvel lettercol answers, Special Announcements, and Bullpen Bulletins. While another editor might have delegated these things to freelancers or assistants early on, Stan realized how important it was that Marvel's readers heard what was going on behind the scenes, and the general tenor around the office, from the guy running the show.

*Stan wrote all the answers to letters and the Special Announcements beginning with the first lettercol (in **Fantastic Four** #3), only giving up answering letters when other regular writers took over specific titles and also their lettercols. When the Bullpen Bulletins page debuted in 1965, Stan then wrote that entire page, not just his signed Soapboxes, until 1972. As busy as he was with writing and editing, as well as speaking and touring on behalf of Marvel, clearly this regular, direct communication with readers was of great importance to him.*

*In this meticulously researched article, **David Kasakove** explores the fascinating saga of how Stan's and Marvel's voices became truly synonymous in readers' minds, and how this bonded them each other in a way never before seen.*

—DF & RT

[This article first appeared in **Write Now!** *#18.]*

Cover to ***Fantastic Four*** #3 (March 1962), the mag that featured the first Marvel superhero comic letters page. Pencils by Jack Kirby, inks by Sol Brodsky. [© 2011 Marvel Characters, Inc.]

Stan Lee's editorial voice—at once frantic, comic, self-deprecating, tongue-in-cheek, good-natured, wildly self-congratulatory and (sometimes) moralistic—was a years-long tour de force, the glue that held the Marvel Age of Comics together. As writer Mark Evanier once put it, "[Stan] put himself on a first-name basis with the readership at a time when the rival DC editors generally came across not only as adults, but stodgy adults."

I started reading Marvel comics in 1966, and was instantly hooked by Stan's voice. The Marvel Bullpen Bulletins page, including Stan's Soapbox, was the most concentrated expression of that voice. When the new Marvels hit the newsstand, it was the feature I would immediately turn to. Learning what was going on in the Bullpen, what artists were working on which stories, or which celebrities had popped in to yack with Stan, was of much more urgent importance to me than the fate of the Fantastic Four.

At the time I started reading Marvel Comics, which coincided with the crystallization of Stan's editorial voice, I had no idea about how the company's point-of-view came to be, and pretty much just assumed that Marvel's comics always existed in that form. Looking back at the evolution of the Bulletins and Soapbox, in the context of the run of ***Fantastic Four,*** Marvel's first, and longtime flagship, title, during Lee's editorial tenure from 1961 to 1972 (although, of course, he had been editing publisher Martin Goodman's comics from 1941 on), it becomes clear that the development of Lee's editorial voice took several years before it evolved into its trademark style. Only in hindsight does ***FF*** #1 (cover-dated Nov. '61—note that while I use cover dates in this article, the comics referred to were usually on sale two to three months before those dates), a stand-alone superhero title amid a modest line of monster, Western, and humor titles, signify the launch of "the Marvel Age of Comics" and the birth of a distinctive editorial voice that would transform the industry, and, ultimately, have a wide impact on popular culture.

The Fantastic 4 Fan Page

The Fantastic 4 Fan Page—the letters page that premiered in

FF #3 (March '62)—was a stepping-stone that would lead to the Bullpen Bulletins page. It was a laboratory for Stan's attempts to communicate with, and develop, a fan base, and in forming his unique editorial voice. The first "F4FP" reveals a glimmer of Stan's agenda. In a P.S. he writes, "We've just noticed something... unlike many other collections of letters in different mags, our fans all seem to write well, and intelligently. We assume this denotes that our readers are a cut above average, and that's the way we like 'em!" Although the letters don't actually support this glowing appraisal, Stan here sets an objective that will be quickly achieved.

By issue #5, with a letter from a Missouri English teacher by the name of Roy Thomas, the fan page became a sounding board for a growing and intelligent fandom. Many letter writers, like Roy (who was first hired by Marvel as a staff writer in 1965), would become future pros. These would include Steve Gerber, Dave Cockrum, and Alan Weiss. Letters were selected with an eye towards demonstrating that Marvel fans were, in Stan's words, a "cut above the average," with college students (particularly English and philosophy majors), teachers, foreign readers, and older readers being well represented.

Stan employed various devices to deepen the bond with readers. In *FF* #11, the unilateral decision is made, effective immediately, to change the salutations from "Dear Editor" to "Dear Stan and Jack" out of a desire to make the pages more personal, not stuffy, like competing comics. (In issue #20, a fan asks, "How come we are supposed to write to 'Dear Stan and Jack' instead of 'Dear Jack and Stan,'" and receives this response: "Because it's Stan's typewriter and so he makes the rules—you troublemaker.") In addition, Stan urged readers to write in about mistakes they spotted, offered "no-prizes" (in contrast to DC's actually giving away pages of then-considered-worthless original art), promoted local FF fan clubs, and (with the emergence of the company's own club, The Merry Marvel Marching Society), listed 25 M.M.M.S. members' names in each letters page. ["No-prizes" were just that, until some winners wondered why they hadn't received anything and so, for a time, empty envelopes labeled "official Marvel No-Prize" were indeed sent to folks, probably confusing some even more.]

In #32, it was announced that Marvel received 3,000 letters per month, and that each superhero magazine would now have its own letters column (prior to this, ***Fantastic Four*** included letters for all Marvel mags).

The Development of the "Marvel Bullpen"

As Stan encouraged fans to write and become part of the "Marvel Age of Comics" (a phrase first coined in *FF* #17, shortly after the debut of the "Marvel Comics" corner-box trade-dress in #14, and also around the time when the 1930s and '40s era of comics was beginning to be commonly referred to as "the Golden Age of Comics"), he increasingly focused attention on the "Marvel Bullpen," not only the writers and pencilers of the comics, but also inkers, colorists and the backroom staff (secretaries, production people) that put the Marvel "mags" together. (While Stan gave the impression that the Marvel Bullpen was a close-knit group that worked together at Marvel's offices, by this point in its history, most Marvel creators—with the exception of Stan and other staffers—worked at home, and the literal Marvel Bullpen consisted mostly of production and corrections folks.) Over time, Stan highlighted (and, in part, "created") a cast of characters—Jack "King" Kirby, Darlin' Dick Ayers, Jazzy John Romita, Genial Gene Colan, among others—that forged a further sense of community with the readership, helped foster fans' appreciation of the art and craft of making comics, and made a generation of comics creators into brand names that generated reader interest. Previously, creators labored in anonymity with not even their greatest fans knowing who they were. Lee's

FANTASTIC 4 FAN PAGE

DEAR EDITOR:
I think the Fantastic Four will become a great success. The Thing and the Torch are very new and different. I would also like to know what the name of your artist is.

Alan Weiss
Pardee Place
Las Vegas, Nevada

It'll become a success?? What do you think it is NOW? Chicken liver?? Considering that our artist signs the name JACK KIRBY on everything he can get his greedy little fingers on, I think we can safely claim that that's his name!

4.

DEAR EDITOR:
The best thing about the comic is the character conflicts. It's nice to see a group of super-heroes who aren't unnaturally buddy-buddy. The cover of #1 was pretty poor, it didn't stand out. I wish the name of Mr. Fantastic were different. It sounds too much like Mr. Clean.

Rick Wood
Ames St.
Cambridge, Mass.

Rick, no two fans ever seem to agree on what cover is best. Same thing applies to characters' names. So, let's hear from you other readers. What type of covers do YOU prefer, and how do you feel about the name Mr. Fantastic? (We'll bet at least ONE joker writes that he'd prefer Mr. Clean!)

4.

DEAR EDITOR:
You've got a heckuva nerve making a doll like Susan Storm invisible!

Unsigned
Dallas
Texas

Listen, Unsigned, with wolves like YOU around, she's a lot better off that way!

4.

DEAR EDITOR:
Before I started to write this letter, I read The Fantastic Four over 50 times! So then I decided to tell you what I thought of it. It is GREAT, WONDERFUL, FANTASTIC, BREATH-TAKING and STUPENDOUS, to say the least!
My biggest request is for more of the Human Torch in action.

George Paul
Park Ave.
Hoboken, N.J.

No WONDER you thought the mag was great, George, after reading it fifty times, brother, you've been BRAIN-WASHED! As for seeing more of the Torch, you've got a treat coming in the next issue!

4.

DEAR EDITOR:
Just finshed reading Fantastic Four and must admit to being disappointed. I expect better things from the team of Lee-Kirby. Jack is capable of better art work, and the Thing ought to revert to human form at will as his teammates do. The story also suffers from "Creeping Monsterism" to paraphrase Jean Shepard, that has dominated most, if not all, of your comics for some time.

Bill Sarill
Colorado Street
Boston, Mass.

See how fair we are? We print the knocks as well as the boosts! (The next time anyone around this office opens another. one of Bill's letters, he's thru!!) As for the Thing reverting to human form, it's not that easy, pal. If you don't believe us, take a dose of cosmic rays yourself and see what happens!

4.

DEAR EDITOR:
Are you the same one who also puts out STRANGE TALES, TALES TO ASTONISH, JOURNEY INTO MYSTERY, TALES OF SUSPENSE, AMAZING ADULT FANTASY, and a lot of Westerns like KID COLT, OUTLAW, and teen-age titles like PATSY WAKER? If so, how do you do it?

S. Brodsky
Brooklyn
New York

With great difficulty!

P.S.—We've just noticed something ... unlike many other collections of letters in different mags, our fans all seem to write well, and intelligently..We assume this denotes that our readers are a cut above average, and that's the way we like 'em!

Address your letters to:
THE EDITOR
FANTASTIC FOUR
THIRD FLOOR
655 MADISON AVENUE
NEW YORK 21, N. Y.

IMPORTANT NOTE:
We receive so much mail that it is utterly impossible to engage in correspondence with any readers. As many letters as possible will be answered on this page each issue. Please do not ask us to write to you personally.

Marvel's editorial voice was first revealed to readers in the premiere ***Fantastic Four*** letters page in issue #3. Alan Weiss went on to become an accomplished comics writer and artist. "S. Brodsky" was Marvel's production manager (and sometime inker), "Jolly" Solly Brodsky. Since this was the first-ever Marvel letters page, Stan apparently had to get Sol to write a letter—or else ghosted one *for* him! Before too long, the "important note" at the bottom of the page would become a self-fulfilling prophecy and the company would be deluged with fan mail.

presentation of himself and his collaborators as stars made them just that.

But the project of making the "Marvel madmen" well known, as all things Marvel, started slowly, and very much under the radar. Initially, ***FF*** stories would be typically signed by Stan Lee and J. Kirby, without any further elaboration. With issue #9, the first formal credits appeared, listing Script, Art, Inking and Lettering attributions. The credits remained straightforward and did not include any of the nicknames or joking that became a Marvel trademark until ***FF*** #24. At first, the letters pages did not include much talk about the artists or how Marvel operated. ***FF*** #13's letters page offered the first "Special Announcements Section," about a quarter column in length, which offered news about other Marvel titles. In it, Stan began to focus increasingly on members of the "Batty Bullpen." For example, in ***FF*** #18, Steve Ditko was credited with creating the Marvel corner box, which featured one or more of each title's stars.

Stan revealed a particular fondness for veteran artists who either were joining or re-joining the Marvel Bullpen. Although Marvel gained (and fostered) a reputation for being hip, Stan did not shy away from letting fans know that many of Marvel's artists had professional roots in the 1940s or 1950s. In so doing, he provided a sense of comics history to many readers who, most likely, were largely unaware that such a history even existed. For example, in #25, in announcing ***Daredevil*** #1, Stan noted (writing in the third person) that "One of comicdom's greatest talents, Bill Everett, who gave you the original Sub-Mariner in the Golden Age of Comics, now joins Stan Lee to bring you the newest and possibly greatest creation of the Marvel Age."

The splash page from ***FF*** #11 (February 1963) features pre-comics shop fans waiting on line at a news dealer's to get the super-team's latest issue—and a proud reader plugging the letters page. [©2011 Marvel Characters, Inc.]

The Birth of the Bullpen Bulletins

The Marvel Bullpen Bulletins page premiered in December 1965's comics, with short paragraphs of information about the Bullpen, an ad for Marvel t-shirts and stationery kits, and "Let's meet 25 more M.M.M.S. Members." Stan has noted that the purpose of the "Bullpen Bulletins" was to provide a venue to speak to readers "informally" and "to give our fans personal stuff, make them feel they were part of Marvel, make them feel as though they were on a first-name basis with the whole screwy staff. In a way, I wanted it to be as though they were getting a personal letter from a friend who was away at camp." On a practical basis, since Lee was writing the individual sets of "Special Announcements" that appeared in each comic, in effect often rewriting the same information half-a-dozen or more times per month, the Bullpen Page seems like a way to only have to do it once. By #46, the alliterative headline, which became a hallmark of the Bullpen page, premiered: "More Nutty News and Notes from One Marvel Madman to Another." The title was inclusive: we were all Marvel Madmen.

The Bullpen Bulletins reflected a genuine enthusiasm for the making of comics and for comics' creators. The very first Bulletins story (Dec 1965), which announced the "Big News" that "Jolly Joe Sinnott has rejoined our mighty Marvel team!", is a case in point. At a time in the industry where inkers were barely (if ever) recognized, Stan refers to Sinnott's last (uncredited) inking job for Marvel over three years earlier: "Remember his great inking job on ***FF*** #5? Dyed-in-the-wool Marvelites are still drooling over it!"

In March 1966, what would become known as "the Marvel method" of comics creation is explained, with Stan taking very little credit: "...all Stan has to do... is give [the artists] the germ of an idea, and they make up all the details as they go along, drawing and plotting out the story. Then, our leader simply takes the finished drawings and adds all the dialogue and captions!"

It's interesting to see what Stan writes about Steve Ditko and Jack Kirby, central creators of the Marvel Age of Comics who both eventually resigned. The departure of Steve Ditko is the lead story in the July 1966 bulletin: "It's hail and farewell to sturdy Steve Ditko... Steve recently told us he was leaving, for personal reasons. After all these years, we're sorry to see him go, and we wish the talented guy success with his future endeavors. As for his replacement, all we can say is—since someone else has to draw Spidey, thank Asgard that Jazzy Johnny Romita has returned to the fold!" Ditko is mentioned two more times in the Bulletins pages. There is a fleeting reference in the context of a short Feb. 1970 item exclaiming that Wally Wood recently called and may be returning, which closes with the parenthetical comment: "Now if only a cat named S.D. would dig up our phone number again! Oh well, we can always dream!" Finally, in the Sept. '71 Soapbox celebrating the 100th issue of ***Spider-Man***, Stan refers to Ditko as "Spidey's initial artist, who breathed life and luster into the strip."

Kirby received frequent mention and praise. In April 1967, he was highlighted as being the "Artists' Artist." "...when you talk of superhero illustration; of action drawing; of imaginative conceptions; of dynamic, double-barreled drama; Marvel's many-faceted master simply has no peer! ...Don't be embarrassed, Jack—this is just Stan's cornball way of telling you that it's been a ball all these years, pal—and the best is still ahead!" A little more than a year later (Sept. 1970), in Stan's Soapbox, Kirby's resignation was announced: "Who says lightning doesn't strike twice? Remember a few years back when Steve Ditko suddenly left the hallowed halls of Marvel to seek his fortunes elsewhere? Well, at the time of this writing (early in March) Jack Kirby has unexpectedly announced his resignation from our surprised but stalwart little staff." Lee promises that the Bullpen will "turn ourselves on, knock ourselves out, and do ourselves in to prove once again that, while we may not be the biggest, we're still the boldest and best!" As if to emphasize that Marvel could survive sans Kirby, a half-page ad on the same page announced the debut of ***Conan the Barbarian,*** as "The Comic-Mag Event of the 70s!!" and "proof positive that Mighty Marvel is on the move again!!"

The Bulletin also focused attention on the members of the Bullpen who worked behind the scenes, notably "Fabulous" Flo Steinberg ("our Gal Friday"), production manager "Jolly" Solly Brodsky, and publisher "Merry" Martin Goodman. The pages reveal a special fondness for "Fabulous Flo," who, as Stan's assistant, read the ever-growing mountain of fan mail and helped keep Marvel running. Indeed, she received more frequent mention than Ditko! Not only was her departure "to seek fortunes in another field" noted with sadness (September 1968), but in February 1969, it was announced that she has "a great new job at Rockefeller Center" (although no other information was revealed.) Lee's friend Brodsky's resignation to strike out on his own as a publisher is greeted with best wishes to "this loyal and talented guy—from sorrowful Stan and the whole batty Bullpen" (January 1971). Stan often poked fun at the Bullpen, including himself: noting that publisher Martin Goodman is one of the nation's top amateur golfers, the Bulletin states, "Despite what you might have heard, it's not true that Stan caddies for him on his day off" (January 1966). In January 1970, it is reported, with some chagrin that the only assignment Jim Steranko would accept was for one of Marvel's new romance titles: "That was weeks ago and we haven't seen him since. All we can think of is that the sonofagun is out doing some personal research!"

Love, Death, and Backaches

The Bulletins would also update fans on various aspects of the Bullpen's personal lives, from the serious to the mundane. In the same month, both Larrupin' Larry Lieber and Wild Bill Everett sprained their backs ("You never knew it was so dangerous producing comics, eh?") (April 1967). It was noted that Romita was a volunteer fireman, and that Brodsky was a dangerous poker player (May '67).

Stan is often depicted as frenzied, with hardly a vacation. In May 1966, it is announced that he and "his lovely blonde wife hopped a train to Toronto" for an entire weekend, Stan's first vacation in years. "Why didn't they fly? Because the train gave him time to bat out a couple of scripts on the way, natch!" The next reported vacation is in October 1971, where Roy Thomas (in "Roy's Rostrum") notes that Stan's taking off for the month from editorial work "polishing off a screenplay for world-famous director Alain Resnais' first English-language film."

Bullpen Visits

Stan frequently highlighted celebrity visitors to the Bullpen. As he sought to move the company to the forefront of mainstream media, he often highlighted Marvel's connection with broader currents in the culture. For example, in June 1966, it was reported that "world famous movie writer/director Federico Fellini, stopped in to visit the gang at the bullpen last November... we spent a wonderful couple of hours showing him around and swapping stories! So, the next time someone gives you a disdainful look when you mention being a Marvel Marcher, you might just casually mention the kinda company you're in!" In August 1966, it was reported that Peter Asher

MARVEL BULLPEN BULLETINS!

FACE FRONT! Here's a whole kaboodle of news and gossip straight from your bullpen to you!

BIG NEWS! An old favorite of yours, Jolly JOE SINNOTT has rejoined our mighty Marvel team! He'll be inking the F.F. regularly, working on "Agent of Shield," and doing as many other features as we can straddle him with! (Remember his great inking job on F.F. #5? Dyed-in-the-wool Marvelites are still drooling over it!)

Everybody's favorite guessing game these days is trying to figure out the real identity of the "Sub-Mariner's" powerful penciller, ADAM AUSTIN! As most of you have guessed, Adam Austin is only a nom de plume, and one of these days we'll reveal his real name to you—if we don't forget it before then!

Did you know that our bullpen ramrod, Smilin' STAN LEE, also authors MONSTERS UNLIMITED as well as YOU DON'T SAY! Both are slick paper photo-gag magazines, and Stan the Man seems to have the magic touch—both of those humor sensations seem to sell out as fast as our own Marvel masterpieces—and that's sayin' something!

Everybody's been clamoring for a sample of JACK (King) KIRBY'S inking as well as his pencilling. So, if you'll remind us next spring, we'll try to get him to pencil and ink a special pin-up page for one of next year's Annuals! Of course, it'll mean our buying him a brush, but no sacrifice is too great to make for you Marvel madmen!

How do you like the layout of this page, gang? Pretty jazzy, eh? Any comments, suggestions or (ulp) criticisms? Grab a sheet of your swingin' stationery and let us know! We're waiting to hear from you!

CAN YOU GUESS WHAT'S IN THIS MYSTERIOUS MAILING TUBE?

It's our next Marvel mail order bombshell! You've been demanding it for months, so we're frantically producing a zillion of 'em right now! Next ish we'll let the cat out of the bag and clue you in, but till then send us your guesses, and we'll try to remember you when our next no-prize academy award time rolls around! 'Nuff said!

THE MIGHTY MARVEL CHECKLIST

A Line-Up Of Some Of The Marvel-ous Mags On Sale Right Now!

FANTASTIC FOUR #45: At last! The secret of Medusa's mysterious lost race! More about the grotesque Gorgon! And wait'll you see who the Torch meets!

SPIDER-MAN #31: Under the sea, the Master Planner plots against Spidey! Also, Peter gets a rough introduction to his new college "friends"!

AVENGERS #22: What happens to a world-famous fighting team after they've suffered their first major defeat? This one is a real shocker!

X-MEN #14: See the human race up in arms against the X-Men, as the super-natural "Sentinels" make their first fantastic appearance!

DAREDEVIL #10: A real collector's item! On a dare, Stan let Wally Wood write this one, and it's the most off-beat mystery in years! Wait'll you see the far-out super-villains and the panicky plot twists! Sure to be talked-about everywhere!

THOR #122: Having battled Thor to a standstill, the Absorbing Man now dares to attack Odin himself! Also, learn the secret of the hooded mystery man!

SUSPENSE #72: The most unexpected villain of all poses a daringly different threat to Iron Man, while Captain America faces the macabre menace of "The Sleeper"!

ASTONISH #74: The surprise of the season! Why does Namor give up his quest? And, wait'll you see what happens to the Leader when the Hulk returns to earth!

SGT. FURY #24: This is the one you've been waiting for! The Howlers fly to the U.S.A. for a furlough—but they get a lot more than they bargained for! Sensational!

LET'S MEET 25 MORE M.M.M.S. MEMBERS:

Ronald Fortier, Somersworth, N. H.
Nicky Vroman, Spokane, Wash.
Gary L. Dyer, Hobbs, N. Mex.
Thomas Campbell, Mt. Vernon, N. Y.
Richard Brown, Jr., Kankall, Ill.
Bill Evans, Reno, Nevada
Daniel Cuda, Canoga Park, Calif.
Patrick Webber, Sherwood, N. D.
Brit Vanderford, Garland, Texas
Charles Hopkins, Norfolk, Va.
Mark Bossey, Gary, Indiana
Bernard Cleaves, Colonial Beach, Va.
Lee Allen, Reynoldsberg, Ohio
Arlene Newman, Brooklyn, N. Y.
Jerry Olidenhoff, Lannon, Wisc.
Kenneth Lieberman, New York, N. Y.
Donald Smith, Cincinnati, Ohio
Roger Girard, North Haven, Conn.
Steve Matthew, North Haven, Conn.
Richard Gusenburg, North Haven, Conn.
Dennis Timberman, North Haven, Conn.
Timmp Timberman, North Haven, Conn.
Fritzey Botcher, North Haven, Conn.
Steve Aliprandi, Chicago, Ill.
Gary Seymour, Slidell, La.

NOTE: If you don't want to cut up this classy mag, you can send us a copy of our coupon!

Be the rage of the Marvel Age in a swingin' T-Shirt! Order yours today! Tomorrow we may keep 'em for ourselves!

Treat yourself to a Marvel Stationery Kit! It's packed with envelopes, letterheads, and autographs of your frantic favorites.

DR. STRANGE

YOURS FOR ONLY $1.50

SEND FOR YOURS NOW ONLY $1.00

MARVEL COMICS GROUP

OFFICIAL SWINGIN' STATIONERY

Send check or money order to:
MARVEL COMICS GROUP DEPT. MO
625 Madison Ave., New York, N. Y. 10022

Please add 15¢ per item for postage and handling

Check one: ☐ T-Shirt: $1.50 each ☐ Stationery Kit: $1.00 each

Name________

Address________

City________ State________

For DR. STRANGE T-SHIRT, CHECK SIZE

ADULT SIZES: Small ☐ Med. ☐ Large ☐

YOUTH SIZES: Small ☐ Med. ☐ Large ☐

ST 159

MARCHERS: Write your membership number on coupon for a bonus gift with each order!

The first official Bullpen Bulletins page, from the Marvel comics cover-dated December 1965. [© 2011 Marvel Characters, Inc.]

"of the famous British singing team of Peter and Gordon" stopped by for a visit, and that his friends, the Beatles, were also Merry Marvelites. In the September 1968 Soapbox, it was reported that the rock band Country Joe and the Fish stopped by. [See Gary Friedrich's recollection of the band's visit elsewhere in this book.—DF & RT] In March 1970, Resnais, the noted "French film genius" spent "many pleasant hours rappin' about movies, comic mags, and the arts in general. According to Alain, Marvel Comics are definitely the 'in' thing in the arty circles of Europe today." Clearly, Stan was reaching for an audience beyond that which comics had traditionally courted.

Comics as an Art Form

Stan repeatedly sought to bring attention to comics as an art form, and relentlessly promoted comics, and particularly Marvel, as equal to other forms of popular culture. By the end of his tenure as Marvel's editor, the company has made remarkable progress in terms of being recognized as part of popular culture—and Stan was not shy about celebrating this. Perhaps because Stan had done such a compelling job of having fans identity with Marvel, I recall at the time that, as a fan, I felt deep pride in the recognition that Marvel received.

As early as 1964, Stan expressed a desire to elevate the field: "Comics are an art form, as creative and enjoyable as any other" (***FF*** #24 letters page). In the context of explaining why Marvel has taken to criticizing competitors who are imitating the Marvel style: "Marvel has spent years trying to upgrade the art of comic magazines—for, an art it truly is, every bit as much as the cinema, the legitimate stage, or any other form of creative expression."

The Birth of Stan's Soapbox

Stan's desire to reach out and more directly address fans culminated in "Stan's Soapbox," debuting in June 1967, which began in response to "a zillion letters (wouldja believe a couple?) asking us to have Our Leader do an editorial on this page each ish, in order to bring the Marvel Message to all True Believers! Hence, in obvious obeisance to thy slightest wishes, O keepers of the Flame, we hereby inaugurate a forensic new feature, to be known forevermore as: Stan's Soapbox." Stan would later explain it this way: "... I wanted to be able to talk directly to the readers, just the way a fella would talk to a friend. So I initiated a column called 'Stan's Soapbox,' in which I discussed anything on my mind, mainly for the purpose of eliciting responses from the readers."

The first installment discussed "The Marvel Philosophy," in which Stan explained that, "In the process of providing off-beat entertainment, if we can also do our bit to advance the cause of intellectualism, humanitarianism, and mutual understanding... to toss a little swingin' satire at you in the process... that won't break our collective heart one tiny bit!" Stan took another stab at defining the "Marvel Philosophy" in March 1971: "Our theme is justice, tempered by tolerance, honed by humor, and leavened with love. We support people everywhere—people striving to improve themselves and their lives—people working and praying for a better world, a world without war. ... We espouse no cause save the cause of freedom—no philosophy save the brotherhood of man. Our purpose is to entertain—to take the world as it is and show it as it might be–as it could be–and perhaps, as it should be.

The March 1970 Bulletins recounted that French "New Wave" director Alain Resnais had visited Marvel. He and Stan would become friends and creative partners. Pages from a script Stan wrote for Resnais, for the unproduced ***The Monster Maker***, can be seen elsewhere in this book. [Photo courtesy of the French film Office, New York.]

The majority of the Soapboxes, though, were not editorials, but rather, focused on comics or Marvel fandom. The second installment featured a letter from Mark Evanier suggesting that Marvel fans have titles, with the lowest ranking being that of "Real Frantic One" upon the purchase of one's first Marvel comic, and at the top of the food chain, "Marvelite Maximus," for a fan who has earned numerous no-prizes. (After receiving support from other fans, this idea was accepted and various fan-titles were introduced, starting in December 1967).

Comics and Politics

During Stan's editorial tenure, the United States experienced a time of unprecedented political upheaval as it moved through the Cold War, the Civil Rights era, the assassinations of John F. Kennedy, Martin Luther King, and Robert Kennedy, the Vietnam War, and Watergate. Although these issues would certainly be reflected in some of the stories he wrote, Stan's tendency was to shy away from directly editorializing about current events, and as fans clamored for him to take a stand on the issues of the day, he struggled with doing so. In October 1967, Stan noted that "many Keepers of the Faith have demanded that we take a more definitive stand on current problems such as Vietnam, civil rights, and the increase in crime," and asked readers for their votes on the matter. Yet, Stan did not report the results of this poll, and in October 1968 stated that Marvel seeks to avoid editorializing about controversial issues, since the Bullpen has diverse opinions. However, in the next Soapbox, in apparent response to a "flood" of new letters in favor of editorializing, Stan changed course and declared that "from now on, whenever we have something to get off our collective chests, we'll assume we have a magniloquent mandate to sock it to ya, and let the chips fall where they may."

In April 1970, when writing his most "philosophical" series, ***The Silver Surfer,*** Stan addressed "readers who wonder why there's so much moralizing in our mags." In response to those who feel that comics are supposed to be escapist reading, Stan responds: "... a story without a message, however subliminal, is like a man without a soul. ... At every college campus where

I may speak, there's as much discussion of war and peace, civil rights, and the so-called youth rebellion as there is about our Marvel mags."

Despite all the attention Stan paid to whether Marvel should editorialize, in fact, the "Soapbox" featured very few of his political opinions. His spare political comments reflect the general shift in public opinion from the general anti-Communist Cold War era in the early 1960s to the generally more liberal climate of the late 1960s and early 1970s. For example, in ***FF*** #25, cover-dated April 1964, a reader asked why so many heroes are fighting Communists. After providing this flippant response, "We spend billions for national defense. Who do you think we're concerned about—the Eskimos?", fan response is requested and was received, going both ways. After reviewing the responses, Stan reports: "The proportion is heavily in favor of calling a spade a spade, or a red a red." (***FF*** #29)

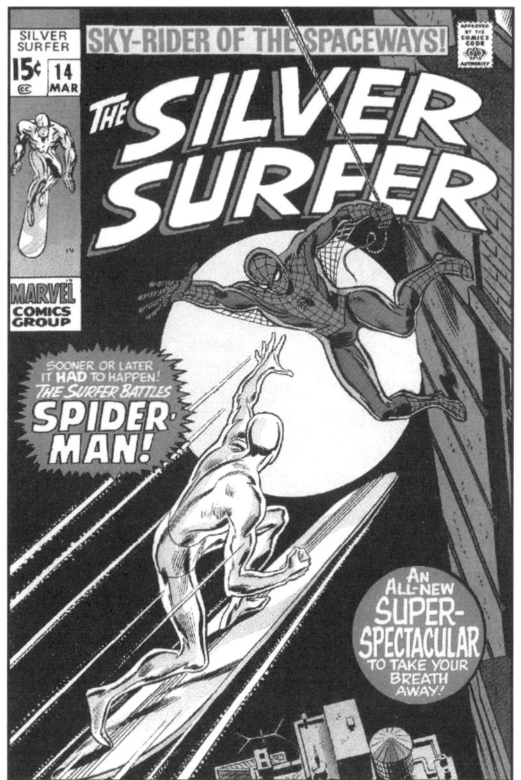

While writing his most philosophical series, ***The Silver Surfer***, Stan would speak in an April 1970 Soapbox about "moralizing" in Marvel's mags. This John Buscema-penciled and John Romita-inked cover to ***Surfer*** #14 (March '70) may or may not be "philosophical"—but it sure is cool! [© 2008 Marvel Characters, Inc.]

On the other hand, Stan rarely mentioned the Vietnam war, and when he did, was exceedingly careful in choosing his words. In March 1968 he promoted Operation Mailcall Vietnam in which people could write to those serving there. But Stan did not indicate any political position concerning the war: "Many of our politically aware readers have divergent opinions about the Vietnam War—as do the Bullpenners themselves. This notice is not intended as an endorsement on our part of any specific policy regarding the war. We simply feel that many American boys have been sent into battle far from home—and anything we can do to make 'em feel that they're not forgotten is surely a worthwhile deed which transcends mere politics. 'Nuff said!"

However, in a few fleeting instances, it appears that Stan did indicate at least sympathy with an anti-war position. For instance, in December 1970, the Bulletins note that Kenneth Koch, the "famous modern idiom poet on the faculty of Columbia University" is a Marvel madman. "It's always fun to spend time with Ken, talking about Marveldom, motorcycles, and making an end to the war overseas." Still, Stan never directly editorialized on the subject.

Stan the Preacher

While Stan showed discomfort in expressing his personal political views in the Bullpen pages, he was at home discussing more general moral, or ethical, concepts. Stan's views in this regard are first expressed in his October 1968 Soapbox. After he expressed discomfort about discussing political views because members of the Bullpen had differing opinions, he nonetheless felt free to speak on behalf of the entire Bullpen with respect to the Bullpen's religious beliefs: "We believe that Man has a divine destiny, and an awesome responsibility—the responsibility of treating all who share this wondrous world of ours with tolerance and respect—judging each fellow human on his own merit, regardless of race, creed, or color. That we agree on—and we'll never rest until it becomes a fact, rather than just a cherished dream." In the December 1968 installment, Stan addressed bigotry and reaffirmed his call for tolerance and, again, spoke in religious terms, concluding that, "... if man is ever to be worthy of his destiny, we must fill our hearts with tolerance. For then, and only then, will we be truly worthy of the concept that man was created in the image of God—a God who calls us ALL—his children."

Stan returned to this theme in June 1969, when he discussed his view that "love is a far greater force, a far greater power than hate... . Let's consider three men: Buddha, Christ, and Moses... men of peace, whose thoughts and deeds have influenced countless millions throughout the ages... men of good will, men of tolerance, and especially men of love. Now, consider the practitioners of hate who have sullied the pages of history. Who still venerates their words?"

In Danny Fingeroth's 2007 ***Disguised as Clark Kent: Jews, Comics, and the Creation of the Superhero,*** Stan, in his foreword, states that religion "never really entered the picture [when we were creating superhero stories]... the one thing I always tried to emphasize was the common bond between people, the fact that we were all passengers on Spaceship Earth, and our ship was never divided into different classes." Yet, Stan could very easily have expressed his views about "Spaceship Earth" without relying on religious concepts of divinity, or man's responsibility to act in God's image. That he chose to do so reveals, perhaps, a deeper religious worldview than Stan himself recognizes. Certainly, his pride in his poem "God Woke" is another possible indication of such feelings.

The End of an Era

The September 1972 Soapbox announced the end of Marvel's "Phase One" and the beginning of "Phase Two," with Stan stepping down as editor and art director, Roy Thomas replacing him as editor, and Stan becoming publisher, devoting his work time "exclusively to dreaming up new, exciting projects for the Bullpen... and new fields for Marvel to conquer in film, TV, books, and you-name-it we'll-do-it!" Although he continued writing the monthly Soapbox through 1980 (and would continue to do so intermittently after that), this would be his last Soapbox as editor. After this point, Roy took over writing the Bulletins, except for Stan's Soapboxes.

In this Soapbox—at almost a full page, the lengthiest he had ever written—Stan gave his own view of Marvel's accomplishments during his tenure, revealing a pretty clear sense of its history: "Until now, mighty Marvel has been a lusty, gusty, irreverent mischief-maker in the wondrous world of commix." [Note the spelling, "commix," influenced by the Underground movement of the era.] He continues: "It was Marvel that first introduced heroes with human hang-ups; Marvel that popularized guest-star appearances till you needed a scorecard to tell you who was who; Marvel that dared create continued stories—and then forgot how to end them, so that they went on forever! It was Marvel who gave you a Bullpen Bulletins page where we can rap together like this; Marvel who liberated the geniuses who bring you these epics from their shadow of anonymity, and bombarded the name of every writer, artist, and letterer until you now know 'em almost as well as we do. Only Marvel could have made satire and sentimentality, relevance and ribaldry a part of the commix mystique. And who but Marvel would have dared make a hero out of the Hulk, or a bald-headed, self-pitying sky-rider called the Silver Surfer? Well, we could go on forever, but it might look like bragging—and you know how much we hate to do that!"

The August 1966 Bulletins informed readers that Peter Asher (right) of the popular British signing duo Peter and Gordon had stopped by the offices. Asher went on to produce records for James Taylor, Linda Ronstadt, and 10,000 Maniacs, among many others. [© the copyright holders]

Through Stan's writing in Marvel's letters pages, Bullpen Bulletins, and Soapboxes—not to mention through the comics stories themselves—we can track the development of Marvel from simply a comics company into a cultural force. We can also chart Stan's progression from a man famously close to quitting the industry he'd toiled in since he was a teenager, to someone who became the driving and defining force in that industry. Whether you read the lines or between them, it's a fascinating look at how a company and a man simultaneously evolved.

'Nuff said, indeed.

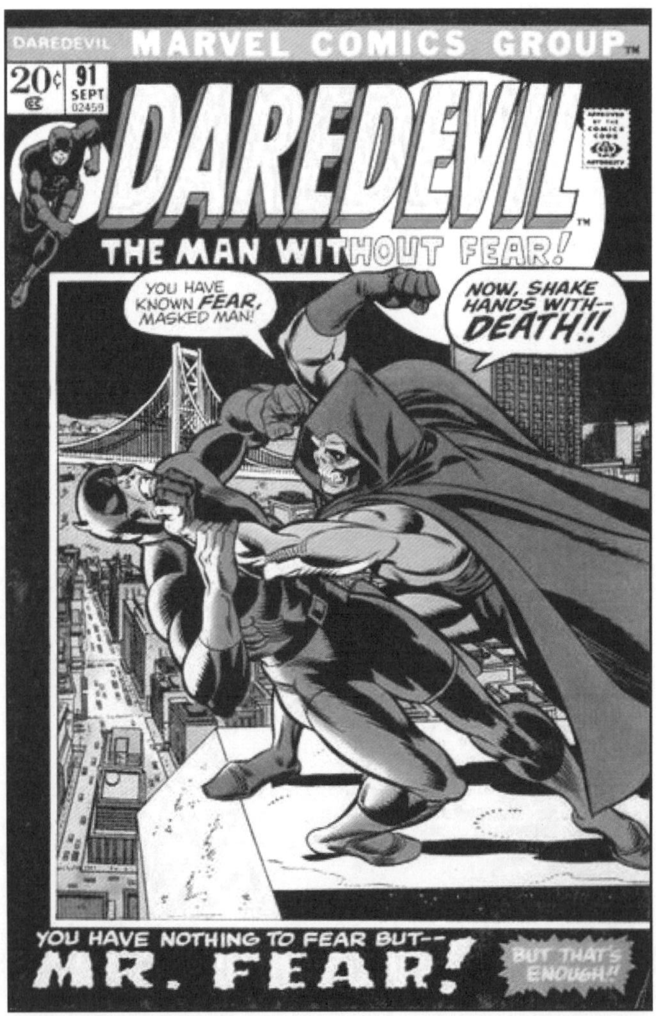

The Marvel comics dated September 1972—such as this Gil Kane-Joe Sinnott covered ***Daredevil*** #91—contained Stan's last Soapbox as editor (though he'd continue writing them through 1980, and then pick them up again at various points). [© 2011 Marvel Characters, Inc.]

David Kasakove *was coaxed out of fan-retirement by* **Stan Lee Universe** *co-editor Danny Fingeroth, long-time friend and fellow SUNY Binghamton alumnus. In the early Bronze Age, David published and edited (with Klaus Janson)* **The Creative Adventure** *fanzine, and co-authored (with John Benson and Art Spiegelman) the definitive study of Al Feldstein and Bernard Krigstein's classic EC story "Master Race." For a short stint (1977-8), David was a Merry Marvel Madman in the company's British Department, and contributed to Marvel's* **Epic Magazine.** *Currently a lawyer residing in New York, he is the father of Sophie, founding member of teenage punk-rock band phenomenon* **Care Bears on Fire.** *[For more on CBOF check out: http://www.carebearsonfire.com] David has attained the Marvel rank of* **PMM** *(Permanent Marvelite Maximus), and, with this article, seeks consideration for the rank of* **FFF** *(Fearless Front Facer), "a purely honorary degree, approved and awarded by Smilin' Stan and a carefully chosen committee" (as defined in the Bullpen Bulletins, June 1968).*

Stan Lee Commends!

A letter of thanks for a job well done

This 1980 letter pretty much explains itself. For a guy as perpetually busy as Stan Lee to take the time to write a letter of commendation for someone who was doing her job says a lot about the subject *and* the writer of the letter.

5/4/80

President
United Airlines
1221 Ave. of the Americas
New York City
NY

Dear Sir,

This is just to commend one of your flight attendants.

Yesterday (5/3/80) my wife and I took your flight #15 from New York to Los Angeles. Towards the end of the flight my wife felt rather ill.

One of your flight attendants, named Yvonne, was most exceptionally courteous, concerned, and helpful. She was not only extremely helpful, but showed such genuine interest and care that my wife and I couldn't stop talking about it.

That young lady, Yvonne, did more to give us a warm feeling towards United Airlines than all the advertising and public relations campaigns put together could ever do.

Very sincerely yours,

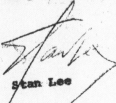

Stan Lee

Stan Lee letter to President of United Airlines, May 4, 1980, Stan Lee Collection, box #14, American Heritage Center, University of Wyoming.

Stan and Joan Lee at the 2008 Hollywood premiere of the first ***Iron Man*** movie.

Just Imagine... Working with Stan Lee

Michael Uslan, executive producer of the Batman movies, on re-imagining DC's top heroes with Stan.

Interview conducted in person by Danny Fingeroth, February 13, 2008
Transcribed by Steven Tice, copyedited by Michael Uslan and Danny Fingeroth

Michael Uslan *is the executive producer of the* **Batman** *films, including the blockbuster* **The Dark Knight**. *He's also the writer of the acclaimed* **Detective #27** *graphic novel and the bestselling* **Archie Marries** *comics. Michael was the instructor of the first for for-credit comics history course offered in a US university. His recent memoir,* **The Boy Who Loved Batman** *(from Chronicle Books), tells of how he made his dreams come true. Michael worked closely with Stan on the 2001* **Just Imagine Stan Lee...** *series, which featured Stan's interpretations of classic DC characters. Michael and I discussed that and other Stan-related topics.*

—DF

[This interview first appeared in **Write Now!** *#18.]*

DF: *How did the* **Just Imagine Stan Lee** *series come about, Michael?*
MU: It was June 1989, and I was at the premiere of our first ***Batman*** movie. While my family was all excited by all the stars that were there, I was excited when I spotted Stan Lee and Bob Kane as I walked in. I spent most of the evening hanging out with those two guys.

DF: *You had met them before, though, hadn't you?*
MU: Oh, sure. I first met Stan when I was in seventh grade. And Bob I had known from when I first was negotiating to buy the rights to Batman from DC Comics, to turn it into a dark and mysterious, serious movie for the first time, which was in 1979.

Anyway, as part of the conversation that night, Stan was giving it to Bob, and Bob was giving it right back to Stan. They had a close relationship. Stan said to Bob, "Gee, Bob, it's really too bad I didn't write ***Batman,*** because if I was writing ***Batman*** and you were drawing it, then we really could have made a success of this thing." And Bob said, "Well, you know, Stan, if I was drawing ***Spider-Man,*** it could have been bigger than it has ever been." So they were giving it to each other pretty good.

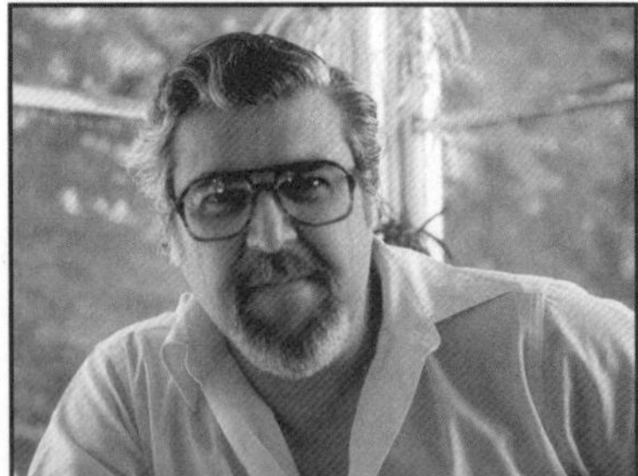

Legendary artist John Buscema, who drew the ***Superman*** issue of the ***Just Imagine*** series. [© 2011 DC Comics]

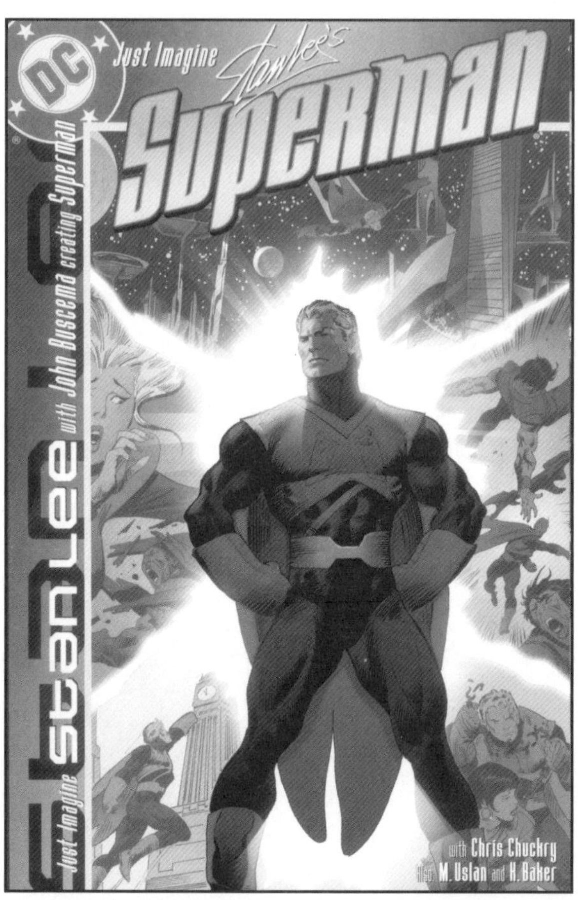

The cover to the 2001 ***Just Imagine Stan Lee with John Buscema Creating Superman***. Stan wrote the story, with pencils and inks by John. Adam Hughes colored the cover. [© 2011 DC Comics.]

I'm listening to this conversation and my head is spinning, because for the first time I'm starting to imagine, "What would ***Batman*** have been like if Stan Lee had co-created it with Bob Kane, and done all the writing?" And that got me thinking. If Stan Lee had been at DC Comics instead of Marvel, what might the pantheon of DC heroes been like under his writing and editorial eye?

I thought about that for a lot of years. When Marvel was in its late '90s bankruptcy, and I knew that Stan was available to potentially do some projects outside the Marvel purview, I went to him. We had had an ongoing relationship over the years, where we would correspond with each other, and talk about possibly doing something together. And, in fact, we worked on an animated project together at Marvel when Marvel had its animation division, around 1986, '87. So I said to Stan, "What if I brought you over to DC Comics and you re-imagined all of their superheroes the way you would have done them? Would that be of any interest to you? And what if I can team you up with the greatest artists who ever lived?"

Stan was absolutely tickled by the idea, and I could see his creative juices flowing. He said, "Well, DC would never go for that." I said, "Leave that to me." So, then, I met with [then-DC President and Publisher] Paul Levitz, and I proposed it to him. And Paul said, "What fun this would be!" So, after all was said and done, I was working with Stan, with Mike Carlin as our editor, on the ***Just Imagine*** series. We lined up absolutely phenomenal artists: Gene Colan, Joe Kubert, John Buscema. It was Buscema's last [published] work, the re-imagining of Superman.

Splash page from ***Just Imagine Stan Lee and Joe Kubert Creating Batman***. This was the first time the two titans had ever collaborated. Stan wrote the story, and Joe did the pencil and ink honors. [© 2011 DC Comics.]

And I'll never forget being in Stan's office in L.A. when Buscema's artwork came in. And, on the one hand, where Stan was raving about how great John is, and what an amazing artist he is, there were a page or two that he was not happy with the way the plot was interpreted. He was trying to explain to John what he wanted, and he wasn't getting the point across. So after the conversation with John ended, I'm sitting there, and Stan brings out tissue paper and tapes it over the pages of Buscema art, and he starts re-sketching the panel borders. Then he hands me the pencil. And he says, "Start drawing." And he gets on a chair and starts striking a pose and explaining to me what the first panel should be. Then he goes into another pose and says, "Now draw this, from this perspective."

Now, I had heard how, in the day at Marvel, he'd be on the furniture and swinging from lamps while Kirby was drawing, and Stan was showing him what he wanted. And I'm sitting there, and there he is, outstretched, showing a pose, telling me to draw it. I'm going, "Holy sh*t. I'm Jack Kirby! I can't believe I'm in this room with my idol, Stan Lee, and he's on the furniture, and he's telling me 'draw this.'" It was one of the most magical moments in my life.

Anyway, when we were through, we had these tissue overlays that he could then send to John to show the changes that he wanted on these two pages. And, oh my God, I was so excited. Talk about dreams come true. It was an incredible moment for me, and I really felt like I was experiencing first-hand the legendary creative process of Stan Lee as a writer, as an editor, as a visual genius in terms of his storytelling. And, boy, it doesn't get better than that.

DF: *What was the plotting process like for that series?*
MU: Well, Stan had his own ideas for backstory. He was re-imagining the backstories and the characterizations of DC's classic superheroes. So it took a lot more explanation on his part than Stan probably was used to giving in the Marvel days.

DF: *Did Stan write up "Marvel style" plots for the stories?*
MU: Yeah, except they were more extensive, I think, than he was used to doing at Marvel. I think they went on a lot longer, with a lot more detail. Now, some artists wanted more leeway, and Stan left it open for them for their creative input. So I think some guys, for example Dave Gibbons, took the plot and twisted it in a lot of different ways, and then brought it back to Stan, and Stan said, "I like what you're doing here." On the other hand, some of the others just took exactly what Stan gave them and went with that.

DF: *How'd you meet Stan?*
MU: The first time I met him, I was in seventh grade. Bob Klein and I—Bob is now a noted comic book historian, and he and I have done a lot of intros to archives editions and other books like that—went up to New York for the DC Comics tour. We took the train in from the Jersey Shore. We were about 12 or 13 years old at the time. We would do the DC tour, and then we used to run around to every comic book company in town and do interviews for fanzines. One day we'd knock on the door at Harvey, and we would wind up having an hour or two with Joe Simon, who was editing the Harvey action line at the time; another day, somebody else. So we went to Marvel and found out, to our chagrin, there was no Marvel tour. So we sat in the lobby for hours, and anybody that came in or out, we jumped up and asked them if they were anybody. Finally, Flo Steinberg

came to our rescue.

You know, originally, we came to find, actually, the Baxter Building. *[laughter]* We figured maybe we could get a tour of that. Not that we thought the Fantastic Four were real, but we thought the Baxter Building was a real building in New York. Flo set us straight on that. We must have seemed so pathetic to her. Thanks to her, Jack Kirby autographed my copy of ***All Winners*** #18, and that's when we met Stan Lee for the first time, and got an autograph, which was about as exciting as things possibly could have been.

I'm guessing this was around '63, around the time of ***X-Men*** #1. The next time I remember seeing Stan, he spoke at a comic book convention. He had the goatee, so I'm thinking maybe it was '67 or '68. It could have been at the Statler Hilton, or the Commodore, or one of those conventions. And I had a chance to listen to him and ask him some questions. Those were the earliest days of the relationship.

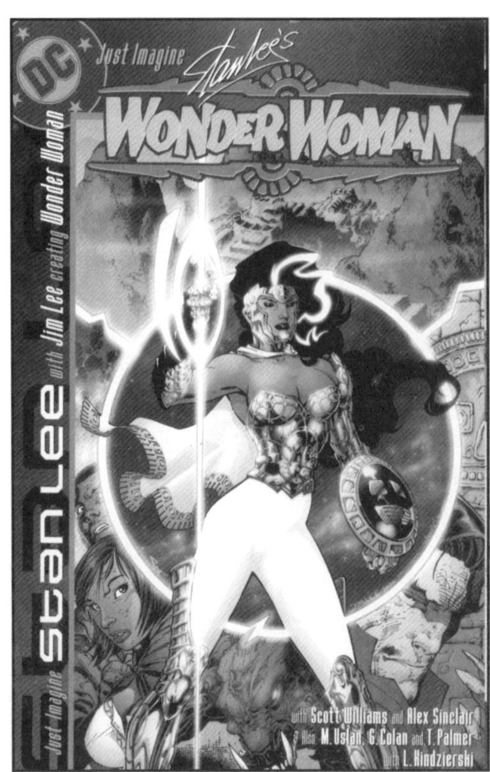

Jim Lee and Scott Williams' cover to the 2001 ***Just Imagine Stan Lee and Jim Lee Creating Wonder Woman.*** [© 2011 DC Comics.]

The way it blossomed, it was 1971, and I had just begun teaching the world's first accredited college course on comic books. I never taught a session of that course that wasn't filled with TV cameras and reporters from every magazine and newspaper you could possibly imagine, because I publicized it, mostly by calling media people as a citizen "outraged" there was a comics course being given for college credit! NBC Nightly News and CBS News were down there. And two or three weeks into it I get a call. I pick up the phone, and this voice says, "Is this Mike Uslan?" And I go, "Yes." He goes, "Hiya, Mike! This is Stan Lee from Marvel Comics in New York City." And this I continually refer to as my "burning bush" moment. He said, "Everywhere I'm looking, I'm reading about you, I'm seeing you on TV, I hear you on the radio. What you're doing is great for the whole comic book industry. How can I help you?"

He began by sending me comics, and then sending out Gerry Conway, and Steve Englehart, who were two of my first lecturers in the course. Then Sol Harrison from DC called about three hours later, and wound up sending me Denny O'Neil. And the floodgates just opened up. But that really began a regular association with Stan. He really loved what I was doing, trying to show that comic books were an art form, were legitimate literature, and could be used in education. He was a very, very strong advocate of that. And things developed from there.

DF: *Was* ***Just Imagine*** *the first thing you actually worked on with him, or did you work on projects with him before?*
MU: Well, the first actual printed creative project that I worked on with Stan was ***Just Imagine.*** But before that, we worked creatively, in '86 or '87, on a new cartoon series for Marvel Animation, which was going to be part of a syndicated Marvel block. It was a brand new version of ***Captain Video.*** I had created it, and Stan loved it, and I began working with him. Margaret Loesch was running the studio at the time, and the three of us worked a lot together to make that thing work. And we took it to NATPE [the meeting of the National Association of Television Programming Executives] and the program was selling great [to advertisers] there, and then, when we were set to go forward and make the show, it was one of those times when Marvel was sold, maybe to New World, who ultimately put the kibosh on a number of projects, including ours. But that was the first time Stan and I really got in the trenches together.

DF: *Do you remember anything specific you learned from Stan?*
MU: I remember him saying specifically that, by creating the new version of *Captain Video,* I'd only done half the job, and that the villains were just as important as the superhero if I wanted this thing to last, if I wanted it to work. He sent me back to really expand on the show's villains. He felt that the thing to tie it into at that moment in time was modern technology, in order to give the show a sense of believability, a way for an audience to suspend its disbelief and jump into it. I think Stan always enjoyed dealing with the scientific world, "science gone mad," versus science when it's properly channeled—which I think, thematically, was probably connected to his feelings about the military-industrial complex. And if you don't believe me, all you have to do is take a look at ***The Hulk*** to get a grasp of that. So it was wonderful—I was getting the Marvel training from Stan in terms of that animation project because it was a superhero type of character.

DF: *How would you sum up what you've learned from Stan over the years, Michael?*
MU: A lot of things, including: Get readers or viewers to suspend their disbelief and buy into what you're doing. Never talk down to them. Incorporate important themes while never once forgetting that the whole purpose of this is to be fun, and that your job is to entertain, whether it's for a 22-minute cartoon, or for a 20- or 30-page story in a comic book. He taught me the importance of characterization, and of making the characters pop and the dialogue ring true, that the dialogue for each person is unique to his or her own voice. I remember him saying that the second you could read word balloons and they could be coming from more than one character, you're not doing your job right. He taught me the importance of proper pacing of a story. And, as I mentioned before, he taught me the very important concept that heroes are defined by their villains, and that the heroes' popularity is dependent on the quality of the villains that they face.

Written By Stan Lee

Comics scholar and historian Peter Sanderson talks about Stan's inimitable writing style

In early 2007, New York's Museum of Comic and Cartoon Art (MoCCA) showcased a retrospective show about Stan and his career. Comics scholar and historian ***Peter Sanderson*** *was co-curator of the exhibit, and while putting it together, gained some awesome insights into Stan's writing techniques. Here, the erudite Mr. Sanderson shares what he observed.*

—DF & RT

[This article first appeared in **Write Now!** *#18.]*

Comics combine words and pictures, but when museums stage shows about comics, the emphasis tends to be on the visual side of the medium. But in 2007, my colleague Ken Wong and I co-curated "Stan Lee: A Retrospective" at the Museum of Comic and Cartoon Art (MoCCA) in New York City, an exhibition focused on perhaps the most highly-regarded comics writer of all. [See photo essay on the exhibition elsewhere in this book. —DF & RT]

In writing the texts that accompanied each page of original art in the show, I developed even greater appreciation of Lee's achievements as a writer. As the section of our exhibit devoted to the "Marvel Method" explained, Jack Kirby and Steve Ditko co-plotted—or even entirely plotted—their collaborations with Lee. But I came to realize that even if, for the sake of argument, we only consider Stan Lee's role in scripting the stories—adding the dialogue and captions after the art was drawn—his contributions are still extraordinary and groundbreaking.

When you consider Stan Lee's writing style, perhaps the first thing you think of is his sense of humor. Not only would Spider-Man puncture a villain's pomposity with cutting wisecracks, but Stan also devised a winning comedic persona for himself, both in the Bullpen Bulletins pages and in the captions through which he narrated his stories. Indeed, I think of Stan Lee as a member of the same generation of urban, Jewish-American comedians of the early 1960s, like Woody Allen and the team of Mike Nichols and Elaine May. He—and Harvey Kurtzman—just happened to work in a different medium.

In recent years, narration in comics has fallen out of fashion. But it's one of the tools that the comics medium provides, and Lee handled it masterfully.

For example, there was the splash from ***Daredevil*** #15 (cover-dated April 1966), drawn by John Romita, Sr. and Frank Ray (a pseudonym for Frank Giacoia), in our exhibit, showing the hero swinging into view on his billy club cable. It is a beautifully drawn splash, dramatically telling the visual aspect of the story, leaving Lee free to enhance the reading experience with a caption and dialogue, explaining how much Matt Murdock loves to escape from his everyday existence as a blind lawyer into the thrills, the sheer joy, of his life as a costumed superhero. Through his introductory captions, Lee turns the page into an exciting overture to Daredevil's latest adventure, and perhaps even an added inducement to a potential purchaser to buy the issue.

Splash page to ***Daredevil*** #15 (April 1966), where the omniscient narrator—a.k.a. "Stan"—leads us into the story, and enhances the already-sensational art by John Romita and Frank Giacoia (still going by his soon-to-be discarded "Frank Ray" pseudonym).

We also had on display a full-size reproduction of the opening page to the Thor story "The Power of the Thunder God" from ***Journey into Mystery*** #111 (December 1964), with Thor facing off against the team of Mr. Hyde and the Cobra as he attempts to rescue the unconscious Jane Foster. Jack Kirby provides powerful artwork, but through the dramatic tone of his opening captions and dialogue, Lee endows the confrontation with an epic quality.

One of the highlights of the exhibition showed just how the "Marvel style" worked. We were loaned some originall art pages in which the celebrated "border notes" that Kirby used to write, to tell Lee what was happening in each panel, were clearly visible.

One of them was a page from "And Soon Shall Come the Enchanters" from ***Thor*** #143 (August 1967). Describing one panel, Kirby wrote, "Then only the smoking footprints remain." Lee transformed this simple line into a caption that read: "Naught now remains but the slowly-fading impression of smoldering footprints," which, to me, is far more expressive.

To begin with, "naught" strongly conveys the idea that there is nothing remaining of the maker of these footprints but the footprints themselves; all else is a void. Furthermore, though Lee's witticisms in his scripts are very modern, a phrase like "naught now" seems intentionally old-fashioned, and hence suitable for the ***Thor*** series, which transplants Norse mythology into the present day. Even the use of the British spelling of "smouldering" adds to the Shakespearean sense Lee liked to give his Thor stories. And, although Lee could revel in humorous alliteration, here he employs it subtly, for poetic effect, making use of the similar sounds of "naught" and "now," also "slowly" and "smouldering," as well as of "fading" and "footprints."

While it was probably Kirby's idea to put in the visual detail of the smoking footprints, here we can see how Lee uses language to strengthen the dramatic impact of Kirby's image and even to endow it with a poetic feel. This is an example of Lee and Kirby working in perfect accord, with Stan's script complementing Jack's visuals, and vice versa.

But another piece of original art that we displayed in the "Marvel Method" section of the exhibit showed Lee and Kirby at loggerheads. This was the second page from the landmark "Bedlam at the Baxter Building," the tale of the wedding of Reed and Susan Richards, from ***Fantastic Four Annual*** #3 (1965). We see Doctor Doom, enraged by the news that today is Reed and Sue's wedding day, tearing a newspaper into shreds. In the next panel, he wears a look of angst as he holds out his hands and soliloquizes.

According to Kirby's border notes, the act of tearing up the paper sent pain shooting into one of Doom's hands. In his last appearance, in ***Fantastic Four*** #40, the Thing had crushed Doom's hand in one-on-one combat. So that is why Kirby drew Doom wearing a literally pained expression as he holds out his hands. According to Kirby's notes, it is Doom's rage over his ignominious defeat and injury by the Thing that motivates him to want to launch his attack on Reed and Sue's wedding ceremony.

But wait—the story is about the wedding, not about the Thing. Surely that is why Stan chose to reinterpret this sequence with Doctor Doom. In Lee's script, Doom vents his hatred of Reed Richards, not the Thing. After all, despite the humiliating defeat the Thing inflicted on him, it was Richards Doom had always regarded as his greatest enemy. So, in Lee's telling, Doom is out to take vengeance on Reed by wrecking his wedding. This is a far stronger premise given how the rest of the story unfolds. In this case, I believe Lee was right in overriding Kirby's intentions.

Lee has made no secret of his love of Shakespeare, whose characters speak in a range of different styles, from the high poetry of his tragic heroes to the earthy prose of his clowns and rustic characters. In his own fashion Lee was following the Bard's example.

With characters like Thor, the Sub-Mariner, and the Silver Surfer, Lee strove to devise an elevated style of language that suited the nobility of his characters. Whereas so many DC Comics villains of the 1960s were, in effect, costumed bank robbers, Lee used language to put his great criminal masterminds on a higher dramatic plane. In the very first ***Fantastic Four*** comic I ever read, #58, Doctor Doom thundered at the Thing, "You insufferable—unspeakable blot on the escutcheon of humanity—prepare to meet the fate you so sorely deserve!!" I knew then that Doom had a sort of majesty I'd never seen in any comics villain before. (And I had to look up "escutcheon." Maybe you will, too.)

Dr. Doom plots revenge in 1965's ***Fantastic Four Annual*** #3. Stan scripts over art by Jack Kirby and Vince Colletta. [© 2011 Marvel Characters, Inc.]

Much of Lee's brilliance lies in his ability to delineate characterization through dialogue. Of course, the colloquial, down-to-Earth dialogue that Stan gives to characters like the Thing or Nick Fury provides a sharp, often funny, contrast with the grandiose bluster of the villains or the formal diction of characters like Reed Richards. Similarly, Lee's narration can poke fun at his characters, his stories, and even himself, without ever subverting their drama or descending into "camp."

That brings me to the most important thing about Lee's narration. His skill with narrative captions can draw readers deeply into a story. Yet he can also "break the fourth wall" and address the readers directly, reminding them it is "only" a comic book story. He can even take both approaches on the same page, yet they don't contradict each other. Somehow it all works as a seamless whole.

Through his narrative voice, Stan Lee casts himself in the archetypal role of storyteller. We suspend our disbelief and believe in his stories, even as we are aware that Lee is telling them to us, despite—or perhaps because of—his peppering his narration with ingratiating jokes. In terms of his 1960s work as seen in the MoCCA exhibit, no matter who drew and co-plotted the stories, it was Stan as editor, scripter and voice of the narrator-storyteller who bound the story's elements together, and bound our affections to his new Marvel Universe as well.

Peter Sanderson *is a comics guru in his own right, penning books, journal articles, and criticism, teaching courses at New York University, and producing documentaries on comics. Peter joined the Marvel Comics staff as an assistant editor, later becoming Marvel's first archivist. He was main writer of* **The Official Handbook of the Marvel Universe** *and writer of* **The Marvel Saga: The Official History of the Marvel Universe.** *His recent work includes the 2010* **Obsessed with Marvel**.

My Lunch With Stan

Jeff McLaughlin tells the (sort of) sensational story behind an interview with Stan

*As one of the growing number of academics who study comics seriously, **Jeff McLaughlin** has added to our knowledge base with his book,* **Comics as Philosophy.** *Stepping outside the ivy-covered walls of Thompson Rivers University, where he teaches, to research his recent book,* **Stan Lee: Conversations,** *McLaughlin ventured not merely to Cheyenne, Wyoming, home of the fabled Stan Lee Archives, but to Los Angeles, CA, home of the fabled Stan Lee. Here, Dr. M tells us the story of his day interviewing Stan. Talk about meta-events!*

—DF & RT

[This article first appeared in **Write Now!** *#18.]*

I don't consider myself a writer, but rather someone who writes. It is part of my job description as an Assistant Professor of Philosophy. When I write it's usually with the intent to convince others of a particular thesis.

And so it was with a fair deal of intrepidity, fear, and excitement that I, a non-writer, met Stan Lee on January 21, 2005. The Los Angeles weather was warm, the sun was shining, and my heart was up somewhere around my throat. This was, at last, my opportunity to do a current interview that would cap the book of collected Stan Lee interviews I was researching and editing. Yet within minutes of seeing "The Man" stand up from behind his desk to greet me, my heart would sink...

A striking page from ***The Silver Surfer*** graphic novel. Copies of the script and pencil art from this landmark Lee-Kirby work—some of which are seen elsewhere in this book—are in Stan's Wyoming archives. [Story ©1978 Stan Lee and Jack Kirby. Silver Surfer © 2011 Marvel Characters, Inc.]

"We've been trying to reach you all morning." He said. "We've tried to leave messages at your hotel."

"I've been out exploring." Actually I was too nervous to sit in the hotel room until the appointed hour.

He'd been busy with emergency meetings all morning. "I know we scheduled to meet today," he continued, "but can we do this some other time?"

"Some other time... " I had flown thousands of miles and had no other time. It was Friday, and I was to be back in the classroom Monday morning.

"I have an important meeting at ABC at 2 pm," he added.

I explained that I was leaving the next day. I tried not to show my utter disappointment as I felt this rare opportunity starting to slip away from me.

"Maybe we can cover some of your questions during lunch and you can e-mail me the rest?"

This was definitely not what I had hoped for. E-mail?

"Or maybe after lunch you can ask me the rest of your questions in the car as Gill" [his business partner, Gill Champion] "and I drive to the meeting on the other side of town... "

Things were starting to improve. My heart was beginning to go settle back into its normal place within my chest.

So we marched off to find a nearby restaurant. I was surprised to see Stan walk faster than a man half his age (namely me). He picked some restaurant, the name of which I can't remember, but I remember the waiter never said so much as a word about whom he was seating. I figured he must have been used to it since it was Beverly Hills, after all. We ate lunch what seemed like quickly, though it was probably more like an hour. "You eat, I'll talk." he said. So I did. And he did.

You can well imagine the range of questions that I might have formulated after spending endless days tracking down interviews from long out-of-print magazines and newspapers and going through some 90-odd boxes of Lee's own paperwork from his archives housed at the University of Wyoming. It seemed to me as I waded through those files that he saved every letter ever written to him from his millions of fans. These letters were compelling, and some were quite touching, but they got in my way of looking for what I considered the real treasures: the little-seen interviews that were to make up my book, and hopefully—material for a future book?—classic plots, scripts, and so on. Reading 30- and 40-year-old letters from kids who don't understand why there are so few ethnic representations in comics, or from soldiers in Vietnam either thanking him or complaining to him about something or other might have been intriguing and insightful socio-political fodder—but for some other time. There were Photostatted pages of the ***Spider-Man*** newspaper strip from the John Romita period, a few from ***The Silver Surfer*** graphic novel he did with Jack Kirby, but no "lost masterpieces." Besides, Stan is a writer, not an artist. So perhaps then I might find a stash of his original comic book scripts... ? Yet, sadly, I only came across two such examples—actually more like one-and-a-half. "Why would I save those?" he would rhetorically ask me at our lunch. "Why *wouldn't* you?" I thought. Indeed, why would a writer find it more important to keep a letter from some 12-year-old kid saying that the Hulk was his favorite character and yet not keep a single ***Hulk*** comic script?

Frankly, it was hard trying to eat lunch with Lee sitting across from me as he talked about his work. His accomplishments were intimidating. He was (without meaning to be) intimidating. Direct and very purpose-driven. *If you're here to interview then let's get on with it.* So how could I pretend that this was a normal lunch? I wanted to show him that I wasn't just an enthusiast, but a serious and objectively interested scholar. This was my one and only chance to impress this man who had shaped an important part of American popular culture and worked with some of our great creative minds over the majority of the last century. Here we were two strangers having a conversation, but I knew him because I grew up with him.

I had studied him more than most. I came armed with photocopies of some of his work that hadn't seen the light of day since they first left his hand. Having seen internal Marvel memos and notes, and having already read hundreds of interviews, I also hoped to be able to rebut any of his standardized replies and perhaps throw something new at him along the way. I showed him some of the artifacts I found in his archives. A letter from the U.S. Department of Health asking him to write an anti-drug story. An unproduced ***Silver Surfer*** screenplay. Samples of his non-comic book photo magazine ventures. He realized, I think, how thorough I had been. So I relaxed a bit. I asked and he answered at a rate that pleased both of us.

Following lunch, I found myself asking questions for posterity, while sitting in a well-kept 10-year-old Mercedes convertible with the top down, crawling in typical Southern California traffic, with the most famous name and face in comic books as my driver.

"Yes, I see... Interesting... Hmm. Good point, but what about... " Those are probably some of the things I was saying. But inside I was thinking: I am in Stan Lee's car, being driven by Stan Lee! And he's talking to me!

He never kept the scripts. Damn. I can hear you all now saying that in unison. I guess personal correspondence from kids, parents, and school principals discussing his work, either positively or negatively, meant more. Once a script is completed, what reason would there be to keep it? Just move on to the next story. Heck, if you wanted to see the script, just grab a copy of the comic off the newsstand. Funny, though, he did appear to keep every creative idea that entered his head. In with his typed-up Stan's Soapbox columns I would find 8½" x 11" sheets of paper with quickly jotted down notes such as: "Write a story about a turtle." "Write a story about a shopping mall." Not quite earth-shattering. But just imagine what they might have been if he ran with them? Perhaps there were others that I missed. Perhaps there was a note: "Write a story about some ordinary teenagers with ordinary problems but with unique talents..." A whole industry was reborn with those kinds of simple ideas.

There is one thing that he did say to me a couple of times on that memorable day that puzzled me for the longest time. Whenever he would make a point that he thought could, somewhere in the far off reaches of the universe, be misinterpreted, he would tell me to be sure to write how he said what he said, and not just what he said. That is, hypothetically speaking, if he stated that I was the brightest human being on the face of the Earth (but he didn't—remember this is hypothetical), and I simply wrote down: "Stan Lee says I am the brightest human being on the face of the Earth," the reader would not know whether it was intended as a joke, as a sarcastic putdown, or as a serious statement.

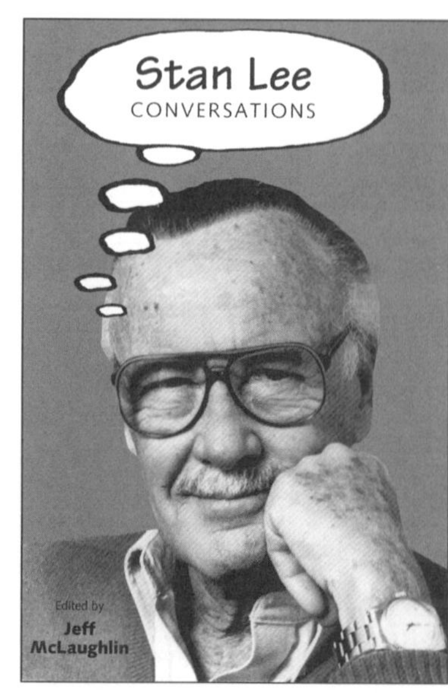

Cover to the McLaughlin-edited ***Stan Lee: Conversations***, the book Jeff discusses in this article, a collection of interviews from over the decades with Stan. Published by University Press of Mississippi. [© 2007 by University Press of Mississippi.]

Of course, one reason for his concern was about being misrepresented or misinterpreted or having statements taken out of context. But it was more as if he needed, or saw the need for, a visual or auditory accompaniment to his text. Did he laugh when he said it? Was there a twinkle in his eyes, or did he just roll them at me? What sort of intonation was there in his voice? Here was one of the most prolific and popular writers of any time telling me that what a person utters isn't sufficient to capture what they mean when we put those words down on paper. Here's a writer saying that words, that transcribed speech, alone can't do the trick. Might this be a theory about the value of comic books—that the writer without the artist can only suggest? Or possibly Lee was simply pointing out that the writer has to be clear and truthful, and that if he does that well enough, he doesn't have to be writing philosophy to get his ideas across. He could be writing a novel, or a comic book.

Or an article about meeting a childhood idol.

Jeff McLaughlin *is assistant professor of philosophy at Thompson Rivers University in Kamloops, British Columbia, and editor of* **Comics as Philosophy** *and, of course,* ***Stan Lee: Conversations,*** *both published by University Press of Mississippi.*

Jeff found copies of ***Spider-Man*** newspaper strips in the Archives. Here's part of the strip's Spidey origin, written by Stan, with art by John Romita, Sr.

Meanwhile, down the hall...

FROM THE STAN LEE ARCHIVES

Stan's writing and editing for Martin Goodman's non-comics publications

by Danny Fingeroth

Publisher **Martin Goodman** produced not only Timely/Atlas/Marvel comics, but also (via his Magazine Management Company) a line of magazines aimed at men. Mag. Mgmt. would ultimately become one of the largest producers of such magazines. Often, staffers and freelancers worked for both parts of the company.

Here, we see the cover and contents page of the October 1942 premiere issue of ***The Male Home Companion***. Note a contribution to the mag by Jerome Weidman, author of the novel, ***I Can Get It For You Wholesale*** and the musical ***Fiorello!***

MHC's contents page shows that Stan had two prose short stories in the issue. "... Where is Thy Sting?" is credited to "Stan Lee." "The Madman of Peekskill Point" is credited to "Stanley Martin," which is the first two-thirds of Stan's original name, Stanley Martin Lieber.

Here, the beginning of "Sting," including illustrations by Don Rico:

THE male HOME COMPANION

ROBERT L. RICHARDS
Editor

GEORGE DAUGHTRY
Associate

MELVIN DONALD
Art Director

A MALE IS BORN

In This Issue

COVER DESIGN BY CARDWELL HIGGINS

THE MALE HOME COMPANION is published every other month by Select Publications, Inc., at Washington and South Avenues, Dunellen, N. J. Application for second-class entry pending at the Post Office at Dunellen, N. J., under Act of March 3, 1879. Vol. 1, No. 1. October 1942 issue. Contents copyright 1942 by Select Publications, Inc., 164 Madison Ave., New York, N. Y. Subscription $1.50 for six issues. Manuscripts and drawings must be accompanied by sufficient return postage, but no responsibility will be assumed for loss or damage to unsolicited material. Reproduction or use of editorial or pictorial content is prohibited unless the publishers give written permission. Use of a person's name in fiction, non-fiction or humorous articles is purely coincidental. Printed in the U. S. A.

"....Where is Thy Sting?"

STAN LEE

BURTON was undeniably dead. From the top of his head to the tip of his toes he was five foot three of lifelessness. His heart had been still for hours and he distinctly remembered that the last breath he had drawn was in O'Brian's Tavern just as dawn was breaking. It was now twelve noon of the next day and Burton began to take stock of the situation.

To begin with, he felt a little bit foolish walking around the streets without breathing. Burton was the living soul of convention. In all of his fifty-two years of living existence he had never missed taking a breath at regular intervals. But now, everything was different. He was dead!

Harry turned to him with a grimace. "Say, Burt," said Harry, "I'm getting tired of walking the streets with you. Just because you got your wish and now you're dead you want to show off and have everybody see you! It's getting annoying."

"Don't be silly," answered Burton, reproachfully. "I'm just walking around because I don't know what else to do." Burton flung out his hands in a gesture of helplessness. "I haven't been dead for very long, you know."

"I still don't think that Minerva will like this idea." Harry changed the subject. "Your being dead will prove to be a shock to her."

Burton manfully threw back his narrow shoulders. "I don't care! Minerva brought this upon herself. If she hadn't scolded me last night I wouldn't have gone to O'Brian's Tavern. And if I hadn't gone to O'Brian's Tavern I wouldn't have gotten good and drunk. And if I hadn't been good and drunk I wouldn't have said that I wished I was dead. And if I hadn't said that I wished I was dead I wouldn't be dead now."

"But you did say that you wished you were dead," interrupted Harry. "And now you've got to go home and explain the whole thing to Minerva. And I still say that I don't think she'll like the idea."

"Well, here we are at my house," said Burton sadly. "Will you come in with me, Harry?"

"No thank you," replied his friend. "I'll leave you here. Good luck with your wife, Burton, and please accept my consolations."

"Thank you," answered Burton as he left Harry and started up the brief walk which led to his little cottage. He wondered about the propriety of Harry offering his consolations to a corpse.

* * *

"So there you are!"

Those words rang out sharply, forming a truism as Burton closed the door behind him. "Yes, dear, I'm home," he muttered, hesitantly.

"I might have known that as soon as my back was turned you'd run out of the house! You were out with that no-good bunch of friends of yours, of course!" Burton didn't know whether that was a question, an accusation or a feeler designed to make him give away valuable bits of information. "Come here, you worm!"

More from force of habit than from a desire to oblige, Burton walked closer to Minerva. Never had she looked so formidable as at this moment, hovering above him with malicious intent. For a moment he was glad he was dead.

WOODCUTS BY DON RICO

[Copyright 1942, Select Publications, Inc.]

box 31, folder 1, American Heritage Center, University of Wyoming.

Here, the cover and contents page to 1950's ***Focus*** # 5, edited by Stan, at the same time he was writing end editing a zillion comics. The guy has always liked to keep busy.

Focus

DECEMBER

VOL. 1, NO. 5

STAN LEE, Editor
BONNIE HERMAN, Assistant Editor

MEL BLUM, Art Director
BILL GREG, Art Associate

WHO IS THIS GIRL???

She's one of the breath-taking beauties you'll find in the following pages of this month's Focus. See if you can recognized her in this magazine.

contents

And ya have to love the ad for ***The Wrestling Scene***, a book written by Guy LeBow, a then-prominent New York radio and TV sportscaster. [Focus ©2011 by Non-Pareil Publishing Corp.]

1950 *Focus* magazine materials, Stan Lee Collection, box #31, folder #2, American Heritage Center, University of Wyoming.

Script pages from *The Monster Maker*

A glimpse at the screenplay Stan wrote for Alain Resnais

In James Monaco's 1978 book ***Alain Resnais: The Role of Imagination,*** Resnais speaks about Stan and ***The Monster Maker*** in one chapter. [Seeker & Warburg, London; Oxford University Press, New York. Copyright © James Monaco 1978.]

Stan met **Alain Resnais** in 1969 when the famed director of ***Hiroshima Mon Amour, Night and Fog,*** and ***Last Year at Marienbad*** sought him out on a visit to New York. Born in the same year, the two men became good friends and worked on several projects together. One was a proposed film, called ***The Monster Maker***, a movie that tied the story of a film producer's midlife creative crisis into a cautionary tale about the dangers of pollution. In 1971, Stan wrote a screenplay for it, of which we reproduce a few pages here. While ***The Monster Maker*** never got made (a fate that befalls 99% of film scripts), Stan would use the metaphor of pollution years later in his ***Ravage 2099*** comics series.

Not unlike Stan's many accomplishments and Resnais' acclaimed film résumé, producer Martin Ransohoff's Filmways (note the credit at the bottom of the screenplay's title page) also has an impressive roster of achievements including the movies ***Catch-22, American Pop, Silver Streak, Save the Tiger,*** and ***The Cincinnati Kid***, and the classic TV sitcom, ***The Beverly Hillbillies!***

Poster for perhaps Resnais's best-known film, 1959's ***Hiroshima Mon Amour.*** [©2011 the copyright holders]

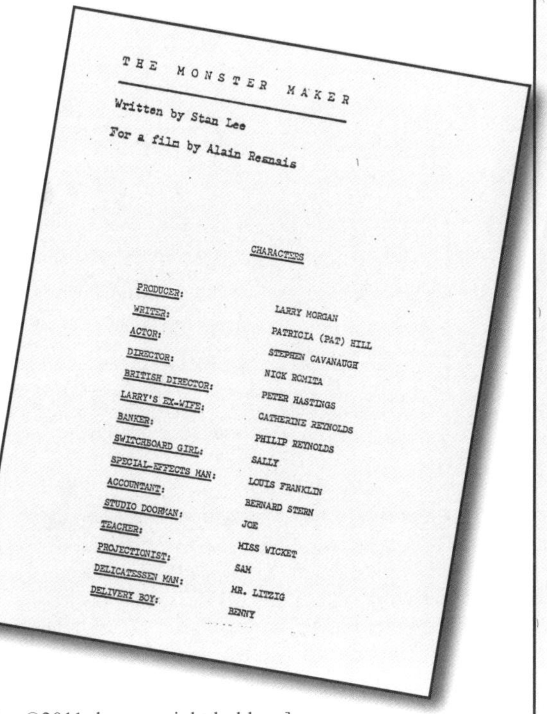

THE MONSTER MAKER

Written by Stan Lee

For a film by Alain Resnais

CHARACTERS

PRODUCER:	LARRY MORGAN
WRITER:	PATRICIA (PAT) HILL
ACTOR:	STEPHEN CAVANAUGH
DIRECTOR:	NICK ROMITA
BRITISH DIRECTOR:	PETER HASTINGS
LARRY'S EX-WIFE:	CATHERINE REYNOLDS
BANKER:	PHILIP REYNOLDS
SWITCHBOARD GIRL:	SALLY
SPECIAL-EFFECTS MAN:	LOUIS FRANKLIN
ACCOUNTANT:	BERNARD STERN
STUDIO DOORMAN:	JOE
TEACHER:	MISS WICKET
PROJECTIONIST:	SAM
DELICATESSEN MAN:	MR. LITZIG
DELIVERY BOY:	BENNY

The title page and first page of Stan's script for ***The Monster Maker***, the product of many discussions between him and Resnais.

1

1 EXT. OZONE PARK, N.Y. DAY

Monday, Oct. 19, 1970. An unwieldy, ponderous garbage truck rumbles through the narrow streets like some monstrous, mechanical behemoth. We follow behind as it inexorably pursues its dreary, deafening, never-ending course.

Finally, it shudders to a stop as a bored garbage man rolls a battered can of refuse to the stationary but still roaring vehicle which is blocking traffic on the gloomy, one-way street.

Behind the smelly, grinding truck waits a silent hearse, followed by a two-car funeral cortege. Directly behind the sombre hearse is a black limousine with three occupants-- the chauffeur, the minister, and a gaunt, grim cadaver of a man who stares unblinkingly ahead; his sharp, hawk-like features and piercing, deep-set eyes mirroring his obvious grief. He is STEPHEN CAVANAUGH.

Bringing up the rear of the little convoy is a Pontiac convertible, driven by forty-year old LARRY MORGAN. Next to him, sharing the wide bucket seat are PAT HILL, a brightly attractive, hip-looking career girl in her early thirties, and NICK ROMITA, whose gruff, uncompromising honesty makes up for the lack of polish which his thirty-seven years of living have never gained him.

The time is two PM. The occasion a gloomy one. Each of our characters is silently lost in his own sober thoughts.

2 EXT. OZONE PARK, N.Y. DAY

Finally, the garbage truck moves on. As it turns the corner, the three-car funeral procession continues straight ahead, on its slow-moving journey to the cemetery.

3. EXT. CEMETERY DAY

At approximately 3 PM, the small cortege reaches Evans Road in the Jamaica section of New York and passes through the gates of the cemetery-- this grim, gray repository for the human residue, the human waste, the human garbage of the world.

4. EXT. GRAVE SITE DAY

As the four mourners stand by, the minister intones the final rites for the deceased. We can hear the mourners' comments over the minister's dull and droning voice. In the background, as if to point up the commercialistic quality of the ritual, a gigantic gas tank looms over the scene, throwing its huge, misshapen shadow over the solemn ceremony.

[*The Monster Maker* ©2011 the copyright holders.]

Script pages from *The Monster Maker* screenplay, Stan Lee Collection, box #53, folder #7, American Heritage Center, University of Wyoming.

2

MINISTER (this dialogue will be heard behind voices of other speakers)
The Lord is my shepherd; I shall not want. He maketh me to lie down in green pastures. He leadeth me beside the still waters. He restoreth my soul. He leadeth me in the paths of righteousness for His name's sake.

CAVANAUGH (grief-stricken)
Mary-- Mary. How can I live without you? Mary-- why were you taken from me?

ROMITA
C'mon, fella-- get ahold of yourself.

PAT (pointing in shock)
Look out!

Cavanaugh is attempting to hurl himself into the grave, as though to be with the casket forever. Larry and Romita reach out, grabbing his arms, restraining him.

CAVANAUGH
Let me go. I must go to her. She was my life. I can't let her leave me. Mary! Mary!

The minister has halted his ritualistic chant and reaches out towards Cavanaugh. But, seeing that Larry and Romita have him in hand, the minister contents himself with a few ad-lib words--

MINISTER
The Lord giveth, and the Lord taketh away. Let us not question the will of the Lord.

Having said the preceding, the minister resumes his prepared reading.

MINISTER
Yea, though I walk through the valley of the shadow of death, I will fear no evil; for Thou art with me. Thy rod and Thy staff they comfort me.

3

But, just as the minister begins the foregoing reading, Cavanaugh again cries out, and the following dialogue is heard over the minister's chant.

CAVANAUGH (as Larry and Romita continue to restrain him)
It wasn't the Lord. You can't blame it on Him. He didn't kill her. It was man. Man is the killer. Man! Man!

LARRY
This is no good. We've got to get him home. He's going to pieces.

PAT
Yes. He's bound to get better once we get him away from the grave site.

Still holding Cavanaugh's arms, Larry and Romita, followed by Pat, turn and lead him away-- as the minister continues to drone on.

5. EXT. CEMETERY, NEAR EXIT DAY

CAVANAUGH (weakly)
She's never been alone before. I was always with her. She was all I had.

LARRY
Just a little further. The car's just ahead.

One of the cemetery workers, tending flowers on a nearby grave, hears their voices and turns to look at our little group. Cavanaugh catches his eye, and the worker calls out to Larry as they pass.

WORKER
Hey, mister-- who is that guy? I got a feeling I seen 'im somewhere before. His face looks real familiar.

Larry and the others walk past without replying.

WORKER (bitterly)
Big shot!

4

6. EXT. LARRY'S CAR, DRIVING THRU STREETS DAY

The burial now a thing of the past, the small funeral party drives Cavanaugh to his home in the Broad Channel area of the Rockaways, in the vicinity of Jamaica Bay and Kennedy Airport. As car drives over the bridge, we hear the voices of its occupants.

LARRY
We'll have to find you a new place to live, Stephen.

STEPHEN
No. I want to stay here. It's where I've always lived-- with Mary.

PAT
But that's just it. You won't want to remain where every sight, every sound will remind you of her.

ROMITA
He won't have much choice. This whole place'll soon be condemned, anyway. They're gonna level it off to make room for more runways for the airport.

CAVANAUGH
I don't care. I'll never leave.

They reach Cavanaugh's house. It's an old, lonely, two-story structure at the end of an isolated, long-neglected street. They leave the car and walk to his door with Cavanaugh.

LARRY
No point in talking about it now. There's plenty of time. What he needs most is rest-- and a chance to forget.

7. INT. CAVANAUGH'S LIVING ROOM DAY

Cavanaugh paces restlessly, unable to rationally marshal his thoughts, unable to calm himself down. He rambles on emotionally, on the verge of hysteria. The others listen patiently, hoping he'll soon get his sorrow out of his system and then lie down to rest.

Resnais's 1955 documentary on the Holocaust, ***Night and Fog (Nuit et Brouillard),*** remains to this day one of the most powerful films on that horrific subject. [©2011 the copyright holders]

In 1961, Resnais made ***Last Year at Marienbad,*** a romance/mystery that became popular in the United States. [©2011 the copyright holders]

[Pages 2-4 of ***The Monster Maker*** script.] As in the pages of Marvel's comics, Stan called for authentic New York area locales for the drama of the script to play out against. Note that the protagonist is named "Larry" (Stan's brother's name) and that there's a character whose last name is "Romita," the same as Stan's longtime collaborator on countless comics.

[*The Monster Maker* ©2011 the copyright holders.]

BUT THE PRODUCER CONTINUES TO STARE OUT OF THE WINDOW, AS THOUGH UNAWARE OF THE ENTRANCE OF THE FANTASTIC FOUR, UNTIL...
EXCUSE ME, BUT I THINK YOU WERE EXPECTING US!
AND THEN, SLOWLY, CALMLY, HE TURNS, AND...
LOOK!
HOLY COW!
YOU!
IT'S THE SUB-MARINER!!
AT YOUR SERVICE!
7

Stan had written stories about movie producers before ***The Monster Maker's*** Larry Morgan—for instance in ***Fantastic Four*** #9, in which the producer who offers to solve the team's financial woes by starring them in a movie turns out to be their deadly foe, the Sub-Mariner. Script by Stan, art by Jack Kirby and Dick Ayers. [©2011 Marvel Characters Inc.]

```
                                                        5

                    CAVANAUGH
          Those years-- those long, long
          years that we've all worked
          together-- what do they mean?
          What do they matter now?
          They've added up to nothing.
          They're useless... wasted.
          Everything is wasted.
          Everything.

                    LARRY
          Look, we know how you feel, and--

                    CAVANAUGH
          No! You don't know how I feel.
          You can't know. I'm the one
          who'll have to live with this--
          live with this guilt-- all the
          rest of my life.

                    PAT
          But you've nothing to feel
          guilty about.

     Cavanaugh walks to window. He looks out of the window as
     he continues to speak.

                    CAVANAUGH
          I am guilty. We're all guilty.

8.   EXT.      JET PLANE, 747, FLYING                    DAY

     We see a 747 passenger jet flying over Cavanaugh's house,
     belching clouds of dark, smoky exhaust, as we hear Cavanaugh's
     voice/over.

                    CAVANAUGH
          Look. Look up there. We're not
          content with having polluted our
          planet. No. Now we have to
          soil the sky as well. Every
          hour-- every minute-- the flying
          death floats over us.

9.   INT.      CAVANAUGH'S LIVING ROOM                   DAY

                    CAVANAUGH
          It's above us. It's at our feet.
          It's all around us. We're
          fouling the world with our own
          garbage. And you speak to me
          of guilt.

     Cavanaugh sinks into a chair-- head buried in his hands--
     his shoulders heaving with silent, anguished sobs.
```

```
                                                        6

                    ROMITA
          Poor guy.

                    LARRY
          Look, maybe it'll be better if
          we leave you alone now. It'll
          give you a chance to pull
          yourself together.

                    PAT
          If there's anything we can do.
          Anything.

                    LARRY
          Don't even think about coming
          back to work for the next
          couple of days. We'll try to
          manage with---

                    CAVANAUGH
          Work? I'll never work again.
          Not your kind of work.

                    LARRY
          But you must. You--

                    ROMITA
          Let it lay, Larry. He doesn't
          know what he's saying now.

                    LARRY
          Yeah. I guess you're right.
          (they start to exit)
          Take it easy now, Stephen.
          I'll call you in the
          morning.

                    CAVANAUGH
          No. Don't call me. Don't
          ever call me again.

10.  EXT.      OUTSIDE CAVANAUGH'S HOUSE                 DAY

     They pause a moment to speak, after having walked out of
     Cavanaugh's house and having shut the front door behind them

                    ROMITA
          Him and Mary-- I knew they
          were close, but I never
          figured he'd go to
          pieces like that.
```

[Pages 5-7 of ***The Monster Maker*** script.] While it's unlikely ***The Monster Maker*** will ever get made, perhaps someone—Stan? Alain? The Sub-Mariner?—will find a way to one day get it on the screen. Love, loss, and humanity's relationship with the Earth are certainly eternal topics.

```
                                                        7

                    LARRY
          You'd think he'd almost be
          glad that it's finally over.
          I mean, the way she suffered
          those last few weeks.

                    PAT
          I hate to leave him like that.
          You saw how agitated he was.
          Look, just give me another
          minute. I want to go back
          and make sure he's all right.

     Pat turns and re-enters the house, the door not having
     locked behind them.

                    LARRY
          I didn't like it-- the way he
          said he'd never do our kind
          of work again.

                    ROMITA
          Aw, he'll get over it.
          Everybody does. Anyway,
          I can fix it so we can
          work without him till
          the end of the week.
          Of course, if he's not
          there next Monday, we'll
          be in big trouble.

                    LARRY
          It was sort of sad, how
          few people were at the
          burial. You'd think, at
          a time like that--

                    ROMITA
          Cavanaugh didn't notice.
          He was always a loner. Why
          else would they have lived
          in a place like this all
          these years?

     Pat comes out the front door again and rejoins the waiting
     men.

                    PAT
          I think he'll be all right
          now. He was making himself
          some hot chocolate, and
          promised to go to bed.
```

The Saga Of...

The Silver Surfer Graphic Novel

Lee & Kirby's last team-up has the groundbreaking duo going out with a bang!

by Danny Fingeroth

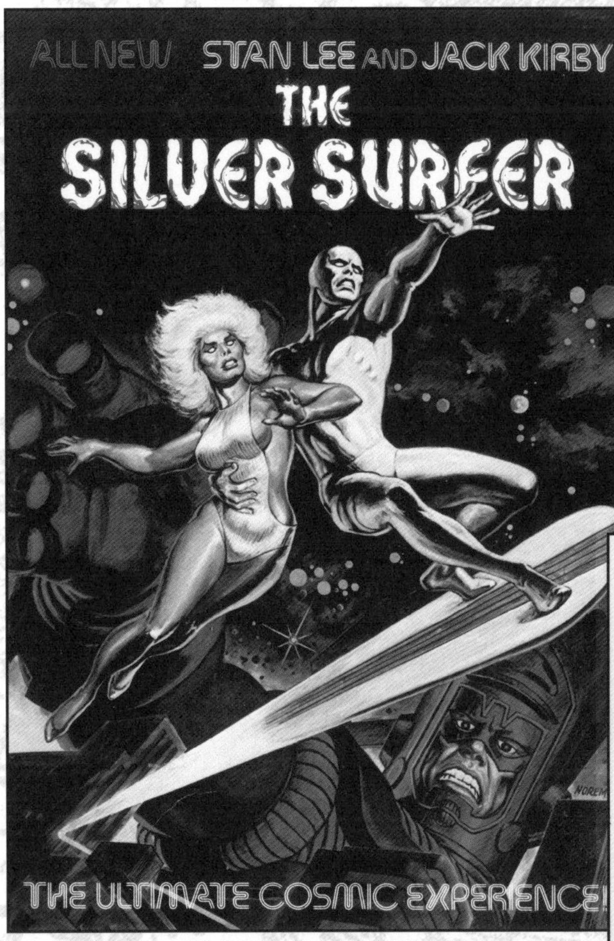

[Story ©1978 Stan Lee and Jack Kirby. Silver Surfer © 2011 Marvel Characters, Inc.]

Jack Kirby, who with Stan co-created the Fantastic Four, the Hulk, the X-Men and so many other groundbreaking cultural icons—including the Silver Surfer—had left Marvel in 1970 to spearhead his own line of comics at DC.

Stan's response to Frederic Frees about what it would take for the Surfer to return was written a year before Kirby did indeed return to Marvel in 1975, where he would work until 1978.

Kirby's return would indeed mean that he and Stan would combine for another Surfer project, this time in the then-new graphic novel format. The book was worked on in 1977 and published in 1978. The cover is painted by Earl Norem, based on a Kirby drawing. The line "The Ultimate Cosmic Experience" seems to be promotional copy, not a subtitle, since it's not seen anywhere in the interior of the book.

April 22, 1974

Mr. Frederic Frees
Imagination Inc.
443 Jackson Street
San Francisco, Ca. 94111

Dear Frederic:

Yes, there's a slim chance that the Silver Surfer will return.

If----

If Kirby comes back to draw him.

If I have the time to write the new stories.

If the world seems ready for Norrin Radd to once again zoom and soar above our woebegone world!

Excelsior!

SL/fl Stan Lee

Letter from Stan Lee to Frederic Frees, dated April 22, 1974, Stan Lee Collection, box #12, folder #5, American Heritage Center, University of Wyoming.

Preface

Well, we finally did it!

After all these years, Jolly Jack and I actually managed to complete the one book we've always been threatening to foist upon a stunned and startled public.

Y'know, it's a funny thing. The two of us have created a whole kaboodle of superheroes and supervillains during our many years of collaboration at the good ol' Marvel bullpen; and yet, the Silver Surfer seems to have a special meaning to us both—a special significance, which goes beyond the normal fascination for a bigger-than-life cosmic-powered character.

Perhaps it's the symbolism bit. Ever since his first appearance in the *Fantastic Four* issue of March 1965, he seems to have symbolized more than just a high-flying hero who got his kicks by battling bad guys. We've received countless letters from readers in all parts of the country—all parts of the world—commenting upon the Surfer's gestalt, comparing him to everyone from Ulysses to Gandhi, and likening his suffering to a pictorial depiction of the agonies of the early religious martyrs.

Well, I won't deny that such descriptions and comparisons absolutely delighted me. Ever since I first saw our gleaming sky-rider, when Jack placed the initial drawing upon my desk, I felt that he had to represent more than the typical comicbook hero. Somehow or other, King Kirby had imbued this new, unique, totally arresting fictional figure with a spiritual quality, a sense of nobility, a feeling of almost religious fervor in his attitude and his demeanor. As I studied that first drawing, and the ones that soon followed, I immediately realized that there was something very special about this solitary figure upon the high-flying spaceboard—something seemingly mystical, and totally compelling. I knew I couldn't give him the sort of dialogue I'd write for any other colorful supporting character in one of our fanciful little epics. No, the Surfer would have to receive very special attention, very special treatment. It was one of those rare cases where the character himself actually seems to determine how his creators will depict him...

In Stan's preface to the graphic novel, he describes how the Surfer came to be, how he and Jack work together in general, how the Surfer's unique style of speaking developed, and how he and Kirby worked out the plotline for this particular story.

Normally, in days of yore, an artist and writer had a very simple method of producing a comicbook epic. The writer would simply type the script and then hand it to the artist. Upon receiving the complete script, with panel descriptions and dialogue all spelled out, the artist merely followed the writer's written instructions and rendered the illustrations, much in the manner of a director structuring a stage play after receiving the author's manuscript. Yes, that was the way it used to be done. But, in the late 1950's, while collaborating on a myriad of fantasy tales, before the dawning of Marvel Comics, Jack and I had evolved another system of working, one which proved far more satisfying to us.

Since my cigar-smoking colleague has always had the greatest creativity, the greatest imagination, and the greatest visual story sense that one could hope for, I realized that there was really no need for me to labor over a fully developed script if Jack was to be the illustrator. All that

The Silver Surfer made his first appearance in ***Fantastic Four*** **#48** (March 1966), searching out planets for Galactus to devour. Script by Stan, art by Jack Kirby and Joe Sinnott. [©2011 Marvel Characters Inc.]

By ***FF*#50**, the climax of what has come to be known as "The Galactus Trilogy," the Surfer had decided to defend Earth, the planet he had chosen for Galactus, and turns against his master. Here, the Surfer fights and philosophizes simultaneously. Script by Stan, art by Kirby and Sinnott. [©2011 Marvel Characters Inc.]

was necessary was to discuss the basic plot with him, turn him loose, and wait until he brought me the penciled drawings. And that's what we did. Jack and I would discuss the high points of whatever story we intended to create, and then he'd trot off to his ivy-covered little inglenook to complete the drawings while I'd occupy myself with other bits of mischief elsewhere till he returned with the drawings done.

Once I received the penciled pages, it was then my task to write the dialogue and captions, giving the story the proper rhythmic mood and establishing the necessary characterization...

But what about today? I seem to sense the more curious amongst you wondering aloud how this very book itself came to be written. Since you've been so subtly prepared by the foregoing explanation, surely 'twill be no shock to you to learn that this very story was produced in the self-same manner. Ever eager for a trip out west, I bravely journeyed to Jack's idyllic aerie high in the hills of southern California. There, during a fateful visit while I waxed envious over the sunny weather and the sensational view, we hammered out the main elements of the phantasmagoric parable soon to unfold before your bedazzled eyes. Then, I took my leave and returned to the real world, where I waited with bated breath until, months later, the penciled pages finally arrived. And then, the whole process began again.

For days on end I studied the artwork, thrilled by the variety, the depth, and the quiet power of Jack's drawings. I tried to absorb and digest the various nuances and implications of each individual scene and sequence. And then, finally, the moment of truth arrived. The fun part was over. Now I had to write the thing!

Well, I won't bore you with the dreary details of the time spent determining how to set the mood, how to set the tone, how to provide the proper pacing, which elements to stress and which to subdue, where to insert lengthy bits of copy and where to let the pictures do the talking. Suffice it to say that it was a labor of love, and it was finally accomplished.

Now, all that has gone before is but prelude to this particular moment. Jack and I have done our part; the rest is up to you.

So join us now in the rapturous realm of fantasy, where the limits of time and space are bounded only by the shackles of your own imagination. The yawning, unending cosmos beckons, and—somewhere out there, beyond the farthest star—the Silver Surfer soars!

Excelsior!

Stan Lee
New York 1978

The splash to the first-ever Surfer solo story, which appeared as a backup in 1967's ***Fantastic Four Annual*** #5. Script by Stan, pencils by Kirby, inks by Frank Giacoia.

Stan says in the preface that, while he was out in California, he and Jack "hammered out the main elements of the phantasmagoric parable soon to unfold before your bedazzled eyes." The mystery of how these two combined their talents to come up with stories remains as mysterious—perhaps even to the two of them—as it does to a reader eager to be a fly on the wall.

(Note that Stan makes a point of saying how much he loves the Los Angeles climate, and, indeed, within a couple of years he'd have moved there permanently.)

On this page and the next, we find Kirby's January 24, 1977, letter to Stan, that describes the pencil art for the first part of the story, which the letter indicates it was included. It also discusses the remainder of the story, which apparently had not yet been worked out in detail. As we will see, Kirby also sent brief panel descriptions. In their earlier collaborations, Kirby would have written these in the margins. Perhaps knowing Stan would be writing the dialogue from reduced photocopies the art, Jack used this method to make sure Stan would be able to know what he intended in each panel.

JAN 24-77

Stanley,

Just in case a little reiteration is needed in view of our discussion, I believe that the over-riding points of the story lie in the Galactus- Surfer relationship and our own helter-skelter position in the universe. It's the Surfer's story, of course, and his experience should be dominant (his love story-his life among Earth people- his decisions). However, I believe the reader will clearly be intrigued by the larger question of his own vulnerability in the scheme of things.

Thus the symbolic arm of Galactus in the opening shot. Its shown in a field of death. He's just made mincemeat of a planet and is ready for another meal. Although, he is omniprescent by our standards, he's just another large beast living in the context of "kill to survive". The Surfer's just the opposite. He a small animal with less of an appetite and with thoughts of life and beauty. The universe, to him, is more of a playground than a hunting ground. That's why Galactus follows him. He knows the Surfer will find with ease, the succulent forces which keep Galctus alive.

At any rate, that's what the battle for Easth is about. I'm ceratain that if you studied the initial synopsis I sent you, panel for panel, the hurried typing will not obscure the meaning og the continuity. I list the Surfer's approach to Earth, the reavealing of

2

detail as he descends to the city. First, the buildings--then, the noise--and finally, the crowds the faces, the reaction of types and age groups.

When, he runs across an individual girl, she bears a striking resemblance to his sweetie pie from earlier days. And taking advantage of author's license allowed in the legitimate novel, I cause him to reflect and imagine that this girl is actually his forsaken love. She becomes Shalibal. Her surroundings changeto become the decor of her home planet and, as Shalibal, she expresses her horror at what the man she loved has turned into. She accuses him of giving up his humanity to take up a life of eternal wandering among the stars. She accuses him of being a hunting dog for Galactus and bringing death to millions. She is frightened of him. And, despite all his pleading to the contrary, she rejects him for what he is---something alien and fearsome.

The girl flees and the bubble bursts. The Surfer finds him--self on a city street among a crowd of gaping, apprehensive people..

But, in this one incident, he finds the motivation to buck Galactus and face the truth about himself. He looks at the crowd and knows that because, of him, they're going to die. --That in coming to Earth, he has doomed the planet. That this kind of thing will go on for all of eternity unless he can change it.

A display of power in the sky and the ominous rumbling of strange forces announces the arrival of Galctus. He materializes on a

Letter from Jack Kirby to Stan Lee, dated January 24, 1977, Stan Lee Collection, box #55, folder #4, American Heritage Center, University of Wyoming.

A full-pager from the classic ***Fantastic Four*** #57 (December 1966), in which Dr. Doom steals the Surfer's cosmic power! By Lee, Kirby and Sinnott. [©2011 Marvel Characters Inc.]

Masters of the spoof, even of their own stories, Lee & Kirby lampoon the Doom/Surfer ***FF*** story in the pages of August 1967's ***Not Brand Echh*** #1, in the story that could only be called, "The Silver Burper!" Inks by Frank Giacoia.

Jack's letter is pretty self-explanatory. We will note that it does contain perhaps the greatest P.S. in the history of human correspondence!

3

tall building from which he can survey the horizon and plan to strip Earth of its vital energies with the equipment he's brought with him.

When defied by the Surfer, Galactus tells him that this is the way of things. He's a power being. He sees power, not people. He needs power and simply takes it. What falls by the wayside, be it the lives and achievements of smaller animals is not his concern.

Surfer, of course, decides to fight him. We are all witness to the battle (which will be shown in the following installment)

And, when the deal which saves Earth is made between the Surfer and Galactus is consumnated, the memory of this battle will be erased from our minds. We will merely find the chipped, smoking buildings, the debris-littered streets and clean up the mess while wondering how it all came about. The cameras which recorded the battle will explode. The video-tapes will burn. The incident will be just a bothersome blank in our memory.

Then, exiled to Earth, the Surfer will begin to make a life among us. He will mystify us with his powers and dare us to penetrate the disguise he creates in order to circulate without attracting at--tention. This is the substance of the succeeding synopsis and I hope to achieve a proper insight for you in explaining the panels. In regards to the further chapters, where Galactus returns to win the Surfer back by manufacturing a female lure, I am certain that we shall have the op-

4

-portunity to discuss it again and nail down the details and dramatic relevance to the story.

At any rate, I'm going to work on the next chapter and should have it for you as soon as possible.

Meanwhile, give our regards to Joan and stay away from cheap cigars.

Your Pal,

P.S. I forgot to mention that in the panels before the Surfer finds Earth, he is traversing space and time and reaching places in the universe where strange conditions exist. He ignores the galaxies where civilizations have developed to a degree where they can give Galactus a stand-off fight.

The Surfer reaches Earth when he leaps into a dimensional warp and finds himself in our solar system.

The Surfer as portrayed in the 2007 movie ***Fantastic Four: Rise of the Silver Surfer***.

Here's the letter from March 14, 1977, which Kirby sent along with a second batch of pages. The page he asks about, in which he uses "the illusion gimmick," is shown here. Looks like the "gimmick" worked pretty well. The page is inked, of course, by Joe Sinnott.

March 14th '77

Stanley,

This is the second batch of continuity for the "Surfer" book. If you can overlook an occasional typing error, you'll find the pages explained in what I feel is the proper per--spective in consideration of realistic rendering and dramatic value. Of course, its all done within the areas we dicussed and I hope it comes across. I've also tried to cover all loose ends and set the stage for the Surfer's life among the humans.

I'll use as many interesting gimmmicks as possible to play up his powers and accent the differences between him and us. I also hppe that you concurr with the illusion gimmick I used on Page Twenty Seven. In a movie sequence it could be very effective(he turns to face the reader who sees his human image for the first time.

The next batch should ALSO set the stage for the return of Galactus and some real heavy stuff. Everything should begin to move faster now, I'm doing my best to implement it.

If you have any questions or suggestions, I'd ap--preciate a call.

Your Pal,

Jack

Letter from Jack Kirby to Stan Lee, dated March 14, 1977, Stan Lee Collection, box #55, folder #4, American Heritage Center, University of Wyoming.

And now, with the preliminaries out of the way, let's take a look at the nuts and bolts creation of some pages from ***The Silver Surfer*** graphic novel...

THE SILVER SURFER by STAN LEE & JACK KIRBY

The Making of an Epic

Page One (Either inside cover typeof

arrangement or page facing title page)

Illustration : Arm of Galactus or symbol of

Life and Death principle which is part of the universe

and governs all its inhabitants, both large and small.

Here's the opening page to ***The Silver Surfer*** graphic novel. As with the rest of the pages from the book in this article, Jack's notes that accompanied the art are reproduced at the top of the page, Stan's typed script is at the bottom. Stan's handwritten notes are in the margins of the photocopies of the pencil art. We also see the lettered and colored pages from the book itself.

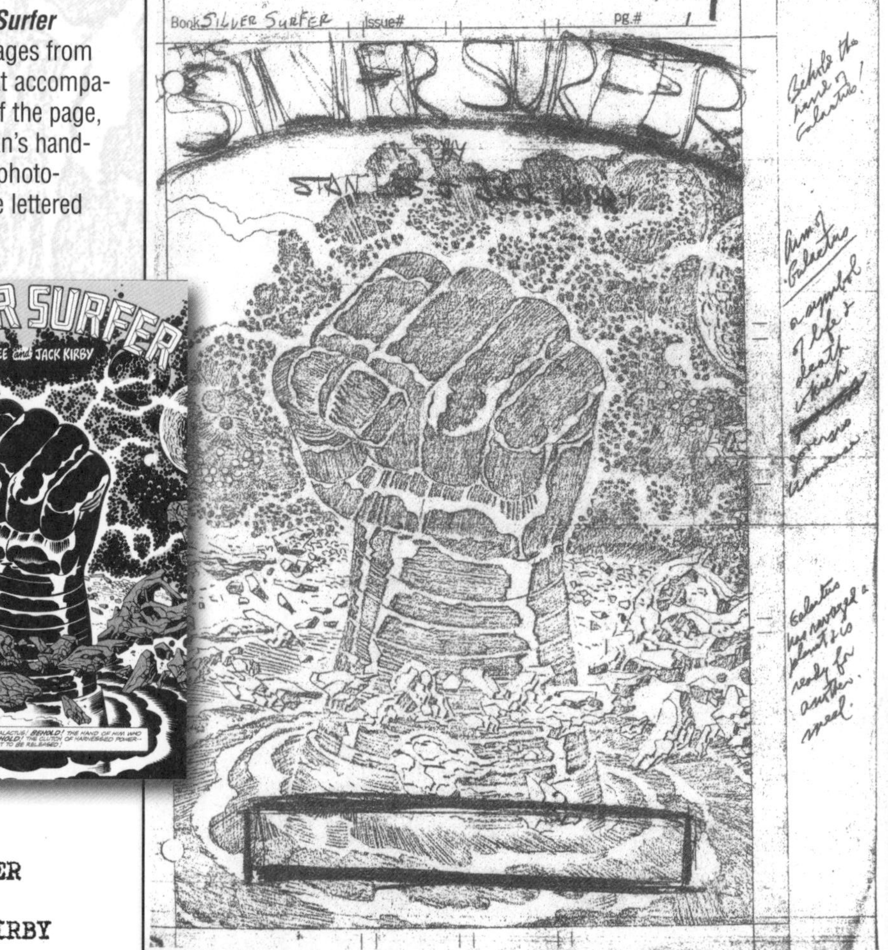

SILVER SURFER

PAGE 1

TITLE: THE SILVER SURFER
by
STAN LEE & JACK KIRBY

CAPTION: (At bottom of page)

BEHOLD! The hand of Galactus! BEHOLD! The hand of him who is like unto a God! BEHOLD! The clutch of harnessed power-- about to be released!

Panel descriptions for *Silver Surfer* graphic novel, Stan Lee Collection, box #55, folders 2 & 4, American Heritage Center, University of Wyoming. Photocopies of pencil art with balloon placements; script for *Silver Surfer* graphic novel, Stan Lee Collection, box #55, folder #1, American Heritage Center, University of Wyoming.

Page Two

Lead in---Title---Credits

Silver Surfer is released from the hand of Galactus.

The drama of Life and Death begins--but on a giant scale.

Here's page two of the story. Note how, since Stan, when scripting, decided the title would go on the previous page, the space Jack left for a title was no longer needed, hence the instruction on the art to raise up the section of the page with the Surfer and extend the artwork along the bottom. Note also that the second caption in Stan's script isn't in the finished story. He must have decided that it wasn't necessary, possibly because we don't see Galactus again for another ten pages.

PAGE 2

CAPTION: (ATOP PAGE) Somewhere in the endless cosmos, the hand is opened!

Somewhere in the swirling mists of space, the power is unleashed!

CAPTION: (At bottom of page) That Galactus may live, a world must die!

But who shall find the star-crossed planet?

Who but THE SILVER SURFER!

Page Eleven

Panel One--- In the air, the Surfer looks at everything about him. It will soon vanish in a fiery holocaust. Can he regain a measure of his own humanity by saving these people?

Panel Two--- The Surfer can feel the arrival of Galactus. The sky begins to rimble. He must make his decision to defy a mighty power.

Panel Three---Galactus' presence begins to maifest itself. Lightning flshes in a display of frightening energy. The Surfer zooms up to confront his master.

Panel Four--- As fireworks cease, Galactus appears. He surveys city from high building."He says"you've done well, Surfer,. This planet will do fine for my purposes."

Although the art is clear and powerful on page 11 of the story, Kirby's notes establish the subtext he intends for the art. Stan works out in the margins the rough dialogue that the Surfer will speak as we see Galactus' face for the first time in the story. As was often the case in his collaborations with Kirby and other artists, Stan here puts his own spin on the tone and nuance of the narrative

Pg. 11

1. SS: It has happened so OFTEN in the past! But now, it is DIFFERENT!
   SS: This time I stand upon a planet peopled with beings who think, who feel, who STRIVE!

2. SS: Yet, if I am true to mission-- the time is come for them to DIE!

3. SS: THERE! In the sky! The moment is at hand!

4. SS: GALACTUS IS HERE!

Page Fourteen

Panel One---The Surfer takes off to challenge Galactus.

Panel Two---He tells Galactus that the universe must be more than something to look at. It must also contain the values that give a being pride.

Panel Three--- The Surfer shouts that his journey will end here if it must. But the attempt to regain his own value will make his death worthwhile.

Panel Four--- More of the same. The Surfer prepares to charge.

Panel Five--- The Surfer unleashes his power. A battle starts that we all should remember., because many of us were there. Yet, somehow, its been erased from our minds.

(The battle will be shown and the deal between Galactus and the Surfer will be made before Galctus departs. The ensuing panels will also deal with the Surfer's stay on Earth and his attempt to study and gain a closer relationship with the people)

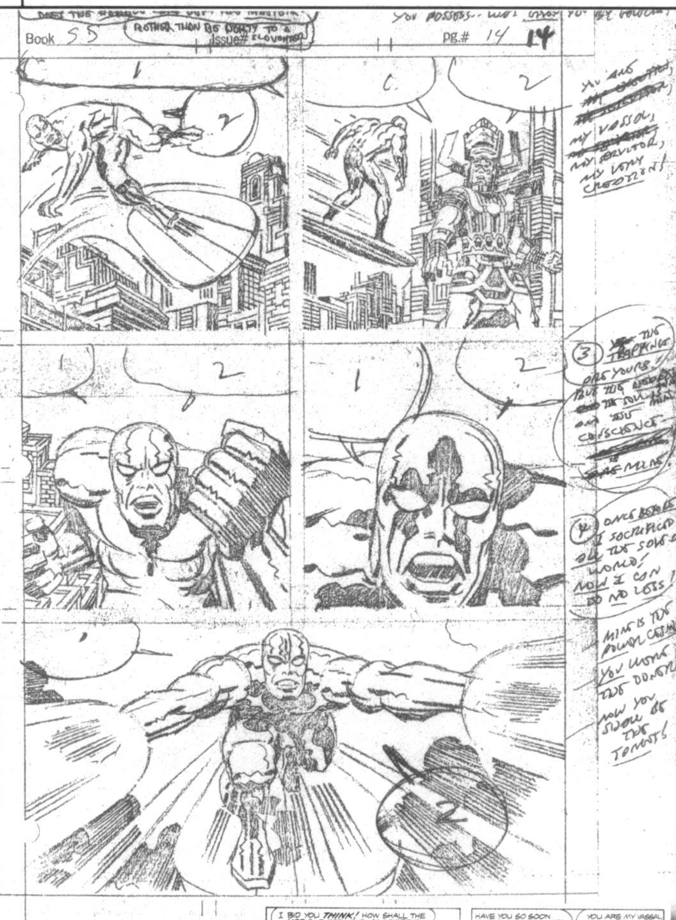

The handwritten dialogue in the margins of page 14 has Stan's writing—and rewriting—of the verbal battle that parallels the physical one between the two cosmic beings. And his typewritten text—created in the days before personal computers—shows how he further refined the Surfer's dialogue.

PAGE 14

1. GALACTUS: I bid you THINK! ~~Shall~~ How shall the HERALD defy the MASTER?
   SS: How shall the herald be party to SLAUGHTER?

2. GALACTUS: Have ~~ye~~ you so soon forgot? I GRANTED you the ~~xxxx~~ power you possess!
   GALACTUS: You are my vassal, my servitor, my very CREATION!

~~3. SS: XXXXXxxxxxxxxxxxxxxxxx Yours are the TRAPPINGS!~~
   ~~SS: But what of the xxxxx HEART, the SOUL, the xxxx CONSCIENCE? Are they not MINE?~~

3. SS: Yours are the TRAPPINGS!
   SS: But the HEART is mine! The SOUL is mine! And remember you this-- the CONSCIENCE is mine!

4. SS: Once before, did I not sacrifice ALL that my native world might live?
   SS: NOW I can do-- NO LESS!

5. ~~XXX~~ SS: You have given me the POWER COSMIC!
   SS: In the name of ~~XXXXXXXX xxxxxxxxxxxxxxxxxxxxTARGET~~ justice-- let the DONOR feel its sting!

[Story ©1978 Stan Lee and Jack Kirby. Silver Surfer ©2011 Marvel Characters, Inc.]

On page 15, it's evident that a lot went into Stan's picking just the right words to heighten the drama of Jack's drawing, while advancing the story and giving whatever exposition is not obvious in the images.

Page Fifteen

Panel One--------The epic battle between the Silver Surfer and Galactus begins. As throngs of people watch from below, strange forces explode with dazzling brilliance against the building upon which Galactus stands. Baloons of surprise and dismay from unseen audience below are suggested here. However, the dialogue can concentrate upon the defiance of the attacking Surfer and a profound response from Galactus.

Panel Two---------Galactus, arrogant, proud and almost god-like is shocked by the fury unleashed against him. He storms at the Surfer as waves of unnameable power engulf him.

Panel Three------- Whatever is happening to Galactus is, of course, incomprehensible to the watching public. They see him vanish in a whirlwind of blazing particles. They hear his voice diminish as the particles thicken and form a crackling cocoon never seen before by human eyes.

Panel Four-------- Hardening like some sort of alien cocncrete, the smoking cocoon , still glowing like red flame, replaces the towering figur of Galactus on the building ledge. (All this happened in the original encounter. But seen from the public's view instead of ours, saves us from lofty scientific explanations and makes the happening more realistic. If we saw this actually take place, we could never explain it, but instead find it highly interesting)

Panel Five--------- The thing has completely hardened. Has the Silver Surfer changed Galactus into another form or is that cosmic

Page Fifteen (2)

being imprisoned within this unexplainable object. The reader doesn't have to have an answer. Like any witness in the story, he is mystified and fascinated by this product of cosmic force.
What will happen now/? Somehow, every watcher senses a frightening response from the vanished Galactus will surely come.

PAGE 15

1. CAPTION: So begins one of the most incredible battles of all time, as a blinding flash of unearthly intensity blankets the city and lights up the sky!

2. CAPTION: Then, like the raging roaring ~~xxxx~~ of a thousand thunderclaps, the awesome voice of GALACTUS hurls forth his fateful challenge!
   GALACTUS: You dare threaten ME with power?
   GALACTUS: I-- who am POWER INCARNATE?!!

3. CAPTION: But, even as the gigantic figure ~~xxxxxxxx~~ advances...
   SS: Power comes in MANY forms! Even the gossamer CLOUD may challenge the storm!

4. CAPTION: Hurtling past the towering figure, the soaring SURFER enmeshes his inhuman foe in a ~~xxxxxx~~ glowing cocoon of shimmering, seething ~~xxxxxxxxx xxxxxxxxxx~~ ENERGY!

5. CAPTION: Instantly, it forms itself ~~xxx~~ into a solid, rock-hard ~~xxxx~~ SHELL, which grows STRONGER with each passing second...

And that's it for this glimpse into the nuts-and-bolts workings of one of the most unique creative combinations in the history of graphic storytelling.

Silver Age Stan and Jack (or: "Will Success Spoil Spider-Man?")

FROM THE STAN LEE ARCHIVES

Lee & Kirby, March 3, 1967 Interviewed on WBAI radio, New York, by Mike Hodel

Transcribed by Steven Tice, copyedited by Danny Fingeroth

__Mike Hodel__ briefly hosted a science fiction program on New York's WBAI radio in the late 1960s, where he interviewed Stan Lee and Jack Kirby (in an episode of of the program entitled "Will Success Spoil Spider-Man?") in 1967. Shortly after this interview, Hodel moved back to his native Los Angeles, where he hosted "Hour 25," a science fiction program on that city's KPFK radio from 1972 until his untimely death in 1986. The show continued, often with guest hosts such as Harlan Ellison and J. Michael Straczynski, and, since 2000, "Mike Hodel's Hour 25," named in his memory, has continued to be broadcast via the internet at www.hour25online.com.

MIKE HODEL: *Who goes around saving maidens, preventing banks from being robbed, and committing deeds of that type, under an alter ego for the name "Peter Parker"? How about "Tony Stark"? Would you believe "Reed Richards"? "Stan Lee?" "Jack Kirby?" Well, except for the last two, they're all superheroes and they belong in Marvel comics, and they are written and drawn by Stan Lee and Jack Kirby. And Mr. Lee and Mr. Kirby are going to be answering questions about their superheroes. And I guess the first one would be addressed to Stan Lee, and it's the title of this program. Stan, will success spoil Spider-Man?*

Mike Hodel circa 1984.

STAN LEE: [chuckles] Well, I don't think anything could spoil old Spidey, as we lovingly call him. Just have to correct one thing you said, though. You said that, except for Stan Lee and Jack Kirby, the others are superheroes. We like to think of ourselves as superheroes, too. I might add also that there are other artists and other writers who do some of the other books, too. Jack and I don't do them all, although we do the ***Fantastic Four*** and ***Thor. Spider-Man*** has been a success since he started, and, luckily, I don't think he's been spoiled yet, so we just have our fingers crossed.

MH: *I ran across Marvel comic books about six or eight months ago, and one of the things that drew me to Marvel comic books, and* **Spider-Man** *in particular, is a panel that showed Spider-Man swooping down on some bank robbers, and they said, "Whoops, here comes Spider-Man!" And he replies, "Who were you expecting? Vice President Humphrey?" Now, this is not a line you expect to find in a comic book, and it sort of symbolizes your whole approach to the field, which is offbeat and interesting. Was it your idea, Stan? Where did it come from?*

SL: Well, I guess, in that sense, in was my idea, since I write the dialogue. In a nutshell, our theory is—although maybe I shouldn't give the theory in a nutshell, because then I don't know what we'll talk about for the rest of the half hour. But, at any rate, in a nutshell, our theory is that there's no reason why a comic magazine couldn't be as realistic and as well-written and drawn as any other type of literature. We try to write these things so that the characters speak the way a character would speak in a well-written movie, well-produced television show, and I think that's what makes our book seem unique to a person who first picks them up. Nobody expects, as you say, that sort of thing in a comic book. But that's a shame, because why shouldn't someone expect reasonable and realistic dialogue in a comic book? Why do people feel that comic books have to be badly written? And we're trying to engage in a one-company crusade to see to it that they're not badly written.

MH: *Jack, you drew and invented, if I'm not mistaken, Captain America, one of the earliest superheroes, who's now plying his trade in Marvel comics. How did Captain America come to be, and does he have any particular relationship to your other superheroes?*

JACK KIRBY: I guess Captain America, like all of the characters come to be, because of the fact that there is a need for them. Somebody needed Captain America, just as the public needed Superman. When Superman came on the scene, the public was ready for him, and they took him. And so, from Superman, who didn't exactly satiate the public's need for the superhero, so spawned the rest of them.

Stan and Jack at a National Cartoonist Society event in 1966.

A surreal look at Lee & Kirby's creative process, seen in "This is a Plot?" from ***Fantastic Four Annual*** #5, 1967 (the same year as this interview). Written and penciled by Jack. Inks by Frank Giacoia. [©2011 Marvel Characters, Inc.]

The rest of them all came from Superman, and they all had various names, and various backgrounds, and they embraced various creeds. And Captain America came from the need for a patriotic character, because the times at that time were in a patriotic stir. The war was coming on, and the corny cliché, the war clouds were gathering, and the drums were beginning to beat, and the American flag was beginning to show on the movie screens. And so Captain America had to come into existence, and it was just my good fortune to be there at the time when we were asked to create superheroes for the magazines that were coming into creation then, for the new magazines.

MH: *Well, Captain America fought valiantly against the Axis from 1940 until after the war. Then what happened? When did he die off or go into hiding until he was revived by Marvel Comics?*
JK: Well, I believe that Captain America went into hiding like all ex-soldiers. I know I went into hiding. I didn't show my face for quite a few years. In fact, I went out to Long Island with my wife and I got happily lost there and never found my way back to Manhattan. And so, feeling like I, myself, am Captain America, because of the fact that his feelings are mine when the drawings are created, and because his reactions are my reactions to the specific situations in the story, why, I have no compunction to say that we both were hiding for all those years, and were quite happy about it.

MH: *Now that Captain America is back in the fight, has there been any talk about sending him to Vietnam? They could certainly use him.*
JK: Well, that's Stan Lee's department, and he can answer that. The editor always has the last word on that.
SL: Well, the Secretary of Defense and myself just haven't yet made up our minds. *[laughs]* I don't know. I don't think we'll be sending him to Vietnam, really, because... It's a funny thing. We treat these characters sort of tongue-in-cheek, and we get a lot of laughs out of them, we have a lot of fun with them. I somehow don't know if it's really in good taste to take something as serious as the situation in Vietnam and put a character like Captain America—. We would have to start treating him differently and take the whole thing very seriously, which we're not prepared to do. The time that Jack talks about, when Captain America was first created, the books were written a little bit differently then. There wasn't this type of subtle humor. The stories were very serious, and at that time I think it was okay to have Captain America fighting the Nazis and so forth, because they were done very seriously. But right now, I don't think I'd feel right writing the stories about Vietnam.

MH: *All of these superheroes—not all of them, but many of them—have hang-ups. You have one character, one superhero, who is blind, named Daredevil, otherwise known as Matt Murdock. You have Spider-Man, Peter Parker, who is perhaps the most guilt-ridden teenager I've ever run across. And there are many others. How did you decide that these were going to be something more than superheroes, that they were going to have problems of their own?*
SL: Well, it was just the idea of trying to make them realistic, as we mentioned before, trying to write them a little bit better. It seems to me that the best type of story is the type of story a reader can relate to. The average superhero published by some of the other companies, you can't really relate to them because

Although Stan tells Mike Hodel, regarding Captain America, "I don't think we'll be sending him to Vietnam," and indeed Marvel would not send him there in the near future. Cap had already been there in the January 1965 ***Tales of Suspense*** #61. At that point, the Vietnam War had not become as controversial as it would be by 1967, and even in this story, Cap goes there on a mission to rescue one man in a tale that took all of ten pages. As for why there was a Sumo in Vietnam—don't ask, just buy it! [©2011 Marvel Characters, Inc.]

Stan tells Hodel that he knew the Hulk would be popular because "it had the idea of a monster who was sympathetic." Here, the Hulk's alter ego, Bruce Banner, at the beginning of his nightmarish double life in the May 1962 ***Incredible Hulk*** #1, script by Stan, pencils by Jack, inks by Paul Reinman. [©2011 Marvel Characters, Inc.]

they're living in a vacuum. They just have a superpower, they can fly through the air or whatever, and that's it. Other than that, they're two-dimensional. Now, in order to make a person three-dimensional, he has to have a family life, he has to have personal problems, and so forth. I've said this so often that it's almost becoming a cliché with me, but what we try to do is, we know that these superhero stories are really fairy tales. They're fairy tales for older people. We think of them that way. We don't really write them for young kids.

And what we ask the reader to do, and hope he will do, is accept the basic premise, the basic fairy tale quality, such as the fact that Spider-Man does have the proportionate strength of a spider if a spider were his size, and that Spider-Man does have the ability to cling to walls, which, obviously, nobody does. However, once we accept that basic premise, that fairy tale quality, we try to make everything else very realistic. The idea being, what would a real person do? How would he react? How would his life be if he had the proportionate strength of a spider and could cling to walls? Wouldn't he still have sinus trouble, possibly, trouble with girls, a sick relative that he was worried about, have to worry about his school marks, and so forth? So once we get beyond the fairy tale quality, we try to write realistic stories. We try to have the characters speaking in a realistic way. To me, I feel that this gives it a great deal of interest. You have the combination of the fantasy mixed with the most realistic story you can get, and, well, we've found sort of a winning combination.
JK: Well, a prizefighter can win the championship of the world, and go home and be very inadequate at home, inadequate enough to have a lot of family trouble.

MH: *Which may be one reason for his fighting.*
SL: *[chuckles]* Very good.

MH: *You've also created something unique in comic books, that I know of. You've come up with an antihero, a physicist by the name of Bruce Banner who periodically becomes the Hulk. He destroys things a lot, as somebody said to me. What made you think that an antihero who goes around tearing down bridges and buildings and things like that, could sell comic books?*
SL: Actually, I think we knew when we started that he could sell comic books better than anybody. I don't think it's that we're this brilliant. Don't forget, we've had so much experience that we'd have to be stupid not to have learned by all these years of experience. And we get a lot of fan mail, and you learn a lot by what the readers write, and we learned that the villains are usually at least as popular as the heroes are. They have a great appeal.
JK: Well, what makes you think that Boris Karloff can't be a great star in movies? It's the same analogy, I imagine.
SL: Right. And what happens is, after a while, we have a lot of trouble, by trying to humanize our heroes and giving them faults and failings. We do the same with our villains. We try to give them understandable qualities and reasons why they are the way they are. We've even had villains who reformed and became heroes. One standing joke among our readers, and among the artists and writers who work with us, our so-called bullpen, is, after a while, we don't know who the heroes and who the villains are. There's such a fine line, you see, dividing them. Well, when we started with the Hulk, we just knew he had to be popular because he had everything in his favor. It had the Jekyll and Hyde format. It had the idea of a monster who was sympathetic, the way Frankenstein really had been in the first movie. Frankenstein's Monster, that is. He wasn't bad, he was misunderstood. All he wanted to do was be left alone. I would have bet my bottom dollar the Hulk would have to be well-received, and he was. And he still is one of our most popular characters, probably the most popular one with our college readers, college-age readers.

MH: *That's what I was going to ask. You say your books are aimed not at children, but at young people and adults. Is there any way that you can check for magazine sales and so forth as to what your readership is?*
SL: No, our only check, really, is through the mail. Which is a very good check, because we get thousands of letters a week. I would guess we must get almost as much mail as the Beatles, and we don't even sing. And by reading all this mail, a monumental task in itself, we've learned a lot about who are readers are, what they like and dislike, and almost half of our mail is from college students and college-age people.

MH: *What do they like, and what do they not like?*
SL: Just what you'd think they like. They like whatever we do that seems to be original, unexpected. They like the degree of satire we put into the books. They're mad for the quality of artwork, which I think is far superior than has ever been presented in any other comics over the years. They like the realism, which it's always a difficult thing to say, because somebody who isn't familiar with our books would think, "This guy must have flipped. He's talking about comic books, and he's talking about realism." But the readers know what we mean. They like whatever quality they find, good writing, good drawing, good editing, and sincerity. I think they can detect a note of sincerity. Even though the stories have some humor, quite a bit of humor, to them, there is an underlying sincerity. We take them seriously,

and I think the readers are aware of this.

MH: *Did you also innovate the letters page? It adds to your stories, and frequently I sometimes find in the blurbs you run that you advance the stories by means of these letter pages.*
SL: The letters pages are one of our most successful devices. It also established a rapport between ourselves and the readers, and I'm happy to say most of our readers feel that we're all friends. When they write a letter, they don't say, "Dear Editor." They say, "Dear Stan and Jack," "Dear So-and-so." They call us by name. And we give ourselves nicknames. We started this as a gag, and they've caught on. The fellow here on my right isn't just Jack Kirby. He's "Jolly Jack."
JK: I'll get you for it. *[laughs]*
SL: Or Jack "King" Kirby. And I'm "Smilin' Stan." This is kind of cute, too, because, as I mentioned to you earlier, I think before we were on the air, we sort of think of the whole thing as one big advertising campaign, with slogans, and mottos, and catch phrases, and things that the reader can identify with. And besides just presenting stories, we try to make the reader think he's part of an "in" group. In fact, we've discussed before, we're always a little worried about being too successful, where the readers will feel, "Oh, gosh, now everybody's caught on to it. We have to find something new."

MH: *Is there a real Irving Forbush?*
SL: Oh, I don't think that it would be right for me to answer that. *[Jack laughs]* When we're off the air, I might hint at it. He's real in our imagination, I'll put it that may.

MH: *I think you also pioneered the use of mythological superheroes. I'm talking about* **Thor***, which you two come up with every month.*
SL: Well, you've got the right guy here, because I always say that Jack is the greatest mythological creator in the world. When we kicked ***Thor*** around, and we came out with him, and I thought he would just be another book. And I think that Jack has turned him into one of the greatest fictional characters there are. In fact, I should let Jack say this, but just on the chance that he won't, somebody was asking him how he gets his authenticity in the costumes and everything, and I think he gave a priceless answer, Jack said that they're not authentic. If they were authentic, they wouldn't be authentic enough. But he draws them the way they should be, not the way they were.

Ego, the Living planet, as portrayed in one of Kirby's amazing photo-montages, this one from ***Thor*** #160, January 1969. [©2011 Marvel Characters, Inc.]

MH: *Did you do a lot of homework on that, a lot of Norse myths, and so forth?*
JK: Well, not homework in the sense that I went home one night and I really concentrated on it. All through the years, certainly, I've had a kind of affection for any mythological type of character, and my conception of what they should look like. And here Stan gave me the opportunity to draw one, and I wasn't going to draw back from really letting myself go. So I did, and, like, the world became a stage for me there, and I had a costume department that really went to work. I gave the Norse characters twists that they never had in anybody's imagination. And somehow it turned out to be a lot of fun, and I really enjoyed doing it.

MH: *Isn't it rather tough to come up with villains that are a suitable match for a Norse god?*
JK: Not if they're Norse villains.

MH: *You've also dragged in some Greeks. I remember one epic battle with Hercules.*
JK: Well, Hercules had Olympian powers, which certainly are considered on an equal basis with the old powers of the Norse gods, and therefore we felt that they were an equal match for each other, and by rights they should contend with each other.
SL: These college kids who are so hooked on these stories, and they like ***Thor***, also, and not long ago I was speaking at Princeton, and one of the questions that I was asked was, how do we reconcile the idea of Norse gods and Greek gods in the same story? Now, obviously, Zeus and Odin are really the same god, but in different mythologies. And it occurred to us that what we do is, we create our own mythology, and we create our own universes, and, in our minds, there is an Olympus, and there is an Asgard, and Odin is the boss of his little god-dom, and Zeus is the chief of his, and we may someday bring in the Roman gods or whoever else. And we figure that, as Jack said, we don't have to be that accurate, because we think we can do better. After all, mythology is mythology, and who's to say that we can't make up our own myths? Which is what we're doing, just basing them on the past ones, and having a heck of a good time doing it.

MH: *Well, you have to draw your villains to scale. You can't give Spider-Man and Thor the same villain to fight. There has to be sort of a Class A, B, and C, for villains, so it must be a bit of a hardship to come up with a villain who can give satisfactory battles to Thor.*
JK: Well, I found out that villains seem to have their limits, too, because I came up with a few on a galactic scale, and soon reversed my direction.

SL: The trouble with Jack is, he's too darned imaginative, and he gets himself absolutely trapped. The last thing he did, and finally we both said we have to stop and retrench a little, is he had Thor fighting a whole planet. Jack came up with an idea, a fellow named Ego, who is a living planet in—what was he, a bioverse instead of a universe?
JK: Which I'm sure we're all very familiar with.

MH: Just the other side of the Negative universe.
JK: Yes, and not just presenting the reader with a living planet. There had to be cause and effect. So we made him into a multiple virus, which we felt could be accepted, maybe not on a friendly basis, but certainly on a realistic basis, and that was our jumping-off point. And we went on from there, and he was acceptable to the reader due to the fact that he could contend with Thor on Thor's level.
SL: He was acceptable due to the fact that Jack drew him so well. But the problem was, where did we go from there? *[laughs]* After you fight a living planet, you can't fight a littler bug. So we do have our problems in that respect. Now we have to, we're trying to humanize these characters again, a little bit, because they've been too far out. We've had him fight the whole troll empire in Asgard, and he fought—Well, in ***The Fantastic Four***, for example, we had a fellow named Galactus who's practically God. I mean, he could do anything. We realized after Galactus that we'd better take it a little bit easy with these villains, too. In fact, a lot of readers would write in, and they'd say, "Where do you go from here? Who's he going to fight next after that?"
JK: And not only that, we felt it was disrespectful to Galactus to even destroy him in any manner, so we had to just respectfully find a way for him to leave and then go on to another adventure, because we couldn't even touch him, I believe. And there might have been an outcry if we had.
SL: One other thing I think that we've innovated that has been pretty successful is overlapping characters and books. For example, this Galactus, he first appeared in ***The Fantastic Four***. Now, this is interesting to me. The ***Fantastic Four*** books that he appeared in were three in number, three consecutive issues. We have continued stories. In fact, all our books are one big continued story. And in the mail we received from so many college kids, they now refer to those books. They'll say, "By the way, regarding your 'Galactus Trilogy'... " And, you know, they're referring to this as though it's ***The Rise and Fall of the Roman Empire***, which I love! This is wonderful! It means we're really reaching them.

At any rate, he appeared in ***The Fantastic Four,*** and then he went off to another universe, and that was the end of Galactus. But we didn't leave him there. In Thor, which is another publication of ours, and has no relationship to ***The Fantastic Four*** except that we publish them both, what we did was, when Thor was finishing off with this living planet that he had battled, on his way back to Earth he passed Galactus, who was wandering around in the sky up there. And Galactus was on his way to meet the fellow, Ego, who was the living planet, and so forth. We just kind of left it at that, and someday, when we run out of plots, we'll have the fight between Galactus and Ego.

But we very often do that because we feel it gives a feeling of realism. Also, if we have a villain who fought the Fantastic Four, or Spider-Man, or Daredevil, or the X-Men, or Captain America, or whomever, why shouldn't he eventually meet another one of our heroes? Or why shouldn't our heroes meet, as they often do, and guest star in each other's book? Because, according to the gospel as preached by Marvel, they all live in the same world, you see?

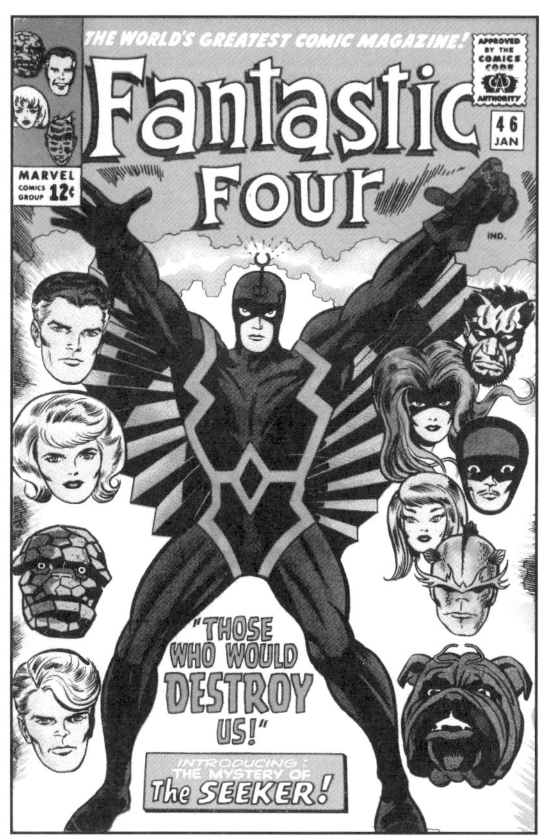

Black Bolt made his first cover appearance in ***Fantastic Four*** #46, cover-dated January 1966, although he debuted at the end of #45. He and his fellow Inhumans were yet another Lee-Kirby innovation. [©2011 Marvel Characters, Inc.]

JK: I would advise any astronomer listening to what we have to say here to take another hard look at the quasars, because we think one of them is Galactus. *[laughter]*
SL: And we dare them to disprove it.

MH: If anyone wants to disprove it, please call WBAI and we'll set up a program. I wanted to talk about your guest-starring villains and superheroes in each other's books. Do you feel that this, well, besides giving continuity and realism, do you think this saves you the trouble of creating more villains?
SL: Oh, it certainly is helpful. It's like a repertory theater where you've got your actors, and you know what they can do, and you can use them as needed. Once we have our cast of characters, whether heroes, or villains, or both, it makes it easier for us to base stories. If we're sitting around dreaming up a plot, Jack might say to me, "Gee, you know, we haven't used the Silver Surfer for a while. How would it be if he was doing this, that, or the other?" Or I might remember, "Gee, what about Galactus?" Or whoever. So it does make it easier, but that isn't the reason we do it.

We do it because, again, it seems to me that you enjoy things you're familiar with, and the readers eventually get to know these characters, and they're interested in these characters, and why just get rid of them? It's very hard, it takes months to build up that interest in a new character. So what we do is, while we're developing a new character, we'll still have old ones reappearing to give a thread of continuity here and there. In fact, in ***The Fantastic Four***, we have absolutely gotten ourselves into such a hole that I don't know if we're ever going to get out. We

Stan, Jack and Mike discuss how complex ***The Avengers*** had become, just in time for Roy Thomas to be handed the writing reins. Here, the cover to issue #42, dated July 1967, on sale around the time of this interview. Cover by John Buscema and George Roussos. [©2011 Marvel Characters, Inc.]

have so many continuing characters that ***Peyton Place*** [a popular primetime soap opera of the era.—DF & RT] seems simple next to our situation.

MH: *I walked into the* **Fantastic Four** *line about three or four months ago, and every couple of pages you drop one of the Fantastic Four. The Human Torch—Johnny Storm—he will go off someplace looking for the Inhumans, for a girl. And I'm very curious to know where the Inhumans first popped up. It looks as if you had an idea for a hero, there, in Black Bolt, who is the leader of the Inhumans, I found out in I think it was one of* **The Avengers** *books, of all places. And they sort of weave in and out over a period of, well, it must be at least a year, now. And that must—*

SL: These things aren't always planned. They grow. Now, what happened was, I think, Jack, the first Inhuman that we brought in was Gorgon, wasn't it? Did we have a story, "The Gentleman's Name Is Gorgon?"

JK: Yes.

SL: And he was a fellow who looked a little like a centaur or something. He could kick his foot very hard and he had great power. He could shatter a mountain by kicking his foot. He started out as a villain. We liked him so much—I should say, *Jack* liked him so much that he kept using him. We figured he has to come from somewhere. We decided let him come from some strange land over in Europe where there are a whole group of people like him, and, well, what else could you call them except the Inhumans?

Then Jack had to create a whole bunch of Inhumans, and I think he did a great job. All these characters are really very imaginative. When it came to doing the leader, we decided, well, there's no need for them all to be villainous. And, you're right, I think we did have in mind that Black Bolt would eventually be a heroic type. And, again, we always try to give a character a hang-up, so his hang-up is he doesn't speak. Now, I'm quite sure he's the first non-speaking superhero, or super villain, we don't know quite yet, in history.

But, anyway, they evolved. We didn't sit down one day and say, "Let's do a group of Inhumans, and these are their names, and we'll present them in this fashion." As with everything we do, we just sort of stumble into them as we go along. I might add, as something that you may not be aware of, we don't do the stories the way most other outfits do. We kick around a plot very, very loosely and generally, for a story, just discuss it for a few minutes. I might say, "Jack, in the next ***Thor***, how about bringing back Galactus fighting the planet Ego or something?" And Jack'll say, "Great," and off he goes. I don't know where he goes. But off he goes. I don't see him for a week. He comes back a week later and the whole strip is drawn. And nobody knows what I'm going to see on those pages. He may have come up with a dozen new ideas, you see. It'll have something to do with Galactus and Ego. Then I take it, and I write it, on the basis of what Jack has drawn. He's broken it down to continuity for me. He's drawn the whole thing, actually. I put in the dialogue and the captions. So he doesn't know exactly what I'm going to write, what words I'm going to put in their mouths. I don't know what he's going to draw. The whole thing is virtual chaos. But somehow, when it gets together, it seems to hold together pretty well, and we kind of like working this way.

MH: *Well, my own favorite book is* **The Avengers**. *I guess I have a hang-up over a group of superheroes rather than individuals. And each one of the Avengers, which number six, I believe, and I believe the official count is eight, although I gather they're changing—*

SL: Always.

MH: *You're bringing some new ones in. I remember in one book that you toyed with the idea of making Spider-Man an Avenger and then decided, "No, we'd better not, because he works best alone." When you start out with, well, with the Avengers, sometimes do they get ahead of you?*

SL: Oh, I'd say all the characters get ahead of us. I sometimes think they write their own stories. The Avengers, we have almost the same problem as Jack has with the Fantastic Four. There are so many of them, and they all have so many of their own problems. And we have another fellow writing that now, Roy Thomas, who's just been added to our writing staff recently, and *[laughs]* I don't know how the poor guy is doing it. I got out of ***The Avengers*** when it began to get complicated, and Roy inherited them. There are now a million more characters there than there ever were when I wrote the book. In fact, I can't even

keep track. If you say there are eight, I'll take your word for it. I thought there were around 35 by now. Every character we have, we don't know what to do with them, we'd throw him into the Avengers.
JK: Not only that, we have to make sure that they're not involved in situations which won't conflict with the one we want to create at that moment.

MH: *You took care of ones of those very nicely in the newest* **Avengers** *strip. I don't recall the number, but the subplot concerns getting, I think it's the Red Witch--?*
SL: The Scarlet Witch. The Scarlet Witch, of course.

MH: *—the Scarlet Witch, into the Avengers. And this causes its own hang-ups, because, unlike most of comicdom, there are people who don't like her and don't think she should be a member of the group. And, meanwhile, in another book, you have sent Captain America off looking for somebody else, and you tied off one of the loose ends by, in* **The Avengers**—*this is getting complicated* [Stan and Jack laugh]—*by saying that he was off. It was very nicely done. I was curious when he left his post in his own book, which is* **Strange Tales**, *or* **Tales of Suspense**?
SL: Captain America is in ***Tales of Suspense***. Free plug. And ***Strange Tales***, since you asked, features Dr. Strange and Nick Fury, Agent of SHIELD, who also stars in his own book, ***Sgt. Fury and his Howling Commandos***, which is probably the nuttiest title ever conceived of.

MH: *I wanted to ask you about Mr. Fury, sergeant, colonel.*
SL: Well, in ***Strange Tales*** he's Colonel Nick Fury. I think I can anticipate your question, the fact that he's in two books concurrently. What happened was, we put out this war book sort of as a gag a long time ago. When our superheroes were doing so well, I mentioned to our publisher, Martin Goodman, that it seems to me we seem to have a formula for these books now, and it doesn't much matter what the subject matter is, as long as they're written and drawn in this style, I think that the readers would like them, this sort of realistic style. And I said, "To prove it, I bet if we put out a war magazine," which were no great shakes at that time, "we could still sell just as well, and we could make the public like it, as well." And just sort of on a gamble, we did it, and we came up with the most unlikely name, ***Sgt. Fury and his Howling Commandos***. I think I was always captured by the name Screaming Eagles from World War II. This was the closest I could get.

At any rate, we gave them a lot of personality. They weren't just a bunch of soldiers who fought heroically, and that was it. They quarreled among themselves, and they had their own—They were a squad. Everything was wrong, too. For example, Americans weren't Commandos during the war, they were Rangers. The English were Commandoes. We made them Americans, and we still called them commandos, and they were based in England. And, in our usual bumbling way, all the facts were pretty inaccurate, but the characterization was there. And they were led by this rough-and-tough sergeant, and nobody can draw rough-and-tough sergeants better than Jack, who did the first few books, Sgt. Fury, Nick Fury. And there are a lot of other interesting characters with him.

Well, at any rate, the stories took place during World War II. The readers loved them so much that they said, "Why don't you have stories of—. What's Sgt. Fury—?" They begin to think he's a real person. "What is Sgt. Fury doing today? That was 25 years ago. Is he alive today? What's he doing? Why don't you have a book of Sgt. Fury in the Vietnamese War today?" And so forth. I didn't want to put him in the Vietnamese War, but at that time the James Bond things were popular, and we figured it might be very logical for Fury to be in intelligence, or a counter-spy, or something of the sort. Not *that* logical, because he's a very rough and tough, hard-bitten guy, without nearly the polish of your average secret operative, which also is typical of the way we do things. He'd be the last guy you would expect to be a debonair head of a secret organization. So we made him Colonel Fury, the head of S.H.I.E.L.D., which is like any of those other—like U.N.C.L.E. or anything else. So now we have stories of Sgt. Fury in World War II, and the same fellow today as Colonel Fury, the head of S.H.I.E.L.D.

MH: *Do you ever get an overwhelming impulse to kill off the sergeant and let them wonder how the colonel got there?*
SL: You know, I never thought of that, but that's a very, very good point. That would drive everybody crazy. *[laughs]*

Lee and Kirby updated Nick Fury by making him a James Bond/Man from U.N.C.L.E. style superspy. Here, as the cover to ***Tales of Suspense*** #78, June 1966, informs us, is the first "modern" (as opposed to WWII era) teaming of Fury and Captain America! Art by Kirby and Frank Giacoia. [©2011 Marvel Characters, Inc.]

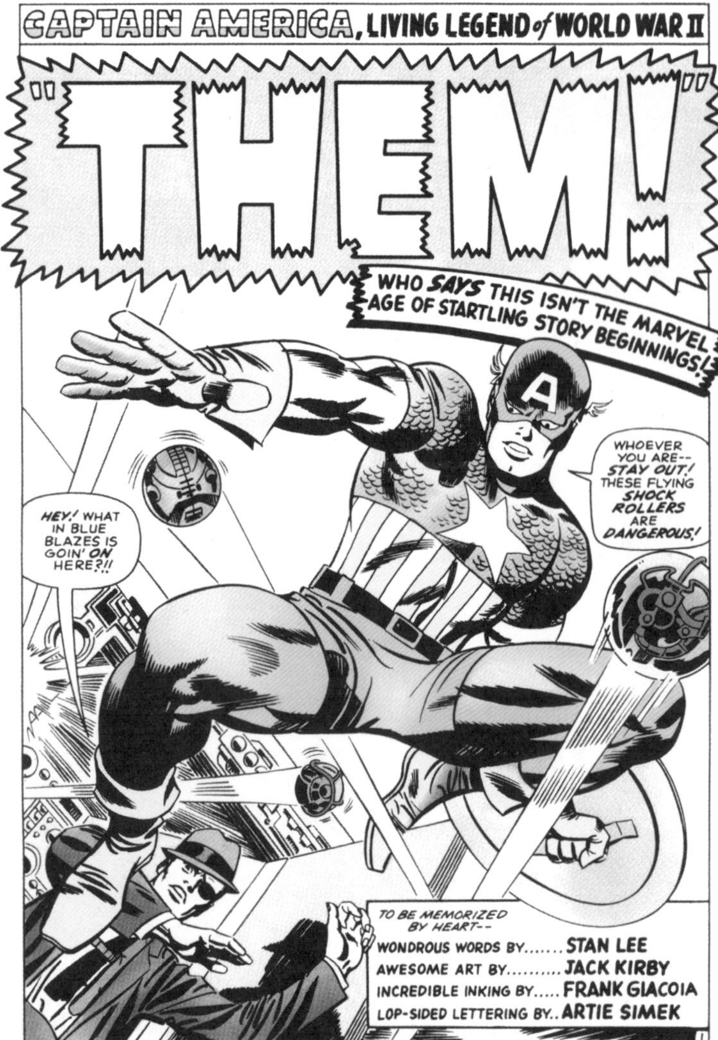

Interior art from ***Tales of Suspense*** #78 shows off some classic Lee-Kirby action and dialogue. Inks by Frank Giacoia. [©2011 Marvel Characters, Inc.]

JK: It's like killing your own grandmother.

MH: *Do your books run in trends, or are there plots that run in trends that you have to anticipate or try to keep up with?*
SL: This was the case for 25 years, for 20 years, before we started with the so-called Marvel Age of Comics. In the past, if the war books were selling, we would put out war books, and we'd sell our share. If the crime stories, cops and robbers type of things, were selling, we'd put those out, and we'd sell our share, and so forth. Now, fortunately, we seem to feel that we are creating the trends. I think if we put out a book of romance stories, or aviation stories, or what have you, we would create a trend in so doing, because we have a loyal following among fandom, and as long as we can write them well and draw them well, I don't think it much matters what the subject matter is. And I know there are a lot of people who will disagree with me, but I feel that the important thing is how well you do it. So we think of ourselves as being at the top of the trends right now, instead of just following them.

MH: *Well, if you're making the trends, what do you think is going to be next? Where do you go from here?*
SL: You know, I'm afraid—I could answer it, and I daren't, because we are working on a new magazine, and if you invite me back here about a month or two from now, I'll tell you then. But I know if I mention it and any of the competition hears it, they might just beat us to it. But we do have a new type of magazine that we're working on right now. It should be on sale in about four months.

MH: *I wanted to ask you, what is the time element involved from your and Jack's idea to the time it hit the stands?*
SL: Well, I'd say from the time Jack and I do a strip to the time it hits the stands must be about three-and-a-half to four months.

MH: *What causes that great a lag? Just mechanics?*
SL: Yeah, the script comes into the house and it sits around for a while, while it's proofread and edited, and then it goes out, and the Photostats are made, and the stats are colored for the engraver, then the matte maker as far as I know. I don't know too much about this, I think Jack knows more than I do, the printer, and so forth, and the distributor, and it's shipped around the country. It's just a complicated thing that takes a long time.

MH: *Does it cost a lot of money? How much per book, would you say?*
SL: You know, I'm embarrassed to have been in the business so long and not to know, but I—Jack would know, wait a minute.
JK: It's higher today than it used to be. I can't give you an exact amount, but certainly everything costs more. A magazine that you put out in 1940 might cost you twice as much to put out today, the cost of paper, cost of printing and engraving. But magazines are doing fairly well in the economy, and certainly holding up. So there's no complaints on that score, not from Marvel, as far as I know.

MH: *Well, and you can sell enough books at 12 cents or 26 cents a piece to do reasonably well?*
SL: Well, we have to sell a lot of them because I think that the profit on a 12-cent book is just—again, I don't know. It may be a penny, or two pennies, but it's something in that area. Most of it goes to the printer, the wholesaler, the distributor, the store-keeper, and so forth, and just a little bit of it trickles back to the publisher. Fortunately, we sell hundreds of thousands of them, so I don't think there's too big a problem as far as making a dollar here and there.

MH: *Before we went on the air, you and Jack were involved in a slight argument over whether Marvel should remain number two in superheroes, or whether you should take advantage of the fact that you are selling more books than, should I say, the other leading publisher?*
SL: Well, I don't know that we're selling more. I think they're printing more. They have more books, consequently they sell more in total volume. I think our percentage of sale is higher. For the books we print, I think we sell more copies of them. Yes, we are having an argument. The argument, in a nutshell—

then I'll let Jack speak his peace—is, I feel that I don't want to lose our image of being the underdogs, which we've had for years, the little outfit that came along and we're challenging the big fellows. The American public being the way it is, once we're known to be the leaders, they're liable to sympathize with another outfit. It's not that I don't want us to be on top, but I'd like, with the public, I'd like them to think of us as the little, homey, fun outfit that, you know, we're not quite that big and successful, we're not that fat-cattish yet. Jack feels differently, though, I think.

JK: Well, we may be number one, but we still retain the type of character that we've always had. If people like you at first, there's no reason why they shouldn't continue to like you, unless there's some sort of a radical change in your makeup. If you're a good magazine, I imagine that they'll keep reading you, and your readers will be faithful to you. Certainly, they don't expect you to get the arrogance that you might expect from a champion of any kind. There have been champions that have been humble, and that have had fine characters, and been likeable. People have had the admiration of the public for years. And there have been champions who have had color, and arrogance, and have been disliked, and have retained the quality that have made them champions. So it doesn't matter what kind of character the magazines have.

My contention is that it must be the content that the readers like. Although each magazine certainly has an individual personality, which Stan has instilled through his cultivation of the readers, we still have a content that is superior to any of the magazines on the market, and I, as a reader, would like to read Marvel. And when I do a strip for Marvel, I feel that I *am* a reader. I'm certainly never bored with the stuff I read in Marvel. And [a reader] may get to dislike anybody... in the organization, but that won't deter [him] from buying the magazine. So I feel that we are number one, we should be number one, and say we're number one, and have no regrets about it. I feel that we should take the criticism and use it for our own improvement. It's as simple as that.

SL: Well, I think Jack is a real pussycat to say that, and I know what he means, and I certainly want us to be number one, too. And I agree with everything he says. I think the quality should be as good as we can make it, and I think the readers always will read our material if it remains what they want to read. My feeling is, as I mentioned, I like to think of this whole thing as an advertising campaign, and I just know that the public generally likes an underdog. And while I'm not sure that we'll lose anybody if they think we've grown terribly complacent and successful, I think it's more fun for the reader to think he's latched onto something that is sort of his little discovery, and it's a little bit far out, and the general public hasn't quite discovered it yet, and he can tell his friends about it. But the minute the reader feels everybody knows about Marvel, and everybody likes Marvel, then I'm just afraid, while they'll still read us, as far as their sympathies are concerned, they may try to find something else that nobody has discovered yet to lavish their affection on.

JK: I think what the reader does not like is false humility. The reader by this time knows that Marvel is number one, he knows that Marvel is superior, he knows that Marvel has quite a number of readers, and if we were to tell him that we are humble and that we're not quite number one, he won't believe it. He really will not believe it.

Fantastic Four #62 (May 1967) was on newsstands—there weren't any comics shops then—around the time of this interview. The mystery figure isn't the Silver Surfer, by the way. It's Triton of the Inhumans out to save Reed from Blastaar the Living Bomb-Burst! (Hope we didn't ruin the surprise for you!) [©2011 Marvel Characters, Inc.]

SL: I think the one thing we have never been accused of is humility, whether false or otherwise, because our readers figure we're the most conceited group in the world, and they get a kick out of it, because we're always bragging.

JK: That's true! *[laughs]*

SL: We call ourselves, "Marvel, the House of Ideas." We have phrases like, "Who says this isn't the Marvel Age of Comics?" And they're always writing letters to us, "You guys may be the most swell-headed guys in the world, but you've got a right to be, and we still love you!"

JK: And there you are.

SL: I'm not talking about humility. I'm talking about the fact that I think it would be better for us if the reader does not think of us as being on top of the heap as far as being a rich, successful outfit. And I might be dead wrong, but I don't know that that's the image I think I'd like the public to have of us.

***MH:** You've been listening to two of the most humble and sincere underdogs in the number one spot in the comic business, Jack Kirby and Stan Lee of Marvel Comics. And this is Mike Hodel for WBAI.*

[End of interview.]

[Not] The Last Fantastic Four Story

Stan and John Romita Jr. team up to tell a tale of Marvel's First Family

Since elsewhere in this book we saw the plot for the first ***Fantastic Four*** story, it's only right to also show a couple of pages of the making of ***The Last Fantastic Four Story***, although, fortunately, that's just the title of this 2007 graphic novel.

In this opus, Stan and John Romita Jr. teamed up for the first time to imagine what the team's final mission might be like. While writer and artist had known each other since John was a kid, the two had somehow never worked together on a complete story.

The Adjudicator tells us (actually he "thinks" rather than "tells" because his thoughts can be understood by everyone no matter what language they speak. However, I'll use the word "tells" or "speaks" from now on because it's a simpler way to convey what's happening) –he tells us he's come to announce the end of human life on Earth, to give us a short time to make our final farewells.

(The Adjudicator doesn't think of himself as a villain, or the Cosmic Tribunal as being evil. They're just doing what they feel they have to do).

The Adjudicator says we have one week (Earth time) to prepare for our final fate before he will signal the Cosmic Tribunal to destroy mankind..

The Sub-Mariner, suddenly aware that the oceans are getting dangerously warm, thinks Reed Richards is responsible, thinking it's Reed's way of attacking Namor and destroying Atlantis.

So Sub-Mariner attacks the FF in their headquarters.

During the battle, Reed tries to make Namor look at a video tape he took of The Adjudicator when The Adjudicator was gigantic. He wants Namor to realize that The Adjudicator is the enemy. But Namor won't stop fighting.

Suddenly, the Black Panther appears. He has flown from Wakanda to help. . He tells Reed that he'll battle Namor—Reed must return to his lab because it will take all his scientific knowledge to find a way to save humanity.

We have an interesting Black Panther/Sub-Mariner battle until the Panther makes Namor look at the video and Namor realizes who the real enemy is.

Before he can be warned, Namor leaps out of the FF's window to dive down and attack The Adjudicator. The Adjudicator just gestures at Namor and Namor falls to the ground, injured.

Sue sees that he's hurt. She gets the Pogo Plane and she and the Black Panther go down and pick Namor up.

When he comes to, it's decided that Namor must return to his people and look after them in this time of crisis. The Black Panther will do the same to his people. It will require more than mere battle skill to defeat The Adjudicator. It's up to Reed to find the way.

Johnny asks Reed if he wants to get little Franklin and put him in a safe place. Reed says, "No. There will be no safe place in Earth unless we can find a way to stop The Adjudicator. We can only save those we love by staying in the battle."

Many people on Earth still think it's all a gigantic hoax. Perhaps the set-up for a new, big-budget movie. Besides, with all the superheroes around there can't be anything to worry about.

Reed sends out an emergency call to the Silver Surfer.

Working "Marvel-style" (a.k.a plot first), Stan provides JRJR with a written breakdown of the tale, telling him the story, which John then breaks down into panels and pages. Stan then adds dialogue and captions to John's images. Here, we see pages 18 and 19 of the story. The inks are by Scott Hanna.

PAGE 19

1.
CAPTION: Yet, the best they can do is approach the area in an effort to surround the Adjudicator.
CAPTION": For, how do you fight a being whom weapons cannot harm?

2.
JOHNNY: We're cuttin' out for now, guys.
JOHNNY: Ol' Reed says he has an idea!
SOLDIER: It's gonna take more than an idea to bring THAT guy down!
THING: Yeah? Wait'll I give 'im my Sunday punch!

3.
REED: Lucky I stored my intra-spacial communicator in here!

4.
REED: Now, let's hope I can reach the one I'm seeking!

5.
REED: *(The pointer of this balloon should point at Reed's head in the preceding panel)*
REED: He might be anywhere in a thousand galaxies—
But maybe I'll get lucky.

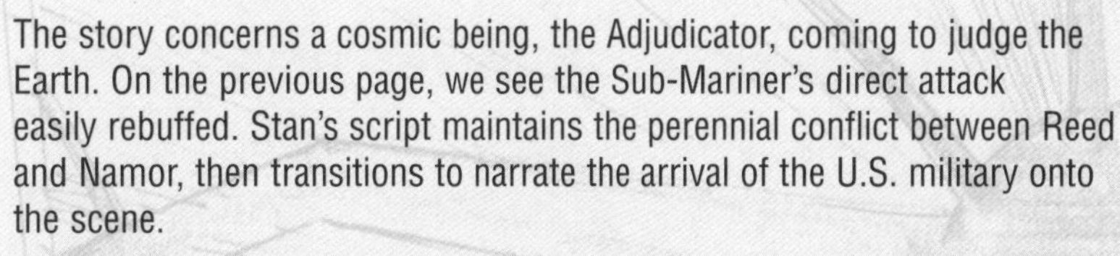

The story concerns a cosmic being, the Adjudicator, coming to judge the Earth. On the previous page, we see the Sub-Mariner's direct attack easily rebuffed. Stan's script maintains the perennial conflict between Reed and Namor, then transitions to narrate the arrival of the U.S. military onto the scene.

Stan and John have Reed summon aid in his own unique manner, befitting his super-scientist persona, by using a high-tech device. Writer and penciler make sure the reader will want to turn the page and find out who Reed is trying to contact. (Of course, since you've read the plot description, you know it's the Silver Surfer!)

Neither Shy Nor Retiring

Stan Lee in the 21st Century

Stan Lee was born in 1922, but on December 28th, so he's younger than most of the people born in that year. He's really just a kid.

Stan's reply when asked why he doesn't retire is that people retire to do what they want to do—but he's doing what he wants to do: generating characters and concepts and entertaining the world.

So as we move through the second decade of the 21st century, it shouldn't be surprising that Stan is involved—mostly through his Pow! Entertainment company—with a plethora of projects. (Of course, he's also Chairman Emeritus of Marvel and does a bunch of writing for the company, including the ***Spider-Man*** newspaper strip.) No doubt, by the time you read this, there will be many more Stan Lee productions out in the world. But here are just a few of Stan's recent endeavors... .

Stan's reality show, ***Who Wants to be a Superhero?***, had him judging the talents of those who thought they had the right super-stuff! [©2011 Universal Television Networks]

Heroman featuring Stan's concepts, is produced by Japan's Studio Bones as both anime and manga series. [©2011 the copyright holders]

"The Guardian Project" is Stan's collaboration with the National Hockey League, for which The Man came up with 30 new superheroes, one for each team in the league! Here, the Carolina Hurricanes' eponymous superhero, Hurricane. [©2011 the copyright holders.]

Stan was the mind behind Boom! Studios' ***The Traveler***, as well as two other concepts. Cover to issue #1 is by Chad Hardin. The story was written by Mark Waid with art by Hardin and Scott Clark. [©2011 BOOM! Entertainment Inc.]

Stan Lee's Superhumans was a reality show that searches out people with unusual abilities that border on the superhuman. [©2011 The History Channel]

Stan and ***Jump SQ.II*** magazine editor Takanori Asada. Stan's collaboration with Hiroyuki Takei, "Ultimo," debuted in the Japanese publication, and is published in multiple-chapter volumes. [photo ©Deb Aoki]

STAN'S STAR

On January 4, 2011, Stan received a "Walk of Fame" star at 7072 Hollywood Boulevard. His decades in L.A. helping shepherd Marvel, Pow!, and other characters onto movie and TV screens were now officially recognized.

The powers-that-be in Hollywood declared it Stan Lee Day, about which Stan quipped, "Some Stan Lee Day—the schools are still open. They're still delivering the mail, too!"

Afterword:
What is a Stan Lee?

Roy Thomas's 1968 tribute to the subject of this book

Wouldn't you know it! Just when it seems like we were only getting started, it's already time for our visit to the Stan Lee Universe to draw to a close—for now, anyway. So as we bid you adieu, this seems like the perfect spot to re-present a piece written by Roy, as he says...

> "... in 1968, about three years after I came to work for Stan. It was scribbled hurriedly (overnight, I seem to recall) for the program book of the SCARP-Con convention [SCARP was the Society for Comic Art Recognition and Preservation], organized by Phil Seuling and Maurice Horn...and I felt thrilled and honored to be the guy asked to write it.
>
> "It's how I felt about Stan and his accomplishments in 1968—and you know what? It's pretty much how I still feel. Stan Lee is still someone I admire and respect... if anything, even more today than I did four decades ago, as I view those accomplishments more and more in perspective...and as I see them loom ever larger, not smaller, on the pop-cultural landscape."

While the words to the intro above and to the piece itself are Roy's, the sentiments expressed in both are wholeheartedly shared by Danny.

What is a Stan Lee?
by Roy Thomas

Many things... not a few of them paradoxical, if not downright contradictory.

An editor much given to belittling his own editing skills... but who can deftly improve a Shakespearian turn-of-phrase written by an ex-English instructor, a couple of sometime journalists, and an experienced movie scripter... among others.

A writer who has long since disavowed any attempt to impose his special writing style on others... but whose style is so strong that it generally does its own imposing.

A bearded non-hippie who has been lauded by conservative publications for his firm anti-radical bias... and who has been toasted by more liberal scribes for his New Left leanings.

A dynamo of energy who doesn't mind taking a short vacation trip... as long as it's by train, so that he can write a few extra pages of Spider-Man

"What is a Stan Lee?" from 1968 SCARP-Con program book, Stan Lee Collection, box #31, folder #3, American Heritage Center, University of Wyoming.

en route.

A self-declared non-artist whose ability to draw even a straight line has been hotly debated... but who can use a few scribbled scrawls to show an artist something he should have seen in the first place.

A devoted husband and father... who nonetheless manages to turn out more work each week than the several bleary-eyed bachelors who write for him.

An accused grand-stander who is supposed to have a tremendous, all-devouring ego... but who is genuinely moved when a parent calls up to congratulate him on the first issue of ***The Silver Surfer***.

A comics-industry figure since the early 1940s... who became an overnight success in 1961.

An idealistic prag-matist who once spent a whole day laboring over four pages of "Forbush-Man"... but wrote twice that many pages of "Thor" by flickering candlelight on the night of the 1965 blackout.

A pragmatic idealist who had to let his other titles languish while he built up the superhero line... then turned around and in two issues made ***Millie the Model*** one of Marvel's best-selling titles.

A businessman supposedly interested only in sales charts and circulation figures... who will delay an already dangerously late book for an hour so that somebody can correct a few lop-sided word balloons.

A Long Island suburbanite who lives father away from Manhattan than most members of his staff... and who is almost invariably at the office before any of them.

A not particularly frustrated actor who can talk like the Hulk till you expect him to turn green... or give an artist an entire synop-sis over the phone in the most solemn tones this side of Churchill.

A mildly myopic perfectionist who pores over each month's covers until the last detail of shading is correct... but who once failed to notice a figure of Captain America with a big white "A" on his chest.

A fantastically busy executive who scarcely has time to speak to his own staff for days on end... then calls them in for the world's most leisurely discussion, over a twin helping of cigars and sourballs.

And, a Stan Lee is quite a few other things, as well...

...Including, most assuredly, a man who will vigorously dis-agree with at least half the things you just read about him.

OTHER BOOKS FROM TWOMORROWS PUBLISHING

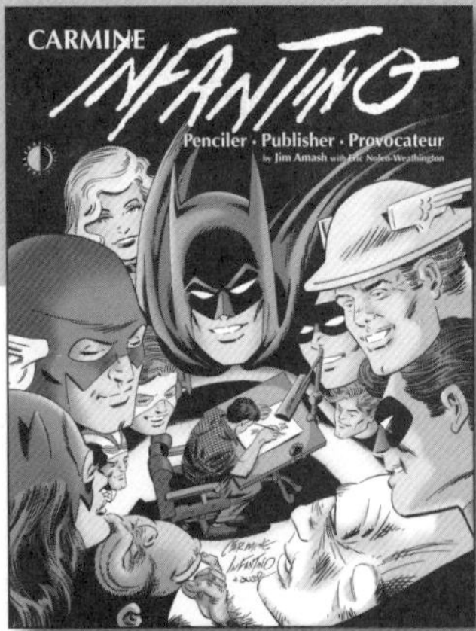

CARMINE INFANTINO
PENCILER, PUBLISHER, PROVOCATEUR

Shines a light on the life and career of the artistic and publishing visionary of DC Comics!

(224-page trade paperback) **$26.95**

SAL BUSCEMA
COMICS' FAST & FURIOUS ARTIST

Explores the life and career of one of Marvel Comics' most recognizable and dependable artists!

(176-page trade paperback with **COLOR**) **$26.95**

MATT BAKER
THE ART OF GLAMOUR

Biography of the talented master of 1940s "Good Girl" art, complete with color story reprints!

(192-page hardcover with **COLOR**) **$39.95**

EXTRAORDINARY WORKS OF ALAN MOORE

Definitive biography of the Watchmen writer, in a new, expanded edition!

(240-page trade paperback) **$29.95**

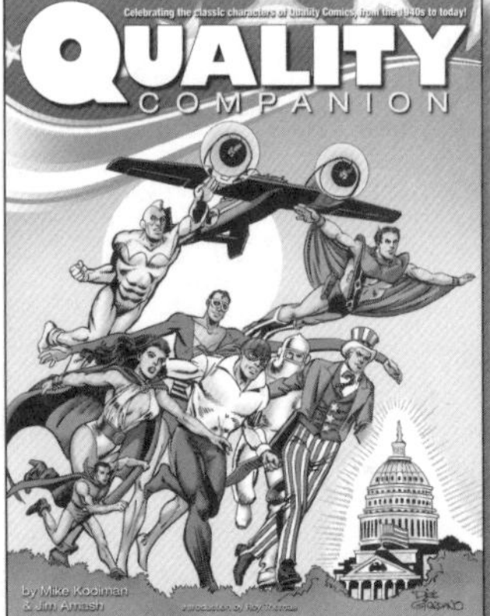

QUALITY COMPANION

The first dedicated book about the Golden Age publisher that spawned the modern-day "Freedom Fighters", Plastic Man, and the Blackhawks!

(256-page trade paperback with **COLOR**) **$31.95**

BATCAVE COMPANION

Unlocks the secrets of Batman's Silver and Bronze Ages, following the Dark Knight's progression from 1960s camp to 1970s creature of the night!

(240-page trade paperback) **$26.95**

ALL-STAR COMPANION

Roy Thomas has four volumes documenting the history of **ALL-STAR COMICS**, the **JUSTICE SOCIETY, INFINITY, INC.**, and more!

(224-page trade paperbacks) **$24.95**

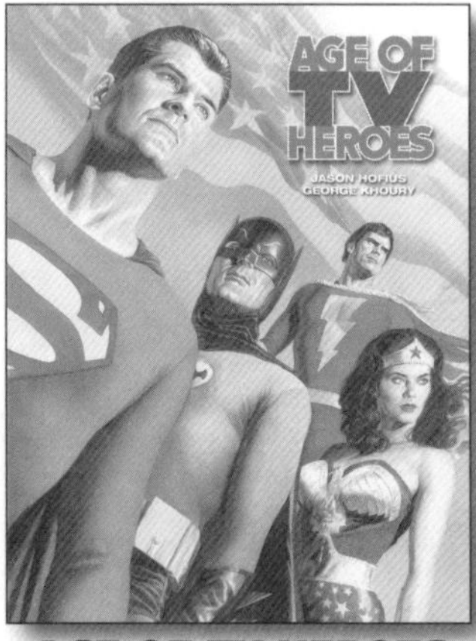

AGE OF TV HEROES

Examining the history of the live-action television adventures of everyone's favorite comic book heroes, featuring the in-depth stories of the shows' actors and behind-the-scenes players!

(192-page full-color hardcover) **$39.95**

MARVEL COMICS
IN THE 1960s

An issue-by-issue field guide to the pop culture phenomenon of **LEE, KIRBY, DITKO,** and others, from the company's fumbling beginnings to the full maturity of its wild, colorful, offbeat grandiosity!

(224-page trade paperback) **$27.95**

MARVEL COMICS
IN THE 1970s

Covers how Stan Lee went from writer to publisher, Jack Kirby left (and returned), Roy Thomas rose as editor, and a new wave of writers and artists came in!

(224-page trade paperback) **$27.95**

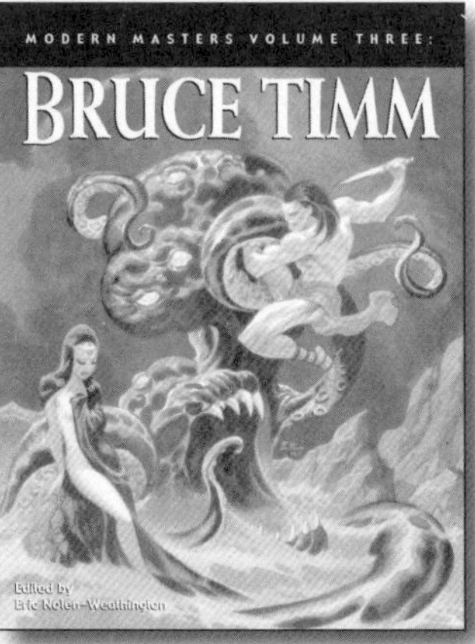

MODERN MASTERS
A BOOK SERIES DEVOTED TO THE BEST OF TODAY'S ARTISTS

20+ volumes with in-depth interviews, plus extensive galleries of rare and unseen art from the artist's files!

(128-page trade paperbacks) **$14.95 each**

HOW TO CREATE COMICS
FROM SCRIPT TO PRINT

Shows step-by-step how to develop a new comic, from script and art, to printing and distribution!

(108-page trade paperback) **$15.95**

FOR A FREE COLOR CATALOG, CALL, WRITE, E-MAIL, OR LOG ONTO www.twomorrows.com

TwoMorrows—A New Day For Comics Fandom!

TwoMorrows Publishing • 10407 Bedfordtown Drive • Raleigh, NC 27614 USA • 919-449-0344 • FAX: 919-449-0327
E-mail: **twomorrow@aol.com** • Visit us on the Web at **www.twomorrows.com**